SHOW ME VETERANS

ISBN 978-1-954095-48-9 (Paperback)
Show Me Veterans
Copyright © 2021 Jeremy P. Amick

All rights reserved.

No part of this publication may be reproduced, distributed, or transmitted in any form or by any means, including photocopying, recording, or other electronic or mechanical methods, without the prior written permission of the publisher, except in the case of brief quotations embodied in critical reviews and certain other noncommercial uses permitted by copyright law.

For permission requests, write to the publisher at the address below.

Yorkshire Publishing
1425 E 41st Pl
Tulsa, OK 74105
www.YorkshirePublishing.com
918.394.2665

Printed in the USA

SHOW ME VETERANS

Jeremy P. Amick, SSG, U.S. Army

TULSA

CONTENTS

Acknowledgements vii
Dedication ix
Introduction xi

Chapter 1: Civil War & Spanish-American War 1
Chapter 2: World War I 51
Chapter 3: World War II 141
Chapter 4: Korea & Vietnam 377
Chapter 5: Cold War & Beyond 515

Works Cited 561
Index 571

ACKNOWLEDGEMENTS

This book would not have come to fruition without the scores of veterans who have been willing to share with me their humble accounts of military service, ensuring their legacy is perpetuated through firsthand recollection. I would also be remiss if I failed to acknowledge the Gold Star Families who have been willing to provide details about their loved ones; your dedication has preserved a treasure trove of records and photographs of many of the Show-Me State's veterans who have since passed on. Your venerable work and dedication to keeping alive their memories have ensured the travesty of forgotten sacrifice never becomes a reality in our communities. The example established by these heroes continues to serve as inspiration to later generations, who, in turn, might someday choose to pursue their own careers in our nation's all-volunteer armed forces. The willingness to volunteer of oneself is what has made our country the most influential in world history, and it is our responsibility to prevent the stories of sacrifice made by our nations' military members from ever being silenced or forgotten.

DEDICATION

To my fellow veterans, past, present (and those in the making), whose stories have not only served to inspire greatness in others but continue to motivate my drive to ensure they receive the recognition they have rightfully earned.

1167 THE ROOKIE OF UNCLE SAM'S ARMY IN FULL FIELD EQUIPMENT.

SHOW-ME VETERANS
THE MILITARY HEROES OF MISSOURI

What a grand period of excitement the last dozen-or-so years have been, providing me with a range of opportunities to travel throughout the state and meet with so many interesting veterans—each with a unique and equally impressive story of military service. There are those who have paused to inquire what my favorite period of military history is, and I might answer… "Vietnam, because both my father and uncles served in combat with the Marine Corps during this conflict and I am proud of their service." But then, as I ponder for a few moments the various wars and military engagements our country has been involved with throughout its history, I am inclined to shift my answer to the "Cold War." This unique period in our nation's history—a period of time that involved many of our Missouri veterans—demonstrated the strength and technological prowess of our nation as we grew our military in response to the terrifying threat of mutual destruction posed by the standoff with the former Soviet Union.

Now, if you were to grant me the indulgence of just a little more time to mull this question, I might be inclined to again change my mind and remark that World War II is the most interesting timeframe in our military legacy. It is fascinating to consider the geographic coverage of this immense conflict and the United States' scramble to out-manufacture any threats that might be encountered in an overseas combat zone. But, as you may have already surmised, the Korean War—the "Forgotten War"—might also emerge as my premiere response because of the stories I have heard from local veterans regarding the Battle of Inchon and the deadly and frozen Chosin Reservoir. Certainly, I cannot be finished (a chuckle on my part) since World War I was a very momentous occasion in not only our nation's grand wartime history but also had many significant implications for our state. It was a transformative period when the entire National Guard was mobilized, and many of Missouri's regiments deployed overseas in mass numbers, some of whom were only recently returned from service in the Mexican Border Campaign. And not to sound too exhaustive and boorish, but there was also the Spanish-American War, which was intriguing in the sense that it acquired new lands for the United States and helped demonstrate our country's military capabilities on a national stage.

So, essentially what I am attempting to communicate through this long and circuitous narrative is that there is no single era of our state's military history that I view to be of more interest or importance than any other. It is the uniqueness of each of these historical moments and the stories of individual veterans that emerge which have helped make writing endeavors such as this book such an informative and enjoyable process.

With the passing of years, my writings have expanded, bit by bit, in geographical coverage. First, it began with the publication of *Jefferson City at War*, which was obviously limited to the narrow confines of our state's capital city. My interviews continued into the surrounding county, and *Cole County at War* was later published. My thirst for learning of the experiences of veterans from other areas in the state was matched only by the growing numbers of readers who absorbed these stories. Eventually, I had written and collected enough veterans' experiences to release *Central Missouri at War*. Now, as my interest and collection of veterans' personal accounts has expanded to cover all four corners of the state, it is my pleasure to present to you *Show-Me Veterans*, which I find to be timely in its release during the year of our state's bicentennial celebration.

One aspect of my storytelling that I am hopeful will be shared with you in the ensuring pages is that you are moved to heartily acknowledge and extend your appreciation to the veterans who have served our state and nation. Some of these men and women may have voluntarily enlisted, inspired by a parent or loved one who pursued military service years earlier. Or, perhaps these individuals were drafted, thus being compelled into service but performing their assigned duties in an admirable manner. These Soldiers, Marines, Sailors, Airmen, Coast Guardsmen, and Merchant Marines—along with our Gold Star veterans who either came home under a flag-draped coffin or whose remains were never recovered—all deserve our unwavering respect for they are the pride of our state and nation. It is my sincerest wish that you will enjoy reading these stories and search within your own family circles for forgotten military legacies that should be resurrected and shared with our future generations. May God bless you all, the state of Missouri, and the United States of America.

Jeremy P. Ämick
Russellville, Missouri
May 2021

CHAPTER 1

CIVIL WAR & SPANISH-AMERICAN WAR

Enoch Enloe Sr. – *Russellville*

At the outbreak of the Civil War in 1861, a seventy-one-year-old Enoch Enloe Sr. had been living near the fledgling community of Russellville for three decades. One of the original pioneers of the area, he eventually set down roots on a farm on property that is now the Enloe Cemetery. He would go on to demonstrate zeal and ambition by establishing the community's first grist mill, running a blacksmith shop, stable, and hotel, in addition to serving as the first postmaster for Russellville.

Enloe and his wife raised a large family despite losing several children at an early age. Records of Enloe Cemetery indicate that prior to the Civil War, he and his wife had already buried three young sons on his farm. After the Civil War erupted, he had older sons who served with the Union army as part of the Enrolled Missouri Militia (EMM), which the State Historical Society of Missouri describes as a "state force" that was "primarily mobilized as needed." Designated as protection for their home areas, members of the EMM were not issued uniforms and were encouraged to use their own weapons.[1]

---

[1] The State Historical Society of Missouri, *Guide to American Civil War in Missouri*, https://shsmo.org.

The elder Enloe, while working the farm and running his various business endeavors, heard accounts of guerilla activity in the area and later learned of the approach of a massive Confederate army. In an effort to protect both his family and property, he erected a location to conceal both his valuables and a firearm, the latter of which he could reach quickly if a threat emerged. Near the gravesites of his sons, the hardy pioneer erected a raised limestone block that possesses all appearances of a burial spot. Under the bulky stone is an area that was dug out where items could be concealed from view.

"One lady told me when Great, Great Grandfather Enoch Enloe heard that Price's army was coming, he hid his old musket gun under a large flat grave rock," wrote Reba Alexander Koester in her 1976 book *The Heritage of Russellville in Cole County*. She added, "At the time he hid the gun, the big rock was surrounded by a thick growth of tall blackberry bushes."

In *The Civil War in Missouri Day by Day: 1861-1865*, Carolyn Bartels explained that Confederate forces "burned the Osage Bridge on the river [near the present community of Taos] on October 6th (1864). After skirmishing near Bode Ferry, these troops, under the command of General 'Jo" Shelby, moved west toward Jefferson City to meet up with General Sterling Price, who intended on capturing Jefferson City. Though leading an army of an estimated 12,000 soldiers, General Price believed the Union forces protecting Jefferson City to be too formidable. Price then began a westward movement following the Old Versailles Road, much of which is now Route C. When passing near Lohman, his soldiers shot and killed two Bavarian immigrants—Erhardt Kautsch and Friedrich Strobel.

Price's army was pursued by a mounted force organized by Union general John B. Sanborn. "On Sunday, October 9 [1864], Sanborn's men covered another four miles and faced 'lively skirmishing' just two miles shy of Russellville," wrote Mark A. Lause in his book *The Collapse of Price's Raid: The Beginning of the End in Civil War Missouri*. The skirmishing passed through the Russellville area and near where the Enloe Cemetery is now located. The fleeing Confederates were pursued throughout much of western Missouri until they were eventually confronted by Union forces in the Battle of Westport.

Local metal detectors Chris Heimsoth and Michael Kisling have tracked much of the route of Price's Expedition through Mid-Missouri. With the permission of the board of Enloe Cemetery, they detected open areas of the cemetery in an attempt to locate evidence of skirmishing—such as dropped coins, cannonballs, fired bullets, and uniform buckles and buttons. No evidence was discovered, leaving the pair of amateur historians to speculate that the Confederate troops took a route a short distance to the south of the current cemetery location.

As noted in the *Russellville Sesquicentennial 150 years* published in 1988, the Enloe Cemetery was founded on October 16, 1866, when Enoch Enloe donated "two acres of land ... to be used as a burial ground for his children, relatives, and friends of the family." The musket Enloe hid under the stone remained in the family for a number of years and was passed down from one generation to the next, explained Ruby Koester in her aforementioned book. Nevertheless, in 1976, it was donated to the Cole County Historical Society "for safekeeping and so other Cole Countians could enjoy it."

Norris Siebert of Russellville, a descendant of Enoch Enloe and longtime member of the Enloe Cemetery board, noted that although many have speculated whether someone is buried beneath the raised stone, his use of a dowsing rod—an ancient process used to locate certain buried objects—demonstrates there are no human remains buried there.

"Sharing tales of those we've lost is how we keep from really losing them," wrote Mitch Albom in his novel *For One More Day*.

The decades after the Civil War saw grand monuments erected to honor those who gave their lives in the deadliest of all U.S. conflicts.

In a cemetery near Russellville, however, exists a small limestone block that to this day serves as a story that continues to be shared in the community and a link to the rough-hewn pioneer who built it. *(Photograph courtesy of Jeremy P. Ämick)*

George P. Gross – *Kansas City*

George Peery Gross (pictured above, sitting upon the left horse) was raised in a military family in Arkansas, listening to stories of his great-grandfather's role in the Revolutionary War while his grandfather shared tales of fighting the British during the War of 1812. The younger Gross would support the Confederate cause during bloody years of the Civil War and, more than three decades later, command a regiment in a near-forgotten war that helped reunite a divided nation. Born in the community of Van Buren, Arkansas, on November 21, 1847, Gross grew up attending area schools. His education was cut short with the eruption of the Civil War in 1861, and, despite his youth and impressionability, he made the decision to join both his father and brother in enlisting.

"He was but fourteen and a half years of age when he joined the Confederate army, serving three and a half years in defense of the southern cause," noted the second volume of *Kansas City, Missouri: Its History and Its People, 1800-1908*. Participating in several notable battles and campaigns of the war, the aforementioned book explained, "At the close of the war he surrendered at Little Rock and took the oath of allegiance to support the constitution of the United States, being at the time eighteen years of age."[2]

Nine years after the end of the war, he collected his belongings and moved to Kansas City, Missouri, where he was employed by hardware businesses and traveled throughout several western states conducting sales for those companies. He later continued the pursuit of business interests, becoming a manufacturing agent for a number of companies. In 1889, he married the former Martha Vincil and, although the couple never had children of their own, they raised one of Gross' nephews. In addition to his employment activities and responsibilities as a husband, Gross soon made the decision to return to a part-time military career.

Gross was appointed quartermaster of the Third Regiment of the Missouri National Guard in 1892 and later served with an artillery battery in Kansas City before returning to the regiment as their first lieutenant. Eventually, he became the regiment's lieutenant colonel. The October 25, 1895, edition of the *Kansas City Times* explained, "George P. Gross ... was last night elected colonel of the Third Regiment. Colonel Gross was named after a spirited contest..."

At the time, Colonel Gross held the distinction of being the only ex-Confederate officer in the regiment. There was still much discord in the country over the Civil War, but in 1898, nearly thirty-three years after the war's end, the nation united against what they perceived as a common threat. On February 15, 1898, the *USS Maine*, a U.S. battleship, exploded while moored in Havana Harbor, Cuba. The ship had been sent as a symbol of protection for Americans living in the country. At the time, there was much civil unrest and revolutionary activities on the island nation since the Cubans sought to achieve independence from Spanish control.

---

[2] History of Kansas City, Missouri, *Colonel George Peery Gross*, 98-108.

The Naval History and Heritage Command explained that 266 sailors died from the explosion and a board of inquiry concluded a mine had been placed under the ship, resulting in outrage by the American public with blame assigned to the Spanish government. Later speculation and research determined the likely cause to be the spontaneous combustion of coal in a bunker next to a magazine.[3]

"War was declared by Congress by resolution of April 21, 1898, and on April 22, the President called for 126,000 volunteers," noted the 1939 historical annual of the Missouri National Guard. "Missouri's allotment was placed at 5,000. The National Guard of the state was accepted as 'volunteers.'"[4]

Commanding the 3rd Missouri Volunteer Infantry, Col. Gross and the soldiers of the regiment left their civilian jobs and mustered into federal service at Jefferson Barracks in St. Louis on May 14, 1898. At the time, the regiment was comprised of forty-seven officers and 1,237 enlisted soldiers. After ten days at Jefferson Barracks, Gross's regiment was sent to Camp Algers, Virginia. It was here they spent more than two months in training and combated diseases such as typhoid, which claimed the lives of thirteen of the regiment's soldiers. In early August, they transferred to Camp Meade, Pennsylvania, and were soon advised the war had ended with the armistice between U.S. and Spain on August 12, 1898. Following the mustering out of the regiment in the fall of 1898, Gross later made the decision to sever his connection from military service and pursue private interests.

"Colonel George P. Gross ... has at last received his discharge papers," reported the *Kansas City Star* in the July 30, 1899, edition. "Colonel Gross expressed himself as being grateful to the officers and men who rallied around him during his service..."

---

[3] Naval History and Heritage Command, *Navy and American Remember the Maine ...*, https://usnhistorylive.navylive.dod.mil.

[4] Historical Annual National Guard State of Missouri, *The Spanish-American War*, XXI.

In the years that followed, he pursued mining and timber interests while also remaining involved in the Sons of the American Revolution and serving as commander of his local chapter of the United Spanish War Veterans. He later served as superintendent of the former Confederate Soldiers Home of Missouri in Higginsville from 1917-1921. When Gross passed in early 1926, he was interred in Mount Washington Cemetery in Independence. His wife died eleven years later while living at the Confederate home and was laid to rest near her husband.

The Civil War had ripped the nation in two, separating a people who sought some form of reconciliation in the years that followed. As Richard E. Wood explained in the May 1969 edition of the journal *The Historian*, soldiers like Gross discovered a means to reconnect with their northern neighbors through an unanticipated conflict.

Writing on the relationship between the North and the South, Wood explained, "The two sections had in fact been united years before, but some bitter memories still remained. The war against Spain served to wipe away lingering doubts of loyalty and reconstruction, and 'the Civil War faded at last in the great crusade to free Cuba… and it was as a united nation that we faced the enemy.'"[5] *(Photograph courtesy of Jeremy P. Ämick)*

---

[5] Wood, *The South and Reunion, 1898*, 415.

James E. Payne – *Kansas City*

James Edward Payne was raised in Illinois and moved to Kansas City, Missouri in 1857. The following year, he went to work for the D.M. Boland & Company, with whom he remained employed until the outbreak of the Civil War. While serving with the Sixth Missouri Infantry (Confederate), he was shot through the right hand in the Battle of Corinth. During this battle, Payne carried a severely Stephen Cooper off the battlefield, the latter of whom became State Senator Cooper.[6] In later battles, he was wounded in the left hip and lost two fingers on his right hand in a shell blast.

After the war, he was engaged in journalistic work in Kansas City and went on to found the *Cass County Courier* in Harrisonville. He later purchased an interest in the *Independence Sentinel*, and, in January 1891, purchased the *Lexington Intelligencer*. In 1897, Payne was elected colonel of the 2nd Regiment of the western brigade of Missouri United Confederate Veterans.

---

[6] February 19, 1899 edition of the *Kansas City Times*.

During the Spanish-American War, he recruited the soldiers for Company B, 5th Missouri Volunteer Infantry Regiment in Kansas City, and was elected captain of the company. He mustered into federal service with the company at Jefferson Barracks but fell deathly ill while they were in camp in Chickamauga and was sent home to Kansas City, where it took him two months to overcome his affliction.

In the years after the war, he became a clerk with the U.S. Bureau of the Census, from which he later retired. The ninety-six-year-old veteran passed away in 1937 and is interred in Arlington National Cemetery. *(Photograph courtesy of Jeremy P. Ämick)*

Sandford Sellers Sr. – *Wentworth Military Academy in Lexington*

There are many who have chosen to dedicate their lives to educating the nation's youth, selflessly striving to produce generations of citizens armed with the knowledge to go forth and make their communities a better place. Many of these educators passed away—along with institutions they supported—never fully realizing the positive impact made in the lives of countless students. For fifty-eight years, Sandford Sellers devoted the full measure of his energies in "providing the best in education to young men seeking a thorough foundation for professional study or for business life," noted the 1925-1926 catalog for Wentworth Military Academy.

Born in Anderson County, Kentucky, on July 24, 1854, Sellers' family later moved to Texas, where his father passed away in 1857. When young Sellers came of age, he went to work in local cotton and sugar cane fields to help support his mother.

In the book, *The Story of Wentworth*, written by Raymond W. Settle in 1950, a young Sandford Sellers is described as being "(l)ike every other boy in the country, he wished to be a cowboy." However, despite his interest in a rough-and-tumble lifestyle, Sellers realized the schools in the Texas countryside were lacking on many levels, leaving him longing for a more thorough education.[7]

His mother remarried in 1861, and following her death in 1870, arrangements were made for Sellers to live with his aunt and attend school in his native Kentucky. The fall of 1872 was the beginning of a nearly decade-long period of instruction when "he entered the private boarding preparatory school of Dr. W.F. Junkin, a Presbyterian minister, at Danville, Kentucky," wrote Settle.

Sellers went on to earn his bachelor's degree in 1877 and master's degree in 1879 from Central University (now Centre College) in Danville, Kentucky. In later years, he continued his education at Westminster College in Fulton, earning his doctor of law degree. He taught one year at a public school in McAfee, Kentucky, and served briefly as an instructor at a military school in Waco, Texas. From there, he went to teach for one session at Austin College in Sherman, Texas. While in Texas, he met Lucia Rogers, whom he married in 1882 and would become the greatest supporter in his educational endeavors.

The Sellers' residence in Texas ended when communication was received in 1880 from Benjamin Hobson, a former classmate of Sellers' at Central University, inviting the aspiring educator to move to Lexington, Missouri, and help establish the Wentworth Male Academy.

Founded by Stephen G. Wentworth as a memorial to his son William, who died in 1879, the board of trustees for the academy was established in 1881. It became a military school in 1882 after Principal Sandford Sellers observed from an upstairs window of the school building "students marching in formation, conducting the military

---

[7] Settle, *The Story of Wentworth*, 29.

manual of arms using broomsticks borrowed from local citizens," wrote Settle.

"The school has steadily grown in public favor, as its students have gone forth into public life, or to distinguish themselves in universities for which it prepared them," wrote Blanche E. Little in the September 5, 1903 edition of the *School Journal* magazine.[8]

Little added, "The Missouri legislature had made it a part of the National Guard and provides for the commissioning of its graduates as second lieutenants.... The United States government has selected it as one of the three schools, including the state university, apportioned to Missouri by Act of Congress entitling to the detail of a regular army officer of military instruction ..."

As the June 2, 1905 edition of the *Lexington Intelligencer* noted, "Wentworth Military Academy began its existence twenty-seven years ago as a day school with eight pupils. It closed out its session ... with an enrollment of one-hundred and seventy-four."

The newspaper did not hesitate to levy the credit for the academy's growth upon a man who had moved to the area twenty-five years previous, noting that, "Colonel Sandford Sellers has been at the head of the institution from the first, responsible for its policies and to be credited with its successes ..."

The Sellers raised three sons and two daughters; all three of their sons became graduates of Wentworth Miltary Academy. One son, James Sellers, succeeded his father as superintendent of Wentworth, while another son, Sandford Sellers Jr., became superintendent of Morgan Park Military Academy in Chicago. Another son, Dr. Ovid Sellers, served as dean of the Presbyterian Theological Seminary in Chicago.

---

[8] Little, *The School Journal*, 204.

The elder Sellers' association with Wentworth came to an end upon his passing in 1938. He had been conferred the rank of colonel by the Missouri National Guard in 1899 and, as such, was laid to rest with full military honors in Lexington's Memorial Park Cemetery. Following her husband's death, Mrs. Sellers maintained her association with Wentworth until her passing in 1949, dedicating an impressive sum of sixty-eight years to the academy. In her golden years, she had enjoyed supervising the planting of campus gardens and was reputed to have been a staunch supporter of Wentworth athletics with the exception of boxing, which she considered too rough a sport.

The academy to which Sellers dedicated fifty-eight years of his life closed its doors in May 2017 after one hundred and thirty-seven years of operations, citing "declining revenue." It was an end of an era to the legacy of educators such as Sellers, who submitted their full devotion to an institution that for decades served as an outlet to mold young minds rather than an instrument through which to gather personal fortunes.

"He has built up a grand school, but not at personal pecuniary profit by any means," reported the *Lexington Intellingencer* in their May 30, 1896 edition. "His ambition is to educate, not to amass fortune. Such educators are safe, indeed, and the academy could but prosper under the direction of such a man." *(Photograph courtesy of Jeremy P. Amick)*

Sweet Springs, Tackett & Hagan, Missouri.

Marmaduke Military Academy – *Sweet Springs*

This photograph features an unidentified cadet from the former Marmaduke Military Academy in Sweet Springs, Missouri. Established in 1891 by Charles T. Farrar, Frank R. Tate, and Colonel Vincent Marmaduke, the latter of whom was the brother of former Confederate general and governor of Missouri, John S. Marmaduke, the academy was built on the grounds of what was previously had been a resort hotel.

The *King City Chronicle* reported in its February 5, 1943 edition, "During the winter months, Marmaduke Military Academy drilled cadets. Summer came, and the barracks were converted into a vacation resort where socialites came to drink from the nearby salt and sulphur springs, to dance, and to meet at night under the gas lanterns on the lawn."

Robert Frank James, the nephew of famed outlaw Jesse James and son of Frank James, became a pupil at the academy after winning a scholarship in a voting contest conducted by the *Dallas Times-Herald* in 1891. The armory and barracks of the academy burned to the ground in early March 1896, and the owners chose not to rebuild. Instead, many of the remaining assets were sold to nearby Wentworth Military Academy in Lexington while the forty acres of property were sold to business interests out of St. Louis. *(Photograph courtesy of Jeremy P. Ämick)*

Herman Abels – *Houston*

A native of Houston, Missouri, Herman Abels was one of several Texas County men who decided to enlist in Springfield's Company M, Second Missouri Volunteer Infantry, following the president's call for volunteers during the Spanish-American War. The regiment remained stateside during their entire period of wartime service. After being mustered out of federal service on March 3, 1899, Abels was employed by the Franklin Life Insurance Company of Springfield, Illinois. In later years, as his health began to deteriorate, the veteran moved to San Diego, California, where he passed away in 1941.[9]

---

[9] May 1, 1941 edition of the *Houston Herald* (Houston, Missouri).

Edwin Batdorf – *St. Louis*

The Missouri National Guard has many times in the past struggled with unique political concerns due to a blending of both state and federal authorities. This long-standing organization has labored to maintain its distinction as the state militia, which has led to some curious situations, such as one characterized by a conflict between a former state governor and the late Colonel Edwin Batdorf during the Spanish-American War. Born near Dayton, Ohio, on October 4, 1853, Batdorf moved to Kansas in 1871, where his father operated a hotel. Years later, the July 28, 1898 edition of the *Newton Daily Republican* (Newton, Kansas) reported, the young Batdorf moved to St. Louis to clerk in a hotel and "afterward engaged in the commission business ..."

In addition to working full-time, Batdorf became a private with the First Regiment—a former Missouri National Guard regiment located in St. Louis—and quickly rose through the ranks to become an officer. The budding officer soon discovered, however, that military organizations were subject to funding uncertainties that originated from the state capitol in Jefferson City.

"On May 23, 1887, the First Regiment was disbanded owing to the fact that the State Legislature failed to provide for its support," notes the 1934 book *History of the Missouri National Guard*. The book adds, "In the late summer of 1887, through the efforts of Lieutenant Edwin Batdorf, a battalion was organized, which was later expanded into a regiment and became the First Regiment, National Guard of Missouri."[10]

After becoming colonel on June 21, 1893, Batdorf did not enjoy a peaceful tenure in uniform, and his reputation was scarred by altercations with the state leadership over his vocalized concerns, the most notable relating to the formation of the Missouri National Guard Association. During the meeting that formed the association in January 1897, Adjutant General of the Missouri National Guard, Brigadier General Joseph Wickham, became the organization's chairman. As noted in the January 3, 1897 edition of the *St. Louis Post-Dispatch*, it was proposed that the colonels of the state's (then) four regiments and the captains of the two artillery batteries serve as vice-presidents.

Col. Batdorf "at once took violent objection to it on the grounds that Battery A, which had only seventy members, was awarded as great a representation to the First Regiment, with its membership of 700," the newspaper explained. Following this incident, Batdorf and many officers of the First Regiment chose to boycott the newly formed association.

The expression of Batdorf's concerns certainly did not endear him to state authorities, but the arrival of a major mobilization of troops the following year would provide him yet another opportunity to distance himself from any favor with both the adjutant general

---

[10] History of the Missouri National Guard, *Chapter III*, 28.

and governor. As noted in the 1939 edition of the *National Guard Historical Annual, State of Missouri*, during the Spanish-American War, Missouri was given the allotment of 5,000 volunteers as part of the president's call for 125,000 volunteers on April 22, 1898, one day following Congress' resolution of war with Spain.[11]

The First Regiment became one of six Missouri regiments, and a light battery of artillery mobilized during the conflict. Colonel Batdorf and the men of the First mustered into federal service at Jefferson Barracks on May 13, 1898, and then left their St. Louis assembly site on May 19, 1898, bound for Camp George H. Thomas at Chickamauga Park, Georgia. Despite the rather lackluster circumstances the regiment experienced while at camp in Georgia, any privations they were forced to endure were overshadowed in the newspapers by altercations between Batdorf and Missouri Governor Lon Stephens.

Appointed as an acting brigadier general during the greatest part of his Spanish-American War service, Batdorf and several officers of First Regiment quickly drew the ire of the Missouri's governor when they refused to accept the commissions of officers in their companies that were issued from the governor. Gov. Stephens received more unwanted news when Secretary of War Russell Alger submitted a ruling essentially nullifying the state commissions and affirming "the regiments were to remain as mustered in from the Stated Guards…," as reported by the *St. Louis Post-Dispatch* on June 16, 1898.

Months later, the First Regiment returned to St. Louis, never having left the United States during the brief war. It was at this time Gov. Stephens gained somewhat of a small victory over Batdorf when he reorganized the regiment and excluded Batdorf from the new command structure. Batdorf again set the newspapers abuzz when he filed suit against the governor, seeking $50,000 in damages because of a

---

[11] Historical Annual National Guard State of Missouri, *The Spanish-American War*, XXI.

"number of interviews with Gov. Stephens printed in various newspapers of St. Louis reflecting [unfavorably] upon Col. Batdorf as an officer and a gentleman," wrote the *St. Post-Dispatch* on September 21, 1899.

The lawsuit was later dismissed, and the colonel faded from public light until 1903, at which time Adjutant General W. T. Dameron, following the expiration of Gov. Stephens' term, added Batdorf's name to the honorary roll of retired officers of the Missouri National Guard. In the years after his release from the National Guard, Batdorf's life gained some semblance of normalcy as the married father of one son served as treasurer for the former Forest City Building Company in St. Louis.

The retired colonel received further recognition in 1920, seven years prior to his death, when Adjutant General Harvey Clark issued him a special medal authorized by the Missouri Legislative Assembly for the state's veterans of the Spanish-American War. Col. Batdorf passed away on January 14, 1927, when seventy-three years old, at Westgate Hotel in St. Louis and was laid to rest in his native state of Ohio. Though much of his embattled service with the National Guard has been forgotten, the words of another Missouri governor twenty years following Batdorf's death stressed the importance of preserving the state's military legacy despite any controversy that may have occurred.

In a letter to the Forty-ninth Annual National Encampment of the United Spanish War Veterans in 1947, Gov. Phil Donnelly stated, "We revere the memory of the men who volunteered in Missouri Regiments in the Spanish-American War ...," adding, "[and] I am sure the pages of history will record your services, and the campaigns in which you engaged ..." (*Photograph courtesy of the Museum of Missouri Military History*)

Charles A. Preis Jr. – *St. Louis*

Born May 3, 1881, Charles A. Preis, Jr. came of age in St. Louis, Missouri. Military records indicate he served as a private first class after enlisting with Company D, 3rd Regiment of the United States Volunteer Engineers on July 28, 1898. This regiment mustered into service between July 25 and August 20, 1898, at Jefferson Barracks, Missouri, and eventually saw service in Puerto Rico, arriving on the day peace was declared in the Spanish-American War.[12] Many of the soldiers recruited for the regiment were in their civilian employment steam engineers, blacksmiths, carpenters, plumbers, draftsmen, telegraphers, photographers, miners, and railway workers. Some of the assorted special duties that were to be performed by the companies of this regiment included "defending the coast with torpedoes, sapping, mining, demolition, military bridge-building, field forti-

---

[12] November 21, 1899 edition of the *Times* (Philadelphia, Pennsylvania

fications, military surveys, and military map printing."[13] Preis was mustered out of federal service on August 1, 1899.

Following his discharge in 1899, Preis was employed as a metal polisher, married Ida Shroeder, and raised a son, Robert. However, the veteran fell ill at a young age and was granted a military pension in November 1922, when he was only forty-one years old. His wife passed away on November 2, 1928, and Preis died the following month, on December 9, 1928. Both he and his wife are buried in Gatewood Gardens Cemetery in St. Louis. *(Photograph courtesy of Jeremy P. Amick)*

---

[13] July 22, 1898 edition the *Tennessean* (Nashville, Tennessee).

Charles Sansone – *Springfield*

Charles Sansone is pictured in 1898 while serving as a soldier in Springfield's Company K, 2nd Missouri Infantry Regiment. Pursuant to the orders of Governor Lawrence V. Stephens of Missouri, the regiment mobilized for service during the Spanish-American War at Jefferson Barracks on May 6, 1898, and was mustered into federal service six days later. The senior regiment in the state, the Second Missouri had the priority for foreign service and were issued the Krag-Jorgensen rifles and other new equipment; however, the order to make the crossing to Cuba was never given. The regiment, which was comprised of twelve companies and one band, spent most of their nine months and twenty-one days of federal service at Chickamauga Park in Georgia. After the Spanish surrender on July 17, 1898, the regiment was stationed briefly at other stateside locations and was mustered out of federal service on March 3, 1899.

Sansone, who had immigrated from Sicily to St. Louis and then moved to Springfield in 1892, spent his time in military service during the war as a quartermaster (supply) sergeant with Company K. After the war, Sansone acquired a reputation as a prominent businessman and owned such interests as a fruit company, restaurant, pharmacy, and hotels. The veteran passed away on December 7, 1954, when eighty years old and was laid to rest alongside his wife, Angelina, in St. Mary's Cemetery in Springfield. *(Photography courtesy of Jeremy P. Amick)*

Robert Chester Langston – *Springfield*

Robert Chester Langston, pictured in 1898, when serving as a young corporal enrolled with Company A, 1st Regiment Missouri Volunteer Infantry during the Spanish-American War. The regiment mustered into active service at Jefferson Barracks in St. Louis on May 13, 1898, and never left the United States, spending their five months of federal service at Camp Thomas in Chickamauga Park, Georgia—the site of a Civil War battlefield. Although they remained stateside, the Spanish-American Centennial website notes the regiment was occupied "fighting the enemies of boredom and disease."[14] The Souvenir Book of the Forty-Eighth Annual Encampment of United Spanish War Veterans stated the regiment lost a total of thirteen soldiers from disease during their period of Spanish-American War service.[15]

---

[14] The Spanish-American War Centennial Website, *2nd Missouri Volunteer Infantry*, https://spanamwar.com.
[15] United Spanish War Veterans, *Souvenir* Book, 25.

After mustering out of service on October 31, 1898, in St. Louis, Langston married the former Lela Landreth in Springfield in 1909. He later moved from his hometown of Springfield, became the father of a daughter, and was eventually employed as a traffic manager in Kanas City. The veteran died of pulmonary tuberculosis on June 20, 1914, when only thirty-five years of age. Langston was laid to rest in Maple Park Cemetery in his native community of Springfield. *(Photograph courtesy of Jeremy P. Ämick)*

Spanish-American War Medal – *St. Louis*

This stunning medal captures some history of the participation of both St. Louis and the Missouri National Guard in the Spanish-American War. The medal was presented in 1899 by the citizens of St. Louis to the soldiers of the state who had served with the Second Missouri Volunteer Infantry Regiment during the Spanish-American War. The regiment mustered into federal service for the Spanish-American War at Jefferson Barracks in St. Louis on May 12, 1898, and spent their entire term of service stateside. The regiment was at the time comprised of twelve companies and mustered out of federal service at Albany, Georgia, on March 3, 1899. *(Photograph courtesy of Jeremy P. Amick)*

Edwin S. Morall – *University City*

Born in St. Louis on February 10, 1873, Edwin S. Morall became a sergeant with Company G, First Regiment of the Missouri Volunteer Infantry, and is pictured in the above photograph taken on July 4, 1898. The regiment was mustered into service for the Spanish-American War at Jefferson Barracks on May 13, 1898, "for the period of two years unless sooner discharged," noted the description on the company's muster rolls.[16] Company G spent nearly their entire time in federal service at Camp George H. Thomas on Chickamauga Park in Georgia, where they received intense training under the Third Army Corps in preparation for overseas service. Several factors that included a lack of proper uniforms and equipment in addition to strained relations between state and federal authorities prevented the regiment from deploying overseas, and they were mustered out of federal service on October 31, 1898.

After the war, Morall married the former Margaret E. Steber on September 26, 1900, and lived in University City, Missouri, where

---

[16] Missouri Digital Heritage, *Edwin S. Morall*, https://s1.sos.mo.gov.

he served as a deputy sheriff for St. Louis County from 1940 to 1945 and was the owner of a women's clothing manufacturing company. Morall later remarried and was the father to both a daughter and step-daughter. He passed away when eighty-three years old on July 27, 1956, and is buried in Valhalla Cemetery in St. Louis County. *(Photograph courtesy of Jeremy P. Ämick)*

Colonel Jay Torrey – *West Plains*

Prior to becoming president of the United States, Theodore "Teddy" Roosevelt entered political circles as the Assistant Secretary of the Navy, but it would be his service with the 1st Volunteer Cavalry during the Spanish-American War that would, in essence, secure his reputation as a leader and help catapult him to the White House. Yet one name that is often overlooked from the annals of Spanish-American War history is that of former Missourian, Colonel Jay Torrey, who is reputed to have conceptualized the idea for the Rough Riders and was later involved in a tragedy that cut short his military career and prevented his own path to the presidency.

Born in the community of Pittsfield, Illinois, in 1852, an article appearing in the January 4, 1921 edition of *The Columbia Evening Missourian* noted that Torrey "was left an orphan while still a small boy" and later "went to St. Louis where he began selling newspapers, thus earning enough money to continue school." He followed the path of education and personal responsibility when he went on to attend Washington University, earning his law degree in 1876. For the next fourteen years, Torrey remained in St. Louis and became active with civic groups and fraternal organizations while also petitioning Congress to pass bankruptcy reform, which, according to law journals of the period, resulted in the "The Torrey bankrupt act."

Torrey's interests soon shifted to those of a more rugged nature when he left Missouri in 1890 to join his brother in Wyoming to establish the Embar Cattle Company. The American Heritage Center at the University of Wyoming notes that although Torrey remained politically active by serving in the Wyoming legislative assembly, it was his idea to form a cowboy regiment that would earn him a level of national notoriety.

On February 15, 1898, an explosion occurred aboard the *USS Maine*—a U.S. battleship that had been sent to Cuba under the auspices of protecting the interests of Americans living on the Spanish-controlled island. The responsibility for the explosion, which resulted in the deaths of an estimated two hundred and sixty American sailors, was believed to have been a mine placed in Havana Harbor by the Spanish. Two months later, on April 25, 1898, war was declared against Spain, thus uniting against a perceived common enemy, a country still healing from the wounds of the Civil War.

President McKinley issued a call for 125,000 volunteers and Torrey soon "laid his plans before the officials at Washington and they were approved and he was commissioned to organize a regiment of rough riders," as his obituary appearing in the December 6, 1920 edition of the *St. Post-Dispatch* described. Commanding the second of three regiments of "cowboys," the *Kansas City Journal* wrote on April 28, 1898, that Colonel Torrey's Second U.S. Volunteer Cavalry (which became known as "Torrey's Rough Riders") would "be comprised of frontiersmen who have special qualifications in horsemanship and marksmanship." (The first regiment was commanded by Colonel Leonard Wood with Teddy Roosevelt as his second in command.)

Newspapers throughout the U.S. continued to chronicle his preparations, and on June 21, 1898, The *Salt Lake Herald* reported that Colonel Torrey and his anticipated complement of "800 or more well-equipped cavalrymen, mounted on the finest horses produced in the west," would soon depart Cheyenne, Wyoming, bound for Jacksonville, Florida, and eventual service in Cuba. After loading on three separate trains (comprised of twelve cars each) to haul the men and an additional three trains (of twenty-five cars each) to haul the horses and equipment, the regiment began their southeasterly journey. Though they lost a soldier who fell to his death from the train in St. Louis, their journey was relatively uneventful until reaching Mississippi.

On June 26, 1898, Torrey's opportunity to establish his mettle as a battle-hardened commander was dashed when, near Tupelo, Mississippi, the first train in their column stopped to take on water when the second train rounded the curve and struck the rear of the first train. The accident resulted in a derailment of several cars, the death of five men, and fifteen injuries, which included Colonel Torrey, who had to remain on crutches for several weeks due to injuries sustained in both his feet.

Several days later, Torrey and his group of Rough Riders finally made it to camp in Jacksonville, Florida, where they remained for the duration of the war while Roosevelt and his Rough Riders secured their reputation in Spanish-American War history during their charge up San Juan Hill in Cuba. Shortly after his return from military service, Torrey was considered for nomination as running mate for President McKinley in 1900; however, Roosevelt eventually received the nomination, boosted by his fame from military service in Cuba.

Torrey returned to Missouri in 1906 and established a large farm near West Plains. Until his death in 1920, he remained an active participant in political and social affairs, leaving behind a legacy often shrouded by the legend of a fellow Rough Rider who later became president. Elections have at times erupted in heated and inflated rhetoric, but the adoration the public maintained for Torrey during the search for McKinley's running mate is described in an article appearing in *The Colored American* newspaper on June 16, 1900, in which the editors noted a common perception of Colonel Jay Torrey as "a man of the people."

"[He is] not a man who confined his patriotism to 'hot air' during the recent war, but one who put on a uniform; not a man from Wall Street, but from the West. The man named thus far who fills this bill and who perfectly answers the demand of the times is Jay L. Torrey." *(Photograph courtesy of Museum of Missouri Military History)*

Kirkwood Military Academy – *Kirkwood*

The Kirkwood Military Academy, once located at Washington and Fillmore Avenues in Kirkwood, Missouri, was established in 1882. During the height of its operation, the academy had an impressive faculty and offered a well-rounded course of study that included instruction in such subjects as English, ancient language, piano, arithmetic, and athletics—all of which was supplemented by military drill and instruction. The beautiful three-story brick building that once housed the educational institution was closed for the holidays when it was completely destroyed by fire on December 29, 1910. According to an article in the *St. Louis Post-Dispatch*, the loss of the building was estimated at $17,000 with only $7,000 in insurance coverage.[17] For twenty-five years, the academy was owned by Colonel Edward A. Haight, who formerly served as superintendent of schools in Alton, Illinois. Following the destruction of the academy, Col. Haight made the decision to not rebuild. In later years, Haight became vice president of a company that operated a chain of banks in the Southwest United States before spending the last ten years of his life employed by the Federal Intermediate Credit Bank

---

[17] December 29, 1910 edition of the *St. Louis Post-Dispatch*.

in Spokane, Washington. Following his death on March 2, 1947, he was laid to rest in Santa Barbara, California. *(Photograph courtesy of Jeremy P. Ämick)*

Arthur Gill Caffee – *Carthage*

Arthur Gill Caffee had large shoes to fill when he decided to pursue a career in the United States Navy. For nearly three decades, his father, Colonel William Caffee of Carthage, Missouri, commanded the Second Regiment of the Missouri Infantry, which included service during the Spanish-American War. Although the elder Caffee was certainly proud that his young son was inspired to follow his soldierly example, it became a decision resulting in a great deal of emotional turmoil for the patriarch.

Arthur Caffee was born on December 20, 1882, and raised in the community of Carthage. His father, William Caffee, "procured (for Arthur) an appointment to the United States Naval Academy … in 1900," reported The *St. Louis Star and Times* on November 20, 1910. The newspaper article goes on to explain that at a time when the course of study at the academy spanned a period of six years, the young Arthur Caffee was able to graduate in only four "because of the pressing demand for officers in the rapidly increasing American Navy."

An article accessed through the website of the Naval History and Heritage Command notes that after the end of the Spanish-American War, "the United States was thrust into the mainstream of international affairs and gained status as a world power, acquiring as possessions the Philippines and Guam in the Pacific, then Puerto Rico in the Caribbean." The article further notes that in 1904, the same year Caffee graduated from the academy, the U.S. Navy established a naval base at Guantanamo Bay, Cuba. This, along with the United States' acquisitions from the Spanish-American War, inspired President Roosevelt to stress "the upgrading and expansion of the U.S. fleet to protect American interests abroad."[18]

Upon graduation from the academy, Caffee was appointed as an ensign aboard the *USS Missouri* (BB-11)—a Maine-class battleship that was commissioned in December 1903 and the second U.S. Navy vessel to carry the name of Caffee's home state. Shortly after his assignment to the *USS Missouri*, an unexpected tragedy unfolded, resulting in the death of nearly three dozen sailors, but at the same time demonstrating the heroic spirit of the young ensign from a rural Missouri community.

The *St. Louis Star and Times* wrote that the ship was in Pensacola Bay, Florida, on April 13, 1904, when it "was shaken from stem to stern by the explosion of 2,000 pounds of powder in a 12-inch gun of the after-turret and handling room of the battleship Missouri." The sailors then scrambled to flood the after-turret with water to stifle the fire, and orders were issued for no one to venture into the "death chamber," the newspaper revealed. Ensign Caffee reportedly ignored these commands and dove into the water to pull out any survivors but was "overcome in his efforts" and had to himself be pulled to

---

[18] Naval History and Heritage Command, *Cruise of the Great White Fleet*, https://history.navy.mil.

safety by his fellow sailors. On that depressing day, a reported thirty-two sailors lost their lives in the explosion. Despite his disregard for the orders given to not attempt a rescue, Caffee was later recognized for his efforts and decorated with medals from Congress in honor of his bravery.

The young ensign served in other naval assignments, including service aboard the *USS Connecticut*, soon reaching the rank of lieutenant. However, he was later appointed an inspector of ordnance at Indianhead Proving Grounds in Washington, D.C.—an assignment that heralded the final chapter in Caffee's brief naval career.

"FOUR MEN KILLED IN EXPLOSION" shouted the headline of an article in the *Daily Arkansas Gazette* on November 20, 1910. The article went on to explain, "Four men were killed today by the premature explosion of a five-inch, 51-caliber gun at the Indianhead Proving Grounds ... The breech lock of the gun, which, being tested, flew backward into the crew which was firing the gun."

Lt. Caffee, who was the officer in charge of the testing of the gun, was killed alongside his battery foreman, battery attendant, and an ordnance man. Survived by a wife and two young daughters, the body of the twenty-seven-year-old Caffee was laid to rest in Arlington National Cemetery. Several months later, on March 16, 1911, Lt. Caffee's mother passed away after a stroke she suffered the previous day. Her obituary in the *Carthage Evening Press* reported that her health had suffered greatly since the loss of her son.

Colonel Caffee would not only have to suffer through the loss of his spouse and eldest son but in 1918, he had to bury his only surviving son when he died after developing pneumonia. In 1923, Colonel Caffee passed away and was laid to rest alongside his wife in Park Cemetery in Carthage. Even though his death appeared to herald the beginning of a succession of tragedies for the Caffee household, the passing of Lt. Arthur Caffee represented a legacy of service and sacrifice made by one family on behalf of their state and nation and demonstrated the impact of loss endured by a proud father.

"Col. Caffee's lifelong ambition," reported the *St. Louis Star and Times* on November 20, 1910, "has been to see the day when his seagoing and warring son would wear with grace the insignia of an American Admiral." The newspaper added, "These hopes were shattered Saturday in the reports of the deaths of Lieutenant Caffee and three subordinates …" *(Photograph courtesy of Nancy Brewer)*

Robert T. Kerlin – *Newcastle*

Missouri has long been home to many notable soldiers who have left a clear and indelible mark on the nation's security. Yet eclipsed by this list of well-known leaders are several individuals whose military service has not been memorialized to the extent of others such as John J. Pershing and Omar Bradley, but who nonetheless went on to live interesting and inspirational lives. Robert Thomas Kerlin is one such veteran whose name is rarely recalled despite his service ministering to the troops as a chaplain during the Spanish-American War, championing for equal rights, and his active involvement with the Socialist Party.

Born in Newcastle, Missouri, in 1866, Kerlin was the son of former slaveholders; however, an article appearing in the *Journal of Negro History* in 1950 noted that his parents "were not defenders of the institution [of slavery]" and "were offered additional slaves but refused to accept them." The journal article further noted that young Kerlin studied at Central College (now Central Methodist

University) in Fayette and later completed a year of studies at John Hopkins. He also went on to attend the University of Chicago and Harvard, eventually earning his doctorate in from Yale.[19]

Though he was away from his native state for many years, Kerlin returned to Missouri in 1890 and received an appointment as Professor of Modern Languages at Missouri Valley College, according to The John Hopkins University Circular dated November 1890. In 1894, he took a break from teaching and instead chose to pursue a career in divinity. From 1895 to 1898, Kerlin served as a minister in the Southern Methodist Episcopal Church where he later participated in the compiling of a new church hymnal," wrote Fredrick Walker in an article appearing on the website of the Virginia Military Institute.

His endeavors in the church soon mixed with the patriotic furor swirling about the country in 1898 when he exchanged his pastoral accouterments for a military uniform when joining the 3rd Missouri Volunteer Infantry Regiment as they prepared for service during the Spanish-American War. The 3rd Missouri was a National Guard regiment that "(m)ustered in at Jefferson Barracks, May 12, 1898," noted a souvenir booklet from the 49th Annual National Encampment of the United Spanish War Veterans held in Kansas City, Missouri, from August 24-28 1947. As the booklet goes on to explain, the regiment never made it overseas during the Spanish-American War but rather served in several stateside locations. This included service at Camp Alger, Virginia, Camp Meade, Pennsylvania, and Fairmount Park, Kansas City, until the regiment mustered out of federal service at Graham Barracks in Kansas City on November 7, 1898.

During the nine months and twenty-seven days the regiment spent in active military service, Chaplain Kerlin took copious notes and wrote to Missouri newspapers to keep the citizens informed of the activities of daily camp life. After the war, Kerlin compiled many of

---

[19] Journal of Negro History, *Robert Thomas Kerlin*, 230-231.

these letters and published the accounts in a book titled *The Camp Life of the Third Regiment*.

Following his release from military service, Kerlin eventually returned to teaching and serves as a professor at several educational institutions, the most notable of which was the Virginia Military Institute. During his teaching career, he championed the cause of equal rights and penned such books as *The Voice of the Negro*—an in-depth reflection of the race riots that occurred after WWI. Kerlin gained a level of nationwide notoriety when he "was dismissed from the Virginia Military Institute because of a letter he wrote to the governor of Arkansas protesting against the treatment of negroes involved in riots in that state," reported *The Bee* (Danville, Virginia) on August 7, 1922.

When defending his actions, the *Wilmington Morning Star* (North Carolina) reported on August 25, 1921, that Kerlin affirmed his actions were "solely to promote such inter-racial adjustments as would secure to both races the fullest measure of prosperity and happiness with good will and cooperation instead of perpetual friction …"

During the summer of 1922, Kerlin was hired to fill the position of head of the English department at the State Normal School in West Chester, Pennsylvania. He was dismissed less than four years later for what the school's principal, Andrew Thomas Smith, defined as his "overemphasis of social amalgamation and [Kerlin's] attitude toward Socialism," reported the *Evening Journal* (Wilmington, Delaware) on April 5, 1927. As the years passed, Kerlin continued to demonstrate his inclination toward free speech and thinking, spending many years involved in the Socialist Party while remaining actively focused on labor initiatives that included the establishment of the American Federation of Teachers.

In addition to becoming a Quaker in his later years, Kerlin penned many books and remained engaged in activities to help represent

Black Americans, eventually becoming a member of the National Association for the Advancement of Colored People. The retired professor passed away in Maryland on February 21, 1950, having pursued many varied career paths and social causes during his existence. Yet as the former soldier explained in his own words in his book *The Camp Life of the Third Regiment*, it was the end of his service in the Spanish-American War that highlighted the associations he viewed as a key aspect of his life experiences.

Kerlin wrote that "now at parting [I] would seek to give them a message of friendship, a token of perpetual comradeship in spirit, and would make known to them (my) great solicitude for their individual welfare ..." He added, "... [I] would entreat them to be courageous in the days of peace and in civic duties as they were in times of war and in the exactions of a military camp. Having faith in the boys, believing them to be [my] friends and prizing their friendship ..." *(Photograph courtesy of the Museum of Missouri Military History)*

Mound City Jubilee – 1900

This decorative medal was presented to many of the veterans who attended the Mound City Jubliee that was held from August 13-18, 1900. (Mound City is located in the northwest corner of Missouri.) The *St. Joseph Weekly Gazette* hailed the event as "a week of royal entertainment" that was attended by former Civil War soldiers (both Union and Confederate), veterans of the recent Spanish-American War, and members of the National Guard from four states. The community's city park was used as a campground for those attending the jubilee, and included many joyous activities such as baseball games, fireworks, campfires, and theatrical performances.

USS Missouri (BB-11)

The USS *Missouri* (BB-63) has garnered a grandiose reputation through its decades of sea service but is often remembered for hosting the surrender of Japanese forces on September 2, 1945, heralding the official end of World War II. The Iowa-class battleship was, however, a descendant of another fine battleship also carrying the state's name. Its predecessor was a vessel whose naval legacy boasts many interesting encounters that intersected with important moments in our country's naval history. According to naval records, the USS *Missouri* (BB-11) was a 13,500-ton Maine class battleship built in Newport News, Virginia. The vessel became the second ship of the U.S. Navy to carry the Missouri name. The previous USS *Missouri* was a sidewheel frigate destroyed by fire in August 1843.

"The battleship Missouri was launched at the shipyard here today at 11:12 a.m.," reported the December 29, 1901, edition of the *Boston Globe*. "Mrs. Roosevelt, wife of President Roosevelt, came up from Old Point on the U.S. dispatch boat Dolphin with her guests and viewed the launching from the steamer's deck," the newspaper further explained.

Miss Marion Cockrell, daughter of former Confederate military commander and then-U.S Senator from Missouri, Francis Marion Cockrell, was designated the sponsor of the new battleship, and with it came the time-honored privilege of performing the christening duties. She ceremoniously shattered a bottle of Missouri wine across the vessel's bow, declaring, "I christen thee, Missouri." Captain William S. Cowles was in command of the Missouri upon its commissioning on December 1, 1903, and initially trained his sailors during operations along the East Coast; however, only a few weeks passed before tragedy struck on April 13, 1904.

"By the explosion of 2,000 pounds of powder in the after 12-inch turret and the handling room of the battleship Missouri ... twenty-nine men were instantly killed and five injured, of whom two will die," reported the *Gazette* (Montreal, Canada) on April 13, 1904. The newspaper stated that the ship was engaged in target practice off the Florida coastline along with the USS Texas and USS Brooklyn when the explosion occurred. In the days following the tragedy, 36 members of the crew lost their lives, and three Medals of Honor were awarded for heroism to those who risked their lives rescuing the injured and dying.

Though not receiving a Medal of Honor, Arthur Gill Caffee, a midshipman from Carthage, Missouri, and son of Colonel William Caffee, noted commander of the Second Missouri Infantry Regiment, was decorated for his efforts in the rescue of injured sailors. Sadly, young Caffee was killed six years later while leading a crew during the testing of naval guns in Maryland. The USS *Missouri* would undergo repairs and later performed duty in the Mediterranean, followed by operations along the East Coast and in the Caribbean. In late 1907, the vessel embarked upon a worldwide journey intended to demonstrate the growing naval strength of the United States.

"The Great White Fleet, consisting of 14,000 sailors on 16 battleships and accompanying vessels, was sent around the world for fourteen months by President Roosevelt," noted the Theodore Roosevelt

Center at Dickinson State University. "The fleet's journey started on December 16, 1907, and concluded on February 22, 1909."[20]

The fleet received its nickname from the white paint on the hulls of the ships instead of the gray paint seen on modern naval vessels. During their fourteen months at sea, the fleet sailed 43,000 miles and made twenty ports of call on six different continents. After undergoing upgrades and modernizations, another distinction came for the USS *Missouri* in 1915 when it became the first battleship to pass through the recently constructed Panama Canal, which had opened to waterway traffic the previous year. As the vessel passed through the canal, Captain Robert E. Coontz, a Hannibal, Missouri, native who later became the second chief of naval operations and commander of the U.S. Fleet (and achieved the rank of four-star admiral) watched as the USS *Missouri* made the historic passage.

In his 1930 biography, *From the Mississippi to the Sea*, Admiral Coontz wrote, "While passing through the canal, most of us spent the time on deck (of the USS *Georgia*) in order not to miss any sights." He went on to explain, "… my son was fortunate enough to be aboard (the USS *Missouri*) at the time."[21]

The Naval History and Heritage Command explained, "During World War I, Missouri served as a training ship in the Chesapeake Bay area. Her final duties, in 1919, included four voyages to Europe to bring U.S. servicemen home."

The ship was decommissioned in September 1919 and sold for scrap in 1922. Years later, a silver set used aboard the USS *Missouri* found renewed purpose and continues to help share the legacy of the former battleship. The State of Missouri appropriated $10,000 in 1947 for a new silver service delivered to the third battleship USS *Missouri* (BB-

---

[20] Theodore Roosevelt Center, *Great White Fleet*, https://theodorerooseveltcenter.org.
[21] Coontz, *From the Mississippi to the Sea*, 392.

63) in 1948. The silver service from the previous USS *Missouri* (BB-11) was consolidated into the new set, while the punchbowl for the earlier battleship is displayed in the Missouri Governor's Mansion.

The USS *Missouri* (BB-11) may have faded into relative obscurity after being overshadowed by the more recent accomplishments of its successor. However, its accomplishments are deserving of remembrance despite what some may have viewed as an inauspicious beginning.

"A great wave rolled seaward as the Missouri sank into the waters, but the entrance was too graceful to cause a splash," noted the *Washington Times* on December 29, 1901, when reporting on the ship's launching. "Slowly, the ship drifted a few hundred yards into the sea, and then her anchors held her fast." *(Photograph courtesy of Jeremy P. Amick.)*

CHAPTER 2
WORLD WAR I

Enoch H. Crowder – *Edinburg*

General John J. Pershing was a Missourian who perhaps gained his greatest notoriety during World War I when leading the American Expeditionary Forces in Europe. His fame, however, has over the years eclipsed that of a fellow Missourian whose distinguished career was defined by his role in establishing a system of registering and classifying more than four million Americans for military service in WWI.

A native of Grundy County, Enoch Herbert Crowder was born on April 11, 1859, in the farming community of Edinburg near Trenton, Missouri. As noted in David Lockmiller's book aptly titled *Enoch H. Crowder: Soldier, Lawyer and Statesman*, during his boyhood, Crowder "preferred reading to plowing and found from experience that a combination of the two produced crooked rows."[22]

---

[22] Lockmiller, *Enoch H. Crowder*, 21.

Crowder completed a course of study at a local college at the age of sixteen and later taught at a rural school near Chillicothe. At the urging of his mother, he took the examination for the United States Military Academy at West Point and, as luck would have it, earned an appointment to the academy in the fall of 1877 after the first nominee resigned his appointment. During the next four years, he received a well-rounded education and, in his senior year, "studied civil and military engineering, Spanish law, military tactics, ordnance, and gunnery," Lockmiller wrote. Crowder "enjoyed listening to addresses and debates but disliked speaking in public," the author further explained, but in the time leading up to his graduation from the academy in 1881, he "gradually overcame his shyness..."[23]

The young officer was soon assigned to the 8th Cavalry at Fort Yates, North Dakota, with whom he remained until April 19, 1891, noted the 1890-1900 edition of the *Biographical Register of the Officers and Graduates of the U.S. Military Academy*. He was briefly reassigned to serve as the professor of military science at the University of Missouri in Columbia. While serving in this capacity, he chose to continue his education and earned his bachelor's degree in law, which would prove beneficial in later military appointments.

Returning to cavalry duty, Crowder then received the assignment to the Army's Judge Advocate Corps. He was later transferred to the Phillippines during the Spanish-American War and received promotion to lieutenant colonel. The budding officer had several responsibilities, including drafting a new criminal code for the islands while also serving on its supreme court. The ensuing years of his military assignments have filled the pages of history books; however, this period was highlighted by his service in 1904 as a senior American observer during the Russo-Japanese War. (John J. Pershing served as an observer during the latter part of this conflict.)

---

[23] Lockmiller, *Enoch H. Crowder*, 32.

Eventually, Crowder would go on to complete several assignments, arguably the most important of which would be his service as chief of the Judge Advocate Corps, the "... smallest, and in no invidious sense the most select, of the Army Staff Corps," as stated in Volume XXIV (June 1917-May 1918) of *Case and Comment: The Lawyer's Magazine*. The legal publication went on to assert Crowder's "great ability as a lawyer, and his immense capacity of a captain of men, are attested by his brilliant success as provost marshal general of the United States ..."

This reputation became well-earned by Crowder after the United States declared war on April 6, 1917. It was at this time that Crowder and his team of lawyers were charged with finding a replacement for "the old volunteer system to which America had been committed since the days of the Revolution," wrote Crowder in his book *The Spirit of the Selective Service*. Crowder went on to describe the "volunteer system" as one that "broke down in wars with a foreign foe upon American soil in 1776 and 1812, and just as it failed in a foreign war in 1846, when put to the test in the Civil War, it collapsed decisively, finally and completely."[24]

Six weeks after the declaration of war, Congress passed the Selective Service Act of 1917 requiring all men between twenty-one and thirty to register for military service; the act was later expanded to include the registration of men between ages eighteen to forty-five. The draft that resulted from the act was structured in such a fashion that great responsibility fell upon the 4,628 local draft boards, which were often operated at the county level. As noted by the National Archives, "The local boards were charged with the registration, determination of order and serial numbers, classification, call and entrainment of draftees."

During WWI, there were three registrations held, each with its own draft lottery in which certain quotas of recruits were selected. By

---

[24] Crowder, *The Spirit of Selective Service*, 77.

the end of the war, more than 24 million men had registered, of which 2.7 million were sent to the U.S. Army through conscription. After WWI, Crowder went on to serve as Acting Minister of State and Justice in Cuba in addition to other diplomatic responsibilities. He retired at the rank of major general and, in the years following his death in 1932, received confirmation of his legacy when Camp Crowder in Neosho, Crowder Park in Trenton, and Crowder Hall at the University of Missouri-Columbia were named in his honor.

With a career spanning fifty years of service to the United States, Crowder is best remembered for his role in implementing and administering the draft in WWI. Though many of his efforts during the war may have been shrouded by the overseas accomplishments of fellow Missourian General John J. Pershing, reflections by military leadership continued to mark the true measure of his contributions.

"The magnificent services he rendered his country in peace and war have often been described," said Major General Blanton Winship, army judge advocate, on the passing of his predecessor. "They will be appreciated to the full(est) only as time gives us a perspective."[25] Secretary of War Patrick Hurley, who earned a Silver Star medal for gallantry in WWI, stated upon the passing of his fellow soldier, "None could have served his country more honorably or more efficiently." *(Photograph courtesy of the Grundy County Historical Society)*

---

[25] May 8, 1932 edition of the *Chattanooga Daily Times*.

Everett Reeves – *Caruthersville*

Born January 18, 1877, in Ruthville, Tennessee, Everett Reeves went on to serve in the U.S. Cavalry during the Spanish-American War from 1898-1899. Following his discharge, he returned to school and earned his law degree from Southern Normal in Kentucky in 1901. The same year he graduated college, he was married to his fiancée, the former Erin Pinkley.

In 1905, the couple moved to Caruthersville in the "Bootheel" of Missouri, where Reeves eventually entered into a partnership with the late Robert L. Ward and formed the law firm of Ward and Reeves. Active in politics at both the local and state level, Reeves served twelve years on the Caruthersville School Board and was a member of the local Odd Fellows Lodge.

For a number of years, he served with the Missouri National Guard and became captain of Company B, Fourth Missouri Infantry Regiment. The company assembled at Camp Clark in Nevada, Missouri, along with the rest of the regiment in late June 1916 for service in the Mexican Border Campaign, arriving in Laredo, Texas, on July 6, 1916. The regiment endured intense heat, storms, and flooding and later participated in patrols along the Rio Grande. The regiment's service along the Mexican border came to an end on February 21, 1917.

Captain Reeves was known to have made a number of interest-free loans to area youth who wished to attend college but could not afford to do so without assistance. His obituary notes that although he charged interest on these loans, he never lost a cent on any of these educational investments. The eight-nine-year-old veteran passed away in Hayti, Missouri, on January 31, 1966, and was laid to rest in Little Prairie Cemetery in Caruthersville. *(Photograph courtesy of Jeremy P. Amick)*

Milo H. Walz – *Jefferson City*

The Milo H. Walz Sr. name has become a memory woven into the fabric of communities throughout Mid-Missouri. As a well-known, successful and honest businessman, years before his commercial endeavors and investment of hard work yielded appreciable financial returns, Walz joined thousands of his fellow Missourians and countrymen called to serve overseas in World War I. Born January 19, 1894, in Jefferson City, Walz's father was "connected with the furniture and undertaking business," wrote James E. Ford in the 1938 book *The History of Jefferson City*. Ford also noted that when the younger Walz finished school, he "worked in the plant of the Hugh Stephens Printing Company as a bookbinder."[26]

---

[26] Ford, *A History of Jefferson City*, 572.

Shortly after the U.S. entered WWI, Walz was required to register for the military draft on June 5, 1917. Several months later, the twenty-three-year-old left his job as a bookbinder when his number was selected during a draft lottery, followed by his induction into the U.S. Army on February 26, 1918. He then traveled by train to Camp Funston, Kansas, to begin his initial military training. During this period, he received assignment to Battery A, 342nd Field Artillery Regiment of the 89th Division. His regiment had been organized at Camp Funston on September 5, 1917, and comprised of young men largely from rural areas of several counties throughout the state.

It was not long after Walz reported to his battery that "training began more intensively ... when service practice took place on the target range: first with three-inch guns and later with 4.7 (inch) Howitzers," wrote Robert Walston Chubb, regimental historian, in his 1921 book *Regimental History, 342nd Field Artillery, 89th Division*. Chubb further explained, "When the regiment left Camp Funston on June 3rd, 1918, it was considerably below strength, having contributed an average of one hundred men a month to replacement detachments, during the previous five months."[27]

Preparing for their overseas departure while at Camp Mills on Long Island, New York, Walz and the soldiers of the regiment spent the next three weeks receiving equipment and training alongside approximately three hundred new recruits. On June 28, 1918, the regiment departed the East Coast aboard the British transport *Justicia*. Following their arrival in Liverpool, England, on July 10, 1918, the next three days were spent traveling by foot, ship, and train to the destination of Le Havre, France. A few days later, the regiment was issued a battery of 1915 model Schneider 155-millimeter Howitzers, training with the weapons for the next several weeks.

Walz received his introduction to the fierce realities of warfare when the regiment began firing artillery in the latter days of September.

---

[27] Chubb, *Regimental History*, 13.

Although Battery A, to which Walz assigned, survived this period relatively unscathed, four soldiers in Battery D were killed and eight wounded by German artillery on the evening of September 25, 1918.

Despite "frequent short bursts of reprisal fire," Chubb, the regimental historian, affirmed that "the first three weeks in October were very quiet." However, the lull in combat intensity soon evaporated with the arrival of what remains one of the deadliest military campaigns in American history.

"The Meuse-Argonne Offensive was the largest operation of the American Expeditionary Forces (AEF) in World War I, with over a million American soldiers participating," notes an article on the website of the National Archives. "It was also the deadliest campaign in American history, resulting in over 26,000 soldiers being killed in action (KIA) and over 120,000 total casualties."[28]

On the evening of November 2, 1918, during the latter days of the Meuse-Argonne Offensive, Walz helped fire the howitzers that kept enemy soldiers clambering for cover while a raiding party went forward of their lines and captured forty-two enemy enlisted soldiers and two officers. According to the regimental history, the 342nd expended an impressive 2,142 artillery rounds during this single raid. When the war ended on November 11, 1918, the regiment joined the rest of the 89th Division in Germany as part of the Army of Occupation. The next several months consisted of activities such as patrols in the German countryside to confiscate firearms, attending various schools and athletic competitions between the troops.

Military records reveal that Walz left Europe early aboard the transport ship *Mercy* on January 7, 1919, because of complications related to pneumonia. The vessel was carrying military personnel suffering from various illnesses and diseases, all of whom required med-

---

[28] The National Archives and Records Administration, *The Meuse-Argonne Offensive*, https://archives.gov.

ical attention. Walz recovered and was discharged in April 1919. In the years following his return to Jefferson City, he married the former Esther Beck, and the couple became parents of eight children. In 1922, Walz founded his first store and, with the help of family, "built the business into one of the largest, most successful, and most respected in the area," reported the *Jefferson City Post-Tribune* on July 24, 1976.

The eighty-eight-year-old veteran passed away in 1982 and was interred in Riverview Cemetery in Jefferson City; his wife joined him in eternal rest five years later.

With the level of notoriety Walz acquired through his business accomplishments, coupled with a humble personality focused on addressing the needs of his customers, the former soldier went through life as a man with a proud record of military service. However, there are few, with the exception of his fellow WWI veterans, who realized the depth of his experiences.

Fellow Missourian General John J. Pershing boasted of men like Walz in a letter to the soldiers of the 89th Division dated April 27, 1919, explaining that they helped contribute to a "splendid record in France." Pershing added, "They will return home ... safe in the assurance of the admiration and respect of their comrades in the American Expeditionary Force." *(Photograph courtesy of the Walz family)*

The Call of Missouri – *Kansas City*

Edwin Howland Blashfield possessed many talents and abilities, the most notable of which involved his creation of various murals that adorn the interior of state capitols and associated buildings throughout the United States. With a keen eye for both historic grandeur and symbolism, it is of little surprise that his reputation drew interest from the Kansas City Chapter of the Daughters of the American Revolution (DAR) during World War I. A native of New York, the February 13, 1917 edition of the *Kansas City Times* reported that Blashfield visited "Kansas City to consider plans for murals here."

In her book aptly titled *Edwin Howland Blashfield: Master American Muralist*, Mina Rieur Weiner wrote that Blashfield, an "exemplar, and advocate of classic tradition in America, rose to prominence as a muralist during the 1893 World's Columbian Exposition in Chicago and the 1917 United States entry into World War I."[29]

---

[29] Weiner, Edwin Howland Blashfield, 19.

At the time of his visit to Kansas City, the artist had already begun documenting on canvas the war that embroiled much of Europe, having recently completed the painting referred to as "Sisters of Liberty," which "allegorically represented America, France, and Russia, the greatest Democratic nations of the world, all of whom shed their blood for freedom," reported the *St. Louis Post-Dispatch* on May 6, 1917.

The Kansas City Chapter of the DAR soon commissioned the artist to paint a mural in honor of the citizens of Missouri who answered the nation's call to arms in the First World War. The result was a painting that measured 79-1/2 inches by 108 inches and, as described by the *New York Times* on June 16, 1918, served as a "historical outline of the development of the State." The foreground features a woman symbolizing Missouri, seated and clad in armor while watching her sons depart for war. Further historical symbolism emerges with a group of trumpeters in the background, "representing Old France, Old Spain, and the Union and Confederate forces, while in the front of her is a figure in khaki representing the Union of the present time, sounding the call to arms," the New York Times further clarified.

"The idea that we should commemorate on canvas the veterans of World War I was really part of a larger cultural discourse of that period," said Derrick Cartwright, associate professor of art history and director of galleries for the University of San Diego. "In the early 1990s," Cartwright added, "I was writing my doctoral dissertation on murals in public libraries, and that's when I discovered the Blashfield painting was one such mural that had essentially gone missing."

The *Twenty-Second Annual Report of the National Society of the Daughters of the Amerian Revolution* (printed in 1921) stated that Blashfield's "Call of Missouri" was commissioned by the Kansas City Chapter of the DAR at the cost of $20,000.[30]

---

[30] Twenty-Second Annual Report, *Special Memorials*, 150.

Following its completion in 1918, the artwork was briefly displayed at an art gallery in Blashfield's home state of New York, but later that year was presented by the DAR as a gift to the Kansas City Public Library to be hung in its facility at Ninth and Locust Streets. For decades, the Blashfield painting adorned a wall above a grand fireplace mantel in the library building; however, David Disney, a senior vice-president of a major Kansas City area construction company who has been tracking the painting's whereabouts, noted its initial disappearance from the Kansas City area.

"The library building was purchased by U.S. Trade School, and the painting was in there when it was purchased, but it disappeared sometime in the 1980s," Disney said. "No one really knows what happened to it, and the trade school has since closed, and the building is now home to Ozark National Life," he added. Disney explained that he has invested countless hours searching for Blashfield's masterpiece, and his research most recently led him to an art dealer in Dallas, who was selling the painting for a customer. However, the painting again went absent when it was sold to an anonymous collector at an auction.

According to the website for the auction service of Christie's New York, the Blashfield painting, which they referred to as "Trumpets of Missouri," was sold at auction in 2014 to a private bidder for a substantial $149,000.

More than three decades have passed since the "Call of Missouri" first departed from its Kansas City home, and although it was later discovered, it has again managed to slip from the public eye. Disney, however, remains hopeful that this World War I work of art will someday be returned to the state for which it was created to honor.

"The painting has always been important to me personally because the first time that I saw a picture of it, I realized the commitment that was made by the people of Missouri to go and fight the battles of World War I," Disney said. "It was one of those pieces that once you view it, you never forget it." Pausing, he concluded, "And, it is my personal opinion that this piece is still the property of the Daughters of the American Revolution here in Missouri, and I can only hope that it will someday be returned to the people of Kansas City." *(Photograph courtesy of Jeremy P. Ämick)*

Jasper Cadice – *St. Louis*

Vic Cadice of Jefferson City recalls admonishments from his father that included staying out of trouble as not to defame yourself, your country, your family name and remain focused on earning a good education. These teachings were the result of his father's challenging experiences in his native Italy and were highlighted by two brothers serving on separate continents for the same cause during WWI in addition to their immigration to the United States. Gaspere "Jasper" Cadice was born on December 17, 1898, in the historical city of Marsala in western Sicily in Italy. When he was only ten years old, Jasper's own father traveled to the United States to find employment and earn enough money to bring over his wife and four children.

"My grandfather settled in north St. Louis (in 1908) because there were others from his area in Sicily that had already come there and had established a small Italian community," said Vic Cadice.

Between 1911 and 1912, Cadice explained, his father's older brother, Vito, was drawn into military service in Italy and served during the Italo-Turkish War. However, shortly after his discharge, he followed his father to the United States to find work and help raise the funds to bring over the rest of the family.

"It's a fascinating story because they finally earned the money to bring the rest of the family to America for a better life," said Vic Cadice. "My grandmother, father and his two older sisters went down to the docks in Palermo in 1914 to board the ship but during an examination, they found my grandmother had pink-eye and wouldn't let her go."

As the ship prepared to leave port, the agreement was made that another family immigrating to the U.S. would escort Jasper Cadice's sisters to St. Louis while he remained in Sicily with his mother. Once recovered, she and her son would make the trip overseas together.

"My grandmother recovered, but World War I erupted, and my father was inducted into the Italian Allied Army," said Vic Cadice. "My grandmother could have gone ahead and made the journey to St. Louis, but she told my father that since he waited for her, she would now wait for him to complete his military service."

In a voice recording made in the years prior to his passing, Jasper Cadice explained that he would first have to spend fifty-four months in the Italian military and endure untold hardships before finally having the opportunity to reunite with his family.

"I was in the First Regiment Engineers with headquarters in Rome … five blocks from the Vatican City," said Jasper Cadice in the recording. "Five days later, they transferred us to Palestrina—a mountain town where we learned to make mines, bridges, and explosives." From there, Jasper continued, they were transferred to Sulzano in northern Italy, where they were constantly harassed by artillery and bombs.

"Everybody was scared ... especially of gas," he recalled. "You had no choice but to make the best of it, and that's what I did."

Several months later, Jasper developed a horrible toothache, and his face swelled up to the extent that seeing a dentist became his only option. He had to walk a day and a half to meet up with a truck that carried him to a city, where he then waited in a line of soldiers to be seen by an army dentist. After a long wait, the young Italian soldier was shoved into a metal chair while the doctor struggled to extract the tooth without any painkillers. The tooth broke in two during the process, and the dentist had to make a second attempt, finally removing the remainder of the shattered tooth.

"He shoved me out with no water to wash my mouth and no cotton," Jasper Cadice said. "I could hardly see and walked out into the street and laid down on a bench."

While involved with his own military responsibilities in Italy, his older brother, Vito, was inducted into the U.S. Army while living in St. Louis. He would go on to serve in France during the war but never crossed paths with his younger brother. Shortly after returning to his company in northern Italy, Jasper Cadice participated in other major campaigns of the war. He noted that he and his fellow soldiers were often so starved that they would dig up wild roots for nutrition.

Following the armistice of November 11, 1918, he remained on duty for several months while his company helped rebuild structures damaged in the war. In 1919, he was finally able to reunite with his mother, but it was not until 1921 that they were able to sail for the United States.

"I think it's fascinating that my grandparents were living on two different continents during World War I and had one son in the Italian (Allied) army while another was serving in the United States Army," said Vic Cadice. "And," he added, "it was 12 years before the entire family was reunited."

His father settled in St. Louis, had many odd jobs, enjoyed a career as a partner in a corner grocery store business and later in real estate before retiring when he turned seventy years old. He met and married the sister of an Italian grocer, Corrine, while living in St. Louis, and the couple raised three sons together (two of whom are veterans).

"Education was very important to my father, and two of us became teachers while my other brother became a doctor," said Vic Cadice.

Jasper Cadice had attained the impressive age of ninety when he passed away in Florissant on October 8, 1989. The blessings he encountered after moving to the United States resulted in an enduring appreciation and love for his adopted country.

"Thank the almighty God who gave me the possibility and the open mind to raise a nice family," he said. "I thank God and the beautiful country of America that gives you a chance if you work hard and apply yourself.

"God bless America."

Elmer T. Pitts – *Pittsburgh*

Elmer T. Pitts of Pittsburgh, Missouri, was inducted into the U.S. Army at Hermitage on October 2, 1917. He initially trained with the 164th Depot Brigade at Camp Funston, Kansas. While still in the service, he married the former Icel Byler of Linn Creek in May 1918. The soldier was later assigned to Battery A, 336th Field Artillery of the 87th Division. Although the 336th served overseas during the war, they did not see combat. After the war, Pitts was employed as a school teacher for several years and later engaged in farming.

The veteran was two days shy of his sixty-seventh birthday when he passed away on October 22, 1954, and was laid to rest in the cemetery of Pittsburgh Missionary Baptist Church. *(Photograph courtesy of Jeremy P. Amick)*

William Lewis Krenzer – *Kansas City*

Born in St. Joseph, Missouri in 1893, William Lewis Krenzer is pictured while serving with the hospital corps of Kansas City's 3rd Missouri Infantry Regiment of the Missouri National Guard prior to the outbreak of World War I. During the First World War, they became part of the 140th Infantry Regiment, and Krenzer rose to the rank of sergeant while serving overseas with the regiment's medical department from April 25, 1918, to April 28, 1919. In later years, he was employed at the dairy operation known as Meade L. Merrell Farms in Pleasant Hill, Missouri. The eighty-one-year-old veteran passed away on December 14, 1974, and was laid to rest in Mount Moriah Cemetery in Kansas City.

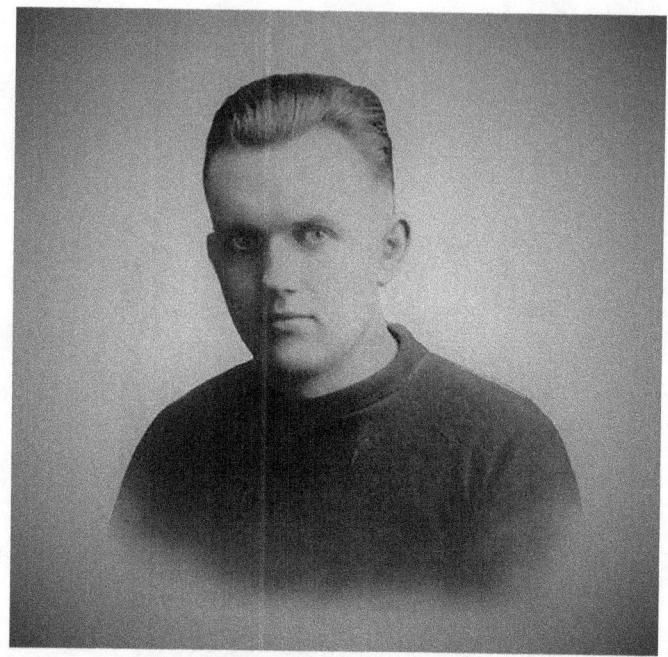

Paul A. Hamilton – *Harrisonville*

Born on November 15, 1896, Paul A. Hamilton, a native of Harrisonville, Missouri, is pictured in 1917 while serving as the captain of the University of Missouri-Columbia football team. He was quite popular as both a student and a player and was elected to serve as the team's captain by his fellow teammates during an election held in December 1916.

The December 7, 1916 edition of the *Evening Missourian* reported, "Hamilton had played little or no football when he entered the university three years ago. Since that time, he has put Harrisonville on the athletic map."

Records from the Missouri State Archives indicate the twenty-one-year-old played a role in supporting the nation's efforts in World War I when he entered military service at Camp Pike, Arkansas on January 5, 1918. He went on to attend officer training school with the 87th

Division and earned his commission as an infantry lieutenant. He was stationed at Camp Jackson (now Fort Jackson), South Carolina, and later served at Camp Gordon (now Fort Gordon), Georgia; however, he received his discharge from the Army in the fall of 1919.

In the years after the war, Hamilton worked briefly as a traveling salesman for a company out of Alabama but later became a realtor in the Kansas City area, establishing the Paul Hamilton Realty company and Hamilton-Crawford Company. Active in civic affairs, the World War I veteran served as president of the Kansas City's Board of Police Commissioners from 1945-1949 and was later appointed by the Kansas City mayor to serve on the City Plan Commission.[31]

The married father of two sons passed away in April 1980. (*Photograph courtesy of Jeremy P. Ämick*)

---

[31] April 20, 1980 edition of the *Kansas City Star*.

Lue Carruthers Lozier – *Carrollton*

Lue C. Lozier is featured in his official photograph taken in 1938 when he served as commander of the Roscoe Enloe American Legion Post 5 in Jefferson City, Missouri. The following year, he was elected state commander of the American Legion.

Born February 23, 1893, Lozier graduated from high school in Carrollton before enrolling at the University of Missouri-Columbia. While in college, he was elected as president of the student body prior to his graduation from law school in 1918. He went on to practice law in his hometown for a number of years and later became chief counsel for the Missouri Highway Commission. He would go on to serve as a commissioner for the Missouri Supreme Court for more than five years in addition to practicing law and lecturing at the University of Missouri. On March 3, 1958, Judge Lozier was appointed official Supreme Court reporter.

Inducted into the U.S. Army on July 25, 1918, Lozier trained stateside as an enlisted soldier during World War I with ambulance companies until receiving his discharge at Camp Zachary Taylor, Kentucky, following the armistice. Lozier was called to active duty as a captain in the U.S. Army in July 1941 and served four years during World War II with the Corps of Engineers—first in Washington D.C. and later in the Pacific Theater, where he handled litigation for the corps and earned a Legion of Merit for his efforts. He was discharged from the U.S. Army at the rank of lieutenant colonel. The veteran became quite active in the American Legion and was a founding member of Post 5 in Jefferson City in addition to being a member of the Veterans of Foreign Wars, the Military Order of World Wars, and the Society of Military Engineers.

It is interesting to note that he was the Democratic nominee for the 2nd Missouri District seat in Congress by two hundred and seventy votes in the 1944 election; however, he spent the entire campaign period deployed to Europe for service during World War II.[32] The seventy-nine-year-old veteran passed away on February 24, 1972, and was laid to rest in Oak Hill Cemetery in his native community of Carrollton, Missouri. *(Photograph courtesy of American Legion Post 5)*

---

[32] April 25, 1945 edition of the *Honolulu Star-Bulletin*.

Jay G. Hollingsworth – *Lexington*

Born December 28, 1890, in Lexington, Missouri, Jay Hollingsworth was employed as a miner by the McGrew Coal Company. His military service record indicates he was inducted into Company A, Sixth Missouri Infantry Regiment of the Missouri National Guard, on June 4, 1917. The following day, he registered for the military draft at the Lafayette County Courthouse in Lexington.

The Sixth Missouri Infantry Regiment was mobilized at Camp Clark near Nevada, Missouri, on August 5, 1917, and the following month moved to Camp Doniphan, Oklahoma, for further training. While at Camp Doniphan, the Sixth Regiment was consolidated with the Third Missouri Infantry Regiment to form the 140th U.S. Infantry under the 35th Division. During the war, Private Hollingsworth would serve with Company A, 140th Infantry Regiment.

The regiment departed the United States aboard troop ships on April 24, 1918, arriving at the wharves of LeHavre, France, on May 9,

1918.³³ Hollingsworth witnessed a lot of action during his six months in combat, most notably during the Meuse-Argonne Offensive when he was slightly wounded on September 27, 1918. He remained overseas after the armistice, leaving France on April 28, 1919, and returned to the United States to receive his honorable discharge.

According to his death certificate, the forty-year-old veteran was married and living in Kansas City, Missouri, when he died on January 10, 1931, from gangrenous appendicitis and was buried in Mount Muncie Cemetery in Lansing, Kansas.³⁴ *(Photograph courtesy of Jeremy P. Ämick)*

---

[33] 1939 Historical National Guard Annual, *140th Infantry*, XXX.
[34] Missouri Digital Heritage, *Missouri Death Certificates*, https://s1.sos.mo.gov/Records/Archives/ArchivesMvc/.

Victor Theodore Malloure - *Caruthersville*

Victor Malloure was born on June 27, 1887, in Evansville, Indiana. His family moved to Caruthersville when he was ten years old, and he went on to graduate from Caruthersville High School in 1906.

Malloure began his military career on March 16, 1906, when he enlisted as a private with Company I, Sixth Regiment of Infantry with the Missouri National Guard. He later served with Company B, Fourth Missouri Infantry, with whom he deployed to Texas in 1916 during the Mexican Border Campaign. He received his discharge as a second lieutenant on February 19, 1917, but two months later became a member of Company B, 139th Infantry. Although willing to serve in World War I, on March 21, 1918, Malloure received his discharge as a first lieutenant at Camp Doniphan, Oklahoma. As noted in the March 28, 1918 edition of the *Caruthersville Journal*, Lt. Malloure "was rejected from foreign service being disqualified on account of his eyes." Ten of his fellow soldiers in the regiment were similarly rejected for foreign service for medical reasons.

In the years following his military service, Malloure was the waterworks commissioner for Caruthersville and spent thirty years as fire chief. He also enjoyed twenty-six years as a U.S. Weather Observer for Pemiscot County and was an active member of American Legion Post 88. The married veteran was father to one daughter. He passed away at the age of seventy-three on July 1, 1960, and is interred in Little Prairie Cemetery in Caruthersville. *(Photograph courtesy of Jeremy P. Amick)*

George Florea – *Knox City*

For many years, a military portrait of George Florea has hung in the home of Jefferson City resident Dot Baker, representing a great-uncle that she never met because of his death in World War I. Acknowledging that she will one day pass the portrait on to one of her children, she hopes to learn more about her relative's military service in an effort to better understand the sacrifice he made on behalf of the nation.

"I didn't ask a lot of questions about him when I was growing up," said Baker when discussing the military service of her great uncle. "I would like to know more about where he fought and served in the war," she added.

Born in the community of Knox City in northeastern Missouri on April 24, 1895, Florea was one of nine children. Due to his age, the twenty-two-year-old cattle farmer was required to participate in the first draft registration day that was held on June 5, 1917. His draft order number was drawn during the first draft lottery held in Washington, D.C., on July 20, 1917. Several weeks later, on October 4, 1917, Florea was inducted into the U.S. Army at the nearby county seat located in the small town of Edina.

Following his induction, Florea was assigned to Company G, 354th Infantry Regiment—a company of the 89th Division comprised primarily of troops from eastern Missouri. According to the U.S. Army's Center of Military History, the regiment began forming at Camp Funston, Kansas, in August 1917 under the early guidance of Major General Leonard Wood. Florea and the soldiers of the 89th Division underwent several months of intense training that helped introduce them to many evolving threats of the war raging in France, including trench warfare. However, survival in combat under threats of gas attacks and shellfire launched by enemy troops were not the only possibility for which the soldiers were prepared.

"When a case of contagious disease, such as meningitis, measles or scarlet fever, appeared, all the men of the company were quarantined, were required to drill separately and were not permitted to join any assembly with other men," noted the book *History of the 89th Division*. The book further explained that when such situations occurred, "The floors of all buildings were washed daily with disinfectants. Every utensil used at the table was sterilized after each meal with scalding water" in an effort to halt the spread of the diseases occasionally racing through the camp.[35]

The young Florea made it through the training unscathed and, according to *Order of Battle* published by the U.S. Army's Center of Military Service, his division boarded transport ships on the east coast bound for overseas during the waning days of May 1918.[36]

---

[35] English Jr., *History of the 89th Division*, 25.
[36] Order of Battle, *Regiments*, 1398.

Following their arrival in France in early June, they participated in several weeks of strenuous training before entering into their baptism of fire in late summer.

"It was announced recently that the 89th Division had taken over trenches in the Toul sector about August 15 [1918]," reported the *St. Louis Star and Times* on September 20, 1918. Nine days later, the paper further explained, the 354th incurred their first casualty when William Unland of St. Louis was severely wounded in action.

In early September, the division took part in the St. Mihiel offensive in northeastern France. This battle lasted several days and was the first major offensive in which the American Expeditionary Forces—led by Missouri native Gen. John J. Pershing—operated as an independent army. Three weeks later, the St. Louis newspapers were full of reports of area soldiers serving in the 354th who were either killed or wounded in the campaign. As the calendar passed through the middle of September, U.S. forces began to shift their resources south toward the Argonne Forest and Meuse River. Throughout the next several weeks, Gen. Pershing commanded what became known as the Meuse-Argonne Offensive—the largest American-run offensive of the war with the ambitious goal of cutting off the German 2nd Army.

On September 25, 1918, during the transition into this new offensive, Florea was killed in action. Although the specifics of his death are not specified, evidence seems to indicate he died as a result of a gas attack. The *St. Louis Star and Times* reported in their October 22, 1918 edition that Pvt. Francis Crowley—a fellow soldier of Company G, 354th Infantry—was wounded by a gas attack the day after Florea's death.

The *War Diary of the 354th Infantry* notes that Florea was killed at Xammes and that on "September 21 we moved into front lines near Xammes. We suffered some gas casualties here. On the 28th, we retired to Boullioinville." The 89th Division history book also describes in great detail a couple of raiding parties that were made in enemy territory by soldiers of the 354th Infantry during the timeframe of Florea's death, which resulted in a handful of casualties from enemy artillery barrages.[37]

"The remains of George Elliott Florea, a Knox County soldier of Company G, 354th Infantry, who was killed in France in the Argonne Forest drive ... arrived Friday morning at Knox City from Hoboken, N.J.," reported the *Edina Sentinel* on June 30, 1921, describing the reinterment of remains of the local resident who had been buried overseas for nearly three years.

In the years after the war, Baker's grandmother, who was one of George Florea's three sisters, continued to honor the memory of her late brother by displaying a simple reminder of him in her northeast Missouri home.

"I remember the picture always hung in my grandmother's living room in LaBelle, and it has hung in my house since my parents passed away," said Baker. "Growing up, I knew he was very important to my grandmother, and being that he is family, it now means a lot to me." With a heavy pause, she added, "It's a connection to our past, and I will some day pass it down to one of my children as a continuance of his legacy." *(Photograph courtesy of Dot Baker)*

---

[37] McGrath, *War Diary of the 354th Infantry*, 98.

Ovid Sellers – *Lexington*

Fictional cinema characters have often romanticized the search for ancient fortunes, creating sensational images of archaeology and generating renewed interest in learning about past cultures. Yet the search for lost artifacts was a reality for one Missourian who not only served as a chaplain overseas during World War I but later became a renowned archaeologist and played a role in the discovery of a piece of Biblical history—the Dead Sea Scrolls.

Born August 2, 1884, in Texas, Ovid Rogers Sellers was raised on the campus of Wentworth Military Academy in Lexington, Missouri, where his father became superintendent and president of the institution. He was the oldest of the five children of Sandford Sellers Sr. and the former Lucia Rogers. The *Kansas City Journal* reported on June 3, 1898, that Sellers graduated from Wentworth, becoming the school's youngest graduate at the age of thirteen. He chose to continue his education at Morgan Park Academy in Illinois before becoming a student at the University of Chicago in 1901.

"Ovid Sellers returned home ... from the University of Chicago where he has been studying for the past four years," wrote the Lexington Intelligencer on June 18, 1904. "He was one of the graduates this year receiving the (bachelor's) degree."

The aforementioned newspaper reported on September 3, 1904, that the 20-year-old Sellers became assistant principal at a high school in Rockford, Iowa, affording him the opportunity to teach Latin, an educational direction "more in line with the studies he is pursuing and the intentions he entertains for the future."

Along with his father, the younger Sellers became a partial owner of the Lexington Intelligencer but sold his interest in 1912 when he entered the McCormick Theological Seminary. Earning a bachelor's degree in divinity in 1914, Sellers became an ordained Presbyterian minister for a church in Chicago. During World War I, he was appointed a chaplain at the rank of first lieutenant with the U.S. Army. Serving during the same timeframe as his two younger brothers, Sellers' military records indicate he served overseas from June 15, 1918, to May 23, 1919, with the 17th Field Artillery, 2nd Infantry Division.

Days prior to his departure for overseas service, the twenty-nine-year-old officer married the former Katherine Wilson at the home of the bride's parents in Lexington. Sellers WWI service coincided with that of his brothers—both of whom were officers, one with the U.S. Army and the other in the Marine Corps. As chaplain, he attended to the spiritual needs of the troops in his regiment, including the unenviable responsibility of notifying parents whose children died while in the military.

Following his discharge on May 26, 1919, Sellers continued his academic endeavors, earning a "Ph.D. from Johns Hopkins University in 1922," noted his obituary. "His studies concentrated largely on the Old Testament and ancient languages including Greek, Latin, Hebrew, Aramaic, Egyptian Hieroglyphics, Syriac, and Akkadian Cuneiform."

He returned to Chicago as Professor of the Old Testament at McCormick Theological Seminary and later fulfilled the role as dean for the school. According to the April 20, 1975 edition of the *Sante Fe New Mexican*, he also "enjoyed extended residence in the Holy Land where he was chosen by the American School of Oriental Research for in-depth study of various documents and artifacts going back 19 centuries and more."

While in Jerusalem "(e)arly in September 1948, Mar (Samuel) brought Professor Ovid R. Sellers ... some additional scroll fragments (from the Dead Sea Scrolls) that he had acquired," explained the website of the Messianic Prophecy Bible Project. "By the end of 1948, nearly two years after their discovery, scholars had yet to locate the original cave where the fragments had been found." [38]

Dr. Sellers attempted to locate the cave where the first four Dead Sea Scrolls were discovered, but political turmoil in Israel prevented his trip. He then attempted to secure assistance from the Syrians in finding the cave, but the price they charged was greater than Sellers could at the time afford. On January 28, 1949, the cave was located by a United Nations observer, and Sellers became the first person to take photographs of the discovery. Shortly thereafter, his photographs were published in Life magazine. His obituary states he was a staff member on ten archeological expeditions in Palestine and published several books on the Old Testament and Biblical archaeology.

Retiring from teaching in 1954, Sellers, his wife, and their daughter moved to Sante Fe, New Mexico, where he remained for the next

---

[38] Messianic Prophecy Bible Project, *The Dead Sea Scrolls*, https://freemessianicbible.com.

two decades. He made the decision to return home to Lexington in April 1975 and passed away nearly three months later at the age of ninety. The renowned Biblical scholar was laid to rest in the city's Machpelah Cemetery. Dr. Ovid Sellers was one of many Sellers descendants whose lives left an indelible mark not only on the world at large but also on their home community of Lexington. In 1972, three years prior to his death, Dr. Sellers had the privilege of joining his two brothers and their children, grandchildren, and extended family for a well-publicized reunion in their hometown.

"Sixty of the 87 descendants of Sandford and Lucia Sellers paraded the length of Main Street (in Lexington) ... in one of the typically untypical events of a weeklong Sellers family reunion," reported the *Kansas City Times* on August 19, 1972.

Days prior to his return to Lexington in 1975, the *Sante Fe New Mexican* issued what would soon become one of the last tributes to Dr. Sellers, describing the scholar and his wife as "filled with enthusiasm for a full and productive life ... (having) backed educational projects, religious programs and other organizations making for a better community for all to enjoy." *(Photograph courtesy of Wentworth Military Museum)*

Sandford Sellers Jr. – *Lexington*

Many young men have their entire lives struggled to crawl out from under the long shadow cast from a successful father. For decades, Sandford Sellers Sr. ushered the former Wentworth Military Academy in Lexington to academic success and international renown, a feat that virtually eclipsed the military and career distinctions his three sons, including Sandford Sellers Jr., would achieve in later years. Born February 5, 1892, Sellers Jr. went on to graduate from Wentworth Military Academy in 1908. He then enrolled at the University of Chicago, where, reported the *Lexington Intelligencer* on November 22, 1912, the young Wentworth graduate distinguished himself in football by representing his former school well "in the great gridiron battles ..."

The *Lexington Intelligencer* reported on June 20, 1913, that Sellers Jr., who recently graduated from the University of Chicago, was preparing to return to Lexington to join "the academic staff of Wentworth and coach" the school's football team. While in college, the newspaper further noted, "Sandy," as his classmates referred to him, received his training under Amos Alonzo Stagg—the legendary head football coach for the University of Chicago from 1892-1932 who led his "Maroons" to seven Big Ten Conference championships.

Shortly after returning to his hometown, explained Raymond W. Settle in his 1950 book, *The Story of Wentworth*, the junior Sellers purchased an interest in the academy and in 1914 became a partial leaseholder along with his father and Colonel W.M. Hoge, the latter of whom served many years as the school's superintendent.[39]

In the brief period leading up to World War I, Sellers Jr. wore many hats at the school, including a teacher of mathematics and science; coaching football, basketball, and track; director of athletics; assistant commandant and commandant. The year 1915 would also serve as an important period in the life of the Lexington native. Described as a "man of commanding presence and character," reported the *Climax-Madisonian* on June 16, 1915, the 23-year-old Sellers married Miss Marian Logan Kean—the granddaughter of Dr. J.V. Logan, who for many years was the president of Central University where Sellers' father acquired much of his formal education.

While Sellers Jr. was serving as commandant of Wentworth in 1917, World War I erupted, and he soon said goodbye to his wife and infant daughter, making the decision to enter an officer's training program with the U.S. Army at Camp Funston, Kansas. On August 15, 1917, he received his commission as a captain in the infantry. He completed a machine-gun school at Ft. Sill, Oklahoma, and was then assigned to Company C, 342nd Machine Gun Battalion of the 89th Division, with whom he would deploy overseas in late May 1918, boarding troop ships at Hoboken, New Jersey bound for England.

As described in the *History of the 89th Division*, the 342nd Machine Gun Battalion "received men from South Dakota, New Mexico, and

---

[39] Settle, *The Story of Wentworth*, 69.

Arizona," however, it was supplemented with "men from all of the states," many of whom came from Missouri. The battalion trained in France for several weeks before they "moved into the lines for the first time" at Mandres, France, north of Toul on August 7, 1918, as is noted in the record of Company C, 342nd Machine Gun Battalion. It was here that Sellers and the soldiers of the company "became familiar with the burst of shells and continuous gas alarms." [40]

The 342nd went on to participate in major engagements of the war, most notably the St. Mihiel Offensive and the Meuse-Argonne Offensive. Records of Company C indicate three soldiers from the battalion were killed in action, and five died from wounds suffered in combat. When the war ended, the battalion remained in Germany for several months before returning to the United States in late May 1919. Sellers Jr. was discharged from the U.S. Army on June 3, 1919, and returned to his family and career in Lexington. He was reinstated to his position at Wentworth Military Academy, where, in 1923, he succeeded his father as superintendent.

Sellers Jr. and his wife raised four children, and in 1933, he resigned his position at Wentworth to return to the University of Chicago and complete his master's degree. Throughout the next several years, he was employed as an educational advisor with the Civilian Conservation Corps and later became superintendent of Morgan Park Military Academy in Chicago.

"It might be said that Mr. Sellers has devoted his life to education among young men, and it would be difficult to find one more fitted by training, experience and temperament..." stated a biography of Sellers Jr. that appeared in the *1937 Annual of the Civilian Conservation Corps*. It was further noted that the educator "has always been active in community welfare and development work." [41]

---

[40] English Jr., *History of the 89th Division*, 22.
[41] Justin Museum of Military History, *Biography of Sandford Sellers Jr.*, https://justinmuseum.com.

In his later years, Sellers Jr. retired to Florida but remained associated with the school his father helped establish decades before. An article appearing in the *Sante Fe New Mexican* on September 10, 1972, explained that the sons of Sandford Sellers Sr., though achieving many independent successes, would always be connected to the Lexington community.

"We're always interested in what the Sellers's do," the newspaper quoted one Lexington resident. "They're an institution in this town," she added.

Sellers Jr. passed away on January 27, 1982. His body was returned to his hometown of Lexington and interred in Memorial Park Cemetery—the same cemetery where his father had been laid to rest decades previous. *(Photograph courtesy of Jeremy P. Ämick)*

James Sellers – *Lexington*

Colonel Sandford Sellers was a name synonymous with quality, military-focused education during his fifty-eight-year association with the former Wentworth Military Academy in Lexington, Missouri. In the years after World War I, his son, James McBrayer Sellers, demonstrated his own abilities to usher the institution into a new era of prosperity by using his father's example as a blueprint for leadership. The youngest of the Sellers' three sons, James, was born in the administration building at Wentworth Military Academy on June 20, 1895. As the years passed, he would grow up on the campus, eventually becoming a cadet in 1907.

In the book, *The Story of Wentworth*, author Raymond Settle explained that the youthful cadet demonstrated his aptitude for the military practices when he "won the General Scholarship and Best Drilled Cadet Medals in 1908-1909" and was "second lieutenant and won the Burnap Trophy for indoor rifle shooting" the following year.[42]

---

[42] Settle, *The Story of Wentworth*, 82.

Graduating from Wentworth in 1912, Sellers attended the University of Chicago, where he graduated summa cum laude in 1917. The United States soon declared war against Germany, and Sellers exhibited his interest and gift for leadership when making the decision to enlist in the military. The aspiring officer chose to accept an offer from the Marine Corps to commission ten graduates of Wentworth. "Capt. Sellers entered the Marine Corps as a second lieutenant in June 1917," reported the *Lexington Intelligencer* newspaper on December 26, 1919.... He commanded the 78th Company, 2nd Battalion of the 6th Marines from October 1918 to the demobilization of the regiment in August 1919."

His service card accessed through the Missouri State Archives indicates Sellers' Marine Corps service began at the rifle range located in Winthrop, Maryland, followed by nearly seven months at the Marine Corps Base at Quantico, Virginia, during which he received a temporary promotion to first lieutenant.

On January 19, 1918, noted the website of the Great War Association, the 2nd Battalion "went to League Island, Philadelphia in order to head out to France as part of the 4th Brigade, American Expeditionary Force." By late May 1918, Sellers and the 78th Company were entering combat as part of the Aisne-Marne Defensive, helping block German advances in the Chateau-Theirry Sector.[43]

This defensive would come to a close after a couple of weeks of fighting, but not before Sellers suffered a gunshot wound on June 6, 1918. As reported by the *Lexington Intelligencer* on July 5, 1918, Sellers "carried messages between Triangular Farm and Bouresches until severely wounded and then refused to accept medical attention until the last message had been delivered in person." The paper further reported, "A recent letter from Mac (Sellers) states that he was wounded ... and that he was in a hospital in Paris receiving the very best of attention and that his wound was healing rapidly."

---

[43] Great War Association, *78th Company, 6th Marines*, https://great-war-assoc.org.

According to his obituary, Sellers spent approximately three weeks recovering before returning to his company and receiving a temporary promotion to captain on September 6, 1918. He participated in additional engagements to include the Aisne-Marne Offensive and Meuse-Argonne Offensive; his bravery in combat earned him the Distinguished Service Cross and two Silver Star medals.

When the war came to a close, Sellers continued in command of the 78th Company until it was demobilized in August 1919. Four months later, in December 1919, he resigned his active duty commission "to enter upon his duties as assistant commandant at Wentworth Military Academy," reported the December 26, 1919 edition of the *Lexington Intelligencer.*

After returning to Wentworth in 1920, Sellers served as commandant until 1933, as superintendent until 1960, and as president until 1990. On December 28, 1925, he married Rebekah Hall Evans—great-granddaughter of Stephen G. Wentworth, the academy's founder—and the couple went on to raise three sons.

Sellers instructed many notable students to include former Congressman Ike Skelton, who, according to the Wentworth website, attended high school at the academy in 1945 and graduated from Wentworth Military Junior College in 1951. Another notable alumnus was the late Marlin Perkins, former host of the program "Mutual of Omaha's Wild Kingdom."

"An active teacher to the end," the September 6, 1990 edition of the *Mount Carmel Daily Republican Register* noted, Sellers "completed his final Latin class last May (1990), just a month before his 95th birthday." He passed away on September 5, 1990, and was laid to rest in Lexington's Memorial Park Cemetery. During his funeral ceremony, Sellers' grandson, Wentworth cadet Mark Sellers, played taps.

Sadly, the legacy of Wentworth, which had been assiduously preserved by the Sellers family, began to dull in the spring of 2017 when the academy was shuttered after 134 years of operations. Through many lean years, Sellers was able to preserve Wentworth, but declining enrollment and rising costs of providing a private education were to assume yet another victim.

The educator is no longer with us to share his experiences in leading one of the finest military academies in the Midwest; however, through sentiments expressed prior to his death, we sense the pride Sellers maintained for the institution to establish, grow and sustain throughout several decades.

"At Wentworth, we train the boys in leadership, responsibility, and self-confidence," said Sellers during an interview that appeared *in St. Louis Post-Dispatch* on May 11, 1972. "The military framework is the easiest way to teach these qualities. Wentworth has produced find leaders in all walks of life," stated Sellers. We're proud of the job we've done." (Photograph courtesy of Jeremy P. Ämick)

Joel Bennett "Champ" Clark – *Bowling Green*

November 11, 2018, marked the centennial of the armistice of World War I—a remembrance of the moment the guns fell silent on the Western Front. It was a victory achieved in large part to the efforts of Missourians such as General John J. Pershing of the small town of Laclede, who helped lead the American Expeditionary Forces to triumph. Additionally, Major General Enoch H. Crowder of the north-central Missouri community of Edinburg helped design the military draft mechanism that built Pershing's army. The dedication of Missourians to their country did not end with the armistice as a group of individuals gathered in Paris, France, in March 1919, for what became the first step in establishing the American Legion.

"The American Legion itself was created in 1919 in two caucuses of veterans," noted *The United States in the First World War: An Encyclopedia*. The book further explained, "The Paris meeting, which was held first [from March 15 to 17, 1919], set the tone for the new organization." … "The Paris Caucus, as the meeting was called, opened at the American Club, an old French residence."[44]

It was during this caucus that "(f)ive hundred officers and enlisted men of the American Expeditionary Forces took the first action … toward the formation of an association of veterans of the world war similar to the Grand Army of the Republic," reported the March 17, 1919 edition of the *Daily Arkansas Gazette*.

During the proceedings, Lieutenant Colonel Joel Bennett Clark (known as Bennett Champ Clark) from Bowling Green, Missouri, was elected temporary chairman of the new organization that would become the American Legion. Because of his election at the Paris Caucus, Clark was not only a co-founder but became the first national commander of the organization. Clark was the son of John Beauchamp "Champ" Clark, who represented Missouri as a member of the House of Representatives in Washington, D.C., from 1893 to 1895 and again from 1897 to 1921. To date, the elder Clark is the only Missourian to have served as Speaker of the House. A twenty-nine-year-old Lt. Col. Clark, while still serving with a federalized National Guard regiment in France in April 1919, received promotion to the rank of full colonel, thus becoming the youngest member of the American Expeditionary Forces to achieve that distinction.

An article appearing on the American Legion website explains the "initial founding caucus had been held in Paris in March and was composed of World War I veterans still in Europe. It was decided that prior to the first national convention of the fledgling organization, a second caucus should be held in the United States to include the input of those who had already returned home." The organizing caucus was held in St. Louis May 8-10, 1919, during which drafts of the Legion's Preamble and Constitution were approved, the structure of various state department and local posts outlined, various resolu-

---

[44] Venzon, *The United States in the First World War*, 29.

tions debated, and Minneapolis selected as the host city for the first national convention the following November.[45]

In the years after the war, the younger Clark not only remained active with the American Legion but also the 35th Division Veterans Association in addition to saving as president of the National Guard Association of the United States. He was a well-known and respected attorney and, in later years, served as the United States Senator from Missouri. He passed away in 1954 and was laid to rest in Arlington National Cemetery.

Returning service members from the Jefferson City area, many whom served under Lt. Col. Clark, did not hesitate in establishing their own local American Legion post. This small group of veterans received their official charter on June 21, 1919 for American Legion Roscoe Enloe Post 5, named in honor of a twenty-three-year-old local soldier killed in action while serving with a federalized National Guard unit during the Meuse-Argonne Offensive. Foster McHenry, a Jefferson City resident, and U.S. Army sergeant, wounded in combat, was elected to serve as the post's first commander in 1919. In 1928, nine years after the establishment of Post 5, Dr. L. David Enloe, the older brother of the post's namesake and renowned local physician, was elected post commander.

"I joined the American Legion in 1971 and have been a member now for forty-seven years," said Charley Goodin, a Navy veteran of the Vietnam War, during an interview in February 2019. "We have a proud history not only at the national level but here in our post as well," he added.

Dorothy Goodin, a long-time member of the auxiliary whose late husband Ben served with the U.S. Navy and National Guard, explained that she and other members of the post auxiliary have worked dili-

---

[45] The American Legion, *What Legion Event Celebrates its 93rd Anniversary in May?*, https://legion.org.

gently to organize a dinner celebrating the 100th anniversary of the founding of the American Legion. The birthday celebration was held at the post home on March 16, 2019. The guest speaker at the event was Dale Barnett of Douglasville, Georgia, a retired U.S. Army lieutenant colonel who served as national commander of the American Legion from 2015-2016.

"This post has been an important part of the community for so many decades, and our members have been actively involved in a number of important programs," said Dorothy Goodin. "That's why we invited members of the community and their special guests to come help us celebrate our proud legacy at both the national and local level." *(Photograph courtesy of American Legion Post 5)*

Walter P. Chalender - *Springfield*

A group of Purple Heart recipients used to meet for breakfast monthly at a Veterans of Foreign Wars post in Springfield, enjoying a meal and fellowship. During one of these informal gatherings, Marine Corps veteran Bryce Lockwood was handed a package by a member of the post containing photographs and documents. Lockwood was advised it had been left by an individual who believed the materials were of some importance and should not be discarded. The package contained information regarding two local veterans—one who, after being drafted in World War I, saw combat in France with a field artillery battery and, years later, witnessed the introduction of airmail service to the Springfield area while serving as a mail carrier.

Walter Penry Chalender, according to his draft registration card, was born and raised in Wellsville, Kansas, but owned and operated his own farm near Springfield when he registered for the military draft on June 5, 1917. Three months later, the twenty-two-year-old was drafted into the U.S. Army and assigned to the 342nd Field Artillery.

"The 342nd Field Artillery was organized September 5, 1917, at Camp Funston, Kansas ..." explained Robert Chubb, regimental historian, in the 1921 book *Regimental History 342nd Field Artillery, 89th Division*. He added, "The regiment was recruited from the first draft of men from Green(e), Polk, Dallas, Stone, Bollinger, and Laclede counties of southern Missouri—men for the most part from farms and rural communities."[46]

For months, the newly formed regiment trained at the Kansas military post, learning such skills as the construction of divisional trench systems similar to those being used in France. They performed road marches around scrap piles of lumber while witnessing new barracks spring up across the surrounding prairie to house scores of fresh draftees being inducted into the military. The regimental historian explained that in April 1918, the regiment began more intense training and practice "on the target range; first with the three-inch guns and later with 4.7 (inch) howitzers." He also noted the regiment was broken down into six batteries and two companies, leaving "Camp Funston on June 3rd, 1918, considerably below strength, having contributed an average of 100 men a month to replacement detachments...."

Records accessible through the Missouri State Archives reveal Chalender departed for overseas service, along with his fellow soldiers of the regiment, on June 28, 1918. Following their arrival overseas, they trained for several weeks in France and received a battery of 1915 Schneider 155mm howitzers to use in combat. They entered service on the front lines during the third week of September 1918, suffering four casualties in Battery D when German shells struck their lines on the twenty-first. Eventually, the regimental historian

---

[46] Chubb, *Regimental History*, 3.

explained, "the regiment began to settle down to the routine of firing at night and working during the day, sleeping between times."

The batteries of the regiment supported infantry along the Hindenburg Line, pounding with their deadly howitzer shells German targets such as command posts and machine-gun emplacements. After the armistice, which occurred at 11:00 a.m. on November 11, 1918, many of the former enemies met in a friendly fashion on the former front lines of the war, which, the regimental historian wrote, was followed by a "general celebration signalized by thousands of rockets and flares."

Chalender remained in Germany for the next several months, assigned to the regimental headquarters while they performed duties as part of the occupational forces. He received a promotion to the rank of "color sergeant" in March 1919, having the responsibility for carrying the regimental colors (guidon, standard or flag). The soldier returned to the states in early June 1919, receiving his discharge and working as a stenographer for a local grocery store. In 1920, he married the former Agnes Rainey, and the couple raised two daughters. As the years passed, the WWI veteran was hired by the U.S Postal Service and was employed many years as a letter carrier.

A highlight of his postal career came more than a decade following his military service. As the *Springfield Leader* reported on October 28, 1930, "transcontinental air mail and passenger service became a reality Saturday." Chalender, a member of the Springfield post office band, helped celebrate "the opening of the Transcontinental-Western Airline with rousing music."

To capture the historic moment, Chalender mailed his youngest daughter, eight-year-old Anetta June, a letter with an envelope marked with a postal stamp celebrating the momentous occasion. On a paper yellowed with age found inside the envelope, he wrote, "Greetings from your father on our first Air Mail flight, Oct. 25, 1930."

The veteran and his wife continued to live and work in the community of Springfield. Sadly, his sixty-seven-year-old wife passed away from complications related to cancer on March 8, 1968; Chalender passed away five years later and lies next to his wife in Springfield's Hazelwood Cemetery. Why many of Chalender's personal effects and documentation were given to the VFW remain something of a mystery, but as Lockwood noted upon receiving the package, he recognized the items represented a unique parallel to another Missouri WWI veteran.

"My understanding is that it may have been a member of the family that brought it to the VFW post because it didn't hold a great deal of importance for them, but they realized it was of some military historical significance," said Lockwood. "And what makes it even more interesting," he added, "is that (Chalender) was a man from Missouri who served in WWI with a field artillery battery." With a grin, he concluded, "I seem to remember another young man from Missouri who served with the field artillery in WWI and went on to become president—Harry S. Truman!" *(Photograph courtesy of Bryce Lockwood.)*

Dr. Newton Enloe – *Moniteau County*

The Russellville area has produced many talented young people who have made great strides in the medical practice. In years past, many of these individuals came from a local branch of the Enloe family tree and includes a respected physician who established an impressive medical center that continues to thrive in the state of California. Newton Thomas Enloe was born on February 3, 1872, in the small community of Lamar, Missouri. (Twelve years later, future World War I veteran and president, Harry S. Truman, was born in the same town.) However, Enloe's family later moved to Russellville, where he attended a local school while his family toiled on their farm.

The third oldest of eleven children, Newton Enloe later attended the former Hooper Institute in nearby Clarksburg—a preparatory school for those interested in continuing their education to become teachers, lawyers, and doctors.

He went on to spend "a year at the Louisville (Kentucky) Medical College, in 1891, and then attended the Missouri Medical College in St. Louis for four years, from which he graduated in 1895, with the degree of M.D.," noted George C. Mansfield in the book *History of Butte County, California*.[47]

Dr. Enloe completed several post-graduate courses in Chicago and New York and, in 1896, married the former Emma Leslie from the Russellville area. Sadly, the following year, tragedy struck when his eighteen-year-old wife passed away unexpectedly and was laid to rest in Enloe Cemetery west of Russellville. Dr. Enloe went on to invest the next six years of his life operating a medical practice in Jefferson City. From there, his migration to points west began with his employment as the physician for the Sierra Lumber Company in 1901.

While living in California, Dr. Enloe met Isabelle Mansfield, a grammar school teacher, and the couple married in 1906. They would later raise one son, Newton Thomas Enloe, Jr.

In the aforementioned book, Mansfield explained that when the lumber company "sold out to the Diamond Match Company, (Dr. Enloe) located in Chico (California), in 1907, for general practice. Immediate recognition of his ability brought him the appointment of Chief Surgeon of the Diamond Match Company...."

In 1908, the *Chico-Daily Evening Enterprise* reported that tragedy again befell the Enloe family when their infant son died at their residence in Chico, California, on October 18, 1908. Yet Enloe remained dedicated to his medical career, later embarking upon the grand crusade of delivering medical care to the masses when opening the Enloe Hospital on Flume Street in Chico.

"The Dr. N.T. Enloe hospital ... opened for business last night and received its first patient," noted the *Chico Enterprise* in the September

---

[47] Mansfield, *History of Butte County, California*, 669.

11, 1913 edition. "The formal opening, in which public officials, doctors, professional men, and the press will be invited to inspect the building, will take place next Monday."

His civilian medical endeavors found pause in late June 1918, when forty-six-year-old Dr. Enloe temporarily closed the hospital to support the scores of fellow Americans serving in the military; he volunteered as a physician with the United States Medical Reserve Corps. Enloe was commissioned as captain and served at the Letterman Army Hospital in San Francisco, treating patients wounded and injured in the war.

The *Sacramento Bee* reported in the August 17, 1918 edition of the newspaper that many of the personnel who were working at Enloe Hospital when it closed for Dr. Enloe's absence volunteered for "war work" and received a transfer to Fabiola Hospital in Oakland, California.

During this same timeframe, Dr. Enloe's son, Newton Thomas Enloe Jr., also served his country. He became a member of the 669th Aero Squadron and had recently passed the examination to attend aviation training school at Wilbur Wright Field in Ohio. Returning to his medical practice and the operation of Enloe Hospital after the war ended, Dr. Enloe was again visited by tragedy when his second wife, Isabelle, died from pneumonia in 1921 in the hospital bearing her husband's name. Mrs. Enloe was forty-four years old at the time of her passing and was laid to rest in Chico Cemetery.

"February 8 (1922) has been set as the date for the marriage of Dr. N.T. Enloe and Miss Dorothy Schram it was announced yesterday," shared the January 21, 1922 edition of the *Oroville Daily Register*.

The Enloe Hospital opened at a new location on the Esplanade in Chico, California, in 1937. On December 2, 1954, the hospital received accreditation from the Joint Commission on Accreditation of Hospitals. This achievement was tempered by the death of eighty-two-year-old Dr. Enloe less than three weeks later, survived by his wife, son, and two daughters.

Interred in Chico Cemetery, Dr. Enloe's third wife, Dorothy, died two years later and was laid to rest alongside him. His hospital has since grown to become the Enloe Medical Center and is now a "298-bed nonprofit hospital with the mission of improving that quality of ... life through patient-centered care," explained the hospital website. Additionally, the hospital now houses the region's only Level II intensive care unit and operates a FlightCare air ambulance service.

More than a century ago, a young man from the Russellville area resolved to pursue an interest in practicing medicine. This quest eventually led him to the West Coast, where, to this day, the hospital he established continues to enrich the lives of its patients.

Until his death, Dr. Enloe looked with great hope toward the future of medical care in his community. As reported by the Chico-Enterprise Record on December 22, 1954, he remarked, "When a man retires, he is through, and there is yet much to be done." He added, "I love my work, and I shall continue in it as long as I live, and I shall hope to make even greater strides in the future than I have in the past." *(Photograph courtesy of Jeremy P. Amick)*

Louis A. Gates – *St. Joseph*

Since the founding of the United States, African Americans have served in the armed forces. During World War I, with scores of young men being drafted while others made the decision to enlist, these brave individuals often found themselves placed in an assortment of non-combat support roles and being treated as second-class citizens despite providing first-class contributions. However, as noted in an article by Jami L. Bryan on the website of the National Museum of the U.S. Army, by the end of WWI, black volunteers "served in cavalry, infantry, signal, medical, engineer, and artillery units, as well as serving as chaplains, surveyors, truck drivers, chemists, and intelligence officers."[48]

Louis Adam Gates, born November 17, 1890, grew up in the predominately white community of Hastings, Nebraska, where his father worked for the local railroad. His parents passed at a young age, leav-

---

[48] Bryan, *Fighting for Respect*, https://armyhistory.org.

ing him to help raise his younger brother and sister. Eventually, he met the former Martha Williams of St. Joseph, and the couple married in February 1915.

On June 5, 1917, the twenty-six-year-old was required to register with his local board for the military draft under the auspices of the Selective Service Act. At the time, his registration card (mistakenly citing his first name as "Lewis" rather than "Louis) showed he was living in Kansas City and employed as a porter with one of the former Owl Drug Stores of the city.

More than a year passed before he received his call to the colors, undergoing his induction into the U.S. Army on August 5, 1918. He was soon on his way across the state border to begin training with Company M, 806th Pioneer Infantry Regiment at Camp Funston, Kansas, which is located on present-day Fort Riley. The *Kansas City Star* reported on July 26, 1919, that "the 805th and 806th Pioneer Infantry regiments (were) negro units which were organized at Camp Funston of drafted men from Missouri and Kansas…"

According to the *History of the 805th Pioneer Infantry* by Major Paul S. Bliss, the formation of both the 805th and 806th was from a directive by Pres. Woodrow Wilson, in May 1918, authorizing the organization of "eight colored infantry regiments," followed by a War Department letter explaining that "(t)wo of these were to be raised at Camp Funston, Kan."[49]

Following his induction, Gates accompanied the regiment to Camp Mills, New York, where they received several additional weeks of training. As Margaret McMahon explained in *A Guide to the U.S. Pioneer Infantry Regiments in WWI*, these soldiers "were trained in infantry tactics, but they were also trained in combat engineering."[50]

---

[49] Bliss, *History of the 805th Pioneer Infantry*, 11.
[50] McMahon, *A Guide to the U.S. Pioneer Infantry Regiments in WWI*, 14.

A passenger list reveals that Gates' company boarded the USS *Powhatan*—a German ocean liner secured by the U.S. at the outset of the war—at the Port of Embarkation in Hoboken, New Jersey on September 15, 1918, preparing to set sail for the war raging in France. The vessel arrived at the port in Brest, France, on September 27, 1918. Initially, the 806th was attached to First Army and participated in the deadly Meuse-Argonne Offensive, which was the largest operation of the entire war that claimed the lives of more than 26,000 U.S. troops.

"Pioneer troops, as the term was used in our Army, may be described as regiments trained and equipped as infantry to be used as troops of emergency, either for combat or simple engineering construction," noted the Philadelphia War History Committee in the book *Philadelphia in the World War, 1914-1919*.[51]

He added, "Overseas (they) operated with the infantry, or as part of the reserve, but usually, they worked with the engineers in building and repairing bridges, roads, camouflage screens, and trenches, cutting wire entanglements and keeping open the communications over the spongy, shell-torn roads for troops, artillery, ambulances, ammunition, and supplies, often under the fire of artillery, machine guns and airplanes, bearing their inevitable share of the casualties."

When the armistice brought an end to hostilities on November 11, 1918, the soldiers of the 806th Pioneer Infantry Regiment remained in Europe with the Army of Occupation until departing St. Nazaire, France aboard the USS *Arizonan* on July 21, 1919. Arriving in Brooklyn, New York, on July 6, 1919, Gates went on to receive his discharge on July 15, 1919.

In the years following his wartime service, Gates spent thirty years as a laborer and butcher with Swift and Company—a meatpacking house in St. Joseph. Additionally, the married veteran became father

---

[51] Philadelphia War History Committee, *Philadelphia in the World War*, 180.

to a son, Louis A. Gates Jr. He maintained pride in his WWI service, helping establish the Roy Curd American Legion Post 51 in St. Joseph, where he served as a post commander and adjutant. (The post was named for a local African American veteran of the 805th Pioneer Infantry who died from pneumonia during the war.) Gates was also active with his local VFW post, serving many years as their adjutant.

"Louis A. Gates, 61 years old, died yesterday afternoon at a local hospital," noted the February 9, 1952 edition of the St. Joseph Gazette. He was laid to rest in Ashland Cemetery in St. Joseph, the city he had called home for 37 years.

As a young soldier, Private Gates had become part of a unique organization that performed many integral tasks in World War I. His regiment represented a large swath of dedicated individuals who never received any appreciable recognition for the scope of the duties they performed under combat conditions. In her aforementioned book, author Margaret M. McMahon explains that their contributions and mettle were ideally described in a simple but bold statement attributed to an unknown Pioneer Infantry officer.

"They did everything the Infantry was too proud to do, and the Engineers too lazy to do." (Photograph courtesy of Jeremy P. Ämick)

Oscar L. Smith – *St. Joseph*

The United States World War I Centennial Commission reported that during World War I, scores of African Americans supported the war effort despite being "assigned menial support roles, due to American society's deep fears and prejudices." The commission further explained that regardless of any racism they may have endured, "at home and in uniform, tens of thousands of black soldiers served courageously and capably in combat."⁵²

This impressive military legacy includes men such as Oscar Lee Smith, who was born March 18, 1895, in the small Carroll County community of Norborne, Missouri. The twenty-two-year-old was living in St. Joseph when the military draft required that he travel to Jefferson Barracks in St. Louis, where he was inducted into the U.S. Army on November 25, 1917.

---

52 The United States World War One Centennial Commission, *African-Americans – World War I,* https://worldwar1centennial.org.

In the article "True Sons of Freedom" written by Jennifer Keene for the *American Legion* magazine, she explained, "Upon the U.S. declaration of war in April 1917, all existing eight black National Guard infantry regiments quickly filled to capacity with volunteers."[53] Keene further noted that this voluntary spirit became the primary reason that more than "96 percent of the 367,710 African-Americans who served during the war were conscripted…" She added that the black draftees and volunteers "eventually formed 13 percent of the wartime Army, even though they represented only 10 percent of the civilian population."

Smith, along with a group of other recent U.S. Army inductees, was assigned to Company I, 303rd Stevedore Regiment, organized at Camp Hill, Virginia. He soon discovered that one of the primary responsibilities of the stevedore regiments was accommodating the movement of supplies through various ports in support of the American Expeditionary Force serving overseas.

In the book *Scott's Official History of the American Negro in the World War* published in 1919, author Emmett J. Scott summarized several of the critical duties that Private Smith and his contemporaries performed in Europe.

"For every soldier who gets even a glimpse of the enemy or risks his life within range of shellfire, there must, in all modern warfare, be from twenty to thirty men working at such commonplace and routine tasks as loading and unloading ships, building piers, laying railroad tracks, making roads, in a thousand other ways making it possible for the fighting men to get to the front, and for the necessary food, ammunition, and other supplies to reach them."[54]

On December 5, 1917, Smith and the regiment were transferred under the 849th Transportation Corps and deployed to France three

---

[53] Keene, *True Sons of Freedom* https://legion.org.
[54] Scott, *Scott's Official History of the American Negro in the World War*, 315.

weeks later aboard the transport vessel *President Grant*. While in France, Smith and his fellow stevedores were employed essentially as dockworkers and laborers, offloading ships when they arrived at their destinations.

An article by Col. Richard Goldenberg accessible through the USO website noted that of the nearly 380,000 African Americans who served in the Army during World War I, nearly 200,000 of these soldiers were deployed to Europe. Col. Goldenberg further explained, "But more than half of those who deployed were assigned to labor and stevedore battalions, assigned to tasks that many Army leaders saw as most appropriate."[55]

Despite not receiving the glory and respect that may have been given to those soldiers who helped win the war through more conspicuous efforts such as trench warfare along the Western Front, Smith and his fellow stevedores performed their duties as assigned and in an efficient and impressive manner.

When the war came to an end, they remained in France for several months continuing to load and offload supply ships. Finally, on July 30, 1919, the 849th Transportation Corps departed Brest, France, aboard the transport ship *Saxonia*. In the years following his discharge and return to Missouri, Smith married and became father to a daughter, stepdaughter, and two stepsons. Newspaper records reveal that the WWI veteran was active with the Boy Scouts while his obituary and death certificate note he retired as a night watchman from Swift & Company - a meatpacking plant in St. Joseph.

The service of African-American troops during the war instilled a sense of brotherhood and pride that resulted in an enduring sense of camaraderie. But, as segregation continued to permeate the military structure and society at large, many minority veterans were not welcomed in the newly formed white American Legion posts. As a

---

[55] Goldenberg, *In World War I* ..., https://uso.org.

result, Smith and many of his fellow World War I veterans resolved to take leading roles by establishing historically black American Legion posts in their communities throughout the United States.

In 1920, Smith became a founding member (and later commander) of the Roy Curd Post 51 of the American Legion, which was named for a local black soldier who died in World War I. Sadly, Smith was only sixty-seven years old when he passed away on June 24, 1962, and is interred in the city's Ashland Cemetery.

Author Emmett J. Scott in his aforementioned book, stressed soldiers such as Smith and his fellow veterans, though often working under segregated and less than glorious conditions in the war, never wavered in their duties, nor was there ever any question regarding the value of their contributions.

"The work of the Negro Stevedore Regiments and Labor Battalions, and their unremitting toil at the French ports—Brest, St. Nazaire, Bordeaux, Havre, Marseilles—won the highest praise from all who had the opportunity to judge of the efficiency of their work." He added, "Every man who served his country in one of these organizations was as truly fighting to save his country as though he had carried a rifle and killed Germans." *(Photograph courtesy of Jeremy P. Ämick)*

Jeremy P. Amick

Coly Karr – *High Point*

Born on January 15, 1892, near the Moniteau County community of Clarksburg, Coly Bridges Karr was living in nearby High Point when he was inducted into the U.S. Army on September 21, 1917, and completed his initial training with the 164th Depot Brigade at Camp Funston, Kansas. The soldier then became a member of Battery B, 130th Field Artillery, with whom he served in France from May 19, 1918, to April 23, 1919. The seventy-year-old retired farmer and World War I veteran passed away at the Veterans Hospital in Kansas City in 1962 and is interred in High Point Cemetery. *(Photograph courtesy of Moniteau County Historical Society)*

Tirey J. Ford - *Independence*

The American Legion Post 21 in Independence, Missouri, was chartered in honor of twenty-year-old Sgt. Tirey J. Ford who was killed in action during the Meuse-Argonne Offensive on September 29, 1918, while serving with Battery C, 129th Field Artillery. The veteran was laid to rest in the Meuse-Argonne American Cemetery in France.

For a number of years, there has been a competition between American Legion Post 21 and American Legion Post 5 in Jefferson City for the bragging rights of being the largest post in the state. However, Post 21 has the privilege of being the home post for another notable Missourian and World War I veteran of the 129th Field Artillery—former President Harry S. Truman. *(Photograph courtesy of Jeremy P. Amick)*

Reuben Hamilton Williams - *Moberly*

Reuben Hamilton Williams was born on February 28, 1885, in St. Clair, Missouri. He would go on to graduate from medical school, and on December 15, 1917, Dr. Williams enlisted in the U.S. Army. During World War I, he served as a first lieutenant with the 40th Field Hospital until April 21, 1918, the 19th Field Hospital until May 1, 1918, followed by assignment to the 80th Field Hospital. The final assignment of his World War I service was with elements of the 6th Division.

At the time of his passing on February 6, 1947, he was living in Moberly as a city physician and was also coroner of Randolph County. The father of a daughter and son, Dr. Williams, was laid to rest in Oakland Cemetery in Moberly next to his wife, who preceded him in death by nearly two years. *(Photograph courtesy of Jeremy P. Amick)*

Henry Robinson Clay Jr. – *Plattsburg*

The men of the United States who took to the skies to fight in World War I demonstrated profound courage to not only crawl into the cockpit of a flimsy airplane and risk being shot down or killed but volunteering to do so with little more than a decade of science and technology to support their fledgling aviation efforts. Despite the lack of an appreciable military aviation program in the United States during the early period of World War I, many embraced the opportunity to fly for the French and British in the war, including a young man from Missouri who earned the coveted distinction of "flying ace."

Henry Robinson Clay Jr. was born November 27, 1895, in the community of Plattsburg, Missouri, a small town north of Kansas City. He went on to graduate from high school in 1913 and later attended the University of Missouri-Columbia, where he participated in Army ROTC and was a member of the Kappa Sigma fraternity.

"In June 1916, he received an A.B. degree... followed with a year of law at Texas State University," reported the *Plattsburg Leader* (Plattsburg, Missouri) in their September 24, 1920 edition. The paper added, "Two months after our country's declaration of war, he enlisted in the ground school of aviation at Austin."

According to the July 27, 1919 edition of the *Austin American-Statesman*, the School of Military Aeronautics of the University of Texas, in which Clay chose to enroll, "was the first effort made by university authorities to aid the Government in the training of aviators." In addition to training pilots, the newspaper stated that "(e)arly in 1919 over 1,200 cadets were in training at the school and it represented the largest air service training school in ground instruction in the United States."

The nation's entry into the air war in Europe was a rather harsh experience, explained David A. Anderton in *The History of the U.S. Air Force*. He wrote, "No American-trained airmen fought in the skies of France until more than one year after the entry of the United States into the war." Anderton also wrote about the perilous conditions Clay and his fellow American airmen were soon to encounter. "The airmen flew castoffs from the French and British air arms, outmoded airplanes whose performance ranged from indifferent to dangerous. Spare parts were lacking; they were improvised ..."[56]

Clay completed his aviation training in July 1917 and was sent to New York to board a troopship bound for England. Following his arrival overseas, he trained for several months to prepare for the combat conditions he would encounter in the skies over France. Sadly, much of the training provided in the U.S. lacked a focus on critical facets of combat, including aerial gunnery.

"He was put over the German lines April 6, 1918, ranking as 2nd Lieutenant and then Captain; July 1st, 1918 he was made Flight

---

[56] Anderton, *The History of the U.S. Air Force*, 21.

Commander of the 148th Squadron of the Royal Flying Corps ..." reported his hometown newspaper, the *Plattsburg Leader*, on September 24, 1920.

The young aviator flew missions aboard a Sopwith Camel, which was "among the most produced, versatile and ubiquitous combat aeroplanes of its time, serving over land and sea from England to Mesopotamia, as well as post-war revolution-convulsed Russia," noted Jon Guttman in his book aptly titled *Sopwith Camel*.[57]

The iconic WWI fighter was a single-seat biplane powered by a rotary engine with two forward-firing Vickers machine guns for its armament. It had the potential maximum speed of 115 miles per hour with a range of 301 miles.

Lt. Clay distinguished himself on a number of occasions, surpassing the five aerial victories needed to earn the accolade of fighter ace. His prowess as an aviator not only allowed him to survive in a deadly battle front but earned him a coveted British medal, the Distinguished Flying Cross, for extraordinary heroism in aerial combat.

Gorrell's History of the American Expeditionary Forces Air Service, 1917-1919, explained that on August 16, 1918, "while (Lt. Clay was) leading his patrol, they were attacked by six Fokker Biplanes near Noyon. Clay shot down one in flames and with his (group) drove the others East." The book went on to describe Clay's aerial victories on August 27 and September 4, 1918, noting that he was responsible for the destruction of five enemy aircraft and proudly citing he "exhibited on all occasions admirable qualities of leadership and has moulded his flight into a most effective fighting unit."

Although the specific number of aerial victories Clay celebrated vary between historical books and newspaper accounts, The Aerodrome, a website dedicated to the history of WWI flying aces and the historic

---

[57] Guttman, *Sopwith Camel*, 2.

aircraft they piloted, credits eight aerial victories to the Missouri-born pilot.

When the war came to an end with the signing of the armistice, the aviator remained overseas on the staff of Col. Harold Fowler, chief of the Air Service for the occupational forces. He later spent time in Chaumont, France, to assist in writing a manual for aviation tactics; however, on February 1st, 1919, he reported for his new duty assignment in Coblenz, Germany. The aviation hero soon fell ill and was instructed to report to the local hospital. He unexpectedly died from pneumonia in Coblenz on February 9, 1919, having reached only 23 years of age. Though initially interred overseas, his remains were returned to the United States the following year.

"Beautiful and fitting was the tribute paid by Plattsburg and Clinton County on Monday, September 20th, 1920, to our hero, Capt. Henry Robinson Clay Jr...." reported the September 24, 1920 edition of the *Plattsburg Leader*. In mournful tribute to their fallen hero, the paper added, "The remains were brought to his old home for burial and a throng of people, estimated at from two to three thousand, came to honor our illustrious American Ace, who fought valiantly through the war ... only to succumb to pneumonia (and) thus ending a brilliant and brief career." *(Photograph courtesy of Museum of Missouri Military History).*

Eugene Earle Amick Sr. – *Kansas City*

Eugene Earle Amick Sr. has been described as a self-made man who achieved career success as the youngest bank president in Missouri while armed only with an eighth-grade education. This career path, his daughter notes, was briefly interrupted by World War I, as he left home to serve with the U.S. Navy and nearly succumbed to the deadly Spanish flu pandemic that gripped the nation. Born December 3, 1886, in the small town of Lone Elm in Cooper County, Amick was raised in the community of Bunceton. His father, Alonzo (Lon), passed away in 1903 and, according to the 1910 U.S. Census, Eugene Amick became the head of the household and sole support for his mother and twenty-year-old sister.

"He was a Horatio Alger-type young man," said Amick's daughter, Joanne Comer, invoking the name of a famous author who wrote about individuals rising above their meager beginnings through hard work, determination courage, and honesty.

In the book *History of Cooper County, Missouri*, author William Foreman Johnson noted that Amick was just fourteen years old when he began working at the bank in Bunceton, rising "from janitor and messenger boy to the position of cashier in eight years ..."[58]

Speaking of her father's dedication to bettering himself, Comer explained, "He took correspondence courses as a young man. They complained about his handwriting, so he practiced the Spencerian Script (a once-popular standard for teaching students handwriting) until he had very nice handwriting."

Amick would later assist in organizing the Boonville National Bank in 1916, wrote Johnson, and "was elected president of this concern, which is the largest, most important and the strongest financial institution of Central Missouri ..."

The following year, on May 23, 1917, he married the former Gertrude Jones, only weeks after the United States declared war on Germany. For the next year, Amick focused his efforts on his banking responsibilities; however, on July 30, 1918, the thirty-one-year-old took leave from his banking position when making the decision to enlist in the United States Navy. Completing his boot camp at the Great Lakes Naval Training Station in Illinois, the young sailor soon fell deathly ill with the Spanish flu, a pandemic that claimed the lives of millions of victims worldwide in a short span of time.

"While my father was in training, he contracted the devastating flu," said his daughter, Joanne Amick Comer. "He spoke of them playing a funeral march all day long while he could hear coffins being stacked outside of his hospital window," she sordidly added.

While the sailor was in the hospital recovering from the illness, the war ended with the signing of the armistice on November 11, 1918. The following month, Yeoman 3rd Class Amick received his dis-

---

[58] Johnson, *Eugene Earle Amick*, 370.

charge from the U.S. Navy and returned to Missouri. His wife, who had become pregnant prior to Amick's enlistment, gave birth to their first child in January 1919—Eugene "Gene" Earle Amick Jr. In the years after the war, Amick moved his family to Kansas City after becoming vice-president of First National Bank. He and his wife welcomed their second child, Lon, in 1920, followed by their third and final child, Joanne, in 1928.

The former sailor, who never finished high school, achieved yet another professional milestone in 1921 when he became a trustee of William Jewell College in Liberty.

"My father was very proud that during World War II, my older brother Gene also trained at the Naval Training Station at Great Lakes," said Joanne Comer. "It was a shock to us all when he was killed on August 9, 1942, while serving as a communications officer aboard the USS Astoria during the Battle of Savo Island."

This loss of a son weighed heavily on her parents, Comer explained, noting that her father was not "afraid to cry and he shed many a tear over Gene's death." She added, "I speak often of my mother's sorrow, but she had the additional challenge of neuritis to contend with and later Parkinson's syndrome ... and it all took a toll on her."

The year following Gene's death, Amick's second son, Lon, entered service with the U.S. Army and, following his infantry training, deployed to France a few weeks after D-Day. His parents, though initially concerned for his safety, learned that Lon became an actor with a special services battalion while overseas, which they viewed as a blessing. In later years, Comer said, her father made the decision to leave his position as vice-president of the bank in Kansas City to help a farm and home loan institution that was struggling to survive during the Great Depression. Failing to succeed in this endeavor essentially ended his banking career, she added.

Loss would again visit her father in 1952 when his wife passed away when only sixty-five years old. Amick followed in 1969 and was laid to rest in Mount Moriah Cemetery in Kansas City.

"I can tell you my father lived," explained Comer. "And as I have said before, he never spoke much about his own service other than how ill he was from the Spanish flu and being in the hospital when World War I ended." She concluded, "But he did his service and was proud his sons also served. Although we lost Gene (Amick Jr.) in World War II, my father was honored when he passed through the same gates he had in WWI, and also when Lon went in the Army not long after." Pausing, she added, "It was a father's proud moment." *(Photograph courtesy of Joanne Comer)*

Millard Brown - *Springfield*

Born January 21, 1893, in Ash Grove, Missouri, Millard F. Brown was inducted into the U.S. Army in Springfield, Missouri, on September 18, 1917, becoming Green County's second draftee of World War I. He served overseas with Headquarters Company, 324th Field Artillery, from June 28, 1918, to May 27, 1919, achieving the rank of corporal. Prior to the war, he was employed as a clerk with the St. Louis-San Francisco Railway Company, but later, he worked for the city street department in Springfield and eventually owned and operated his own real estate business. Brown was also very active in his support for the Ozark Empire Fair and was for many years the superintendent of admissions.[59] In 1941, the veteran was elected commander of the Goad-Ballinger Post 69 of the American Legion in Springfield.

The Springfield veteran passed away on October 16, 1981, and is interred in the city's Maple Park Cemetery.

---

[59] August 17, 1960 edition of the *Springfield Leader and Press*.

Jeremy P. Amick

The Missouri National Guard – *Labor strike near Mindenmines, Missouri*

The governor has, on many occasions, called upon the Missouri National Guard to respond during natural disasters including devastating storms and flooding throughout the state. On other occasions, the state militia was mobilized to provide protection for citizens and property during moments of threatened and actual civil unrest, including a labor strike that occurred in the community of Mindenmines in 1934. The period of the Great Depression was characterized by high unemployment rates in a number of major industries in the United States. The stress of an economic depression created high levels of tension between management and organized labor with many strikes unfolding in its wake.

"As unemployment soared in the early years of the 1930s, the labor movement seemed helpless, unable to protect jobs let alone wage rates," noted an article on the University of Washington's (Seattle) website. The article further explained, "Across the nation, 1934 saw huge organizing campaigns followed by major strikes."[60]

In southwest Missouri, it was not only friction between labor and management that resulted in disputes but disagreements between competing types of miners employed in bordering states. This tension led to a militant response by state leaders to protect against threats to company property and employees. As reported by the *Emporia Gazette* on April 30, 1934, the citizens of southwest Missouri were "(w)arned to expect 1,000 trouble-making miners from Pittsburgh, Kan., mining district, possibly bent on destruction of machinery." In response, the article explained, "… the national guard and state patrolmen were being mobilized at Minden(mines), west of … the Kansas line."

Located in Barton County, Mindenmines, Missouri, had a population of 787 inhabitants according to the 1930 U.S. Census. However, the area became the hub of sensational news accounts when certain mineworkers grew frustrated because of their unemployment.

"Trouble between strip miners and deep shaft miners, both members of the United Mine Workers of America, has been developing for several weeks since the NRA (National Recovery Administration) order for a seven-hour working day and higher wage rates was issued," wrote the *St. Louis Post-Dispatch* on April 30, 1934. The NRA was an agency established in 1933 under President Franklin D. Roosevelt's "New Deal," creating minimum wage standards in addition to setting price controls and maximum weekly hours that employees could work. In 1935, many of the provisions of the NRA were invalidated when ruled unconstitutional by the U.S. Supreme Court.

"The strip mines in this field have put the order into effect, and have continued to employ about 2000 miners in Missouri and in the

---

[60] University of Washington, *The Great Depression in Washington State*, https://depts.washington.edu.

neighboring Kansas field," explained the aforementioned *St. Louis Post-Dispatch* article. "Operators of deep shaft mines, contending their higher production costs makes it impossible for them to comply, have shut down, throwing about 2000 miners out of work."

Rowland Diggs Sr., in his book *The History and Lineage of the 203rd Engineer Battalion*, wrote that the problem for the miners was compounded by the contention of coal mine operators that "coal is cheaper in Illinois and elsewhere," compared to extracted from the deep shaft mines in Kansas and Missouri.[61]

The coal collected through these mining activities was used primarily by companies such as the Missouri Pacific Railroad in powering their locomotives, reported a number of local newspapers. The unemployed deep shaft miners from Kansas, threatening to shut down the strip-mining operations and destroy equipment such as huge steam shovels they believed were used to replace them, created enough concern that the Barton County (Missouri) prosecuting attorney and sheriff requested troops to help maintain the peace.

"As a result of this controversy, the peace officers of Barton County asked for the (National) Guard," wrote Major Leroy Simmons in the book *The History of the Missouri National Guard*.[62] Additionally, several companies, elements of the 203rd Coast Artillery, were mobilized in response, reported April 30, 1934, edition of the *St. Louis Post-Dispatch*. This force consisted of approximately 170 Missouri National Guard soldiers in addition to the dispatch of three airplanes to scout for striking miners in the area.

According to the May 1, 1934, edition of the *Maryville Daily Forum*, "Col. Ray Watson of Webb City commanded the Missouri troops. (He) ... stationed most of his (soldiers) at Minden, but placed a few guards, equipped with machine guns and full fighting materials,

---

[61] Diggs, *The History & Lineage of the 203rd Engineer Battalion*, 84.
[62] History of the Missouri National Guard, *Chapter V: 203rd Coast Artillery*, 78.

at the mines of the Alson Coal Company and the Clemens Coal Company, just this side of the Kansas line."

Maj. Leroy Simmons, in the previously mentioned Missouri National Guard history book, wrote that two batteries were withdrawn after only two days of service and, on May 4, 1934, "the situation had so cleared that it was deemed unnecessary to remain longer, and the rest of the troops were sent to their home stations."

An amicable compromise was eventually achieved through conferences between mine operators and union officials, and threats to the mine sites in Missouri subsided. However, for several weeks, there were recurrent strikes and labor struggles for those once employed by many of the Kansas mining companies. The ensuing decades would find the Missouri National Guard maintaining a frenetic pace of activity in supporting their dual state and federal mission, responding to state emergency duty from the riot at the Missouri State Penitentiary in 1954 to the Great Flood of 1993 and, more recently, deployments in the Global War on Terrorism.

As noted in a 2008 report by the Commission on the National Guard and Reserves, incidents such as those unfolding decades ago near Mindenmines highlight the unique role performed by the National Guard when responding to emergencies.

"The state can … be expected to use its National Guard, which plays a leading role in state emergency response and is commanded by the state's governor unless federalized." The report further noted, "The National Guard operating in state status is generally the 'first military responder' to domestic incidents."[63] *(Photograph courtesy of the Museum of Missouri Military History.)*

---

[63] Commission on the National Guard and Reserves, *Appendix 2*, B-2.

The American Legion Police – *Jefferson City*

On the evening of May 3, 1939, a major fire consumed the former Madison Hotel in Jefferson City, Missouri. The flames spread "rapidly through the seventy-year-old structure," which "at its height threatened the governor's mansion and a block of business buildings along one of the capital's principal streets," reported the *St. Louis Star and Times* the day following the event. While emergency crews scrambled to the site, Harry Mackey was serving as police chief for the Jefferson City Police Department. What he observed were significant traffic difficulties encountered by his police force because of sightseers crowding the surrounding streets to watch the event unfold.

Chief Mackey later affirmed the fire demonstrated that the local police force "was not adequate to handle emergencies, and his men were often over-taxed in handling state affairs, thus the need for some properly trained assistants," reported the *Jefferson City News and Tribune* on September 5, 1943. The newspaper went on to explain that the police chief then "made preliminary arrangements with the [Jefferson] City Council to enact the necessary ordinances to create an emergency police force" comprised of a number of veterans—many of whom had served in World War I. Thus, began the opening moments of what became known as the American Legion Police of Jefferson City.

Permanent officers were soon elected for the voluntary police force, which consisted of a police chief, captain, and adjutant. The captain then selected lieutenants, sergeants, corporals, and patrolmen. Each member purchased a badge to wear while on active duty and was authorized to carry a sidearm. Sworn in by a local judge, members of the American Legion Police were "full-fledged Peace Officers of the City of Jefferson," noted a brief history of the organization that has been preserved in the files of the American Legion Post 5.

The history also notes that the voluntary police force "operates under the direct supervision of the Chief of Police of Jefferson City and are only on duty at his call. While each member of the Legion Police is a duly authorized police officer and has the power of arrest at any time, great care has been taken that the privilege is never abused." The auxiliary police were engaged in a variety of functions such as assisting the Cole County Draft Board in investigations and physical examinations in addition to providing support for the draft registrations that occurred during World War II. However, the American Legion Police would both augment and, on occasion, replace the full-time city police force.

When President Harry S. Truman and Winston Churchill arrived in Jefferson City prior to their visit to Westminster College in Fulton on March 5, 1946, the American Legion Police supplemented the city's full-time police force. The American Legion volunteers also helped direct traffic when the Freedom Train made a one-day visit to the city in June 1948.

Another seminal moment in the history of their service came during the riots at the Missouri State Penitentiary in Jefferson City in 1954. While Missouri State Highway Patrol officers stormed the grounds to put an end to the disturbance, the Legion police "handled most of the traffic on the streets adjacent to the problem area," the *Jefferson City Post-Tribune* reported in the October 27, 1954 edition. Because of the valuable services provided by the Legion Police during the riots, the newspaper further noted, "all members of the unit have been assigned definite points, which they will man in the area around the penitentiary in the event of future trouble."

"The [American Legion Police] has been working home games since the football season started...," stated the *Jefferson City Post-Tribune* on October 25, 1955. "The entire force will be on duty Nov. 4 while regular members of the police department attend the annual policeman's ball."

Oftentimes, respected business and community leaders maintained an association with the Legion police, including the late William Laux, who was reelected a number of times to serve as the organization's police chief. Laux served as a radio operator and instructor with the U.S. Army in World War II and was employed full-time with the Central Missouri Trust Company. Another local notable was the late Lester "Chub" Schulte, a U.S. Army veteran of World War II and retired mail carrier. Schulte could often be seen directing traffic at the corner of East Dunklin and Madison Streets and was so fluid and practiced in his duties, the Missouri State Highway Patrol recorded video of him to use the footage in training films for cadets. Wyman Basinger, a long-time sheriff for Cole County and twice-wounded Marine of World War II, used his experience with the American Legion Police as part of his credentials when first running for the position of sheriff in 1968. At the time, Basinger had served with the auxiliary police force for nearly two decades.

The American Legion Police continued to support law enforcement efforts into the mid-1970s, at which time state funding for local police departments increased to the level that additional full-time police officers could be hired. Regardless, the years of support given by the auxiliary police force were honored and recognized by the community in which it served.

"The city owes a vote of thanks to the Legion police for their splendid work during the past," wrote the *Jefferson City Post-Tribune* on October 31, 1942. The newspaper continued, "During the period this auxiliary police force has existed, services of its members to the city have been of immeasurable value. It is likely that debt will grow in the years to come." *(Photograph courtesy of American Legion Post 5)*

Frederick Hoechst Jr. – *St. Louis*

Coming of age in a community of St. Louis referred to as the "Patch," Fred Hoechst Jr. graduated from high school only to discover the employment difficulties presented in the grim period known as the Great Depression. The scarcity of jobs not only motivated the young man's enlistment in the military but placed him aboard a naval vessel that would help search for a famed American aviator who went missing. Naval records preserved by Hoechst's family indicate the twenty-one-year-old made the decision to embark upon a four-year enlistment in the U.S. Navy on May 5, 1936. The first stop in his new career choice was traveling to the Great Lakes Naval Training Station near Chicago for his boot camp.

"The Great Lakes Naval Training Station, closed two years ago, will be reopened with colorful military ceremonies on July 29," reported the June 1, 1935 edition of the *News-Palladium*. The paper went on to explain that "230 enlisted Navy men and 60 marines will arrive to make up the permanent personnel."

Several weeks later, finishing his training at the newly re-opened naval training site, Hoechst acquired his first experience as a sailor when assigned to the USS *Colorado*—a battleship commissioned years earlier, on August 30, 1923. Records accessible through the U.S. Navy indicate that between "1924-1941 (the) *Colorado* operated with the Battle Fleet in the Pacific, participating in fleet exercises and various ceremonies ..."[64]

Joining the crew while it was stationed with the U.S. Fleet at Pearl Harbor, Hoechst began his climb through the enlisted ranks by working from apprentice seaman to becoming a fireman third class in June 1937, learning to operate and maintain the boilers that provided the steam power for the vessel. The month following his promotion, the USS *Colorado* arrived at Honolulu as part of a one-month training cruise for Naval Reserve Officer Training Corps students from the University of California and Washington, in addition to carrying a number of distinguished guests. However, their plans were abruptly delayed by the disappearance of a celebrated female American aviator.

On the morning of 1 July 1937, (Honolulu Time) Mrs. Amelia Earhart ... and her navigator, Mr. Fred J. Noonan, took off from New Guinea for Howland Island in the Lockheed plane known as a flying laboratory...," reported William L. Friedell, commander of the USS Colorado, in a report dated July 13, 1937.

In the years previous, Earhart merited the reputation as a living legend through her many aeronautical accomplishments. It was on this trip, however, that the aviation pioneer planned to achieve her greatest triumph by flying around the world. On July 2, 1937, the day after her departure from New Guinea, "word was received in

---

[64] Naval History and Heritage Command, *Colorado III (BB-45)*, https://history.navy.mil.

Honolulu that the Earhart plane had not arrived at Howland Island," Friedell further reported. Hours later, the U.S.S. Colorado received instructions to depart Pearl Harbor to participate in the search for the missing aviators.

"AMELIA LOST! This was the newspaper headline thousands of Americans woke up to on July 3, 1937," wrote Candace Fleming in her book *Amelia Lost: The Life and Disappearance of Amelia Earhart*. She added, "And for the next ten days, the lost flier stayed on the front pages as people grasped for any tidbit of information."[65]

The USS *Colorado* was soon placed in charge of all vessels involved in the search. Although Hoechst was one man aboard a ship of more than one thousand sailors, their impromptu mission did not prevent him from earning a time-honored designation that was bequeathed to sailors making an important oceanic crossing. While engaged in the hunt for the lost plane, Hoechst and a group of his fellow sailors underwent the transition from "pollywog" to "shellback" on July 7, 1937, which meant they were initiated during a special ceremony in recognition of their first time crossing the Equator.

"The USS *Colorado* arrived off Pearl Harbor early yesterday afternoon after participating in the Amelia Earhart search and after taking aboard supplies ...," reported the *Honolulu Advertiser* on July 17, 1937. Although the ship discovered no traces of the aircraft, the disappearance has for decades remained a topic of investigation and debate.

While aboard the *Colorado*, Hoechst traveled the world during Pacific and European cruises. His records reveal that he not only enjoyed sightseeing activities in his off time, such as the New York's World Fair in 1939, but he also passed through the Panama Canal with the U.S. Fleet—comprised of 140 ships and 60,000 sailors—in the early weeks of 1940.

---

[65] Fleming, *Amelia Lost*, 106.

Hoechst remained in the Navy until March 1940, at which time he was discharged at the rate of watertender second class. Having survived the closing months of the Great Depression while in the Navy, the veteran returned to St. Louis, was married, and went to work for the National Lead Company in southeastern St. Louis. However, months prior to his discharge, Germany invaded Poland, which led to a stiffening American military posture and increased levels of national spending, helping to spur an economic recovery.

Despite the improving economic conditions, when Pearl Harbor unfolded the following year, the former sailor made the decision to leave his civilian employment and leap into the fray, applying the skills he developed while serving as a sailor in the peacetime naval forces. The sailor has since passed away and is no longer able to share through firsthand recollections his military experiences, yet the words spoken by President John F. Kennedy at the U.S Naval Academy in 1963 seem to summarize the fulfillment Hoechst acquired through his seafaring adventures.

Kennedy remarked, "And any man who may be asked in this century what he did to make his life worthwhile, I think can respond with a good deal of pride and satisfaction: 'I served in the United States Navy.'" *(Photograph courtesy of Judy Thompson)*

CHAPTER 3
WORLD WAR II

Frederick Hoechst Jr. – *St. Louis*

Spending the latter years of the Great Depression serving in the U.S. Navy, Fred Hoechst Jr. returned to St. Louis following his discharge in March of 1940 to embark upon his life as a civilian. Although the previous four years had granted him a worldwide adventure aboard the battleship USS *Colorado*, little did Hoechst realize he would again don a sailor's uniform after the country was drawn into war. In the months after leaving the service, the veteran began working for Laclede Gas and used some of the money he saved to purchase a 1940 Chevrolet. The following year, he and his fiancée, Ruth Gieson, were married before a justice of the peace in Imperial, Missouri, on February 19, 1941. Weeks later, he went to work for the National Lead Company in south St. Louis.

"The Japanese attack on Pearl Harbor in the Hawaiian Islands on December 7, 1941 marked the official entrance of the United States into World War II," noted the Atomic Heritage Foundation. "The attack caught American military personnel by surprise and was certainly costly, but it did not cripple the U.S. Navy as the Japanese had anticipated."[66]

---

[66] Atomic Heritage Foundation, *Attack on Pearl Harbor – 1941*, https://atomicheritage.org.

Still in their honeymoon period, Hoechst was caught up in the patriotic furor gripping the nation and made the decision to return to the U.S. Navy to apply his peacetime naval skills in potential combat. Enlisting on March 25, 1942, he was assigned to the engine room of a ship that would enter service several weeks later—the USS *Meade* (DD-602). A Benson-class destroyer with a complement of 208 sailors, the USS Meade was commissioned on June 22, 1942, at the Brooklyn Navy Yard. According to a keepsake book given to members of the crew after the war, the ship "then had a shakedown cruise to Guantanamo Bay until 22 August."

With the war fully underway, the book goes on to explain that there was little delay in deploying the USS *Meade* as they soon passed through the Panama Canal and "reported for duty to the Commander in Chief, Pacific Fleet on 28 August (1942)."

Hoechst ascended the enlisted ranks, becoming one of only fourteen chief petty officers assigned to the ship. In the early weeks after their arrival in the Pacific, he and his fellow sailors kept the engines in optimal condition through the Battle of Guadacanal in November 1942, during which the Meade destroyed four Japanese transports and rescued 285 U.S. sailors from sunken vessels.

"A rapid change in locale followed," explained a small pamphlet maintained by Hoechst after the war. "After a brief period in Sydney, Australia, the Meade steamed to the Aleutian Islands to participate in the bombardment and occupation of Kiska and Attu. Finally, in September 1943, a respite from duty was given the ship with a short overhaul on the West Coast."

Naval records reveal that the Meade received only a momentary break from the action as she again sailed for the South Pacific, arriving in Wellington, New Zealand, on October 29, 1943. Assigned to the Fifth Amphibious Force, the ship escorted Marines to the Battle of Tarawa the following month and again engaged in shore bombardments. Danger abounded for the crew and contact with a submarine "was made on 22 November," noted the souvenir booklet printed for sailors of the Meade. "With the assistance of the U.S.S. *Frazier* the sub was brought to the surface with depth charges, shelled and sunk," resulting in the capture of one Japanese sailor.

The USS *Meade* then sailed for Pearl Harbor to prepare for a return to the West Coast to undergo a major overhaul but was rerouted to provide close fire support for the Battle of Kwajalein in the Marshall Islands in early 1944. Throughout the next several weeks, Hoechst and the crew of the Meade became part of Task Force 58 and were engaged in attacks against Pacific locations such as Palau, Yap, Hollandia, Truk, and Ponape (Pohnpei). They were detached from the task force in April 1944 and began patrolling islands controlled by the Japanese.

"During a shore bombardment 'practice' on Milli [Atoll], the Meade came the closest in her Pacific career to being hit," recorded the Meade souvenir booklet. "The [Japanese] returned fire for the first time. However, no damage or casualties were received."

The closing of Hoechst's combat service approached when the Meade received orders to report to the West Coast for a much-needed overhaul in July 1944. Months later, they completed a shakedown and were sent to provide shore fire support in the liberation of the Philippines in the waning weeks of the war. Following the Japanese surrender on September 2, 1945, Hoechst received his discharge the following month on October 25, 1945. During his naval career, he completed nearly seven and a half years of active service and earned an Asiatic-Pacific Campaign Ribbon with nine stars, which represented his participation in nine campaigns of the war.

After coming home to St. Louis, Hoechst returned to the National Lead Company, from where he went on to retire decades later. He and his wife raised one son, Jerry, and in their retirement years enjoyed bowling and traveling. Upon his passing in 1995, he was laid to rest in Jefferson Barracks National Cemetery.

A famed painter once explained that men like Hoechst were a dedicated type of individual. Through his actions, he demonstrated that sailors and those who embraced a life on the sea possessed a uniquely brave perspective and, despite being faced with the hardships of life on the water, never made excuses to avoid embarking upon a nautical journey.

"The fishermen know that the sea is dangerous and the storm terrible," wrote the late Vincent Van Gogh, "but they have never found these dangers sufficient reason for remaining ashore." *(Photograph courtesy of Judy Thompson)*

Elliott Woodrow Amick – *Franklin*

Barely thirty years of age, Missouri native Elliott Woodrow Amick had already endured a lifetime of harrowing experiences and amassed an impressive list of accomplishments from his service in the U.S. Army. By this point in his young life, he had attained the impressive rank of lieutenant colonel, earned a Silver Star medal for valor in WWII, and endured disabling combat injuries that soon resulted in his discharge from the service and the search for another career.

Born in the Howard County community of Franklin, Missouri, on March 8, 1913, Amick's father moved the family to Roseville, California, approximately ten years later. A decorated Eagle Scout, the young man graduated with high marks from Roseville Union High School in 1931 and continued his education by earning a two-year degree at Sacramento Junior College.

The *Press-Tribune* (Roseville, California) reported on June 21, 1933, that Amick "will leave the first of the week to begin a four-year military training course at West Point. His appointment came through Congressman Englebright early this spring."

While at the academy, he excelled in both academics and sports. In January 1934, the local newspaper of his hometown boasted that he had been selected for the basketball team at West Point. He later received promotion to cadet corporal and became "responsible for the discipline, neatness of appearance and command of his squad at all formations including drill and parade," reported the *Press-Tribune* on July 5, 1935.

Cadet Amick was appointed to the rank of lieutenant at West Point in the summer of 1937 and graduated the following year as a member of the "Class of '38." Returning home for the summer, he embarked upon his active-duty military career as an infantry officer when reporting to his first duty assignment at Ft. Benning, Georgia, in September 1938.

In the spring of 1939, he wedded the former Muriel Orr, whom he met while attending the academy. "From 1941 onward, he was caught up in the vortex of mobilization, force expansion, and war on a global scale," noted in the April 1989 issue of *Assembly*, the former alumni magazine for graduates of West Point.[67] He and his wife became parents to a daughter in the summer of 1941, but the young officer was soon on his way to Ft. Leavenworth, Kansas, where he graduated at the top of his class while attending the General Staff College. He soon demonstrated his mettle in combat by taking part in the initial landings in North Africa while assigned to General Patton's headquarters in early 1943.

Shortly thereafter, he was given command of the 1st Battalion of the 142nd Infantry. During the invasion of Italy, he proved himself "a magnificent combat leader: outwardly fearless, decisive, adept at outwitting the opposing commander and constantly attentive to the

---

[67] *Assembly, Be Thou at Peace*, 140.

welfare of officers and men under his command," noted the aforementioned issue of *Assembly* magazine.

Major Amick received his first combat wound in February 1944, when struck in the right shoulder by shrapnel while commanding his battalion. His gallantry during the Italian Campaign earned him a Silver Star medal for "leading his men over extremely mountainous terrain ... during an advance toward heavily defended enemy positions under intense enemy fire," and all while wounded, reported the *Sacramento Bee* on June 6, 1944. Recovering from his wound, he continued his rapid ascension through the officer ranks, receiving a promotion to lieutenant colonel. In July 1944, while serving in France with the 36th Division, he was appointed as commander for another battalion whose previous battalion commander was killed in action.

In September 1944, he received severe wounds that resulted in his second Purple Heart. Evacuated from the front lines, Lt. Col. Amick remained in the hospital for several weeks while doctors struggled, unsuccessfully, to fully repair the injuries he sustained. Because of his wounds, reported the *Press-Tribune* on April 25, 1945, Lt. Col. Amick was assigned to West Point to serve as an instructor in the tactical department of the academy. In addition to his two Purple Hearts and Silver Star, he was awarded an Oak Leaf Cluster to his Bronze Medal (denoting his second award of the medal) for "heroic or meritorious achievement."

After achieving the rank of colonel, Amick received a medical discharge from the U.S. Army on June 30, 1947. He and his wife raised three children while remaining in New York. The combat veteran spent nearly the next three decades employed by the United States Military Academy in capacities to include Deputy Director of Athletics and Director of Housing until his retirement in 1975.

The seventy-year-old World War II commander passed away on November 1, 1983, and found his final rest site near the institution he had dedicated a significant part of his adult life—the United States Military Academy Post Cemetery in West Point, New York. Receiving the nickname of "Mick" while attending the academy, the young officer was compassionately remembered by his friends, family, cadets, and soldiers as "always quick to lend a helping hand; and radiated the sincerity and genuineness that are the glue of friendships."

In the *Assembly* magazine, a tribute to the memory of the departed officer provided glowing comments remarking on the characteristics that had drawn soldiers to him as both an individual and leader.

"His warm and winning smile never faded. His concept of service—to professional colleague, personal friend, individual with problem, community-at-large—never flagged. To the end of Mick's course on earth, he was a giver." *(Photograph courtesy of Suzanne Byerly)*

Everett Markway Sr. – *Jefferson City*

Growing up the third child in a family of seven, there was little to distinguish a young Everett Markway Sr. from his siblings during the difficult years of the Great Depression—a time when families struggled to scratch a living in a meager economy. As World War II erupted and three of the four hardworking sons entered the service, the greatest distinction for Markway would be his decision to enlist in the United States Marine Corps.

"My father went to Immaculate Conception School in Jefferson City and graduated from St. Peter High School in 1936, where he played football," said the veteran's son, Everett Markway Jr. "He attended Jefferson City Junior College for about eighteen months before going to work at the post office as a postal clerk," he added.

Markway Sr. soon began dating Lillian Schneiders; however, their budding relationship was placed on hold because of more pressing circumstances. Following the attack on Pearl Harbor, Markway's younger brother, Ulysses, chose to enlist in the U.S. Navy. Three months later, Markway's voluntary spirit resulted in a similar decision.

"His military records show he enlisted with the Marines at Jefferson Barracks on April 15, 1942, when he was twenty-three years old," said the veteran's son. "From there, he was sent to the Marine Corps Recruit Depot in San Diego for his initial training."

After boot camp, he was sent to U.S. Naval Air Station in Jacksonville, Florida, for specialized aviation training. While there, he qualified as an aviation metalsmith and aircraft mechanic. According to the August 1, 1943 edition of the *Sunday News and Tribune*, he "graduated with the highest averages in his class."

While completing his advanced training in Florida, another of Markway's brothers, Francis, was drafted into the U.S. Army in 1942 and went on to serve with a troop carrier squadron. Markway's son explained, "In early February 1943, my father sailed to Midway Island and joined a Marine SBD (Scout Bomber Douglas)—a carrier-based scout/dive bomber) squadron. The unit had already received a Presidential Unit Citation at Midway in 1942 and later received two Naval Unit Citations in the Philippines in 1945."

Weeks later, the aviation mechanic was transferred to the Marine Corps Air Station Ewa on the island of Oahu. This was but another brief stop in his military journey since he boarded the USS *Long Island*—an escort carrier—bound for service in American Samoa in late April 1943. He soon joined his fellow Marines in training for battle in addition to ferrying aircraft to crews stationed on various islands in the region. Assigned to the Marine Scout Bombing Squadron designated VMSB-214, Markway moved to Efate Island in New Hebrides in December 1943 and served with a carpentry and engineering section. The following month, he returned to his aviation mechanic duties and was sent to an airstrip on Bougainville in the North Solomon Islands.

"My father mentioned that while he was in the area, there were isolated Japanese troops found raiding garbage dumps for food, the occasional sniper was discovered and, one time, they even caught a Japanese soldier sneaking into an outdoor movie at night."

The next stopover in his duty assignment brought with it an "incident which changed his life," remarked Markway's son. VMSB-214 was sent to Munda on New Georgia Island in the Central Solomon's near Guadalcanal in July 1944. In this region, Marines were frequently transferred between islands via transport aircraft.

"It is my understanding that my father was scheduled to be on one of the planes, and it crashed into a mountain, and all aboard were killed," said Everett Markway Jr. "Instead, he was away from his unit at the time and attached to a field hospital, but somehow the records showed he was on that plane." He added, "When he returned to his unit, all of his gear was stacked outside his tent so that his personal items could be sent back home, but fortunately, no telegram had yet been sent to his family."

His official military records note that through September 20, 1944, he participated in a major campaign to occupy Munda in the New Georgia Islands. From there, he boarded the USS *Harry Taylor*—a troop transport—for his return to the states in October 1944. When back in Jefferson City on leave, he and his fiancée, Lillian, were married on December 2, 1944.

"My parents loaded up their 1938 Plymouth and drove to my father's final duty assignment at the Naval Air Station in Jacksonville, Florida," said Everett Markway Jr. "He trained airplane mechanics from January through November 1945."

Receiving his discharge on November 7, 1945, Markway remained in the Marine Corps Reserves until 1953. After returning to Jefferson City following his active-duty service in WWII, the veteran resumed his employment with the postal service, and he and his wife went on to raise three sons—Everett Jr., Ronald, and Eric. A member of his local Veterans of Foreign Wars post and the Central Missouri Detachment of the Marine Corps League, Markway passed away January 8, 1979, and was interred in Resurrection Cemetery in Jefferson City with final honors provided by his fellow members of the Marine Corps League.

The perpetuation of Markway's legacy, like many veterans of the WWII era, was impeded due to his hesitancy to share with his children the stories of his military experiences. However, through vague recollections, military histories of several of his contemporaries, and documentation, his sons have been able to chronicle much of his time in the service.

"He only mentioned his time in the Marine Corps in passing with us but never shared many details," said Markway Jr., a veteran of the U.S. Army. "I've spent many hours figuring out where he was in the war and expanding the details into a coherent story. Our family has an intriguing legacy of military service, and it's satisfying to know what he may have gone through while overseas and to be able to share these experiences with others." *(Photograph courtesy of Everett Markway Jr.)*

Clifford Mathis – *Kansas City*

Clifford Mathis has many wonderful reflections of growing up in Kansas City, including selling peanuts and popcorn at the Kansas City Blues baseball games held at the former Muehlebach Field. One of his fondest memories, he explained, was trying to follow in the footsteps of an older brother who had joined the Missouri National Guard.

"Little brother likes to be like big brother, so I fibbed about my age and enlisted in the 110th Engineers in February 1935, when I was only seventeen years old," he recalled, with a grin.

The young enlistee was assigned to the medical detachment and attended drill periods from 7-9 p.m. every Wednesday evening at the old armory located at 3610 Main Street in Kansas City. During these two-hour drill periods, he learned the basics of soldiering in addition to the treatment of a variety of wounds but never attended formal basic training. Working a variety of jobs to make a little money in addition to performing his duties with the Missouri National Guard, Mathis noted that the day of December 23, 1940, is one that remains forever etched in his memory.

"President Roosevelt mobilized the National Guard more than a year before Pearl Harbor, and that's the day we had to report to the armory, suit up and then drive to Joplin," he said. "Then, we were sent on to Camp Robinson (Little Rock, Arkansas) with the entire 35th Division—that was a lot of guys!" he exclaimed.

For the next year, the 110th Engineers participated in training and maneuvers to prepare them for service in an overseas combat zone, which included war games in Louisiana and Minnesota. One day, the veteran noted, an announcement came on the radio declaring: "Attention all military personnel! All passes furloughs and leaves canceled."

Mathis explained, "We returned to base and found out about the attack on Pearl Harbor. Within a day or two after the attack, we loaded on trains and headed west, spending several months in California as coastal defense," he added.

During the summer of 1942, although he had achieved the rank of staff sergeant, Mathis decided he wanted to become an officer and was accepted for officer training. Slotted to become an engineer officer, he was sent to Ft. Belvoir, Virginia, for his officer candidate school.

"I finished the training in late 1942 and became a second lieutenant with a certificate that said 'temporary appointment,'" he chuckled. "I remember there was a U.S. Army colonel involved in our training who said, 'You can't put the wisdom of age in the minds of babes in just three months,'" Mathis mockingly recounted.

Following a brief period of leave back in St. Louis, Lt. Mathis traveled to Camp Gruber, Oklahoma, where he underwent several months of additional training as an engineer officer and learned such skills as the construction of roadways. He later became commander of Company D, 335th Engineer Regiment and, in March 1943, received orders to deploy overseas. Traveling to Ft. Dix, New Jersey by train, the regiment boarded the SS *Sloterdijk*—a Dutch transport converted to a troop carrier—and made the two-week journey to the harbor at Oran, Algeria.

"One of our first responsibilities as an engineer outfit after arriving in North Africa was to set up the water supply for a tent city," said the former officer. "We assembled a large water tank and ran pipes to all of the areas that needed it."

Another important assignment came weeks later when Mathis' company was given the project of repairing a villa that was to serve as a headquarters for high-ranking officers.

"The villa was quite beautiful and sat on a high hill overlooking the Mediterranean," he said. "We checked out everything and made any necessary repairs to the plumbing and electrical in the buildings," he added.

Although Mathis did not at the time realize for whom the repairs were being performed, weeks later, he received a letter of commendation from General Dwight D. Eisenhower—a five-star commanding general of World War II and future president.

"From North Africa, our company was sent to Corsica, and our first job was to build a hospital. Then," he continued, "they sent us to cut lumber for the U.S. Army, which they used for flooring, walkways, and building latrines. We had to use mules to drag the lumber down from the mountains where it had been cut."

Months later, they would enter Southern France and go on to repair docks destroyed by retreating German forces. Victory and Liberty ships then utilized the rebuilt docks to deliver supplies and equipment in support of the Allies.

"When we finally got into Germany, one of our final projects was repairing a bridge that had been damaged by the Germans," said Mathis. "That was memorable because my sergeants came up to me when we were finished, handed me a hammer, and told me I could drive the final nail into the completed bridge."

Returning to the U.S. in November 1945, Mathis received his discharge from the U.S. Army at Jefferson Barracks on February 18, 1946. In 1948, he married Alice, and the couple went on to raise one daughter. In the years after the war, the veteran worked for truck leasing companies, eventually retiring from Rollins Truck Leasing when he turned sixty-five.

When asked if he was proud of his military service, Mathis bluntly explained, "I guess I wouldn't say I'm proud; I'm just glad that I got to serve and do my part." Smiling, he added, "I wanted to be there—I wanted to be part of it all even if it meant lying about my age back when I was seventeen years old." *(Photograph courtesy of Clifford Mathis)*

Warren E. Hearnes - *Charleston*

The legacy of the late Warren E. Hearnes, 46th governor of Missouri, endures through contributions to education, civil rights, and other legislative achievements from his many years as a public servant. Prior to any legislative endeavors, however, was his wish to someday attend the United States Military Academy—a dream that came to fruition through a circuitous set of circumstances. Growing up in the southeastern Missouri town of Charleston, Hearnes and a group of sixteen-year-old boys from around the community made the decision to conceal their true age and enlist in Headquarters Company, 140th Infantry Regiment of the Missouri National Guard on May 27, 1940.

"The boys were sent to Camp Robinson (Little Rock, Arkansas) because their unit got called up," said the late governor's wife, Betty Hearnes. "They did their duty while they were there, but when someone found out their true age, that's when they were discharged and sent back home to finish out their senior year of school.

According to the December 12, 1940 edition of the *Sikeston Herald*, the 140th Infantry Regiment "will be called for encampment December 23, after which they will be stationed at their home armories for ten days before reporting for their year's training at Camp Joseph T. Robinson ..."

Service records obtained from the Missouri State Archives confirm Hearnes was discharged from the National Guard at Camp Robinson on April 11, 1941 for reasons of being a minor, although his discharge document indicated his character as "good" and his efficiency as a soldier "satisfactory." Returning to high school and finishing his senior year several weeks later, Hearnes' wife noted, "Warren was attending school at the University of Missouri in Columbia when he received his draft notice for the U.S. Army."

Prior to his induction into the Army at Jefferson Barracks on February 24, 1943, Hearnes had achieved the first step in pursuit of his dream of attending West Point by taking the academy's competitive examination in his congressional district.

"While he was training at Fort Sheridan, Illinois (a regional induction and training center during WWII), he received a telegram from his congressman and President Roosevelt appointing him to West Point," said Betty Hearnes. "They gave him another discharge from the service, and he went on to the academy," she added.

The "Report of Separation" issued to Hearnes noted that on June 28, 1943, the recent inductee left the service to begin his military education at the academy. For the next three years, while undergoing an accelerated program crafted to train officers for the war effort, Cadet Hearnes was a member of the cadet choir and "studied all day and most of the night, then got up and did it again," said Betty Hearnes.

Graduating from the academy in 1946 with his bachelor's degree and receiving his commission as an officer, Hearnes traveled to Ft. Benning, Georgia, to complete additional training to become qualified as an infantry officer. The war may have been over, but the young officer still had a commitment to the United States Army and was assigned to the 35th Infantry Division in Puerto Rico. Hearnes' wife explained that the young officer was stationed at Henry Barracks—a U.S. Army post near San Juan, Puerto Rico, that was closed in 1965—and remained actively involved in training troops. His duties included conducting drills and ceremonies in addition to going on various types of maneuvers to maintain a state of military preparedness.

The time the troops spent on the island was not entirely dedicated to performing military activities, and they often engaged in friendly games of baseball to help pass the time and build camaraderie. This activity, Betty explained, would lead to the accident that resulted in Hearnes' eventual discharge from the military.

"He and his men were playing another team in baseball in 1947 and (Hearnes) was jumping for a fly ball when one of his sergeants ran into him and broke his (right) ankle," said Betty.

The soldier was sent to the Percy Jones Army Hospital in Battle Creek, Michigan, where he underwent numerous treatments and procedures in an attempt to correct the damage done to his ankle. However, as Betty noted, the injury never fully healed and resulted in a perceptible limp for the rest of Hearnes' life. While undergoing treatment for the injury, Hearnes was allowed to recuperate in his hometown of Charleston and married to Betty Cooper in 1947. Although the Army eventually allowed him to return to his unit in Puerto Rico, his wife noted that it was only for a brief period.

Betty explained, "Warren went on maneuvers in Vieques (an island-municipality of Puerto Rico), and his colonel called him in and said that he couldn't stay in the service because he couldn't pass all of the (physical) tests at a one hundred percent level. He was walking with a cane at that time." Pausing, she added, "It changed his life."

The years following his discharge from the service have become an important part of the state's political history, crowned by Hearnes becoming the first two-term governor of Missouri. The former governor passed away in 2009 and his wife affirms that despite his many successes, he reflected on his time in the Army as the most influential period of his life.

"He loved being in the service and all of his life he wanted to attend the military academy," said Betty Hearnes. "Graduating from West Point was certainly his proudest moment." With solemnity, she added, "I am so proud of his service and thought, as did he, that he would stay in the Army forever … but that didn't work out. But all the lessons he learned from the Army during that time—the focus, discipline and the ability to tell people 'no' when need be—those were all lessons that would later benefit him as governor." *(Photograph courtesy of Betty Hearnes)*

Earl Tisdale – *St. Louis*

While glancing at his wife of nearly seven decades, Earl Tisdale mirthfully explained, "I wouldn't trade her for all the tea in China." He went on to discuss his service in World War II, at which point the fondness shared by the couple becomes evident, having survived the separation of military service and growing ever stronger in their bond throughout the years. Raised in north St. Louis, Tisdale graduated from Ferguson High School in 1943. His father, who was acquainted with a local draft board member, was then informed that his son's draft number would soon be selected.

"That's when I decided to join the Marines because it has always fascinated me, and I figured it would allow me to have at least some control over my military career," said Tisdale.

The seventeen-year-old enlistee traveled to San Diego in early August 1943, where he "went through the routine" while completing his basic training. From there, he was assigned briefly to a Marine Air

Squadron at Miramar, California, before traveling to Norman, Oklahoma, for several weeks of aviation "Ordnancemen's School" at the Navy Technical Training Center.

"We learned how to handle all different kinds of ammunition used on airplanes, including bombs," Tisdale explained. "We learned how to fuse and defuse them ... and that was no fun."

The next destination in his military career was with the 3rd Marine Aircraft Wing at Cherry Point, North Carolina, in the spring of 1944, where he spent several months applying the training he had received while in Oklahoma.

"I stayed at Cherry Point until September 1944, and that's when they sent us overseas aboard a freighter," he said. "Our first stop was at Majuro (Atoll) in the Marshall Islands, and I stayed there for a few months loading ammunition on planes coming in off the aircraft carriers," he added.

On the island, Tisdale recalled, a storm brought with it strong winds that destroyed their food supply. Though a supply ship was dispatched to replace the lost provisions, during the several days that it took for it to arrive, the Marines were forced to rely upon a single, plentiful food source.

"Some of the guys climbed the trees and collected coconuts that we were able to eat until the ship came in to bring us food," he said. "I got so tired of eating coconuts and, to this day, cannot stand to eat one," he grinned.

The young Marine went on to spend several weeks working at an airfield on Kwajalein Island. He was then sent to Guam and detailed to guard Japanese prisoners.

"The Japanese were still up in the hills and occasionally came down into our camp, hiding and killing some of our GIs," he somberly recalled. "Some of them were able to get our boys before we were able to get them ... it was a terrible situation."

While stationed on Guam, Tisdale and his fellow Marines learned of the end of the war with Japan following the use of the atomic bombs on Nagasaki and Hiroshima. Within a few weeks' time, he was sent back to the United States and received his discharge at the Naval Air Station in Glenview, Illinois, in August 1946, after having achieved the rank of staff sergeant. Following his discharge, Tisdale's life focused on two important factors: building a career and continuing his relationship with Ann, the girlfriend from whom he had been separated for three years because of his World War II service.

"We decided not to marry before the war," he said, "just in case something was to happen to me while I was in the service."

On November 21, 1947, he and Ann were married, and a young Tisdale began to provide for his family by selling paint for a company in the St. Louis area. In an effort to establish a more stable income source, he soon enrolled at Washington University and completed an aeronautics course. He was later employed with McDonnell Douglas and spent thirty-five years with the company, coordinating the delivery of completed aviation components for aircraft such as the F-4 Phantom and F-15 Eagle. Following his retirement in 1982, the father of two daughters remained in Ballwin and began working part-time in the funeral business, from which he eventually retired at eighty-six years old. In 2011, Tisdale and his wife relocated to Jefferson City, Missouri, as the advent of age necessitated that they reside closer to their children.

In discussing his service during World War II, Tisdale explained that although he believes that the service he performed in the military was not nearly as significant as that of other young Americans, it was a responsibility that needed to be fulfilled.

"I think that because the Japanese attacked our country, it was our duty as Americans to protect it; I think that's the way most people felt back then. I don't feel like I was in danger like some of the boys that invaded certain areas and such, but I did what I was asked to do." With a slight pause, he noted, "I can remember being overseas and waiting for letters from Ann. We didn't seem to get letters all that often ... they just didn't seem to get to us."

His wife softly added, "Naturally, I was worried about his safety during the war. At that time, all of my friends were in the service, and you just worried about them all and prayed they made it home safely."

Earl Tisdale entered into heavenly rest on September 12, 2018. The ninety-three-year-old veteran was laid to rest in Jefferson Barracks National Cemetery. *(Photograph courtesy of Earl Tisdale)*

The Citizens War Manpower Committee – *Kansas City*

The War Manpower Commission was established by Pres. Franklin D. Roosevelt during the early period of World War II. It called for the "elimination of wasteful labor turnover in essential activities ... the direction of the flow of scarce labor where most needed in the war program ... (and for) the maximum utilization of manpower resources," explained an article in the October 29, 1943 edition of the *St. Cloud Times* (Minnesota).

Early in the war, it was revealed that many industrial centers in the United States were struggling to provide necessary war materials and products because of a labor pool greatly diminished when thousands of former employees were drafted to serve in the United States military.

"Our country saw fit to locate at Kansas City, the Heart of the Nation, the production of large quantities of the most important munitions of war," wrote John B. Gage, mayor of Kansas City, in a proclamation dated May 6, 1944. He added, "At the very time when the greatest battles of this war are to be fought—when planes, engines, explosives, landing craft and other vital material of war produced here are most needed, a shortage of workers fully to man the war plants has developed."

Under the auspices of the War Manpower Commission, Mayor Gage sought to address these labor shortfalls by forming the Citizens War Manpower Committee to aid in supplying an additional 30,0000 workers for local war plants. The mayor called upon Elmer C. Rhoden, president of Fox Midwest Amusement Corporation, to serve as chairman for the local committee. On May 15, 1944, only a week after the formation of the committee, an "advertising approach" was approved that was designed to "appeal to older men who may fear they are not adequate to the jobs that are open."

The committee also noted, "We must appeal to both men and women who are in non-essential or less-essential jobs and convince them it is their duty to surrender their present security and take up work on the production line in the manufacture of the implements of war."

The special committee for advertising was headed by W.J. Krebs of Potts-Turnbull Advertising Company and comprised of volunteers employed in various Kansas City-area advertising specialties. The committee developed a multifaceted approach that included advertising on Kansas City streetcars and buses, a billboard campaign, notices on water and gas bills of 100,000 residents, and brief clips played prior to the showing of films in area theaters.

"The services of the War Housing Centers are available to assist employees of essential industries in finding suitable quarters," explained the booklet titled *War Workers Guide: Greater Kansas City*. "Anyone who has a vacancy can make a real contribution by listing their vacancy with the War Housing Centers ...."

With scores of local men away from home to fight the war, the committee sought to address the concerns of women who might otherwise be willing to fulfill an essential war job but were disinclined from doing so because they had young children for whom to provide care.

"Mothers who feel impelled to take a war job can rest assured their children will be well cared for," the above-cited booklet explained. "There are 32 child care centers operated by the public school system, which can be expanded to meet future needs."

A War Jobs Headquarters was opened at 1120 Grand Avenue in Kansas City, where applicants were received, assessed, and potentially referred to essential war industries by U.S. Employment Service employees and area war plant representatives. Several recognized companies—such as Pratt & Whitney Aircraft, Hercules Powder Company, and North American Aviation—opened employment storefronts to receive potential applicants.

In his final report to Mayor John B. Gage on July 31, 1944, Committee Chairman Elmer Rhoden related, "During the period of the Citizens Committee campaign, 90,000 persons responded to the appeal, 60,000 of these were referred to employers, and 30,000 were placed in jobs."

Rhoden affirmed the committee's success would not have been possible without assistance from a myriad of partner agencies, noting the majority of the new workers resided in Kansas City, thus "proving the claim that the labor supply was available … and the effectiveness of the committee's campaign."

Pratt & Whitney Aircraft also acknowledged the assistance provided through a local campaign in helping them maintain production of their Wasp family of aircraft engines, which were used in a number of military aircraft of World War II. L.C. Mallett, assistant general manager Pratt & Whitney's local offices, wrote Chairman Rhoden on

July 13, 1944, "(T)he members of the (committee) are to be congratulated on their performance. There is no question in our minds that their efforts assisted all war industries in this community and that the results could not have been attained without their assistance."

Further acknowledging the contributions of others and spotlighting the profound achievements of the committee in supporting the war effort, Chairman Rhoden, in the aforementioned letter to the mayor, calmly stepped away from his voluntary wartime endeavor to return to his employment in the private industry.

"Now that the Citizens War Manpower Committee has completed its task, your chairman feels he can resign his responsibilities with sincere and profound thanks to all those who served with him and with renewed faith in the belief that the citizens of Kansas City can accomplish anything they set out to do." *(Photograph courtesy of David Keckler.)*

Joseph Schwaller – *Jefferson City*

With more than sixteen million men and women serving in the U.S. military during World War II, it was not uncommon for families to have more than one child departing home to serve in the military. For the Schwaller family of Jefferson City, they would suffer the anxiety of having three sons inducted into the military, one of whom survived an airplane crash off the coast of Great Britain. Joseph Frederick Schwaller was a 1940 graduate of St. Peter High School and spent the next year and a half working at a local bowling alley. Shortly after the Japanese attack on Pearl Harbor, however, he was filled with patriotic fervor and became the first of the Schwaller sons to enlist.

"He began his active-duty service at Jefferson Barracks (St. Louis) after he enlisted in the U.S. Army Air Forces on January 9, 1942," said Jeanne Schwaller, who has researched much of her late brother-in-law's military service.

Jefferson Barracks not only grew into one of the busiest recruitment centers for the military during WWII but was also the first—and one of the largest—Army Air Corps training centers in the United States. (The Army Air Corps officially became the U.S. Army Air Forces on June 20, 1941.)

Upon completion of his basic training, Schwaller went on to complete several weeks of flexible gunnery training at Las Vegas Army Airfield in Nevada, followed by additional gunnery training at Tyndall Army Airfield (now Tyndall Air Force Base) near Panama City, Florida.

In the *Army Air Forces Historical Studies: No. 31*, it is noted that the type of training Schwaller and his contemporaries were given imbued them with the proficiency to operate a turret gun on a B-17 Flying Fortress—a four-engine heavy bomber. As noted, students learned ballistics, sighting, aircraft recognition, methods of firing, and turret manipulation. Located in the rear of the plane, the tail gunner targeted enemy aircraft through a small window and had the responsibility of protecting the rear quarter of their aircraft through the heavy firepower of twin .50 caliber machine guns.[68]

"When his training was finished in the United States, he was assigned as a gunner and began flying bombing missions aboard a B-17 during Air Offensive Europe, the Tunisian and Sicilian campaigns," said Jeanne Schwaller, describing chronological campaigns of the war.

On October 9, 1942, less than two months following his arrival overseas, Schwaller was thrust into the midst of a situation in which he faced overwhelming odds while serving with the 419th Bomb Squadron of the 301st Bombardment Group. According to the October 16, 1942, edition of the *Spokane Chronicle* (Spokane, Washington), the B-17 Schwaller was serving aboard as a tail gunner

---

[68] Air Force Historical Studies No. 31, *Flexible Gunnery Training in the AAF*, 37-72.

was participating in a bombing mission against targets near Lille in northern France.

During this mission, the newspaper reported, Schwaller's aircraft "was attacked on all sides by (German) yellow-nosed fighters. Two motors were shot up and a third crippled. Losing altitude on the lone good motor and being left farther behind the rest of the American formation ... the Fortress battled its way out of the German fighter screen...."

The crew miraculously reached the English Channel, crashing their Fortress at a speed of more than one hundred miles an hour. All ten members of the crew survived despite spending forty-five minutes in the icy waters before being rescued. *The Ironwood Daily Globe* (Ironwood, Michigan) reported on October 16, 1942, that the crew declared, "All we want is another plane.... We've got a score to settle with those guys ..."

Reflecting on the incident, Jeanne Schwaller explained, "According to stories from the family, Gabriel Heatter, a radio commentator who started each evening's newscast with 'There's good news tonight,' announced that Joseph Schwaller of Jefferson City, Missouri, had been rescued from the English Channel by the British Navy." She added, "His mother, Freida Schwaller, was listening to the news and knew her son had been saved. Some days later, military personnel came to her house to tell her that her son was missing in action. She told them he was in England, safe and recovering in a hospital."

Schwaller was soon back to flying missions and earned a Purple Heart medal for minor injuries sustained in the crash. He would go on to serve as an engineer and gunner during the North African campaign, earning a Distinguished Flying Cross after completing twenty-five sorties against the enemy. Returning to the United States in early July 1943, Tech Sergeant Schwaller became a gunnery instructor at the Rapid City Army Air Base in South Dakota. He finished out the final weeks of his military career at an airfield in Oklahoma, receiving his discharge on September 3, 1945, after nearly two years and nine months in the military.

"While he was stationed at Rapid City, he met Mary Helen Smith, a former Navy nurse," said Jeanne Schwaller. "He moved to Rapid City after the war, and the two were married."

During his residence in Rapid City, Schwaller operated a gaming business and, in the early 1950s, moved to Connecticut, where he expanded his business. Due to the success of his company, he was able to retire at a fairly young age and moved to Sun City, Arizona, with his wife. The eighty-three-year-old veteran passed away in 2005.

Relating that the former airman lived several states away from his native Jefferson City during the latter part of his life and had no children to pass down any tales of his military legacy, Jeanne Schwaller affirms Schwaller's story possesses some unique occurrences worthy of preservation.

"He lived in another state all those years, and I never had the opportunity to visit with him about his military service," said Jeanne Schwaller when speaking of her late brother-in-law. "I find it fascinating that there is this boy out of small-town Missouri who survived a crash and was plucked from the English Channel—and his mother heard about it on a radio program while several thousand miles away.

"It certainly isn't the type of military story you hear about every day," she chuckled. *(Photograph courtesy of Jeanne Schwaller.)*

Leo G. Schwaller – *Jefferson City*

Raised in a family of five children, Leo George Schwaller was not only the oldest of his siblings but possessed more age and experience than most of his fellow draftees called to serve during World War II. When his draft notice arrived in 1944, he was on the threshold of turning thirty-three years old, was married for six years, had two young sons, and was the owner of his own cabinet-making business. A 1927 graduate of the St. Peter High School in Jefferson City, military records reveal that Schwaller registered for the military draft on October 16, 1940. Nearly four years would pass, however, before he would have to say goodbye to his family when he was inducted into the U.S. Navy in St. Louis on April 29, 1944.

"One of his younger brothers, Joseph, enlisted in the Air Force in January 1942, and another of his other younger brothers, Ed, chose to go in the Navy a few months later, in October 1944," said Jeanne Schwaller, sister-in-law to the late veteran.

Completing his basic training at the Naval Training Station at Great Lakes, Illinois, the older recruit was selected to attend a school to train on the operation of several types of naval landing craft. The next point of his military journey carried him to U.S. Naval Amphibious Training Base at Ft. Pierce, Florida, in mid-summer of 1944. Although the D-Day landings, which had taken place weeks earlier, had already become a subject of famed reflection, the base remained busy as a training site instructing sailors and Marines on amphibious combat techniques employed in both Europe and throughout the Pacific.

"After he finished his training in Florida (in late 1944), he was shipped to the island of Saipan in the western Pacific, wrote David Schwaller, one of the veteran's sons, in a brief summary of his father's service. "Part of his duties included supervising and operating landing craft that ran between large ocean-going vessels and the receiving port on Saipan," he added. As noted by Trevor Nevitt Dupuy in his book *Asiatic Land Battles: Japanese Ambitions in the Pacific*, Saipan was part of the Marianas Islands, located "only fifteen hundred miles south of the main islands Japan." Dupuy went on to explain that after significant shore bombardment was conducted, beginning on June 15 (1944), two Marine divisions followed by a U.S. Army division "went ashore" and met what was described as "the most determined resistance yet encountered in the Central Pacific fighting."

Saipan was captured, Dupuy noted, on July 9, 1944, around the time Schwaller was beginning his training in Florida. The fierce fighting resulted in the deaths of 27,000 Japanese soldiers, and 2,000 captured while the U.S. suffered 3,500 killed and an estimated 13,000 wounded, the author explained.[69]

Once Saipan, in addition to the islands of Tinian and Guam, was captured, the airfields previously in possession of the Japanese were now used by U.S. bombers to strike strategic airfields in locations

---

[69] Dupuy, *Asiatic Land Battles*, 58-61.

such as Iwo Jima in preparation for the planned invasion of the Japanese mainland.

David Schwaller went on to explain that during his father's service on Saipan, the landing craft his father used to transfer supplies from Liberty and Victory ships in the harbor was equipped with two large diesel engines, making it quite maneuverable.

"Because my father was significantly older and piloted his own craft," wrote David Schwaller, "the majority of the younger sailors and other servicemen began calling him 'Skipper.'" He continued, "This was later shortened to 'Skip'—a nickname that stuck with him for the rest of his life."

In the weeks following the Japanese surrender aboard the USS *Missouri* in Tokyo Bay on September 2, 1945, Seaman First Class Schwaller, along with scores of his fellow sailors, boarded troop ships bound for the U.S. According to his separation documents, Schwaller was discharged on December 11, 1945, after one year, seven months, and thirteen days of service.

"He was welcomed home for Christmas by his family and friends," noted David Schwaller. "Having started a kitchen cabinet business before the war, he continued this business and many years later retired."

In the years after the war, a third son was welcomed into the Schwaller family. According to his son, David, their father enjoyed spending time with friends and family in addition to being outdoors, primarily hunting and fishing on the lower Osage River. The eighty-six-year-old veteran, having spent a long and full life in central Missouri (with the exception of the short time he spent with the Navy in Pacific), passed away in Jefferson City in 1997; his wife, Matilda, passed ten years later. The former sailor was laid to rest in Resurrection Cemetery and Mausoleum.

In discussing the service of her brother-in-law, Jeanne Schwaller explained that the late sailor's experiences characterize many families during World War II, who invested greatly in the war effort by watching as their children left home, not knowing what awaited them.

"There were four sons and a daughter in the family, but Carl died of whooping cough at a very young age," said Jeanne. "World War II truly was a unique time in the country, and I find it interesting that the Schwaller family sent all three of their sons off to war and, fortunately, all three sons came back home." *(Photograph courtesy of Jeanne Schwaller.)*

Edward Schwaller – *Jefferson City*

When graduating from St. Peter High School in Jefferson City in May 1944, Edward Schwaller had not only witnessed many of his friends leaving for military service but became the only son left at home since one of his older brothers was in the U.S. Army Air Forces and the other in boot camp with the U.S. Navy.

"He worked a few months after his graduation and then decided to enlist in the U.S. Navy," said the late veteran's wife, Jeanne Schwaller. "His older brother, Leo, told him that if he became a sailor like he was, then he wouldn't have to eat dried rations."

Inducted in St. Louis on October 25, 1944, at the enlisted rate of seaman apprentice, an eighteen-year-old Schwaller left Mid-Missouri for the first time when traveling to Farragut Naval Training Station to complete his basic training. Located in northern Idaho, the Idaho Military Museum notes that Farragut Naval Training Station "was the second-largest U.S. naval training station in the world" and was potentially the largest employer in Idaho" during World War II.[70]

When finishing his training around Christmas of 1944, he and a number of his fellow recruits traveled by troop train to Camp Shoemaker, California, where the young man from a small town witnessed one of many exciting "firsts" in his life.

"I remember him talking about the train passing near the Golden Gate Bridge, and he then saw all the water of the Pacific Ocean for the very first time," said Jeanne Schwaller. "He said that his eyes must have been as big as saucers as he gazed out the window."

The young sailor was soon reporting for duty aboard the USS *Alcyone* (AKA-7)—a former Merchant Marine vessel converted to an Arcturus Class attack cargo ship, with a crew complement of 368 enlisted personnel and thirty-one officers. Prior to Schwaller's arrival, the *Alcyone* had already participated in a number of operations throughout the Pacific. As a member of the crew, Schwaller was appointed to serve as a mail clerk aboard the bustling ship. His duties found him supporting his fellow crewmembers through such duties as postal counter work, sorting incoming and outgoing mail items, routing mail, and maintaining a mail directory.

Naval records indicate that in the months following Schwaller's arrival, the USS *Alcyone* was involved in a number of combat operations to include supporting the landing of troops in the assault on Kwajalein in addition to operations in the Philippines.

"Edward told a harrowing story of a time when a Japanese mine floated close to their ship while they were tied to another ship while unloading their cargo," recalled Jeanne Schwaller. "The crew immediately cut the lines and the cargo in the nets plunged into the sea,

---

[70] Idaho Military Museum, *Idaho Legacy: Farragut, Idaho*, https://museum.mil.idaho.gov/idaho-military-history/idaho-legacy/.

but the ships began to separate and the mine floated past without hitting either of the ships."

The USS *Alcyone* continued to support various assault operations throughout the Pacific, carrying within her holds critical cargo used to replenish the fighting forces. Returning to the United States in early March 1945, the vessel spent several months undergoing an overhaul. The ship was back to sea in June 1945 and was involved in conducting a replenishment mission in the western Pacific when Japan announced its surrender on August 15, 1945. From there, they sailed to Tokyo Bay to unload supplies and were present with the American fleet when the Instrument of Surrender was signed aboard the USS *Missouri* on September 2, 1945.

Schwaller continued his mail duties aboard the ship, which remained in Japanese waters for several months. The vessel returned to the United States in the spring after the war's end, and Schwaller received his discharge from the U.S. Navy on April 22, 1946, having achieved the rating of "Mailman Third Class."

"After the war, Edward came back to Jefferson City and attended the former Jefferson City Junior College while working at the old Southside Supermarket," said Jeanne Schwaller. "He then went to St. Louis and became a union carpenter and then moved to California. He was a carpenter foreman for the City of Los Angeles for fifteen years and took engineering courses at the University of Los Angeles."

Jeanne Schwaller went on to explain that the former sailor returned to Jefferson City in the 1970s and established his own construction company, Schwaller's Inc. Jeanne also noted they married in 1974 and remained so for forty years, raising two children together. Sadly, the eighty-eight-year-old veteran passed in 2014. Noting her late husband was proud of his military service and maintained membership in the Veterans of Foreign Wars and the American Legion, he remained hesitant to share too many stories from his World War II experience.

"He was like a lot of veterans in that he didn't share many details of his time in the service, but when he did, it was of unique moments that had a lasting impression on him," said Jeanne Schwaller. "He always said that he just wanted to get back home from the war." She continued, "And it's odd what you remember, but I can recall him saying that one of the best things about being back from the war was he was happy to finally have a real shower … not the saltwater showers they had on the ships." *(Photograph courtesy of Jeanne Schwaller)*

Ralph Lee Comer – *Kansas City*

The economic morass of the Great Depression had essentially evaporated, and opportunities were unfolding in the Kansas City area as a young Ralph Comer finished his high school education in 1944 when only sixteen years of age. He briefly attended college but, the following year resolved to join scores of his fellow youth by enlisting in support of World War II—a decision that later resulted in five university degrees and a laudable military career.

"He joined the United States Maritime Service in July 1945, when he was seventeen," said the late veteran's wife, Joanne. "In a description, he wrote about his experiences, Ralph explained that he was sent to boot camp at a site on Catalina Island where the Chicago Cubs once had their training camp," she added

The young Comer was soon aboard a train headed east for Sheepshead Bay, New York, in September 1945. Once there, he spent several months in Hospital Corps/Purser School before transferring to the Marine Hospital on the Presidio in San Francisco. His training period as a hospital corpsman ended in June 1946, and he was placed in the Merchant Marines. He soon received assignment to the *SS Helena Modjeska*, a Liberty Ship operated by the Black Diamond Steamship Company with a complement of thirty-eight crewmembers.

For the next year, his personal recollections reveal, the newly trained Comer came of age quickly from the experiences he endured during a year spent at sea under the command of several "salty" sailors of questionable virtue.

"The First Engineer, Mr. Allen, was sixty-seven years old and looked like Abraham Lincoln, and he used snuff," Comer mirthfully wrote in his brief memoirs. "Wherever we were, as soon as the first man hit the dock, (he) had the best-looking girl around. I never did figure out how it worked ..."

The vessel transported various supplies such as coal and oil to international ports in addition to equipment and gear abandoned by the military; they accomplished this mission through the combined efforts of an ethnically diverse crew.

"During the war and immediately after," Comer wrote, "... you weren't supposed to have more than 10% foreigners. Well, this ship was a floating United Nations. We had about 10% American, and the rest were foreigners." He added, "It was so bad that, if you called the engine room and didn't speak Chinese or Greek, you'd had it. There was only one other English speaker down there besides the engineer."

Despite any linguistic challenges presented by the unique crew composite, they continued their travels and Comer collected a lifetime of mirthful reflections. One of the most unforgettable, he recalled in his later years, came on September 12, 1946, when their ship ran aground on the Goodwin Sands off the coast of Kent in southeast England.

"We anchored to pick up minefield charts for the North Sea," Comer wrote. "All around, we could see the stacks of ships that had run on the sands. We elected to go up the inner channel and, on a bright, sunny afternoon about 1:00, we ran aground." He added, "To this day, I don't know exactly whose fault it was."

During the next couple of days, tugboats vainly attempted to drag the ship from the sands. The captain eventually gave the order to evacuate the ship, and on September 14, 1946, the *USS Helena Modjeska* broke in two.

Comer continued in his seafaring service until returning to civilian life in August 1947. Coming home to Kansas City, he enrolled in the University of Kansas, where he met the former Joanne Amick. The couple married on April 8, 1950, following their graduation.

"The next several years were focused on continuing his education," said his wife, Joanne Comer. "He received his master's degree in human anatomy from the University of Kansas and worked on his Ph.D. in human anatomy in Charleston, South Carolina, while also teaching anatomy."

Earning his doctorate in 1955, he went on to complete medical school in December 1957. His return to uniformed service came when he was accepted for active duty with the U.S. Navy in 1958 and went on to complete additional education that included a master's in public health from Johns Hopkins University.

A highlight of his naval career was assignment as commanding officer for the Navy Medical Science Unit at Gorgas Memorial Laboratory in the Republic of Panama, where he spent time with the Chocó Indians. He later served as a medical officer aboard the USS *Halsey* before retiring in April 1979, following a stint as commanding officer of the Drug and Alcohol Treatment Center for the San Diego Naval Hospital.

"During the latter part of his naval service, he became interested in the treatment of alcoholism and chemical dependency," said his wife. "In the years following his military service, he was director of the Alcoholism and Drug Abuse Treatment Center at the state hospital in Austin, Texas. In 1983, he and I opened "Living Well," which was a marriage and family counseling service."

The former sailor later moved to work part-time for another alcoholism treatment facility in Texas, but after retiring in 1994, he and his wife moved back to Austin. Sadly, Comer passed away on March 10, 2018, survived by his wife (who passed away on June 21, 2020) and their four children.

Possessing a bounty of remarkable experiences from his military service, Comer described in writing one memorable moment from his time in the Merchant Marines that left quite an impression on a young man, barely eighteen years of age, who had only recently graduated from high school.

"Well, the captain's favorite food was pickled fish," he wrote. "(He) ran around in shorts and undershirt and barefooted, and was just filthy from the knees down." In mirthful reflection, he added, "Drunk and smelling of pickled fish, his favorite sport was to come to my stateroom and talk to me. My stateroom wasn't any bigger than a kitchen. He would come in and sit on the edge of my bunk and bang his filthy heels against it, and breathe pickled fish and whiskey at me and tell me his troubles …" *(Photograph courtesy Joanne Amick Comer)*

Colonel Andrew R. Duvall - *Rolla*

While serving as a second lieutenant with the Tennessee National Guard, Andrew R. Duvall had already accrued nearly a decade of military experience when his unit was federalized for service in World War I. During the war, he experienced combat when serving with the 30th Infantry Division and, in the years that followed, chose to focus on a career in the U.S. Army. Years later, when the Second World War erupted, the now-seasoned colonel found himself in the position of providing focused leadership to troops who were facing a unique type of enemy on the home front—venereal disease.

"Maj. Gen. Frederick E. Uhl, Seventh Corps Area commander announced yesterday the appointment of Col. Andrew R. Duvall as post commander of Fort Leonard Wood, Mo.," reported the *St. Louis Post-Dispatch* on July 9, 1942. "Col. Duvall, who until recently was executive officer at Fort Francis E. Warren, Wyo., succeeds Lieut.

Col. Austin F. Anderson, who continues as executive officer...," the newspaper further noted.

As Dr. Larry Roberts, a historian with the United States Army Engineer School, explained in a brief article aptly titled *History of Fort Leonard Wood*, ground was broken for the new Army post on December 3, 1940—a little more than a year prior to the attack on Pearl Harbor—in anticipation that the "country would be drawn into what was rapidly becoming a global conflict."

The fort, named for Congressional Medal of Honor recipient and a former "Rough Riders" commander of the Spanish-American War, Major General Leonard Wood, soon grew to encompass approximately 63,000 acres of land. During World War II, noted Dr. Roberts, "more than 300,000 soldiers passed through (the fort) on their way to service in every theater of operation."

Prior to his assignment at Ft. Leonard Wood, Col. Duvall studied "operations methods and procedure at the corps area headquarters in preparation for his assignment as commanding officer...," reported the May 29, 1942 edition of the *Casper Star-Tribune* (Casper, Wyoming). The newspaper additionally noted Duvall's involvement with the community as a member of his local Kiwanis Club. Community engagement, Duvall discovered, became an important aspect of the myriad of his command duties as soldiers passing through the post pursued recreational opportunities offered in the various local towns and cities. These off-post adventures, often absent from any restrictions imposed by the U.S. Army, included towns such as Lebanon situated nearly thirty miles away.

"An ultimatum that the city of Lebanon must undertake to clean up vice conditions or be declared 'off limits' for Fort Leonard Wood soldiers has been delivered here by Col. Andrew R. Duvall, commander of the Army post," reported the *St. Louis Post-Dispatch* on August 15, 1944. The newspaper went on to explain, "Col. Duvall told representatives of civic groups in Lebanon Aug. 8 [1944] that there were 27 women in Lebanon known to have venereal disease who had infected Fort Wood soldiers," adding that the colonel viewed it as his "duty to protect the health of soldiers under his jurisdiction."

It was a challenging situation for the military commander, rife with contrasts and political overtones. During the war, the community of Lebanon banded together to demonstrate their support for the fort by establishing a local USO Club where service members could relax, write letters home and enjoy various forms of entertainment such as dances. However, the *Sikeston Standard* reported on August 25, 1944, that Jean Paul Bradshaw, the Republican nominee for governor of Missouri, was at the time prosecuting attorney of Laclede County, of which his hometown of Lebanon was the county seat. The newspaper stated that although he promised during his campaign to keep "politics ... free from the faintest suspicion of graft and vice," he had failed in such enforcement in his own hometown.

Adding another interesting twist to the allegations of vice was the fact that his Democratic opponent for governor was Phil M. Donnelly, an attorney who resided in Lebanon. In the news reports that followed, Donnelly declined to comment with regard to the allegations made by Col. Duvall and would go on to win the 1944 gubernatorial race. In his defense, reported the *St. Louis Post-Dispatch*, Bradshaw asserted he had "personally participated in the raid on (a) residence" where questionable activities had taken place, adding, "We can't grab somebody and lock him up without a specific charge. We must have a violation of the law.... That is what we have tried to explain...."

The vice was eventually resolved, media attention faded and Col. Duvall was again able to focus on his duties of preparing soldiers for potential combat overseas. As the war ended, Duvall retired from the military, and he and his wife made the decision to live out their remaining days in the community of Rolla. The struggle against the spread of venereal disease became one of many foes fought by commanders at numerous military bases in the United States and abroad during the war, and officers such as the late Col. Duvall went to great lengths in maintaining a healthy, ready fighting force.

The desire of Col. Duvall to work in unison with a local town in resolving a serious health concern was revealed in a statement he released on August 15, 1944, in which he affirmed, "My statements were in the nature of a report to the community (of Lebanon) by an officer deeply concerned for the well-being of his command." Days earlier, he noted, "Your relationship with Fort Leonard Wood has always been close, and I feel certain the good people of this community are willing to cooperate to the fullest extent in solving this problem." *(Photograph courtesy of Jeremy P. Ämick)*

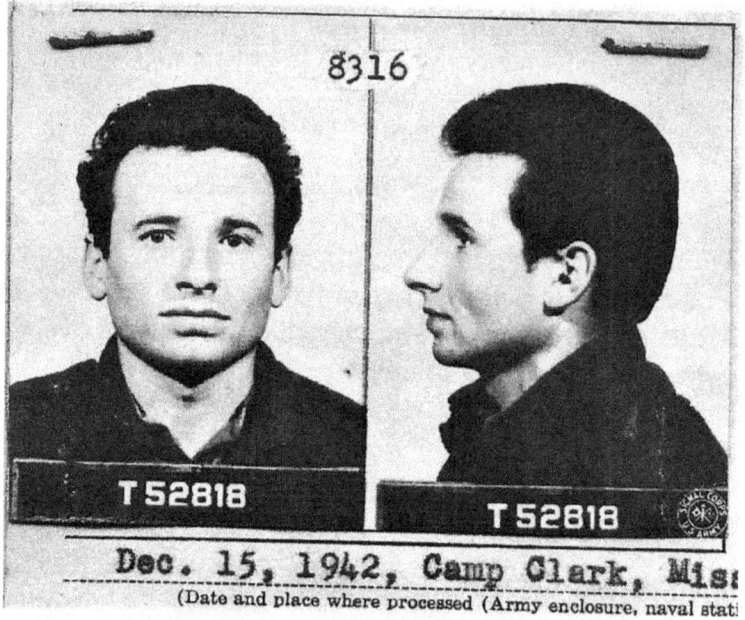

Enrico Sesenna – *Italian Prisoner of War*

Born in January 1920 in a small village in northern Italy, Enrico Sesenna grew up the youngest of nine sons. As a child, he toiled in the vineyards owned by his family while also maintaining the fields where they grazed their cattle. It was a peaceful time, with World War I behind them and most Italian families unable to foresee the changes that would affect their beloved country. Soon, they would experience a new war and the imprisonment of thousands of Italian soldiers in distant locations such as Missouri.

"My father was only three years old when his father died (in April 1923)," said Sesenna's daughter, Augusta, who still resides in Italy. "My grandmother was a widow with nine children to support, and she kept working in the fields with the help of the older children," she added.

Entering World War II in 1940, as part of the Axis powers alongside Germany and Japan, Italy quickly began to build its army through conscription of young men. In January 1941, a twenty-one-year-old Sesenna was compelled into military service and assigned to the 3rd Assault Platoon of the 66th Motorized Infantry Regiment. The following year, he was moved from his duty station in Sicily and sent to fight in North Africa. In stories shared with his daughter, Sesnenna remarked that he and his fellow soldiers were often short of food and water and lacked decent weapons, tanks, and vehicles with which to fight. He bluntly explained, "In the morning, we licked our gun barrels to drink the dewdrops left from the humidity of the night and were surrounded with nothing but sand and scorpions."

There were other instances, Sensenna explained when the Italians were concealed in sandy foxholes surrounded by the stench of rotting corpses from earlier battles that could not be buried without exposing oneself to enemy marksmen. Despite the sparse supplies available to the frontline soldiers of the Italian military, U.S. Army Col. (ret.) Trevor Nevitt Dupuy noted in his book *Asian and Axis Resistance Movements* that there were "some Italian units under Rommel in Africa (that) frequently fought as effectively as the best German units. These Italians were as brave and skillful fighting men as any in the world."[71]

Later transferred to the 28th Infantry Regiment Pavia, Sesenna received an unanticipated reprieve from the Spartan conditions to which he had become accustomed when he was among a group of Italian soldiers captured near El-Alamein, Egypt by New Zealand infantry (who were with the United Kingdom's Eighth Army) on July 15, 1942. For several weeks, he was held as a prisoner of war (POW) in camps in North Africa. The POW was then moved to a camp in the United Kingdom before being placed on a troopship bound for Canada in late November the same year. Detention records maintained by Sesenna show he departed Canada on December 10, 1942, and was with the first group of Italian POWs to arrive at Camp Clark near Nevada, Missouri, two days later. In September 1942, the pris-

---

[71] Dupuy, *Asian and Axis Resistance Movements*, 66.

oner of war was moved to a camp in United Kingdom before boarding a troopship for Canada in October. Upon his arrival in Halifax, Nova Scotia, he was sent by rail to the prisoner of war camp located at Camp Clark, Missouri, arriving in December 1942.

Records of Camp Clark's POW history written by an unknown author state that on December 12, 1942, "Prisoner of war troop train, bearing 499 Italian Prisoners of War for this camp was wrecked about 7 miles north of Nevada. Flying squad of 366th and 344d MPEG (Military Police Escort Guard) Companies was alerted to the scene of the accident."

No Italian prisoners escaped custody; however, two soldiers of the 324th MPEG assisting in the transfer of the detainees perished from injuries sustained in the accident. For the next seventeen months, Sesenna remained at Camp Clark and, in mid-May 1944, he was transferred to Camp Weingarten when the POW camp at Camp Clark was placed on standby status. The POW camp at Camp Clark was reactivated several weeks later to receive German POWs.

"Established at Weingarten, a sleepy little town on State Highway 32 between Ste. Genevieve and Farmington Missouri, (Camp Weingarten) had no pre-war existence, and unlike the other major camps in the state, it never served any military function other than as a pen for Italian POWs," wrote David Fiedler in *The Enemy Among Us: POWs in Missouri During World War II*.[72]

"I know he spent a lot of time in the woods as a lumberjack on POW work details," said his daughter, Augusta. "The trees were sent to sawmills near the camp, and he would talk about the squirrels that weren't scared of men. He said they would come down from the trees and eat food out of his hands." She continued, "Sometime after that, he worked as a cleaner at the hospital and did other jobs. In March 1945, he cut his hand badly while washing cutlery in the kitchen (of

---

[72] Fiedler, *The Enemy Among Us*, 51.

the Officers Mess) and was sent to the outpatient clinic to have it dressed. They sent him for a few days to Schick General Hospital in Clinton, Iowa, for medication according to his medical report."

With the war ended, Camp Weingarten closed and, in September 1945, Sesenna was transferred to Ft. Crooks, Nebraska, followed by his repatriation to Italy in 1946. Like many veterans returning from war, he went on to marry and raised a family of six children. In the years after the war, he returned to his work as a farmer until his death in 1981, when only sixty-one years old.

"My father was buried with his relatives in a small cemetery not so far from the same hills and fields where he had worked his entire life," shared his daughter, Augusta.

Somberly recalling that her father shared few details regarding his service in World War II, she added, "It's a little sad, but in Italy, the stories of Italian prisoners during the war have been forgotten and nobody tries to discover what happened during those years. My father did not like speaking about the war years but he always remembered his period (in the USA) with pleasure," she explained. "He spoke about it with happiness and you could feel how much admiration he had for your great country." *(Photograph courtesy of Augusta Sesenna)*

Willard Ray Johnson – *Independence*

Graduating from Grain Valley High School in 1936, years later, Willard Ray Johnson of Independence, Missouri, married the former Grayce Huffman on December 29, 1942. Less than two months later, Johnson enlisted in the Merchant Marines. During his first voyage, he served aboard the oil tanker *Yankee Arrow* when it struck a mine off the coast of Tunisia in early August 1943. Wounded during the incident, the seaman was evacuated to the U.S. Army's 90th General Hospital on the island of Malta for treatment for multiple severe burns. Despite all the medical care given, Johnson passed away on August 11, 1943.

Johnson was posthumously awarded the Mariner's Medal, the second-highest award that can be bestowed upon a merchant seaman. Although he was initially laid to rest in the Naval Cemetery in Capuccini, Malta, his remains were later returned to the United States and interred in the Oak Grove Cemetery in Jackson County, Missouri. On February 9, 1945, a Liberty ship, the SS *Willard R. Johnson*, was launched in memory of the deceased seaman. *(Photograph courtesy of the Johnson family)*

Fay Holt – *Dixie*

While serving in North Africa and Italy during World War II, Fay Holt did not believe his service to the country to be of any lasting significance. Decades later, he explained during an interview, when programs such as the Central Missouri Honor Flight began recognizing the service of local veterans, he was awestruck by their efforts to commemorate his contributions.

"I didn't think that what I did was all that important, but I got a bunch of letters of appreciation on the (honor) flight from some big shot politicians that said that it was," the veteran grinned.

Born in 1920 in the nearly forgotten Callaway County, Missouri, community of Dixie, Holt finished the eighth grade at a local schoolhouse and then went to work on the farm of a local family until receiving his draft notice in 1942.

"The family that I was working for tried to get me a deferment because they needed me to work on the farm." Chuckling, he added, "But I guess Uncle Sam needed me a lot more than they did."

Inducted into the U.S. Army at Jefferson Barracks, Missouri, on July 24, 1942, the draftee was sent to Ft. Riley, Kansas, and completed his boot camp at a training site known as "Camp Whitside." From there, he received assignment to Company A, 743rd Military Police Battalion—an all-black unit that had been formed only weeks earlier. The young soldier remained at the camp for the next several months, learning how to function as a military policeman and performing guard duty around the post. However, in August 1943, the battalion received orders for overseas service and took a train to the East Coast, where they boarded a troop ship that brought them to their new duty station in Algeria.

"It was pretty much just guard duty as usual (in North Africa)," said Holt. "I was lucky because I never had to shoot anyone."

As the veteran explained, after several months in Algeria and later at a site in Tunisia, the battalion again boarded another troop transport and sailed for Naples, Italy.

"I can remember it still being pretty hot when we got to Italy, with mortars and such exploding nearby," Holt affirmed. "The one thing that sticks out in my mind was us running off the ship with our shotguns and having to take cover," he said.

Though the soldier was never informed of the details of the skirmish that was taking place upon the battalion's arrival in Italy, he recalled that the situation soon "settled down," followed by him and his comrades traveling to their new duty station to resume their responsibilities as military policemen. As they had done in North Africa, the men of the 743rd Military Police Battalion continued performing security and traffic patrols, but it was their guard duty, Holt said, that placed him in one of the most stressful situations he ever experienced while overseas.

"We were pulling a lot of guard duty in a compound that held Italian and German prisoners of war," Holt said. "One time, while I was guarding one of the gates to the compound, an Italian guy came up and wanted to get inside; he was quite persistent about it." He added, "I was ready to shoot him (because of his aggressive approach), but he turned around and walked away, and I was sure glad that he did."

When the war in Europe ended in May 1945, the soldiers of the 743rd MP Battalion believed that their next destination would be somewhere in the Pacific in support of the planned invasion of Japan. However, in the months that followed, Japan surrendered, and the battalion made their return trip to the United States in November 1945. Receiving his discharge at Jefferson Barracks on December 1, 1945, Holt returned to Mid-Missouri and "drove a truck for several years," he said. He then went on to spend a couple of years as a police officer with the New Bloomfield Police Department before going to work for the Department of Corrections, from where he retired in 1985 after twenty-six years of employment.

The father of six children, Holt enjoyed looking through many of the documents and photographs from his days in the military during the interview, pausing to point at a picture of himself in uniform and exclaiming, "I was a young man then, but look at me now!"

Reflecting on the more than two years he served overseas, Holt jokingly recalled that all of his journeys to various locations in North Africa and Italy were made by ship, and it was not until many years later that he would first set foot on an airplane as part of the Central Missouri Honor Flight.

"I had never been any higher than a treetop my entire life," Holt lightheartedly remarked. "When we did the Honor Flight (in November 2013), that was the first time I had ever been on a plane, and they let me sit by the wing over one of those big engines, and I got to see it all—what a great time!"

In describing his experience while visiting the nation's war memorials as part of the trip to the nation's capital, Holt noted, "It seemed like all of this didn't happen until we were too old to do anything about it." He added, "But it was a wonderful trip, and it seemed like we were always on the move to get to the next place—it all happened so fast. But I'm glad I got to see everything because at my age, it was certainly a once in a lifetime opportunity." *(Photograph courtesy of Fay Holt)*

Clifford Holt – *Guthrie*

Clifford Holt became something of a local celebrity in and around the community of New Bloomfield, Missouri. He enjoyed escorting the area children safely to school by serving as a crossing guard and, many years previous, was the town's first black chief of police. Achieving more than nine decades of age, the veteran of World War II displayed no signs of slowing down and was often found in a local convenience store swapping stories about his days in the military over a cup of coffee with several of his close friends. Born in 1925 in the near-forgotten Callaway County town of Dixie, Missouri, Holt recalls coming of age in a small black community and attending a local school held inside a building that he describes as little more than "an old house."

"When I graduated the eighth grade, I went to work on a farm, that is until I turned eighteen and got my draft notice in the mail," he recalled.

The young man then traveled to St. Louis to take a physical and, while undergoing the military induction process, was asked whether he wanted to become a soldier or a sailor.

"I told them that I wanted to be in the Army so they put me in the Navy," he chuckled. "That's how they did things back then."

With his branch of service now identified, Holt was transferred to Norfolk, Virginia, to complete several weeks of basic training.

"When I was in Virginia, they were working on the boat that I was supposed to be assigned to," said Holt. "So, while that was happening, they sent me to a Navy base in (Norman) Oklahoma, until it was finished being built and it was time for me to report to the ship."

During his stay at the base in Oklahoma, the sailor attended a naval gunnery school and, because of his ability to hit the targets, was appointed to serve as the rear gunner aboard his new ship. According to naval records, the USS *LSM-498* was completed by the Brown Shipbuilding Company and launched on April 7, 1945, followed by its commissioning a month later. The ship, Holt explained, was classified as a "Landing Ship Medium (LSM)" and designed to transport troops and cargo in support of the war effort in the Pacific.

After commissioning, the ship was sent to support U.S forces in the Battle of Okinawa—an eighty-two-day long campaign that became the largest amphibious assault of World War II. During this battle, Japan lost more than 77,000 soldiers, with the Allies suffering the loss of more than 14,000 of their troops. As Holt recalls, one of the greatest threats to the safety of the men aboard the LSMs were often the attacks that came from Japanese aircraft; however, he added, though he was prepared to defend the ship from an aerial attack with his 20mm gun mounted on the stern, it never became a necessity.

"We went over there to fight, but most of the time, the Japanese planes were so far off you could hardly see them," he said. "The biggest threat we encountered were those stormy seas—they seemed worse than a tornado. Those waves would push you way up in the air and then would drop out from under you and slam the ship down into the water. Let me tell you, that just about made everybody seasick."

At the close of their service in Okinawa in June 1945, Holt's ship and the "291 LSMs commissioned were preparing for the invasion of Japan," wrote William Craighead in his book *All Ahead Full: World War II Memoirs of an LSM-215 Veteran*.[73]

On August 9, 1945, Holt recalls their LSM operating along the southern coast of Japan when they witnessed a historic event that prevented the U.S. from having to invade the mainland of Japan, a military operation that would possibly have been the bloodiest engagement in modern history.

"We were close enough to see when they dropped the second atomic bomb (on Nagasaki)," said Holt. "That was really something to see," he added.

Days later, following the Japanese surrender, USS *LSM-498* remained in the Pacific as part of the cleanup and occupation of Japan until April 1946, at which time they returned to San Diego where Holt was mustered out of the Navy. Returning to Mid-Missouri, he was married, raised two children, and operated a truck until suffering a heart attack when in his mid-forties.

"I then went to work as a deputy for Callaway County for several years until I was hired as the chief of police for New Bloomfield, which I did for twenty-eight years," he said.

Following his retirement, Holt remained actively engaged with the community by serving as a crossing guard for the New Bloomfield School. With all the veteran was able to see and experience during

---

[73] Craighead, *All Ahead Full*, 162.

his months of service that carried him across the Pacific during a time of war, he proudly exclaimed that the most memorable moment of his service was being able to demonstrate his marksmanship abilities while in his military training.

"Yes, the one thing the military taught me was that you'd better learn to respect others, or they're going to give you a hard way to go," he grinned. "But mostly, what I'm proud of is that I showed them how I could shoot a gun." He added, "I qualified by hitting the airplane target the first time around (in training), and that's why they made me a gunner. It was probably because of all of the rabbit hunting I did back when I was a kid that I was good at it—or at least I thought I was," he chuckled.

Clifford Holt was ninety-four years old when he passed away on May 21, 2019. The World War II veteran was laid to rest in Oak Chapel Missionary Baptist Cemetery in Guthrie, Missouri. *(Photograph courtesy of Jeremy P. Ämick)*

Charles Foster – *Weaubleau*

Following graduation from high school in Weaubleau, Missouri, in 1939, Charles Foster made the decision to attend Southwest Missouri State Teachers College (now Missouri State University). When he ran out of college funds in 1941, he moved to Carbondale, Illinois, where he went to work at a local restaurant and learned valuable lessons that would later help shape the direction of his military experience.

"The owner of the restaurant took the time to show me how to prepare a number of different meals using whatever ingredients were available," recalled Foster. "I didn't realize it then, but his guidance turned out to be a blessing when I was in the military," he added.

After one of his close friends was killed while serving aboard the USS *Oklahoma*, Foster made the decision to enlist in the U.S. Army Air Forces in May 1942, shortly before his twenty-first birthday. Within days, he was at Jefferson Barracks in St. Louis to begin his basic training. The young enlistee was selected to attend aircraft mechanic school, traveling to Glendale, California, for training at the Curtis Wright Technical Institute. For the next several weeks, he learned all aspects of maintenance and repair on the B-25 Mitchell—a twin-engine bomber widely used by the Allied air forces in World War II.

"An interesting part of being at Glendale is that I got to visit the hangar where Howard Hughes stored his famous "Spruce Goose," Foster explained. (The Spruce Goose was essentially a flying boat made primarily from wood and built by the Hughes Aircraft Corporation.)

Graduating the course with a superior rating, he was sent to a B-25 Specialist School with North American Aviation at Inglewood, California. It was there that he received more advanced maintenance and repair training and qualified to serve as a crew chief on the B-25s. Through random selection, Foster was chosen to enter training to become a replacement for anticipated personnel losses in the upcoming invasion of North Africa. He was first sent to Camp Kearns, Utah, for infantry training and then to Camp Kilmer, New Jersey, where he finished his preparations for overseas deployment.

"We left the United States on January 14, 1943, as part of a convoy of ships and were constantly under threat from German submarines," he explained. "We made it safely overseas, but a ship in our group that was carrying my military records was torpedoed and sunk, which caused me problems for several months."

Upon arrival in Oran, Algiers (North Africa), Foster was essentially a "man without a country" for the next several months since he lacked any official records. Although slated to serve as a B-25 crew chief, he was instead detached to work in the headquarters of the 825th Engineers. When his replacement records finally arrived, he was paid for the first time in six months and assigned to the 36th Supply Squadron in Algiers, where he was placed in charge of airfreight operations and managed the receipt and storage of critical war supplies such as munitions. While there, he had the privilege of meeting Winston Churchill and General Dwight D. Eisenhower.

"I requested and was granted a transfer to the 360th Air Squadron on November 7, 1943," Foster recalled "We were part of the invasion of Sicily, Sardinia and Corsica, but our outfit was eventually split up." He added, "We landed in Ajaccio, Corsica, and the first thing they did was put me on K.P. (kitchen patrol) duty."

As the veteran explained, the head cook was drunk, and none of the soldiers on K.P. with Foster knew how to cook, so he took charge and started making assignments, realizing the troops on the base would soon be hungry.

"There were some dried apples that I found, and using the lessons I had learned working in the restaurant before the war, I made an apple cobbler from them," he said. "The troops loved the meal, and because of that, I soon became the acting mess sergeant."

Foster and another soldier assigned to the mess section hunted deer on the island to provide fresh meat for the soldiers in addition to preparing sea bass caught from the ocean. On one occasion, he noted, they even shot a wild boar that was prepared and served in the mess hall. With their unit joining the push toward Germany, they left Corsica on May 5, 1945, for Leghorn, Italy. The war with Germany ended days later, and the military began discharging soldiers for return to the states.

"I was transferred to the 2493rd Quartermaster Truck Company in northern Italy to work as their mess sergeant until my discharge came through," he said. "It wasn't until November 1, 1945, that I got to come home, and I was discharged at Jefferson Barracks about three weeks later.

In the years after the war, Foster married and raised two children, eventually making his home in Jefferson City. He went on to earn his master's degree from the University of Missouri in Columbia and enjoyed a lengthy career in education, much of it spent with the Missouri Department of Higher Education. In 2009, he had the opportunity to travel to Washington, D.C., to see the various war memorials as part of the Central Missouri Honor Flight—a heartwarming experience that inspired him to become a proponent of the program.

"When we got off the airplane in Maryland, and all these people were lined up to shake our hands and thank us for our service, that was a very emotional moment for me because we didn't have any fanfare when I came home from the war," he said.

"And looking back on my time in the service, I'm no hero ... but I'm proud of what I did and would do it all over again. I really feel that it was a miracle that I spent three years overseas during a war and lived to come home when so many were not so fortunate."

Charles Foster departed Earth for his heavenly home on December 6, 2019. The ninety-eight-year-old veteran was laid to rest in Hawthorn Memorial Gardens in Jefferson City, Missouri. *(Photograph courtesy of Charles Foster)*

Robert A. Young – *Green City*

Sitting upon a dusty shelf in a shadowy nook of an antique store in Jefferson City, Missouri, was an ornate copper mug etched with Vietnam War service dates. It held a small U.S. flag and a time-curled military photograph of a soldier from Missouri—all for the meager price of five dollars. This inexpensive purchase of a war memento revealed details about a soldier from Missouri, who, during his thirty-year-career, served as a paratrooper making more than one hundred parachute jumps and achieving the highest of enlisted ranks as a command sergeant major.

Graduating from high school in the north-central Missouri community of Green City in 1942, Robert A. Young's draft registration card dated June 29, 1942, notes that the eighteen-year-old was living in Chicago, where he was employed by the Cleveland Container Company. However, on April 8, 1943, he conceded to a higher calling when leaving his manufacturing job and enlisting in the U.S.

Army. After entering the service at Ft. Leavenworth, Kansas, he was soon assigned to the 17th Airborne Division—one of five airborne divisions formed in World War II.

In his book *World War II Order of Battle*, Shelby L. Stanton explained that the 17th Airborne was "activated at (Camp) Mackall, N.C. and participated in the Carolina Airborne-Troop Carrier Command Maneuvers (from December 6-10, 1943)." He further noted that the division then "moved to the Tennessee Maneuvers Area ... and took part in the Second Army No. 5 Maneuvers."[74]

Young was just a twenty-year-old paratrooper when he arrived in England with the division in late August 1944. Four months later, he received his baptism of fire during the Battle of the Bulge when "the inexperienced 17th Airborne Division was rushed to the front from England and took part in the Allied counteroffensive," noted Matthew J. Seelinger, in an article for the National Museum of the United States Army. Following the Battle of the Bulge, the division was engaged in clearing operations and, in late March 1945, participated in airborne assaults near the Rhine River north of the German town of Wesel. Throughout the next several weeks, they led attacks, cleared towns of pockets of German resistance, and relieved other divisions.

When the war came to an end on May 7, 1945, the 17th Airborne Division received credit for three campaigns of the war after suffering 1,191 of its soldiers killed in action. The division returned to the United States in September 1945; however, Young was reassigned to the 82nd Airborne Division and remained in Germany with the occupational forces. He eventually decided to make a career in the U.S. Army, climbing through the enlisted ranks and moving "to Ft. Campbell, Kentucky, then to Japan to work on 'Operation Gyroscope' before returning to Ft. Campbell to form the 101st ABN (Airborne) Division," noted his obituary.

---

[74] Stanton, *World War II Order of Battle*, 97.

The *Leaf-Chronicle*, a newspaper printed in Clarksville, Tennessee, reported on January 20, 1958, that Master Sgt. Young was among a group of nine battle-hardened soldiers of the 506th Airborne Infantry of the 101st Airborne Division awarded "gold wings" when becoming members of the "century club," by individually have made more than one hundred airborne parachute jumps. The paper noted that Young, who was fulfilling the role of sergeant major for the 506th, was credited with one hundred twenty-six jumps.

Young was called the "Currahee group sergeant major"—a reference dating back to World War II. "Currahee" became the motto of the 506th Infantry Regiment during the war because of Currahee Mountain at Camp Toccoa, Georgia—a former paratrooper training camp. Running up and down the mountain during training helped build camaraderie amongst the airborne troopers. Several weeks later, on March 20, 1958, the *Leaf-Chronicle* printed that Young "thought up the idea" of formalizing the qualification process for Master and Senior parachutists by "issuing qualification cards" signed by the group commander. As the paper explained, the billfold-size cards were to help "develop a closer brotherhood amongst its older jumpers."

The following year, in 1959, Young was promoted to the rank of command sergeant major and, in 1962, married the former Betty Jane Judge. He went on to serve a tour in Korea followed by a stint with the U.S. Strike Command in Florida before returning to the 101st Airborne Division. During the Vietnam War, Command Sgt. Maj. Young led troops of the 101st Airborne Division during two tours. He was revered by those under his command and presented a copper mug by the soldiers of the First Brigade that was emblazoned with the emblem of the division.

According to the September 2, 1969, edition of the *Austin-American Statesman*, Sgt. Maj. Young assumed the top enlisted post at a major military base when he was appointed to replace retiring Sgt. Maj. Willard V. Hunter as the "command sergeant major of III Corps and Fort Hood (Texas)." His thirty-year career came to a close in 1973 when he finished his assignment at the Presidio of San Francisco. He eventually settled in his hometown of Green City, enjoying many years of retirement while seeking escape from the haunting recollections of those lost in his career and personal life, including his wife, who passed away in 1981. Following his death in 2016, having no children to carry forth his legacy, Young's engraved mug from Vietnam, along with other unknown treasures, was sold off and awaited rediscovery.

Although former Vice President Adali Stephenson never met Command Sgt. Maj. Young, his intuitive observation regarding the devotion of those pursuing military careers aptly describes the selfless service of the late paratrooper, characterized in a fascinating story unexpectedly uncovered through an antique store find.

"Patriotism is not short, frenzied outbursts of emotion, but the tranquil and steady dedication of a lifetime." *(Photograph courtesy of Jeremy P. Amick)*

Don Whitehead – *Springfield*

In the spring of 1945, when Don Whitehead was preparing to graduate from high school in Springfield, Missouri, he and more than four dozen of his fellow seniors flooded into the local recruiting office to enlist in the U.S. Navy in support of the country's efforts in World War II. This, he later discovered, was the opening moment of his two-decade medical career spanning two branches of the military. A few weeks later, in late May 1945, an eighteen-year-old Whitehead arrived to Great Lakes Naval Training Station in Illinois to begin his basic training. However, the veteran recalled, the initial training was soon cut short when the young recruit expressed an interest in becoming a medic.

"They pulled me out of boot camp early, and I remained at Great Lakes for several weeks of training as a hospital corpsman because they were badly needed at that time," he said. "I learned to perform some nursing work such as diagnosing and treating patients, administering IVs, and giving shots," he added.

In the late summer of 1945, he was assigned to support part of a U.S. Marine division traveling aboard the USS *Alcor* (AD-34)—a destroyer tender of the U.S. Navy. The vessel was sent to the Philippines, where intense fighting had essentially ceased, resulting in an unenviable responsibility for Whitehead and his fellow corpsmen.

"There was a hospital ship that came in after the invasion of the Philippines, and I, along with eight other corpsmen, prepared for shipment back to the states the bodies of about four thousand service members who had been killed in action," he solemnly explained. "Part of that process was placing the bodies in plastic bags and then putting the dog tags in the mouth of each casualty for later identification."

With the recent surrender of Japan, Whitehead was reassigned in the fall of 1945 to serve with the occupational forces of Japan. His duties found him working in a small building that had been converted into an outpatient clinic near downtown Tokyo.

"The clinic had a Japanese doctor, a Japanese nurse, and myself working there," recalled Whitehead. "We established a regular sick call and treated a variety of things to include venereal disease." He added, "We were treated like kings by the Japanese people while we were there—it was almost like we had never been at war with one another."

After spending several months in Japan, he returned to the United States and assisted in decommissioning the medical department of an aircraft carrier. The sailor was then sent back to Great Lakes Naval Training Station because of a shortage of medical staff at the naval hospital. On December 8, 1946, he received his discharge from active duty. The veteran chose to remain in the Navy Reserve and, following his return to Springfield, enrolled in classes at the former Southwest Missouri State University. While in school, he met Luda, and the two married on June 1, 1948.

"After being out of active service for a year or so, I returned to active duty with the Navy and was transferred to the Olathe (Kansas) Naval Air Station," he said. "I attended a four-month course in aerospace medicine in Pensacola, Florida, in 1953 and became a medic on flying status."

The sailor remained at Olathe until 1956, at which time he made the decision to join the Air Force because of their robust and growing aviation medicine program. His first assignment was with the 3415th Technical Training Wing at Lowry Air Force Base in Colorado, where his duties included helicopter rescues and transporting patients. Whitehead's career in the Air Force continued with his transfer to Eielson Air Force Base near Fairbanks, Alaska, in 1962. For the next three years, he was the non-commissioned officer in charge of flight medicine in addition to his regular medical duties such as assisting physicians with surgical procedures and participating in air rescue missions.

"I received orders in 1965 to report to McGuire Air Force Base in New Jersey with the 539th Fighter-Interceptor Squadron," he said. "When I got there, the pilots and support staff were in training for Vietnam." Pausing, he added, "In 1966, a year after I arrived, I chose to retire because I had twenty years of service and I was ready to move back to Missouri so my son could attend college."

The veteran relocated to Jefferson City after he was hired by the Missouri Department of Health as a public health administrator. He remained employed with the state agency until retiring in 1991. The father of two children, Whitehead beams with pride when discussing the thirty-six-year military career of his son, who, prior to his unexpected death, retired from the Air Force after achieving the rank of colonel.

Decades have passed since Whitehead left high school and began a fascinating journey that carried him across the globe as a member of two branches of the United States military. In retrospect, he humbly stated it was a collection of experiences that provided him with an unanticipated proficiency.

"While I was in high school, I learned embalming while working for a local funeral home," Whitehead said. "I never imagined that within a short period of time, I would be applying some of those skills when working with the bodies of troops who were killed in the Philippines." He continued, "Having the opportunity to work in flight medicine gave me a baseline of medical expertise that qualified me for a career with the Missouri Department of Health years later. All of this," he concluded, "was enjoyable because I liked taking care of people and the overall atmosphere of working in a medical environment." *(Photograph courtesy of Don Whitehead)*

Lon Amick – *Kansas City*

After graduating high school in Kansas City, a young Lon Gilbert Amick followed his older brother's footsteps by attending William Jewell College in nearby Liberty. Two years later, he made the decision to transfer to the University of Missouri in Columbia, where he participated in the ROTC program and gained valuable experience as an actor that would benefit him during World War II. Enlisting in the U.S. Army on July 31, 1942, Amick was granted a deferment until the following year so that he could complete his bachelor's degree in journalism. His military records indicate he entered active service on March 23, 1943.

"My oldest brother, Eugene, was killed August 9, 1942, while serving as a communications officer on the USS *Astoria* during the invasion of the Solomon Islands," said Amick's younger sister, Joanne Comer. "They commissioned the USS *Amick* (destroyer escort) in his honor, and Lon was able to get leave from his training to attend the launching on May 27, 1943."

Amick traveled to Camp Wolters, Texas, in the spring of 1943, spending several months in training to prepare him as an infantryman to replace those lost in combat—a military specialty that he would leave behind shortly after his arrival overseas. The twenty-one-year-old soldier boarded a troopship in early July 1944, making the two-week journey across the ocean. In an undated letter sent home during the war, Amick provided a candid description regarding the unpleasant conditions of his two-week trip across the Atlantic.

"The ship was crowded, terribly crowded," wrote the soldier. "Dice, thick smoke, field equipment, sentiment, homesickness, dirty stories, raucous laughter, and ever-present loneliness amid thousands was much in evidence."

Disembarking the ship in Liverpool, England, in July 1944, his group soon made their way to a marshaling area and days later boarded landing craft bound for Omaha Beach, which, the month previous, served as ground zero for death and devastation during the famed D-Day landings.

"My first job in France was loading ammunition," the soldier wrote. "They needed it badly, and several of the men that came in with me were immediately put to work. The front was six miles away."

The area along the Normandy coastline continued to buzz with activities to provide service and support for soldiers engaged in combat on the front lines of combat. During a rare break in the action, Amick glanced at an advertisement that captured his attention.

"I noticed a (pamphlet) looking for stage talent and walked down to that building—a tent in the field," he wrote in a letter to his parents. "(I) demonstrated a few imitations and 'The Tell-Tale Heart' and was told to perform in a show—I did, and the rest you know," he added.

The young soldier was transferred to the 6817th Special Service Battalion (with whom film star Mickey Rooney was assigned during the war) and began traveling across Europe with a small performance troupe comprised of actors and band members. Their early shows, he explained, "were laughable" with musicians being recruited from foxholes and bandstands constructed from empty rations crates. Their group quickly blossomed with a full band to compose music for their shows. They provided entertainment in venues ranging from theaters to "bomb-cratered villages" in addition to "a circuit of hospital and Red Cross clubs." When the war ended the following spring, he was reassigned to duties more aligned with his journalism degree from MU.

"(I) am putting out a paper for the depot now," wrote Amick to his parents in a letter dated September 22, 1945. "I am enclosing a copy of the paper. I have marked what I have written simply because I know it will interest you .... The paper is exactly what the doctor ordered. I am myself again."

Pfc. Amick remained in Europe for several months after the war, boarding a troopship for his return home in February 1946. On March 2, 1946, he received his discharge from the U.S. Army through the separation center at Fort Dix, New Jersey, having accrued nearly twenty months of overseas service. Integrating back into civilian life, Amick married the former Naomi Campbell in 1950, and the couple raised five children. In the years after the war, he remained somewhat active with local theater groups, but this interest appeared to evaporate when he became president of a national fundraising firm in Kansas City.

According to the November 23, 1972 edition of the *Word and Way*, "Amick joined the staff of William Jewell College in February 1971, as an officer of the administration. At the college, he served as director of development and was in charge of the donor support program, alumni services, and public relations."

"Lon was killed in an automobile accident on October 23, 1972, when he was fifty-two years old," said Joanne (Amick) Comer, the veteran's sister. "He told me when I was younger to spend two years at William Jewell like he did, and then get the experience of a big university." Smiling, she added, "So I ended up at KU, where I met my husband, Ralph."

The veteran can no longer share direct accounts of his experiences during World War II—a fascinating journey that began as a replacement in the infantry and transitioned to service as an actor and work with a military newspaper. He left a legacy behind through letters and reflections that demonstrate a soldier prepared to embrace his circumstances.

From Camp Wolters, he wrote, "Somewhere there must be a wise man of the mountain that knows why the human race can't live in peace. What is, is—and I'm prepared for my share of whatever it is to be, without regret, without enthusiasm." Displaying wisdom beyond his years, he concluded, "Mine is completely a soldier's inevitable attitude. The future doesn't worry me, because I'm resigned to what comes ... if God has endowed me with what talents I possess, I'll use them." *(Photograph courtesy of Joanne Comer)*

Al Davis – *Jefferson City*

The Grapes of Wrath by John Steinbeck is a novel that paints a gloomy picture of a family leaving their Oklahoma roots during the Great Depression to seek work and the promise of opportunity in the state of California. As local veteran Al Davis notes, it was a book unnecessary to read since his family experienced it firsthand. It was circumstances, he added, that he was later able to escape through service in the military. Born in Iowa, Davis was raised in Oklahoma until his family loaded their 1927 Dodge and followed thousands in a migrant caravan to California. For several years, his family toiled on farms harvesting "grapes, tomatoes, cherries—you name it," he said.

"I dropped out of school in the ninth grade to work, and when the war came on in 1941, my family went to work in defense plants," said Davis. "I was itching to get in the war but was too young at the time, but I was able to join the Merchant Marines in June 1945, when I was only sixteen years old."

As Davis explained, there was no formal training program involved with his enlistment. Instead, he simply went to his local union hall, applied for "seaman's papers," and then awaited assignment to a ship. He soon began sailing on tankers out of the harbor in San Pedro, California, making trips to and from sites in Alaska to deliver fuel for Texaco. In December 1945, he recalled, the ship he was serving aboard "ran up on a tidal wave" and ended up stuck on rocks along the shoreline, requiring the Coast Guard to free the ship.

"I remember that we pulled into Seattle on January 13, 1946, the day I turned seventeen," said Davis. "I decided to enlist in the Army because I thought it would be better than freezing in the Merchant Marines," he grinned.

Assigned to the U.S. Army Air Forces (which many veterans of the era continued to refer to as the Army Air Corps), Davis completed his basic training in Texas and then traveled to Boca Raton, Florida, to complete sixteen weeks of electronics training. From there, he was sent to Japan.

"I went through another sixteen weeks of training in Japan and was assigned to the 7th Radio Maintenance Team," said the veteran. "I traveled to different places in the region to work on radar equipment."

On September 18, 1947, Davis clearly recalls, his Army service ended because this was the date that the U.S. Army Air Forces transitioned to the United States Air Force. After nearly two years in Japan, first as a member of the Army and later with the Air Force, Davis finished his enlistment and returned to California. He briefly went to work in quality control for the Hughes Aircraft Company in Culver City, California. However, when the Korean War erupted shortly thereafter, he made the decision to enlist in the Navy in November 1950 after friends and coworkers told him of the opportunities for advanced electronics training.

"Instead of going to Korea," said Davis, "they sent me to the Sand Point Naval Air Station in Seattle. We were a transport squadron with one airplane and ninety-two men, and I spent two years there."

He disappointedly added, "But I didn't get much training there, though."

His next duty assignment was with a patrol squadron in Hawaii with whom he completed the remainder of his enlistment. Since he did not receive the electronics training that he initially requested when joining the Navy, he agreed to reenlist under one condition—they provide him the training.

"They sent me to Memphis (Electronics Training Program actually located in the nearby community of Millington, Tennessee) for the forty-two-week school, and it sure was tough," he grinned. "I sure didn't set the world on fire during that school."

With an in-depth education in electronics now under his belt, Davis was assigned to the USS *Orca*, a seaplane tender stationed in Hong Kong. This was followed by his assignment to the USS *Boxer*, an amphibious assault ship on which he served for two years.

"In 1959, they sent me back to Memphis, this time as an electronics instructor," said Davis. "I guess they figured with all of the flunking I had done there before, I had learned enough to teach it," he chuckled.

After four years of teaching, he was sent to the Naval Air Mobile Technical Training Unit in San Diego, where he finished out his naval career teaching electronics on navigation systems for helicopters. Years previous, while teaching electronics in Tennessee, Davis encountered a friend that taught electronics at the former Linn Technical College (now State Technical College of Missouri). During their conversation, his friend informed him that once he left the Navy, Davis could get a job teaching there.

"My first wife passed in 1967 (the same year he retired from the Navy), and I had a one-year-old son to raise," he said. "I figured that Mid-Missouri would be a good place to raise him, so I got a job teaching there."

Following twenty-one years of teaching, he retired from Linn Technical College in 1988. In later years, he went on to serve a decade as president of the Jefferson City (Missouri) Veterans Council in addition to commander of the Veterans of Foreign Wars post in St. Martins, Missouri. Davis has since remarried and continues to enjoy retirement at his home in Jefferson City. The former sailor acknowledged that the military became an instrument of his success in life, whereby he was able to reach academic heights that might have otherwise remained unattainable.

"I came from being a ninth-grade dropout and got a terrific education," he declared. "All of my education came from the military, and because of that, I later had the opportunity to teach college." His wife, Katie, said, "I think his entire life has been exceptionally interesting—going from *The Grapes of Wrath* to the service providing him a wonderful education." She proudly added, "His story is just fascinating."

Albert George Davis was eighty-eight years old when he passed away on December 27, 2017. He is interred in Hawthorn Memorial Gardens in Jefferson City, Missouri. *(Photograph courtesy of Al Davis)*

Ray Merrell – *Lexington*

As a young man coming of age in the community of Marshall, Missouri, Ray Merrell went to work at a local shoe factory following his graduation from high school in 1941. With World War II continuing to expand and at the same time growing tired of his job, Merrell and a few of his friends enlisted in the Marine Corps—a decision that would soon place him in a newly formed amphibious assault group.

"There was three or four of us that thought we'd rather wear the shoes than make them," Merrell jokingly explained. "We all decided to join the Marines because we had been reading what they had been accomplishing (in combat) on Guadalcanal," he added.

A nineteen-year-old Merrell signed his enlistment papers in November 1942 and was on his way to San Diego for several weeks of basic training. From there, he received additional infantry training at nearby Camp Elliott, a section of which was at the time referred to as "Green Farm."

"While we were on patrol at Green Farm, one of our lieutenants began hollering for us to stop while we were crawling down a hillside," the veteran recalled. "There was a rattlesnake in a culvert near one of the Marines, and the lieutenant pulled out his pistol and shot it."

The final days of his training in the mountains of southern California arrived in early March 1943, at which time he and a number of his fellow Marines traveled to the harbor in San Diego to board the USS *Mount Vernon*—an ocean liner purchased by the Navy and used as a troop transport during World War II. Arriving in New Caledonia, a French territory in the South Pacific, the Marines began practicing amphibious operations. While there, they were approached by a colonel seeking volunteers interested in becoming part of a new group called "Marine Raiders." Considered the earliest U.S. Special Forces operation formed in WWII, the Marine Raiders were to serve as an elite light infantry force that could make amphibious landings behind enemy lines. Igniting his interest, Merrell volunteered and soon passed the physical required to qualify as a Raider.

"We continued to train for several months in New Caledonia doing night hikes, training in jungle operations, setting up defenses, and practicing amphibious assaults," Merrell explained. "When we first started training, I was given a Tommy gun, but before we went into action, I became a BAR (Browning Automatic Rifle chambered for the .30-06 cartridge) man."

A member of a ten-man squad, Merrell saw action in early November 1943 when deployed behind enemy lines in Bougainville—the largest of the Solomon Islands. It was here they remained for several weeks establishing beachheads and relieving troops on the front lines. Next came Guadalcanal, where the Raiders were disbanded, and he was transferred to the 4th Marine Regiment, training as an assistant gunner on a 37mm antitank gun. In June 1944, he boarded the USS *Ormsby*, destined for the invasion of Guam; however, because of intense fighting with Japanese forces at nearby Saipan, he remained aboard ship for forty-seven days. Approaching Guam by landing craft on July 21, 1944, they became stuck on coral reefs and had to drag their 37mm guns to shore through waist-high water.

"It was pretty intense fighting there, and I ended up in the hospital for three or four days from dysentery," Merrell explained. "When the island was finally secured sometime in August, that's when we were sent to Guadalcanal to train for the invasion of Okinawa."

Arriving at Okinawa on Easter Sunday (April 1, 1945), Merrell explained that a "fake landing" was made to the south in an effort to distract the Japanese forces while the actual landing, of which he was part, took place at a location further north.

"We were pretty lucky when he got to Okinawa and landed with little opposition," he said. "However," he grinned, "we stirred up the Japanese over the next day or so."

For the next three months, he and his fellow Marines fought to secure the island and participated in a number of "mopping up" patrols. On July 6, 1945, after weeks of fighting and having lost several friends in combat, he boarded a landing craft bound for Guam and additional training. Boarding the USS *Grimes* on August 15, 1945, Merrell was with a group destined to participate in the invasion of the Japanese mainland, but while he was on the ship, they learned the war in the Pacific had ended. He and many of his fellow Marines were eventually sent to Japan as part of the occupational forces, where he remained until being sent back to the states in November 1945.

Merrell received his discharge from the Marines on December 11, 1945, after having spent thirty-three months overseas. He returned to Missouri and the following year married his fiancée, Helen, with whom he had communicated during his entire period of service. After the war, the combat veteran worked at a local locker plant, was a manager for an MFA location, managed the meat department at a supermarket in Liberty, and sold real estate for a number of years. The father of two children, Merrell affirms his service with the Marines was not only a maturing period but also an opportunity to build a number of enduring friendships.

"I aged and grew up pretty quick after being sent overseas," Merrell said. "For many years, a lot of the guys I served with in the Marine Raiders got together for reunions throughout the country ... but I think I am the only one now left from my squad." With a grin, he concluded, "Helen saved all of the letters I wrote home to her during the war and still has them. The ones she wrote to me," he paused, "are all gone because they got wet when I was huddled in foxholes overseas."

Louis Raymond Merrell was ninety-six years old when he died on September 9, 2019. The Marine Corps veteran was laid to rest with military honors in Resurrection Cemetery in Liberty, Missouri. *(Photograph courtesy of Ray Merrell)*

Lon Douglas – *St. Louis*

During World War II, the military draft became the great equalizer—virtually all young men from various cross-sections of society had the potential to serve. Yet when Pearl Harbor was attacked on December 7, 1941, Lon Douglas never questioned if he would be drafted; instead, he left his employment with the Burroughs Corporation in St. Louis and joined a couple of his friends who chose to enlist.

"I thought we ought to do something," he said. "It seemed like the country could use our help."

As Douglas humorously recalled, he enlisted in the U.S Army Air Forces, clinging to the hope that he would be allowed to explore his interest in aircraft while also having a warm bed to sleep in at night. Following his induction at Jefferson Barracks in St. Louis in February 1942, he went on to complete some of his initial training at Tarrant Field near Fort Worth, Texas. From there, he was sent to Foster Field, Texas, for additional training and was soon classified to work in armament.

"I was sent to Matagorda (Peninsula Army Airfield) to receive training on machine guns," he said. "The base was basically a sandbar off the coast of Texas with an airstrip and some barracks, and they used it to train pilots in fighter aircraft like the P-39s, P-40s, and the P-51s," he added.

The young airman learned to work on .50 caliber machine guns, removing them from the planes, performing any necessary repairs, reinstalling, and then sighting the weapon. After performing that duty for a year, Douglas decided he would like to learn to fly and applied for and was accepted into aviation cadet training.

"That's when they sent me to Santa Ana, California, for a couple of months of pre-flight training," he said. "Since the pilot training program was filled with applicants, they said there were openings for bombardiers or navigators ... so I chose navigator," he noted.

In his new assignment, the regimen of training continued when he was sent to an airstrip near Las Vegas for several weeks of training on the B-17 bomber, first learning to operate and maintain the various machine guns used to defend the aircraft. This was followed by weeks of classroom instruction at Drake University in Iowa, introducing him to all the "bookwork and mathematics" associated with serving as a navigator.

"Several months later, I transferred to San Marcos Army Airfield (Texas), and that's where we started flying," he recalled. "We were assigned to a C-47 (transport aircraft), and I began performing my navigational duties every day using instruments and sometimes navigating by the stars when we flew at night."

Douglas went on to explain that their aerial route would often consist of a "big triangle," with the crew lifting off from San Marcos and then flying to Tyler (Texas) on to New Mexico before returning back to their base.

"They were getting us prepared for service in the South Pacific, I imagine," he explained.

The veteran noted that during their flights, they began to observe ships sunken in the Gulf of Mexico, many of which were Chinese merchant ships that had been torpedoed by enemy submarines. When rumors began to circulate of additional torpedo attacks and threats of an invasion of U.S. coastal areas, Douglas' duties underwent an abrupt adaptation.

"Instead of sending us overseas, we began flying to Florida and back—and sometimes down to Yucutan—to conduct reconnaissance on the coastline and search for anything that looked like enemy submarines," he said. 'If we spotted anything, we reported it." He added, "From the air, there was really no way to tell if they were enemy submarines or ours."

On some of their aerial missions, Douglas recalls the helplessness associated with seeing crewmembers of merchant ships treading the ocean waters after their vessels had been sunk by torpedoes. Sadly, he explained, the only help they were able to offer was reporting the situation to the U.S. Navy.

When the war ended in the late summer of 1945, Douglas remained at San Marcos "doing odd jobs and just awaiting my discharge," he explained. He was sent to Scott Field, Illinois (now Air Force Base) and given his discharge in December 1945. The twenty-three-year-old then returned to St. Louis to begin the process of reintegrating into civilian life.

"Fortunately, I was able to return to my job with the Burroughs Corporation and married my fiancée, Mary Lou, in 1948," he said. "I remained with the company for forty-two years, retiring as a district products manager in 1984. That's when we moved to Jefferson City, and we've been here ever since," he grinned.

Douglas maintains that although he is proud of his military service, performing a necessary duty for his country, there was for him one heartbreaking aspect of the war.

"It just felt like we were doing what needed to be done at the time—we were young, and we accepted it." He added, "But I remember my friend, Bob Barron, who was flying over Tokyo Bay in a P-51 Mustang after the war and had to bail out of the plane. The parachute came down on top of him, trapping him, and he drowned in the water."

In reflection, he concluded, "If there is one thing I resent about my service in World War II, it is situations like that ... knowing that not all of my friends got to come back." *(Photograph courtesy of Lon Douglas)*

Frederick Farr – *Kansas City*

Born in Kansas City, Missouri, on February 9, 1923, Frederick Farr (center) graduated from Paseo High School in 1940. He entered the U.S. Army Air Forces in early 1943 as an enlisted soldier but the following year completed Officer Candidate School at the former Camp Barkeley, Texas. During World War II, he served three years as a cryptographer, military supply officer in addition to a stint as the liaison officer for the 28th Army Air Forces Base Unit in Coral Gables, Florida. Following his discharge, he earned a journalism degree from the University of Missouri in 1947 and went on to achieve the rank of captain while serving in the U.S. Air Force during the Korean War. The veteran later earned a master's degree in liberal arts and was employed for forty years in advertising, sales, and marketing in the southwest Unites States. The eighty-four-year-old Missouri native passed away on October 27, 2004, and was laid to rest in Restland Memorial Park in Dallas, Texas. *(Photograph courtesy of Jeremy P. Amick)*

William Beaman – *New Franklin*

Joan Stubinger was little more than a year old when her father, William Lee Beaman, was killed in action while serving with the U.S. Army in World War II. Though her mother, who is now deceased, shared with her some memories of her father throughout the years, Stubinger wishes to know more about his time in the military so that she can share his story with her own son, who is a veteran of the U.S. Army and National Guard. Born June 24, 1910, in the Howard County community of New Franklin, William Beaman married the former Pauline Moehle at the Evangelical Church Parsonage in Boonville on June 1, 1938.

"In his early years, he worked in some kind of factory in Boonville, where my mother was from," recalled Stubinger. "After they married, there wasn't a lot of work so my mother's brother—my uncle—convinced them to move to Kansas City because he said there was plenty of work available there."

According to Stubinger, while living in Kansas City, her father was employed locally while her mother worked at the Lake City Army Ammunition Plant, where small-caliber ammunition was manufactured for the U.S. Army. However, when it was discovered her mother was pregnant, her supervisors at the plant let her go. Stubinger was born in September 1943, and shortly thereafter, her father received notice that he was to be inducted into the U.S. Army for service in World War II.

"My parents then decided to move back to Boonville so that mother and I could live with her parents while my father was away from home serving in the military."

Records accessed through the National Archives and Records Administration indicate Beaman was inducted as a private into the U.S. Army at Jefferson Barracks on October 20, 1943. It would not be long until the new draftee was assigned to Company B, 318th Infantry Regiment of the 80th Division. In the months prior to Beaman's induction, the 80th Division left their home station of Camp Forrest, Tennessee, to train with the 83rd Division at the Tennessee Maneuver Area south of Murfreesboro, Tennessee. From there, they traveled to Camp Phillips, Kansas, in late August 1943, where Beaman met up with the division.

"Range firing and grueling marches highlighted the three months' stay" at Camp Phillips, as was written in a divisional history. "Nov. 17, the division once more pulled up the stakes … (t)his time it was the California-Arizona Maneuver Area"—a desert training area located in southeastern California and western Arizona that was established in 1942 to prepare soldiers in desert warfare tactics.[75]

In the months that followed, Beaman and the soldiers of the division participated in training exercises near Palen Pass followed by artillery testing at Iron Mountain, California. Their preparatory exercises

---

[75] Lone Sentry, *The Story of the 80th Infantry Division*, https://lonesentry.com.

ended in early April 1944, when the division, following a short stay at Ft. Dix, New Jersey, traveled to Camp Kilmer, New Jersey to board troop ships bound for overseas service. The official history of the 80th Division further explains that on August 3, 1944, "less than one month after landing in the British Isles, the 80th found itself for the second time on French soil (the first time being in WWI), ready to assist in the destruction of the new German dream of world domination."

Entering France through Utah Beach, the division pushed the Germans westward, capturing cities and following "in the wake of the 4th Armored Division to cross the Meuse River at Commercy" on September 1, 1944, as is noted in the book *World War II Order of Battle*.[76] The division met strong opposition in the weeks that followed and incurred significant casualties during German counterattacks. Yet, it would be within days of the division crossing the Seille River in the early part of November that Beaman would lay down his life in combat.

According to a report submitted by Captain Edward Hueske, who at the time was serving in 1st Battalion of the 318th Infantry Regiment, on November 11, 1944 "the [Battalion] jumped off with the mission of taking Morville [Morville-sur-Seille is a small community in northeastern France]." Captain Hueske went on to report, "Heavy resistance was met in Bois Juville woods.... Some fifteen casualties were suffered while fighting in the woods." Sadly, the thirty-four-year-old William Beaman was one of the soldiers killed in action during this encounter.[77]

"I was very young, but I can remember my mother sitting on the edge of the bed and crying," recalled Stubinger. "I somehow knew that she was mourning my father."

---

[76] Stanton, *World War II Order of Battle*, 149.
[77] 80th Infantry Division Veterans Association, *After Action Reports*, https://80th-division.com.

Private First Class Beaman was laid to rest in the Lorraine American Cemetery near Saint-Avold, France. "A Protestant Chaplain held the grave-side service, and a Christian cross, bearing the pertinent information of the deceased, marks the grave," wrote John W. Osberg, chaplain with the 318th regiment, in a letter to Stubinger's mother dated January 10, 1945. Stubinger's mother remarried in 1963 and passed away at ninety-seven years of age in 2009. As her daughter went on to explain, with her mother now gone, there remains no connection to her father, but she is satisfied in knowing some of the details of his military experience.

"My mother told me that she was given the choice of leaving my father's body in France or bringing him back home but she decided to leave him there because she would never really know for sure whether it was his body in the casket." With heavy pause, Stubinger added, "I was always told that my father was on the front lines of combat but never really knew the circumstances of how he was killed. I've thought about this for quite some time, and it was important not only for me to know, but to be able to share it with my son." *(Photograph courtesy of Joan Stubinger)*

Octavian Savu (Sergeant Snorkel) – *St. Joseph*

A rather portly and occasionally grouchy Sgt. Orville P. Snorkel has for decades tried to instill some discipline into the easygoing Beetle Bailey. Few realize that the relationship revealed in the comic strip between Beetle and Sarge is a direct reflection of the association between the strip's creator, Mort Walker, and a sergeant he encountered in St. Louis during World War II. Octavian N. Savu was born in 1914 in Indiana to parents who immigrated to the United States from Romania. At a very young age, the family moved to St. Joseph, Missouri, where Savu grew into adulthood.

"His mom took him to school when he was very young and when the teacher asked him what his name was, he said 'Tavie,'" explained Savu's oldest daughter, Rena Griffin. "The teacher thought he said 'Tommie' and that was his name ever since—Tom or Tommie."

According to his obituary, Savu went on to pursue post-high school education at St. Joseph Junior College, Park College, and the University of Missouri. In 1935, the twenty-one-year-old decided to embark upon what would become a decade-long military journey by enlisting in the U.S. Army at Ft. Leavenworth, Kansas, receiving assignment to the 17th Infantry. Five years into his enlistment, he married his fiancee, Margo. He quickly ascended through the enlisted ranks and, in the early 1940s, became an instructor with the Reserve Officer Training Corps program at Abraham Lincoln High School in Council Bluffs, Iowa. While there, he provided training to the students in first-aid, combat tactics, marksmanship, and map reading.

In 1943, Washington University in St. Louis became Savu's next assignment, where he oversaw soldiers in the school's Army Specialized Training Program. The program was renamed the Engineering, Science, and Management War Training program and ran from 1943-1945, offering 12-week courses to active duty service members with a focus in such fields as foreign language and engineering. It was while he was at Washington University that Sgt. Savu met Mort Walker of Kansas City, a World War II draftee who would later memorialize him through a widely syndicated comic strip.

"Sgt. Snorkel comes from real life, too," wrote Mort Walker in his 1975 book *Backstage at the Strips*. Although occasionally a firm disciplinarian, Walker noted in a 2017 interview, "I remember there was a time that the sergeant wrote all of us (soldiers) a poem titled 'My Boys,' and placed it on each of our pillows. That's when we realized that this man had a heart, and we weren't mad at him anymore." [78]

Walker, who was already a recognized artist prior to his induction in the U.S. Army, drew a caricature of Octavian Savu before the two parted ways in St. Louis in 1944, not realizing at the time his former sergeant would inspire a beloved cartoon character a few years later.

---

[78] Walker, *Backstage at the Strips*, 9.

Discharge papers reveal that Savu, who achieved the rank of first sergeant, deployed overseas from April to August 1945, serving as an administrative sergeant with the 14th Reinforcement Depot in Thionville, France.

"I know that my father had a service-connected disability and came home from France early," said Griffin. "He had cardiovascular disease and was later diagnosed with diabetes."

Discharged for reasons of disability on September 21, 1945, with a little more than 10 years of military service, Savu and his wife eventually relocated to Colorado after adopting Griffin and her younger sister.

"We lived in Denver at first and later moved to Aurora," Griffin explained. "My father found a job as a financial systems specialist with the Air Force Accounting and Finance Center." Griffin recalls that after her father had a heart attack when she and her sister were very young. He then took up gardening and grew "the most beautiful roses and lawn in the neighborhood," she noted, adding that he remained active in the community and served as commander of his local Veterans of Foreign Wars post.

In April 1968, Savu loaded the family in a car and headed east to visit the community of his youth. During the trip, he showed his children the home where he grew up in St. Joseph, in addition to the schools he had attended. He then took his family north to visit a family friend in Council Bluffs, Iowa.

"On the way back to Denver, we stopped at a hotel in Omaha," said Griffin. "My dad had his third heart attack and died in that hotel. I was fourteen at the time, and my sister was eleven." With a somber pause, she added, "He had taken great pleasure in showing us all of those places and really loved Missouri."

The fifty-four-year-old Savu was laid to rest with full military honors in the Fort Logan National Cemetery in Denver.

Although Mort Walker drew a caricature of her father while they were stationed together in St. Louis during World War II, Griffin solemnly explained her father never realized he was the inspiration for the character that became Sgt. Snorkel.

"He never said anything about it, and I don't believe he communicated with Mort Walker before he passed away in 1968," Griffin said. (Mort Walker passed away on January 27, 2018) "My sister and I didn't even know about the connection between dad and Beetle Bailey until recently."

She acknowledges her father possessed many of the bold characteristics portrayed in the Beetle Bailey comic strip, even though some may have been exaggerated for comedic effect, but Griffin affirms the real Sgt. Savu was a man full of character and compassion.

"While he was tough, he was fair, and I think that's why his troops loved him so much," she said. "He was my mentor as well as my father, and some of my best memories are of him." *(Photograph courtesy of Rena Griffin)*

Charles Palmer – *Jefferson City*

All too often, veterans of WWII describe their service in a manner that moderates the importance of the contributions they have made, dismissing any notion of heroism or stellar performance. Though he admits that he is proud of his service as a pilot during the war, Charlie Palmer chose to summarize his own military experience with the simple, straightforward assertion, "I did my bit, what I was trained to do."

Born in Plainfield, New Jersey, in 1924, Palmer explained that the majority of his early years were spent living with his sister and her husband since his father died when he was a child and his mother was in failing health. He went on to graduate from high school in 1942 and, during the heart of World War II, made the decision to take the Air Corps exam "because I wanted to be a pilot," he affirmed.

"There really is no easy answer as to why, but the best way that I can explain it is that I just liked the idea of flying; I liked airplanes, and my heart always seemed to be set on that notion," he said.

After passing the battery of required military exams and physicals, the aspiring aviator officially entered service at the induction center at Fort Dix, New Jersey, followed by his transfer to the Air Corps Training Command in San Antonio, Texas. It was here, the veteran explained that he underwent additional testing to determine his suitability for service as a pilot, bombardier, or navigator.

"I passed all of the tests and qualified for pilot," Palmer recalled. "That's when I started several weeks of pre-flight training, and we began to receive instruction in subjects such as math, Morse code, aircraft recognition and map reading." He continued, "Then they sent me to an airfield in Muskogee, Oklahoma, for several weeks of primary flight training. That's where I learned to fly a Fairchild PT-19, which was a twin-seat plane with an open cockpit."

Soloing on this first aircraft after eight hours of instruction, the aspiring pilot's training progressed when he was transferred to Greenville, Texas, for basic flight training in the Vultee BT-13, learning more advanced techniques including formation flying, cross country, and night flying. He progressed to twin-engine training in Houston, Texas, where he earned his wings and was commissioned a second lieutenant. For the next several months, he continued his training aboard additional types of aircraft at several airfields throughout Texas. Eventually, he received assignment to Barksdale Field near Austin, where he refined his aviation skills aboard a Douglas C-47 military transport aircraft.

"Basically, I spent most of my time in the United States training at several different locations for about six to eight weeks at a time," Palmer said. "I then went overseas from Alliance, Nebraska, to Chalgrove Field in Oxfordshire, England in December 1944."

As Palmer explained, he was assigned to a Pathfinder unit. This duty, he further noted, required the pilots to take off when visibility was limited, fly a mission that included dropping resupplies or paratroopers, and then returning to their home base, all of this under instrument conditions. This overseas assignment also resulted in their aircraft flying supply missions during which Palmer helped deliver hundreds of five-gallon cans of gasoline for the assorted vehicles and tanks that General Patton's Third Army used in its relentless push across Southern Germany.

"One mission that I distinctly remember flying was with the 15th Airborne Division and named 'Operation Varsity,'" he said. "We flew a couple of minutes past the Rhine near Wesel, Germany, and dropped paratroopers to reinforce the British troops that were already there and then returned to base." He added, "There were other groups that had to fly further on to make their drops." Pausing, he solemnly concluded, "They were getting shot up something terrible. I thought for sure that I was going to get hit on that mission, but we all made it back."

Following the war's end in May 1945, Palmer flew several non-combat missions before returning to the United States in early June 1945. He completed the remainder of his service as a C-47 instructor in Battle Creek, Michigan, training new pilots until receiving his discharge on December 5, 1945. The former aviator went on to attend college at the University of Newark (now Rutgers University), earning his bachelor's degree in business administration. In the ensuing years, he pursued a sales career path, which included working for such companies as Warner Lambert, Monsanto, Bank Building in St. Louis, 7-Up in Clayton, and later as an independent training consultant.

He and his wife have resided in Jefferson City for many years, where he has remained active in the community by volunteering with the Lewis and Clark Task Force (serving seven years as the organization's chairman), JC Parks and Recreation, and Missouri State Archives.

The veteran affirms that when reflecting on his service, he does not view himself as having done anything "special" during the war. Instead, he chooses to lavish credit on his fellow soldiers and aviators who did not make it home. However, he recognizes that the brief time he spent as a military pilot did teach him the significance of preparation.

"There were always things that we had to learn so that all of us would be ready," Palmer noted. "During the training, I never felt like we were being rushed through; I could tell that they wanted us to be prepared for whatever we might face. That's demonstrated when I lost an engine on a takeoff and landed safely. You had to master your aircraft and if you weren't prepared, you had a problem. To that end," he affirmed, "I am proud to say that I was a pilot—there's no question about that!"

Charles Franklin Palmer passed away on November 24, 2019. The body of the ninety-five-year-old veteran was donated to the University of Missouri Medical School for research and educational purposes. *(Photograph courtesy of Charlie Palmer.)*

John "Pete" Adkins – *Mexico*

Decades before he was inducted into the Missouri Sports Hall of Fame for his success as a high school football coach, John "Pete" Adkins collected a treasure trove of experiences with his first team—the U.S. Navy—in World War II. These days, however, when it comes time to assemble a team, it is in support of veterans' events to honor those who never made it home from the war. A 1943 graduate of Mexico High School, Adkins and a small group of friends decided to enlist in the U.S. Navy before the military draft process made the decision for them.

Adkins reflected, "We went over to enlist at a recruiting office in Mexico and they sent us to Jefferson Barracks (St. Louis) for our induction in July 1943. Then, a day or so later, they put us on a troop train and sent us to Farragut, Idaho, for boot camp." Established in 1942 as the Farragut Naval Training Station, Adkins said it appeared as though "they took a hillside, some flatland and then carved a naval base out of it."

For the next eight weeks, he and his fellow recruits underwent their initial training. When many of the trainees began to depart for additional training at other locations, Adkins remained at the Idaho base for another eight weeks to become a signalman—a specialty, he recalled, the Navy selected for him.

"Everything in signal training was visual; we didn't use any radios for communication," said the veteran. "We used flags and flashing lights to signal in Morse code. It was our job to learn to direct ship traffic in and out of harbors, making sure they knew where to moor, when to depart and so forth."

Much of their training, he recalled, was spent in the classroom learning skills such as communicating letters of the alphabet using flag signals known as "semaphore." Additionally, they spent time in a mock signal tower, demonstrating they had acquired the skills necessary to direct harbor traffic. From there, the untested sailors were transferred to San Pedro, California, to apply their new skills in a live training environment.

"We were there for about four or five weeks," he said. "They had a signal station in the harbor, and they indoctrinated us into doing live signal work by directing ships."

They spent additional training time in San Francisco before traveling to Treasure Island in San Francisco Bay, where they received an issue of uniforms, weapons, and equipment. They were then sent into the mountains for a brief period of training by the Marines, much of it focused on weapons familiarization, before traveling to Shoemaker, California, to board a troop ship. Following an overnight stop in Pearl Harbor, Adkins and his fellow signalmen sailed for the Marshall Islands in the central Pacific. They arrived in late March 1944 on the Eniwetok Atoll, which had been the site of a brutal battle a month earlier.

Eniwetok "was defended by a garrison of 3,400 men," wrote Trevor Dupuy of the Japanese occupation in his book *Asiatic Land Battles: Japanese Ambitions in the Pacific*. He added, "A combined landing force of Army and Marine units, totaling nearly 8,000 men, landed there on February 19 [1944]. The [Japanese] defenders were overwhelmed in four days of vicious fighting."[79]

"The island was said to be the largest natural harbor between Hawaii and Japan," Adkins said. "When we got there in March, the Seabees had already built a signal tower that rose above a stockade that held a small group of Japanese prisoners of war."

As the former sailor explained, the Japanese prisoners were soon moved elsewhere but he remained on Eniwetok, spending the next two years applying the signal instruction he had received stateside by directing naval traffic in the harbor.

"About the only time I left Eniwetok during the two years I was stationed there was for eleven days of leave in Hawaii—that was it," Adkins affirmed. "We lived in a tent city that entire time, and we had outdoor showers set up on the beach."

In the early days of August 1945, an assortment of naval vessels began to assemble in the harbor, leaving Adkins and his fellow signalman to speculate that a major military operation was in its beginning stages.

"We found out several days later that the ships were there for the planned invasion of the Japanese mainland," Adkins said. "But they ended up dropping the atomic bombs on Japan, and the war was over."

Remaining on Eniwetok until March 1946, Adkins returned to the United States and was discharged on April 3, 1946. After going home to Mexico, he married the former Lorraine Fenner in 1948

---

[79] Dupuy, *Asiatic Land Battles*, 56-57.

and utilized his G.I. Bill benefits to earn his master's degree in education. As the years passed, he become head football coach for Jefferson City High School, retiring in 1995. Throughout the course of his forty-five-year career, he compiled a 405-60-4 record, resulting in his induction into the Missouri Sports Hall of Fame in April 2013 for being the most successful high school football coach in the nation. His victories on the gridiron notwithstanding, Adkins values his service in the U.S. Navy and maintains it helped instill the lifelong aspiration to recognize his fellow veterans while also refining many positive qualities he has embraced throughout his career.

"The military does a lot for a person—the discipline, the work ethic, and the fact that we had to learn to live very sparingly," Adkins said. "I can tell you, living in a tent for two years will make a believer out of you and made me appreciate home." He added, "Since that time, I have always remained active in veterans' events to help honor those men who were killed taking that island before I got there in WWII. And when you go to a veterans' function, it's special because we all have something in common … we have all developed a respect for those who have served." *(Photograph courtesy of Pete Adkins)*

Buck O'Neil – *Kansas City*

The late Buck O'Neil has ascended to icon status in the annals of professional baseball following his days as a player, scout, and coach. He further distinguished himself by helping preserve the history of the days of segregated professional baseball through his instrumental role in the establishment of the Negro Leagues Baseball Museum in Kansas City, Missouri. A lesser-known fact is his overseas service in the U.S. Navy, which unfolded during the height of his professional baseball career in World War II and continued his experiences of segregation on an entirely different level.

John Jordan O'Neil inauspiciously entered the world on November 13, 1911. An article on the website of the Jackie Robinson Foundation explained, "The grandson of a slave, O'Neil was raised in Florida and spent his youth toiling in celery fields." The article further noted, "His baseball prowess proved to be his escape from farm work.

Barred from attending local Sarasota High School and the University of Florida due to his skin color, O'Neil went on to become an electrifying first baseman who won a pair of Negro League batting titles with the Kansas City Monarchs ...." [80]

The twenty-eight-year-old left Kansas City and traveled to his native Florida on October 16, 1940, to comply with the mandate of the Selective Service and Training Act of 1940 by registering with his local draft board in Sarasota County. Although O'Neil returned to the Kansas City Monarchs and, in 1942, enjoyed the first of three appearances in an All-Star game, the war raging overseas soon halted many major league careers. For O'Neil, his call came in August of 1943, when he was inducted into the U.S. Navy and completed his initial training at Norfolk, Virginia.

"The US Navy had traditionally employed blacks only in servile roles, and did not accept black volunteers or conscripts until Roosevelt's Executive Order No. 9279, issued in December 1942, forced all services to end such restrictions," explained an article by Clayborne Carson titled "African Americans at War." Carson went on to note, "Even after this presidential order, more than 95% of the blacks in the navy served as messmen ...." [81]

"(O'Neil) was assigned to a Stevedore battalion" and had the responsibility of unloading ships, explained Bob LeMoine in an article written for Society for American Baseball Research, a non-profit organization. LeMoine further noted that O'Neil's service carried him to the Mariana Islands and later Subic Bay in the Philippines. The article goes on to detail some of the racial injustices he encountered in the segregated Navy. As a boatswain first class, the professional baseballer turned sailor demonstrated his ability to plan and guide the

---

[80] Jackie Robinson Foundation, *JRF Mourns the Death of Baseball Great Buck O'Neil*, https://jackierobinson.org.

[81] Carson, *African Americans at War*, https://web.stanford.edu.

work of the twelve men under his charge; however, he was advised, "If you were white, you'd be an officer by now."[82]

The Philippines was abuzz with military activity in the latter months of 1944 in an effort to free the Filipino people from the occupying Japanese forces and "provide the best possible base for a final invasion of Japan," wrote Trevor Nevitt Dupuy in *The Naval War in the Pacific: On to Tokyo*.[83]

In his duties as a stevedore with a U.S. Navy Seabees battalion, O'Neil and his fellow sailors not only assisted with various construction duties, but helped deliver food, ammunition and other integral supplies as the war progressed closer to Japan.

While O'Neil was overseas, budding baseball superstar Jackie Robinson played five months for the Kansas City Monarchs in 1945. Later the same year, he broke baseball's color barrier when becoming the first African-American player to enter the major leagues after signing with the Brooklyn Dodgers. Robinson's achievements were closely followed by O'Neil and his fellow sailors.

"The commanding officer came over the speaker at 10 one night and told me to come to his office at once," remarked O'Neil in an interview that appeared in the *Atlanta Constitution* on September 21, 1944. The article continued, "I thought, 'Hell, what did I do now?' He told me (the Brooklyn Dodgers) had signed Jackie (Robinson), and I said, 'Thank God, give me that horn.' And I got on the speakers: 'Now hear this! Now hear this!' And they whooped and hollered and shot guns in the air."

A few months following the official end of World War II with the instrument of surrender signed aboard the USS *Missouri* in Tokyo Bay on September 2, 1945, O'Neil received his discharge and trav-

---

[82] LeMoine, *Buck O'Neil*, https://sabr.org.
[83] Dupuy, *The Naval War in the Pacific*, 41.

eled to Kansas City to marry his fiancée. The former sailor returned to baseball with the Kansas City Monarchs and, in later years, became a scout and the first African American coach in the major leagues. However, his greatest passion was sharing the stories and preserving the legacies of Negro League icons such as Cool Papa Bell and Satchel Paige.

The spirit of his positive outlook and foresight has inspired others to share in the effort to enshrine his legacy for future generations. He has since been inducted into the Hall of Famous Missourians at the Missouri State Capitol and had the Buck O'Neil Research and Education Center in Kansas City named in his honor.

Many years of his life were that of division—not being allowed to attend schools for whites in Florida as a child, playing ball in a segregated league followed by service in a segregated U.S Navy. Yet O'Neil lived to witness integration on all of these levels, recognizing the strengths of a united community.

"I've done a lot of things I liked doing," O'Neil remarked during a speech at the National Baseball Hall of Fame in June 2006. "But I'd rather be right here, right now, representing these people that helped build a bridge across the chasm of prejudice—not just the ones like Charlie Pride and me that later crossed it..." He added, "And I tell you what, they always said to me, 'Buck, I know you hate people for what they did to you or what they did to your folks.' I said, 'No, man, I ... I never learned to hate.'" [84]

O'Neil passed away on October 6, 2006, approximately a month prior to his 95th birthday. The baseball legend was laid to rest in Forest Hill Cemetery in Kansas City. *(Photograph courtesy of Negro Leagues Baseball Museum)*

---

[84] American Rhetoric, *John Jordan "Buck" O'Neil*, https:// https://www.american-rhetoric.com/.

Stan Musial – *St. Louis*

The "crack" of Stan Musial's bat produced a staggering 3,630 career hits, ranking him first in the National League when he retired from baseball in 1963 and becoming the inspiration for countless smiles among generations of St. Louis Cardinals fans. Despite the impressive statistics that serve as part of the baseball icon's legacy, the numbers fail to reveal the dedication he demonstrated to his other team—the United States—when called to serve in World War II.

"He missed the entire 1945 baseball season because of the military," said Brian Schwarze, Musial's grandson. "Who knows what kind of numbers he might have put up if he had played professionally that year, but he was called to serve his country, and he did his duty," he added.

A native of Donora, Pennsylvania, Musial married the former Lillian Labash in 1940. The following year brought two major life events for "Stan the Man," with the birth of his son, Richard, and playing his first major league game with the St. Louis Cardinals. Regardless of any prowess demonstrated on the playing field, his draft registration card notes that the twenty-one-year-old was required to travel to Donora, Pennsylvania, to register with his local draft board on February 16, 1942, as part of the 1940 Selective Training and Service Act.

Married with a child, in addition to providing support to an ailing parent, Musial initially received exemptions from service and continued to distinguish himself in baseball, earning the first of three National League Most Valuable Player awards in 1943.

"Stan Musial, Donora's outstanding athlete … passed his pre-induction physical examination today and joined his teammate Danny Litwhiler in awaiting a call to report for service in the Navy," reported the *Morning Herald* (Uniontown, Pennsylvania) on May 17, 1944.

Continuing to play through the 1944 season, Musial explained in his 1964 self-titled biography written by Bob Broeg, "I was really relieved to go into service when my Donora draft board finally called in January 1945." He added, "I chose the Navy and was sent to Bainbridge (Maryland) for basic training."[85]

The *Leader-Telegram* (Eau Claire, Wisconsin) reported on January 24, 1945, "Stan Musial, St. Louis Cardinal slugger, donned a sailors' uniform at the Bainbridge Naval Training Center today, where he will undergo ten weeks of 'boot' training." The paper further explained, "Musial told Bainbridge officials he hoped to resume his baseball career after the war."

Assigned to Company 3023 during his recruit training, the *Bainbridge Mainstreet*—a newspaper printed by sailors on the base—reported on March 3, 1945, that Musial, who was the company's ath-

---

[85] Broeg, *Stan Musial*, 83.

letic petty officer, led his sailors to victory in a regimental basketball competition.

During the four months he remained at the Maryland training site, he also played several baseball games for the Bainbridge Commodores. In late March 1945, the Commodores hosted a three-game series against the New York Giants that resulted in a win, loss, and tie for the Navy team. In early May 1945, Musial returned home for a few days of leave before reporting to San Francisco, from where he sailed for his next duty assignment—Pearl Harbor. Shortly after his arrival, reported the *Bainbridge Mainstreet* on June 2, 1945, he "chipped a bone in his hand driving for a line drive …"

He quickly healed from his injury and continued his duties of running a liberty launch for approximately four hours each morning, transporting sailors to and from ships moored in the harbor for various repairs. In the afternoons, he played baseball in the Hawaiian sun for another four hours.

"By the time I got off that thing (liberty launch) and went over to run around in more sun, I was dead," said Musial in an interview printed in the *St. Louis Post-Dispatch* on February 3, 1957. "I finally told the officer in charge, 'You gotta make a choice, I can ride around on that boat, or I can play baseball. I don't much care which, but it's gotta be one or the other.'"

Musial would play baseball for the remaining months of his naval service.

It was also during this timeframe that the baseball pro adjusted his hitting stance so he could hit more home runs, providing additional entertainment for the service members watching the ball games. This modification would haunt many a major league pitcher in the coming years.

When his father fell deathly ill with pneumonia in the latter part of 1945, Musial's mother made an appeal through the Red Cross for her son to be granted emergency leave. The sailor returned to the states in January 1946 and was assigned to the Philadelphia Navy Shipyard to be closer to his family. Fortunately, the elder Musial recovered.

"Two months later, when Uncle Sam suddenly began to release itchy-footed servicemen, I got unexpected good news. I would be out in time to play the 1946 season," said Musial, as quoted in his aforementioned biography by Bob Broeg.[86]

Receiving his discharge on March 1, 1946, after thirteen months of naval service, Musial returned to his wife and son. The baseball family later welcomed the addition of three daughters—Gerry, Janet, and Jean. In 1963, Musial finished his legendary playing career with the Cardinals and, in 1969, was elected to the National Baseball Hall of Fame in his first year of eligibility.

The WWII veteran and sports superstar died at his home in St. Louis County on January 19, 2013; he was ninety-two years old.

"He has always been known for baseball but he was more than just baseball," said Brian Schwarze, when describing his late grandfather. "Don't get me wrong, he loved baseball, but he was very charitable and, because of his experience, always liked to support three groups of individuals—firefighters, police, and veterans."

Schwarze added, "But few people know about his Navy service because it was brief, and he would often downplay what he did by making the joke that he 'served with the hula girls.' Regardless, he did not run from his responsibility and answered the call during a time of war. His military story is something different than his baseball career, and he was proud that he had been given the opportunity to serve his country." *(Photograph courtesy of Brian Schwarze.)*

---

[86] Broeg, *Stan Musial*, 85.

Joe Garagiola – *"The Hill"* in St. Louis

History is full of examples of overlaps in major league baseball and military service. From Stan "the Man" Musial's naval service in WWII followed by his historic career with the St. Louis Cardinals to Yogi Berra's combat service in the WWII Navy followed by many distinguished seasons as a catcher for the New York Yankees, professional baseball, and the military have often become intertwined. Growing up across the street from Yogi Berra in the historic Italian district of St. Louis known as "The Hill," Joseph Henry Garagiola became a celebrated prospect as a catcher for the St. Louis Cardinals in 1944, around the timeframe he was required to register for the military draft.

"Joe Garagiola, the eighteen-year-old St. Louis boy who has already had two years of professional baseball experience with the Cardinal minor league farms and who was accepted for army service Monday after passing his induction examination at Jefferson Barracks, arrived here tonight," reported the *St. Louis Globe-Democrat* on March 22, 1944. The newspaper added, "Considered one of the finest catching prospects the Cardinals have ever had ... Garagiola will help out with the Cardinal catching here until he is called into service."

Exchanging his Cardinals uniform for that of a soldier in the U.S. Army, Garagiola completed basic training at Jefferson Barracks. From there, he was sent to Fort Riley, Kansas, playing baseball for the Fort Riley Centaurs to entertain troops stationed at the Army base. However, later that year, in mid-December 1944, the Battle of the Bulge unfolded in Europe, and his battalion was sent to Fort Knox, Kentucky, undergoing the conversion from cavalry to tank operators. It was here that his pre-war talents were called upon once again.

As noted in the March 30, 1959, edition of the *Tampa Times*, Garagiola was assigned to Company C, 785th Tank Battalion "because the CO (commanding officer) was a bug on baseball and wanted the best team at Fort Knox." The article further explained, "He got it but he [also] got his sailing orders soon after and we all set out for the Philippines."

Departing the United States aboard a Dutch freighter on July 28, 1945, Garagiola discovered during the thirty-nine-day journey to the Philippines that he possessed the talent to entertain an audience through speaking and storytelling—a revelation that would benefit him in the years following his baseball career. During their journey across the Pacific, the atomic bombs were dropped on Hiroshima and Nagasaki, heralding the end of World War II. Upon arrival in the Philippines, their tank battalion became military policemen and were assigned to Camp Balut near Manila.

In an article by Gary R. Morminos printed as a special to the May 6, 2016, edition of the *Tampa Times*, a fellow 785th Tank Battalion veteran and lifelong friend of Garagiola, Tom McEwen, explained that the battalion was responsible for the establishment of a prisoner of war (POW) camp, which eventually housed 2,000 Japanese POWs. McEwen, who was appointed to serve as a prison officer for the new

POW camp, noted that his new position came with an assigned driver.

"Pfc. Joe Garagiola, reporting for duty!" recalled Morminos in the aforementioned article.

The Cardinals catcher soon received special assignment to play baseball for the Manila Dodgers and helped entertain scores of troops passing through the Philippines, who were completing their paperwork for discharge and return to the United States. When no games were scheduled, Garagiola helped oversee Japanese POWs tasked with unloading ships in the harbor.

"In ... (1945) he caught Pitcher Kirby Higbee, Brooklyn fireballer who managed an army team in Manila," reported the *St. Joseph Gazette* on October 30, 1946. "Joe hit a home run in Manila's Rizal Stadium, and his name is printed in big letters on the outfield wall, not far from spots where Babe Ruth and Lou Gehrig once blasted four-baggers on their way to Japan barnstorming tours."

Garagiola's youngest son, Steve, explained, "He said they would sometimes play four or five games a day because there was always a new batch of soldiers moving through who needed some entertainment." He added, "And for a catcher, that was no easy duty."

According to Garagiola's discharge papers, he returned to the United States on May 7, 1946, and received his separation on May 13, 1946, having achieved the rank of sergeant after completing a little more than two years of service. Following his return to Missouri, he entered the lineup for the St. Louis Cardinals and, as a rookie, went on to make his only World Series appearance in 1946. His major league career would extend nine seasons with him also playing for the Pittsburgh Pirates, Chicago Cubs and New York Giants.

In the years that followed, he married and raised two sons and a daughter. In 1954, he "quit a $16,000-a-year job with the world champion New York Giants ... to begin a career as a $12,000-a-year color commentator on the Cardinals' broadcasts," wrote Bob Broeg, a former sports editor, in the August 3, 1971, edition of the *St. Louis Post-Dispatch*.

The ballplayer's career later blossomed into a successful livelihood as a broadcaster and author, also parlaying the captivating storytelling abilities he discovered in the military into a successful public speaking circuit. On March 23, 2016, the ninety-year-old former St. Louis Cardinal and U.S. Army veteran passed away in Scottsdale, Arizona. His remains were returned to his native St. Louis and are interred in the city's Resurrection Cemetery.

Answering his country's call to service when Uncle Sam drafted him during WWII, Garagiola's stint in the U.S. Army had a lasting impact on his career success and revealed his dedication to a simple, unadorned philosophy of living. In the transcript from an oral history interview conducted between 2007 and 2008 by Historical League, Inc., Garagiola modestly affirmed, "I do what I'm supposed to and try to stay out of trouble, which has been my philosophy." *(Photograph courtesy of Steve Garagiola.)*

Lawrence Peter "Yogi" Berra – *"The Hill" in St. Louis*

The son of Italian immigrants, Lawrence Peter Berra grew up in the historic Italian district of St. Louis known as "The Hill," where he was given the nickname of "Yogi" by a friend noting his resemblance to a snake charmer seen in a movie of the era. Berra spent countless hours of his youth playing baseball in the sandlots of St. Louis, enjoying the company of neighbors such as Joe Garagiola, who himself earned a World Series ring as a St. Louis Cardinal in 1946. Berra went on to establish himself as a celebrated player after entering the New York Yankees farm system in 1942, but his career was initially delayed when he entered the Navy in World War II, and went on to participate in the famed D-Day landings.

In the 1952 book written by Joe Trimble and aptly titled *Yogi Berra*, the late baseball icon noted that he was playing baseball for the Norfolk Tars—a New York Yankees affiliate—near the U.S. Naval shipyards along the coast of Virginia, when he received orders to take his military examinations at the Army Induction Center at Richmond, Virginia. Passing his physical, Berra explained that the inductees were asked what branch of service they wanted to join, with the Yankee prospect finding the U.S. Navy the most appealing.

"But when we finished the physical and knew we passed, the officer told us that anyone who took the Army got a three week's extension of time before being sworn in but that the Navy guys would only get one week," noted Berra in the aforementioned biography. He added, "So I took the Army because I wanted to go home for a while. It didn't quite work out that way, however."[87]

A warrant officer who coached the Norfolk Naval Training Station team heard about Berra and needed replacements for his players who had been shipped to overseas assignments. He was able to wield some influence and change Berra's branch selection. Separation papers accessible through the Missouri State Archives note Berra was inducted into the U.S. Navy in Norfolk, Virginia, on September 23, 1943, a little more than four months following his eighteenth birthday.

Completing his initial training at Bainbridge, Maryland, a twist of fate ensured that Berra never played for the Norfolk team despite the wishes of the warrant officer who changed his assignment. Berra soon received orders for the Navy Amphibious Training Center at Little Creek, Virginia, arriving in January 1944.

"The Amphibious Training Base (also known as 'Little Creek') was the center for all types of amphibious training and the training of ship's crews …," noted an article on the website of the Joint Expeditionary Base Little Creek-Fort Story. The article went on to explain, "In a commendably few months the trained men who were to land fighting forces from Africa to Normandy were ready for sea.

---

[87] Trimble, *Yogi Berra*, 48.

During World War II, over 200,000 Naval personnel and 160,000 Army and Marine Corps personnel trained at Little Creek."[88]

In March 1944, following two weeks of additional amphibious exercises at Lido Beach, Long Island, Berra was aboard LST *508* (Landing Ship, Tank). Traveling in a convoy to Glasgow, Scotland. Following his arrival, Berra spent the next several weeks training for amphibious assaults and, prior to D-Day, was assigned as a gunner's mate aboard the attack transport USS *Bayfield*.

An article by the Naval History and Heritage Command explained, "… (The) *Bayfield* and the other transports reached their designated positions early on the morning of the 6th (June 6, 1944, D-Day) and debarked their troops. Once the troops left *Bayfield*, she began serving as a supply and hospital ship in addition to continuing her duties as a flagship."[89]

As part of a group of vessels launched from the *Bayfield*, Berra was aboard a thirty-six-foot rocket boat operating off Omaha Beach prior to the landing of ground troops, firing upon and neutralizing German shore batteries. Berra noted in his biography, "There wasn't time to be scared. My job was loadin' the gun, which was mounted on a little deck toward the back of the boat."

Surviving a major amphibious assault that cost the lives of thousands of his fellow service members, Berra went on to serve with the Navy in Italy and, in July 1944, arrived in North Africa. He went on to participate in the Allied invasion of Southern France known as "Operation Dragoon." While aboard a rocket boat a couple hundred yards off the coast of Marseilles, Berra and the group of boats in his attack group began firing upon a resort hotel used to conceal a German machine gun nest. During the exchange of fire, Berra

---

[88] Commander, Navy Region Mid-Atlantic, *Former Naval Amphibious Base Little Creek's History*, https://cnic.navy.mil.
[89] Naval History and Heritage Command, *Bayfield*, https://history.navy.mil.

was nicked in the hand by a German bullet—a war wound he never reported. When later asked about the wound, Berra responded that he did not apply for a Purple Heart because "I didn't' want to scare my mother," he recalled in his 1952 biography.

Berra spent the next several months in Bizerte, Tunisia, before returning to the U.S. in January 1945, where he was assigned to the Navy base at New London, Connecticut. It was here that he was placed in "Welfare and Recreation" and began to play baseball for the Navy. He received his military discharge on May 7, 1946. In the years that followed, Berra entered the annals of baseball legend not only because of his abilities as a player, but also for his colorful and unique quotes such as, "It's déjà vu all over again." As with many veterans of the WWII era, the Hall of Famer did not boast of his time in the military despite the pride he maintained for having served his country.

In a June 1, 2005, interview with the Academy of Achievement, the former Yankee slugger known for his simplistic descriptions said of his D-Day experience, "Fortunately enough, nothing happened to us. We were lucky." Berra added, "I wasn't scared. Going into it, it looked like the Fourth of July." *(Photograph courtesy of Museum of Missouri Military History.)*

Samuel J. Salamon – *Crystal City*

Samuel J. Salamon was born April 18, 1918, in Crystal City, Missouri. During World War II, he was inducted into the U.S. Army at Jefferson Barracks on December 21, 1943, and later served in the European Theater with the 128th General Hospital. After returning from the war, he became active in the American Legion beginning in 1946 and remained heavily invested in the organization until his death. For several years, the veteran-owned a store for Pittsburgh Plate Glass Company and later retired from the American National Insurance Company. In addition to his public service on the city council for Crystal City, Salamon was active in many civic organizations and, in 1982, was elected Missouri State Commander of the American Legion at the department convention held in Joplin in mid-July 1982.

The ninety-two-year-old veteran passed away May 31, 2010, and was laid to rest in Sacred Heart Cemetery in his native community of Crystal City. *(Photograph courtesy of American Legion Post 5.)*

Herb Siebert – *St. Louis*

The harsh reality for Herb Siebert when he approached his graduation from Cleveland High School in St. Louis during the height of World War II was that it was likely only a matter of time before he was drawn into the military. Shortly before his graduation in May 1943, his beliefs became reality when he received his draft notice. A few weeks later, the eighteen-year-old traveled to nearby Jefferson Barracks for his induction into the U.S. Army.

"That all happened right in the middle of the war, and I didn't want to rush into the service, but I knew I would go when my time came," said the veteran.

Following his entry into active service on July 28, 1943, he was sent to Camp Wallace, Texas, for his basic training. It was here, Siebert noted, that he and many of his fellow trainees received instruction to prepare them to serve in anti-aircraft artillery units.

"When we finished our training that fall, that's when they sent us down to Camp Claiborne (Louisiana) and transferred us into the infantry," he recalled. "That's also the place where I became a member of Company E, 335th Regiment of the 84th Division," he added.

For the next year, Siebert endured the heat of the Bayou State while participating in maneuvers, battle simulations, and learning to operate a number of different weapons. During this training period, he began as an assistant gunner but eventually was assigned as primary gunner using a .30 caliber machine gun. In late September 1944, the division traveled to Camp Kilmer New Jersey, to board troop ships that would deliver them to the war raging in Europe. Several days later, they arrived in England and, in early November, were entering France through Omaha Beach—the site of the deadly D-Day invasion only five months earlier.

"We got off the LSTs (landing ship tanks) that brought us to Omaha Beach, and I thought they'd bring trucks to take us to our next stop," he laughed. "Instead, we must have walked twenty miles, and I was wearing new boots." Smiling, he added, "I had blisters on my heels and when we finally got there, we pitched our tents in the rain ... and it was miserable."

A booklet about the 84th Division published in the *Stars and Stripes* (military newspaper) during the war noted, "Wasting little time, (they) sped through France and Belgium into Holland. Rarely had a division been moved from the States to the flaming Western Front with such speed as the 84th's." The booklet added, "Within a week after the division CP (command post) was set up, (they) were attacking one of the strongest sectors of the Siegfried Line."

Siebert said, "On November 29th, we were pinned down overnight by machine gun fire coming from a bunker," he said. "The following morning, they ordered us to attack the bunker and I expected return fire, but by the time we reached it, it had been abandoned."

As mid-December 1944 arrived, the last major German offensive of the war unfolded—the Battle of the Bulge. Handwritten notes maintained by Siebert record that on December 17, his company "Repulsed heavy German night attack and … destroyed an entire enemy battalion." Three days later, they were "relieved by the 102nd (Division) and motored to (Marche-en-Famenne), Belgium."

The notes go on to describe Christmas Day being spent in a barn followed by movement to a different assembly area to relieve British troops a few days later. However, the following week, a combat injury would remove Siebert from his unit for nearly a month.

"On January 9 (1945), we had to move on the offensive once again, and I remember we set up our machine gun on a road firing into the woods to provide cover for our riflemen to move in," Siebert explained. "That must not have been too bright because the ground around us was white with snow and we probably stuck out like store thumbs in our olive drab uniforms," he added.

As Siebert recalled, the Germans soldiers had concealed a machine gun nest and soon began firing upon him and his assistant gunner.

"We got up to run to higher ground, and that's when I felt a sting on my arm," he said. "I was shot through the upper left arm but fortunately, it wasn't too serious a wound."

He was evacuated to a field hospital for treatment, and when he was able to return to his unit, the Battle of the Bulge was over. Weeks later, the war in Europe ended and Siebert remained in Germany until January 1946 as a member of the occupational forces. On February 11, 1946, he received his discharge from the U.S. Army at Jefferson Barracks, Missouri. In the years after the war, Siebert was employed by the McDonnell Douglas Corporation, retiring in 1987 after thirty years with the company. He and his wife, Brenda, later resided in a retirement community in his native St. Louis.

Plain spoken about his service in World War II, the Purple Heart recipient avoids any sensational descriptions of his own service that might diminish the contributions of the brave soldiers with whom he served. Despite having survived the frigid European winter and being shot in combat, the veteran still maintains mirthful reflections of his wartime experiences.

"It's been so long that many of my memories of the war have left me, but I remember that they usually fed us pretty good over there," he affirmed. Smiling, he added, "You know how us GI's are—you could feed us steak every night, and we'd still complain."

Herbert Siebert was ninety-four years old when he passed away on May 19, 2019. He was laid to rest with full military honors at Jefferson Barracks National Cemetery. *(Photograph courtesy of Herb Siebert)*

Edwin Jungmeyer – *Lohman*

In reflection, the early years of the late Edwin Otto Jungmeyer were likely built on the promise of better times ahead. Graduating from Centertown High School in rural Cole County in the mid-1930s, he briefly paused to work on his father's farm during the height of the Great Depression, toiling to survive during a period in which many farms were lost to a bank through foreclosure. A short while later, he sought to continue his education by attending La Salle University in Pennsylvania, in addition to participating in a business and farm management correspondence course through a school in Chicago.

Returning to Lohman to work on the family farm in the early 1940s, he began dating a young woman, Norma June Weaver, to whom he was soon engaged. Their marriage, however, would have to wait since he unexpectedly embarked upon the most influential segment of his career when joining tens of thousands of young men registering for the military draft on October 16, 1940.

"His records show that he was drafted into the U.S. Army on January 22, 1941, and completed his basic training at Jefferson Barracks (St. Louis)," said Kevin Jungmeyer, the youngest of the veteran's sons.

While on leave from his training, he returned home and married his fiancée in California, Missouri, on July 15, 1941. Days later, he returned to the 3488th Ordnance Medium Automotive Maintenance Company to continue his training for overseas service. In the spring of 1942, Jungmeyer was temporarily assigned to Springfield, Massachusetts, where he spent several weeks learning how to properly maintain and repair motorcycles at the factory service school for the Indian Motorcycle Company.

"From 1940 until 1945, Indian Motorcycle focused its efforts on contributing to the Allied cause in WWII, at first (by) building motorcycles for the French government and, starting in 1941, producing the Model 841 for the U.S. Army," noted an article on the Indian Motorcycle Company's website. "Very few bikes were built for consumers during this time."[90] The Indian 841 motorcycle was initially designed for desert warfare to provide greater mobility for U.S. troops. Although not adopted for widespread use by the U.S. Army, the motorcycle's intended end use, in a sense, foretold the location of Jungmeyer's upcoming duty assignment in a desert environment.

The maintenance course ended on January 30, 1942; however, five months later, his company boarded troop ships on the East Coast. Arriving in England on July 12, 1942, they conducted additional training for the next several weeks before joining the Fifth Army in Mid-November 1942 for the Tunisian Campaign. Days later, on November 29, 1942, the wife of the twenty-eight-year-old soldier gave birth to their first daughter, Nathalia.

While the Fifth Army made hard-fought gains against Italian and German forces in the deserts of North Africa, Jungmeyer and the

---

[90] Indian Motorcycle, *History*, https://indian-motorcyle.lv.

men of the 3488th performed the necessary automotive work to keep all types of vehicles running for critical missions such as road patrols—a burdensome responsibility requiring creative measures in the face of supply shortages.

"Captain Joseph M. Montgomery of the 3488th reported that the authority to salvage vehicles and reclaim the parts had been the deciding factor in keeping the trucks rolling; 75 percent of the jobs completed by his company were made possible by cannibalization," wrote Lisa Mayo in *The Ordnance Department: On Beachhead and Battlefront*.[91]

In an article appearing in the April 4, 1943, edition of the Des Moines Register, Captain Montgomery said of the soldiers under his command, "They take apparently wrecked trucks and create a breathing monster of transportation to take food, and clothing and ammunition, and gasoline and fighting men to the front lines." The commander went on to explain that mechanics such as Jungmeyer did not accomplish such tasks in a "well-equipped garage"; instead, they performed their critical work where "the sky is their roof, the ground their floor and the horizon the walls."

Jungmeyer and the soldiers of the 3488th later supported the Fifth Army during the Allied Invasion of Italy, admirably performing the strenuous work of repairing inoperable vehicles. He remained in Italy until approximately a month following Germany's capitulation, returning to the United States in June 1945.

"I can remember our father telling us that they had been working on Indian motorcycles overseas and were riding them on the sand dunes," said Steve Jungmeyer, another of the veteran's sons. "Apparently, the kickstand came open on the bike he was riding, and it stuck in his calf." Grinning, he added, "That was his war injury."

---

[91] Mayo, *United States Army in World War II*, 134-135.

Receiving his discharge on June 26, 1945, Jungmeyer reunited with his wife and two-year-old daughter. In the years that followed, the couple welcomed three sons, Dennis, Steve, and Kevin, into their family. Leveraging the automotive and maintenance experience acquired in the Army, he went on to retire from the former McKay Buick in Jefferson City as Service Manager after thirty-two years of employment. His second-oldest son, Steve, explained that his father, who spent more than four years living and working under stressful situations with the soldiers of the 3488th Ordnance Company, developed strong friendships that endured throughout the decades.

"I can remember there were many years when friends from his days in the service would come to our house to visit, and other times, he and mom would take trips to other towns on visits of their own," said Steve.

Kevin, the veteran's youngest son, added, "But our dad never really spoke to us about his service; he didn't like to talk about it, so we never got much out of him. I don't know if it was the experiences he went through—if it was traumatic—but he didn't open up about it." Pausing, he concluded, "To be honest with you, we probably didn't ask him enough about it."

The eighty-four-year-old veteran passed away on June 3, 1999, and is interred in the cemetery of St. Paul's Lutheran Church in his hometown of Lohman. *(Photograph courtesy of Kevin Jungmeyer.)*

Ralph Muessig – *Tipton*

Ralph Roger Muessig of Tipton, Missouri, was born on September 22, 1922. The nineteen-year-old registered for the military draft on June 30, 1942, at the Moniteau County Courthouse in California, Missouri. At the time of his registration, he was employed with A.F. Martin Manufacturing Company in his hometown of Tipton.

On December 23, 1942, Muessig was drafted into the U.S. Army and went on to train at Ft. Knox and Ft. Campbell, Kentucky prior to deploying overseas with the Seventh Armored Division. Sadly, the twenty-year-old soldier was killed in action during the Allied invasion of Sicily on August 4, 1943. His remains were returned to Missouri and laid to rest in the cemetery of St. Andrews Catholic Church in Tipton. *(Photograph courtesy of the Moniteau County Historical Society)*

Camp Weingarten – *Weingarten*

As author David Fiedler explained in his book *The Enemy Among Us: POWs in Missouri During World War II*, Missouri was once home to more than 15,000 German and Italian prisoners of war (POWs). Many of the camps where they were held have faded into distant memory as little evidence remains of their existence; however, one local resident has a relic from a former POW camp that provides an enduring connection to the service of a departed relative.

"Established at Weingarten, a sleepy little town on State Highway 32 between Ste. Genevieve and Farmington, Missouri, (Camp Weingarten) had no pre-war existence," wrote Fiedler. The author further explained, "(T)he camp was enlarged to the point that some 5,800 POWs could be held there, and approximately 380 buildings of all types would be constructed on an expanded 950-acre site."

Camp Weingarten quickly grew into a sprawling facility to house Italian POWs brought to the United States and, explained Jefferson City resident Carolyn McDowell, was the site where one of her uncles spent his entire period of service with the U.S. Army in World War II.

"My mother's brother, Dwight Hafford Taylor, was raised in the community of Alton in southern Missouri," said McDowell. "His hometown really wasn't all that far from Camp Weingarten," she added.

Although her uncle passed away in 1970, records accessed through the National Archives and Records Administration indicate he was drafted into the U.S. Army and entered service at Jefferson Barracks on November 10, 1942. After completing his initial training, he was designated as infantry and became a clerk with the 201st Infantry Regiment. Shortly after Taylor received assignment to Camp Weingarten, Italian prisoners of war began to arrive at the camp in May 1943. Despite the challenges of overseeing the internment of former enemy soldiers, the camp experienced few security incidents, and conditions remained rather cordial, in part due to the sustenance given the prisoners.

It was noted that many of the Italians were "semi-emaciated" when arriving in the United States because of a poor diet. The *Chicago Tribune* reported on October 23, 1943, that the prisoners at Camp Weingarten soon "put on weight" by eating a "daily menu … superior to that of the average civilian."

Pfc. Taylor and his fellow soldiers, most of whom were assigned to military police companies, maintained a busy schedule of guarding the prisoners held in the camp, but also received opportunities to take leave from their duties and visit their loved ones back home.

"During one of my uncle's visits back to Alton, he asked his mother for an aluminum pie pan," said McDowell. "He then took it back to camp with him, and that's when he gave it to one of the Italian POWs."

When returning to camp, one of the POWs with whom Taylor had established a friendship was given the pie pan and used it to demonstrate his abilities as an artist and a craftsman by fashioning it into a cigarette case. The case not only had a specially crafted latching mechanism but was also etched with an emblem of an eagle on the cover with barracks buildings and a guard tower from the camp inscribed upon the inside.

"My uncle then gave the cigarette case as a gift to my father, who was living in Jefferson City at the time and working as superintendent of the tobacco factory inside the Missouri State Penitentiary," stated McDowell. "It is a beautifully crafted cigarette case, but the irony of it all is that my father never smoked," she jokingly added.

As McDowell went on to explain, her uncle remained at Camp Weingarten until his discharge from the U.S. Army in December 1944. The following October, the former POW camp was closed, and many of the buildings were dismantled, shipped, and reassembled as housing for student veterans at colleges and universities throughout the United States. In the years after the war, McDowell said, her mother kept the cigarette case tucked away in a chest of drawers but since both of her parents have passed, she now believes the historical item should be on display in a museum.

Little remains of the once sprawling POW camp located approximately ninety miles south of St. Louis, with the exception of a stone fireplace that was part of the Officer's Club. McDowell notes the cigarette case is not only a beautiful piece that serves as a link to the past but represents a story to be shared of the state's rich military legacy.

"I will someday donate the cigarette case to a museum for preservation and display, and I believe my brother, Harold McDowell, would agree. However, I want to ensure it is recognized for the treasure that it is and it is not simply thrown away," said McDowell. "That's why I want to tell the story of its creation ... its history, so that its association to Camp Weingarten is never forgotten." *(Photograph courtesy of Carolyn McDowell)*

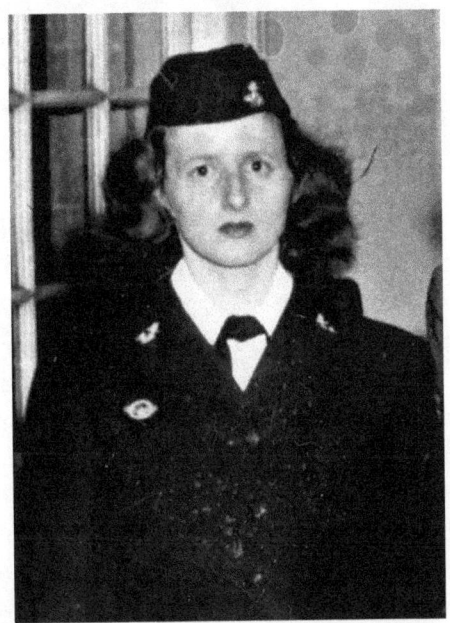

Margaret E. Duss – *New Cambria*

Margaret Elizabeth Duss (who went by the nickname "Dusty") was born March 1, 1923, in New Cambria, Missouri, and graduated from Macon High School in 1941. She later attended Central College in Fayette and worked briefly at the Macon County Social Security Office before accepting a job in Jefferson City in May 1944 with the Manpower Commission Employment Service Office. On December 1, 1944, she enlisted with the U.S. Naval Reserve and became a member of the Women Accepted for Volunteer Emergency Service (WAVES). Upon her enlistment, she became the fourth member of her family to serve in the Navy since three of her brothers were already serving in the Navy Air Corps.

After completing her boot camp at Hunter College in New York, Duss was sent to a naval school in Cedar Falls, Iowa, to train to become a yeoman. When her training was completed in March 1945, she was assigned to the Bureau of Aeronautics with the Department of the Navy in Washington, D.C., until her discharge on June 17,

1946, after having achieved the rank of Yeoman second class. She is pictured several months following her discharge, in December 1946, when becoming first vice-commander of the newly formed Central Missouri Women's Post 496 of the American Legion.

Duss attended the University of Missouri-Columbia after the war, graduating with a Bachelor of Arts degree in journalism in 1950. Weeks after her graduating, she traveled to Hawaii to visit her brother and sister-in-law. The *Macon Chronicle-Herald* reported on September 28, 1950, that she decided to remain in Honolulu and was employed as a secretary to the president of a gas company on the island. While living in Hawaii, she met and married a sailor, Maurice D. Riley, who was serving as a gunner's mate stationed at Pearl Harbor. The couple later raised a daughter and spent much of their married life living in the San Diego area. Margaret Duss Riley was employed as a civil service employee in the Amphibious Force Logistics building at the Naval Amphibious Bas in Coronado, California. The World War II veteran passed away on June 18, 2001, and is interred in Chula Vista, California. *(Photograph courtesy of American Legion Post 5)*

Stephen Boehmer – *Rich Fountain*

The fourth of six children, Stephen Boehmer grew up with an intimate understanding of both hardship and hard work. His mother passed away when he was only five years old and, when not attending the local one-room Reichel School near the Osage County community of Rich Fountain, he joined his siblings in assisting their father in completing various chores around the family's farm. As the years passed, Boehmer graduated from Freeburg High School in 1941 and, several weeks later, registered for the military draft with his local draft board in Linn. Returning to his employment at Uncle Willie's Café in Rich Fountain, he became the first of the four Boehmer sons to enter the service when drafted into the U.S. Army at Jefferson Barracks on February 18, 1943.

"His family was very close, I think because of the passing of their mother," said Diane Rackers, one of Boehmer's nieces. "He also wrote home and spoke about having enjoyed attending dances in the Rich Fountain area," she added.

The nineteen-year-old draftee was sent to Camp Sibert, Alabama, to complete several weeks of basic training. Dedicated on Christmas Day 1942, Camp Sibert became the primary training camp for chemical warfare soldiers during World War II and closed shortly after the end of the war in 1945.

"In June 1943, after three months of basic training, he was sent overseas, headed to North Africa after passing through England," said Diane Rackers.

Following his arrival in North Africa, Boehmer eventually received assignment to Company D, 83rd Chemical Mortar Battalion, who had been in the country since May 11, 1943. A brief period of invasion training ensued, and the young soldier soon entered combat as part of the Allied invasion of Sicily, supporting numerous attacks and counterattacks using such weapons as the 4.2-inch mortar.

Diane Rackers explained, "In a letter that was later sent to Stephen's father by Lt. Alfred H. Crenshaw, he wrote, 'Stephen saw many grueling days of combat. Throughout all of this, he acquitted himself in a manner that is a credit to both you and his country.'"

Remaining stalwart in the face of heavy resistance, Allied forces pushed northward into the Italian mainland and were able to secure the port of Naples in addition to vital airfields as part of a nearly three-month campaign named Operation Avalanche. In a letter dated November 17, 1943, Boehmer indicated he was "sleeping in foxholes in wet clothes and blankets" with bullets "whistling" above his head. Ten days later, he wrote of another "enemy" the men of the battalion faced—the weather, with rain falling regularly and creating "an awfully lot of mud."

In his book *Bastard Battalion: A History of the 83rd Chemical Mortar Battalion in World War II*, Terry Lowry notes that Daniel Shields, one of Boehmer's fellow Company D soldiers, "said it rained so much he could not stay in his foxhole and eventually sought shelter in a church."[92]

During Christmas of 1943, Boehmer wrote home that he received a welcome respite from combat operations and was able to attend midnight mass while on a five-day pass, during which he had the opportunity to sleep in a bed and watch some films. The following month, on January 25, 1944, he was one of more than six hundred men to board LST *422*—one vessel in a convoy of thirteen ships that departed Naples for the Battle of Anzio. Early the next morning, LST *422* encountered inclement weather and high winds, which blew the ship into a known minefield; the resulting explosion caused the ship to break in two and sink off the Italian coast.

"Stephen (Boehmer) was reported missing in action in Italy," said Diane Rackers. "In a letter sent by Lt. Alfred Crenshaw, he explained that Stephen 'was aboard a ship that was destroyed about three miles off the enemy coastline and had to be abandoned.'" Somberly, Rackers added, "The letter went on to state that the water was very rough and after a 'hard fought contest,' he finally 'succumbed to the overwhelming might of the sea.'"

One of several hundred casualties, Boehmer's body was recovered and was initially interred in the Sicily-Rome American Cemetery in Nettuno, Italy. His remains were returned to the United States in 1949 and reinterred at the Sacred Heart Cemetery in Rich Fountain, the veteran's home parish. Following his death, Boehmer's three brothers were all drafted into the military because of World War II, surviving their service and returning home to marry and raise children. Decades have passed since Boehmer lost his life in a violent storm off the Italian coastline; however, his nieces and nephews have found ways to honor the memory of an uncle they never met.

---

[92] Lowry, *Bastard Battalion*, 114.

"Stephen was in the military for only eleven months when he gave his life for ours—a deed we must all remember in thought and prayer," said Betty Dickneite, one of Boehmer's nieces. "That is why we held a special ceremony at his gravesite on November 3, 2018—seventy-four years after his death—to present his Purple Heart, Missouri WWII awards, and a memorial notebook to his brother's son, Stephen, who was named in his honor."

Stephen's sister, Mary Kay Hager, added, "We know that he will cherish these items, and it is our family's hope that they are passed on to his heirs as a remembrance of Stephen Boehmer's sacrifice for the United States of America." *(Photograph courtesy of Diane Rackers)*

Sylvester Boehmer – *Rich Fountain*

The years prior to World War II extracted a heavy price on the Boehmer family as they toiled to maintain a farm near the community of Rich Fountain. Sylvester Boehmer, one of six children, mourned the loss of his mother, who passed when he was only ten years old and was later only able to finish the fifth grade since he was needed to help his father work their farm. Tragedy again struck in January 1944, when Sylvester's younger brother, Stephen, drowned after the vessel he was aboard struck a mine and sunk off the coast of Italy while he was serving with the U.S. Army. This loss remained fresh in the family's thoughts when Sylvester received his draft notice months later and was assigned to the military branch whose primary mission was on the seas that had taken his brother's life.

"My father entered active service with the U.S. Navy on December 6, 1944," explained Mary Kay Hager, one of Sylvester Boehmer's two children. "He entered the service from St. Louis," she added.

The twenty-five-year-old recruit was sent to the U.S. Naval Training Center at Great Lakes, Illinois, spending the next several weeks undergoing the basic training requirements to earn the revered title of "sailor." He was then sent to Camp Peary, Virginia, which at the time was surging with recruits who would serve in naval construction battalions known as "Seabees." Shortly after his arrival on the East Coast, documents maintained by Boehmer's family indicate his temporary transfer to the West Coast and subsequent orders that would lead to overseas deployment.

"We know some of what was going on from letters my father wrote home during the war," Mary Kay Hager said. "He wasn't engaged to my mother, Alvina Pope, at the time, but he would write to her and also to his father and sisters."

In a written summary, Sylvester's son, Stephen (named in honor of his uncle who died at sea in WWII), noted that on April 2, 1945, his father wrote from San Bruno, California and "talk(ed) about being a guard for a WAVES barracks, bank and post office." He added, "In his May 22, 1945 letter, he says he is 'somewhere in the Pacific.'" Correspondence received by family the following month established that Boehmer was assigned to Naval Supply Depot 926 on the island of Guam. According to an article on the Naval History and Heritage Command website, Guam had to be "captured from the enemy and cleared of debris before construction could begin." [93]

In his book *Guam 1941 & 1944: Loss and Reconquest*, Gordon L. Rottman explains, "The seizure of Guam in December 1941 was one of the Imperial Japanese armed forces' first victories in the Pacific War.... The July 1944 battle followed on the heels of the American assault on Saipan and the Battle of the Philippines Sea,

---

[93] Naval History and Heritage Command, *Building the Navy's Bases in World War II*, https://history.navy.mil.

which advanced the U.S. forces into the heart of Japan's pre-war territories." [94]

As the previously cited U.S. Navy article related, Guam was considered a critical military objective, and the subsequent supply depot built there became one of fifteen scattered throughout the Pacific during the war. Additionally, it was "capable of supporting one-third of the Pacific fleet" and possessed "the replenishment storage necessary to restock every type of vessel with fuel, ammunition, and consumable supplies..."

"We remember (Sylvester) telling us that he served in Guam on a small shuttle boat that helped transfer supplies from the larger ships in the harbor to the unloading facilities located on shore," recalled his daughter, Mary Kay Hager.

Boehmer wrote to his family on September 15, 1945, approximately two weeks following the surrender of Japan aboard the USS *Missouri* in Tokyo Bay. He said that he had what his fellow sailors referred to as "the best job on the island of Guam," learning to operate small boats under the guidance of the "Cox" [coxswain]—the sailor in charge of the craft. He would again write in January 3, 1946, advising he was still stationed on the island but looked forward to returning home. Less than a month later, his sister wrote a letter to the War Department pleading for Boehmer to be released from service since their father, Frank, was very ill and hospitalized.

Although there were four brothers in the family, Stephen had died in the service in early 1944, and Louis was stationed in Japan with the U.S. Army, which left only their youngest brother, Andrew, to assist with the farm responsibilities. Sadly, their father passed away from colon cancer on February 5, 1946, and Sylvester did not receive his discharge until April 23, 1946. Less than three months after Sylvester's return home, Andrew was drafted into the service, and

---

[94] Rottman, *Guam 1941 & 1944: Loss and Reconquest*, Introduction.

Louis did not receive his discharge from the Army until October 1946.

"The letters my father wrote back to my mother have been lost," Mary Kay Hager sadly noted. "But it wasn't long after he was discharged that they were married ... on June 15, 1946."

In addition to becoming the father to two children, Boehmer eventually moved his family to Jefferson City. He later became a mechanic and worked a number of years at the former McKay Buick, from which he retired. An active member of the American Legion and VFW, he passed away July 20, 2000, and was laid to rest in Resurrection Cemetery.

"My father and his siblings had a rough upbringing in losing their mother, the death of a brother in the service, and then their father, but I know that he was quite proud of his service," said Mary Kay Hager. "I can remember he saved his uniform and had a display made for his medals." She added, "And even though he never spoke about his service much to me, I think it is an interesting story of four brothers who had to serve and a family that was greatly impacted by war." *(Photograph courtesy of the Boehmer Family)*

Louis Boehmer – *Rich Fountain*

Louis Boehmer was not yet three years old when his mother passed away in 1929. Years later, he joined his three brothers and two sisters in helping their father work the family farm near Rich Fountain. He would watch as one of his older brothers, Stephen, was drafted into the U.S. Army, later deploying overseas and writing home about his experiences in Italy. On January 17, 1944, an eighteen-year-old Boehmer traveled to the courthouse in Linn, Missouri, to register for the draft. Nine days later, his older brother drowned off the coast of Italy after the military vessel he was aboard hit a mine. The family had little time to mourn his loss since Sylvester—Louis' other older brother—received his draft notice in December 1944 and went on to serve in Guam with the U.S. Navy.

"In papers that I have," said Betty Dickneite, one of Louis Boehmer's daughters, "it indicates that our father was scheduled to report for his pre-induction military physical at the Linn County Courthouse on January 4, 1945."

While his older brother continued to serve in the U.S. Navy, Louis Boehmer was inducted into the U.S. Army at Jefferson Barracks on April 19, 1945, leaving only one of the four Boehmer brothers, Andrew, back home.

Betty Dickneite went on to explain, "My father was first sent to Camp Livingston in Louisiana, where he completed his basic infantry training followed by the instruction to become a military policeman with Company A, 140th Battalion of the 35th Regiment."

Named in honor of Chancellor Robert R. Livingston, the individual who negotiated the Louisiana Purchase in 1803, Camp Livingston became an infantry replacement training center during World War II and was the site of training for more than 500,000 troops on its sprawling 47,000 acres. Spending a little more than five months at the Louisiana post, World War II ended approximately a month before Boehmer received orders to deploy to Japan to serve as a military policeman with the occupational forces. Shortly after his arrival overseas in late October 1945, he was assigned to the 237th Military Police Battalion.

As an article from the National World War II Museum explained, "The military occupation of Japan by the Allied Powers lasted from 1945-1952. Supposedly a joint occupation by international powers, it was primarily carried out by U.S. forces under the command of General Douglas MacArthur." [95]

During this transitional and uncertain post-war period, a strong military presence was maintained while trials were conducted for

---

[95] The National World War II Museum, *The United States Occupies Japan*, https://nationalww2museum.org.

Japanese leaders of the war, followed by the demolition of factories that had produced weapons and munitions for the war effort.

"Documents in my father's military records show that he served for six months in the Asiatic-Pacific Theater," said Bonnie Higdon, another of the veteran's daughters. "They also note that part of his duties was patrolling roads and assisting in enforcing military rules and regulations governing traffic and military personnel."

His daughter went on to explain that their father was also responsible for performing a host of additional law enforcement activities, including assisting the civilian police in maintaining order, apprehending lawbreakers and receiving and escorting prisoners to their places of confinement. While in Japan, Boehmer's father fell ill, and the soldier was unable to return home prior to his passing from colon cancer on February 5, 1946. However, he was eventually transferred back to the United States in mid-March 1946 but had to remain in the Army until receiving his discharge at Ft. Riley, Kansas, on October 23, 1946. By the time he received his discharge from the Army, Boehmer's older brother, Sylvester, was already out of the Navy, but their youngest brother, Andrew, had received his draft notice and was inducted into the U.S. Army in July 1946.

"He and my mother, Marie Elizabeth Haller, were married in February 1948," said Betty Dickneite, when speaking about her father. "I'm sure they knew one another before the war because they didn't grow up too far apart."

In the years following his overseas service, Boehmer and his wife settled in Freeburg and went on to raise three daughters. He was later employed by Quaker Windows & Doors, becoming a foreman for the company. Sadly, the fifty-year-old veteran died from a massive heart attack on August 11, 1976, and was laid to rest in Holy Family Cemetery in Freeburg. Betty Dickneite explained that although her father was hesitant to share many details about his time spent with the U.S. Army in post-war Japan, he remained proud of his military police service and, like many veterans, maintained a collection of mementos to remind him of those experiences.

"He was a member of the American Legion, and my mom was a member of the auxiliary," said Dickneite. "Although he never talked about it—it just wasn't something he discussed around the house—he had pictures from his Army days hanging on the front wall of the living room." She added, "We didn't fully realize how important it was to him until years later when we decided to do a little redecorating and took the pictures off the wall and put them in the box in the shed." With somber pause, she concluded, "Although he never said anything to us about it, we could sense how much that collection of military items meant to him." *(Photograph courtesy of Betty Dickneite and Bonnie Higdon)*

Andrew Boehmer – *Rich Fountain*

Born in 1928, Andrew Boehmer of Rich Fountain was little more than a year old when his mother unexpectedly passed away, leaving their father with six children to raise. Difficult years would follow as the Stock Market Crash of 1929 brought about a lean time known as the Great Depression and farmers in Osage County joined scores of their counterparts nationwide struggling to extract a living from their land. The youngest of six children, Boehmer grew up to witness his three older brothers depart for military service because of World War II—one of whom, Stephen, died in 1944 after drowning off the coast of Italy while serving with the U.S. Army.

"As I understand it, my father was basically raised on the farm by his older sister, Catherine," said Gene, the oldest of Boehmer's children.

His son further explained that little information exists regarding his father's early years and his subsequent military service because of a fire decades ago that destroyed many of the family records and mementos. Like his siblings, Boehmer attended Freeburg High School. The young farmhand also followed in the footsteps of his older brothers when he traveled to the courthouse in Linn, Missouri, on March 15, 1946—his eighteenth birthday—to register with his local draft board as required by the Selective Training and Service Act of 1940.

He returned briefly to his work in "self-employed farming," as noted on his draft registration card, while his older brother Sylvester remained in the Navy until April 1946, followed by his brother Louis, who did not receive his discharge from the Army until October 1946. The call to service that had come for his three older brothers arrived for the youngest Boehmer on July 5, 1946, when he was drafted into the U.S. Army at Scott Field, Illinois—a U.S. Army Air Corps training site that became Scott Air Force Base on January 13, 1948.

"By the onset of World War II, Scott Field was well on its way to earning the title of Communications University of the Army Air Forces and adopted the slogan, 'The best damn radio operators in the world,'" according to a fact sheet available on the official website of Scott Air Force Base.[96] An article appearing in the September 19, 2018 edition of the *Belleville News-Democrat* reported that by the close of World War II, "Scott Field Radio School had produced an astonishing 77,370 radio operators/mechanics for the war effort, including Allied nations, such as France, China, the Netherlands, and several Latin American nations."

For several weeks, Boehmer remained at Scott Field to complete communications training and went on to earn the designation as a "Message Center Clerk." In early October 1946, after only three months in the U.S. Army, he was sent to the West Coast to board a troop ship bound for service overseas. Arriving in Japan on November 4, 1946, he was assigned to the 25th Signal Company under the 25th Infantry Division. Following the example of his older brother Louis, who had served as a military policeman in Japan months earlier, Boehmer became a soldier in the Army of Occupation.

---

[96] Scott Air Force Base, *Scott Air Force Base History*, https://scott.af.mil.

The 25th Infantry Division had participated in a number of bloody battles of World War II, including campaigns in the Central Pacific, Northern Solomons, Guadalcanal, and the Philippine island of Luzon. The division was sent to Japan in October 1945, a year prior to Boehmer's arrival. At the time of Boehmer's arrival, the 25th Signal Company was located in the Japanese city of Osaka—an area that "had suffered several bombing damages, but a number of large, modern buildings remained," which were secured for use by the occupational forces, noted the book *The 25th Division and World War 2*.[97]

Throughout the next several months, Boehmer and the soldiers of the 25th Signal Company provided communication support to the military organizations under the command of the 25th Infantry Division scattered across Japan. In early October 1947, after spending a year overseas, a 19-year-old Boehmer received orders to return to the United States. Receiving his discharge as a technician fifth grade (tech corporal) at Fort Lawton, Washington, on October 29, 1947, he returned to Rich Fountain, married, and became father to six children.

"He lived in Freeburg for a while and had a shop where he did mechanic and bodywork," said Boehmer's oldest son, Gene. "We later moved to Jefferson City, and he worked a number of years for McKay Buick."

As Gene recalled, his father was later employed as part of a crew that traveled throughout the United States painting bridges, but in the early 1960s, he moved to the state of California to perform bodywork at a Buick dealership. He eventually settled in Iowa, where he passed on August 31, 1977, when only forty-nine years old. His body was returned to Missouri and interred in the Sacred Heart Cemetery in Rich Fountain. In the years since his passing, his son has come to realize that the fire that consumed many important records was

---

[97] *The 25th Infantry Division and World War 2, Japan*, 166.

a contributing factor to little information remaining of his father's military experience.

"I don't know anything about what he did while he was in the service, and my siblings don't know either," Gene Boehmer said. "He never talked about his Army service while we were growing up, and because of the fire and his death at such a young age, he was never able to give us any insight about what he experienced. It's a relief to know that we can learn a little bit about him through other sources," he added. *(Photograph courtesy of Diane Rackers)*

Theodore Stubinger - *Russellville*

More than three-quarters of a century has transpired since the United States entered World War II following the Japanese attack on Pearl Harbor. In the years since this historic event, many of the men and women who served in the military during the war have passed away and, in some circumstances, were laid to rest before their personal accounts of service to the nation could be shared. Fortunately, some service members, such as local Army veteran Theodore Stubinger, have family members who were devoted to preserving the stories of the sacrifices made by their loved ones during the tumultuous period of the Second World War.

Born on a farm north of Russellville on December 26, 1915, Stubinger was the son of an Austrian immigrant and attended the local school while growing up. As he entered adulthood, he began to explore a vocational interest that would transition to a career several years later, explained his niece, Dorothy Rockelman, prior to her death on August 14, 2017.

"Before he was in the service," Rockelman said, "he worked as an automobile mechanic at one of the garages that used to be in Russellville—the old MFA garage that was once located downtown, I believe."

Stubinger's journey to military service began with The Selective Training and Service Act, which was implemented in 1940 and required the "registration of all males between the ages of 21 and 35," explained Roger William Little in his book *Selective Service and American Society*. The author went on to state that "in the first registration, more than 16 million men registered"—a staggering number that included the twenty-four-year-old Stubinger.[98]

The budding mechanic was married to his sweetheart, Verneda Kirchner, on October 26, 1941. Several weeks later, the nation entered WWII, but it was not until the following year, on December 30, 1942, that Stubinger was inducted into the U.S. Army at Ft. Leavenworth, Kansas.

"I never heard him talk about his time in the service or anything from the war," said Rockelman, describing the modest amount of information the family has regarding her uncle's military service.

The former soldiers' military discharge papers indicate his assignment to the 671st Tank Destroyer Battalion, a unit that was activated at North Camp Hood (now Ft. Hood), Texas, on June 12, 1943, according to an official unit history. The battalion trained at the camp's Tank Destroyer Unit Training Center, whose primary mission was to provide specialized training in maneuverability and armored warfare. This included familiarity with such weaponry as the 75mm gun and the M10, the latter of which was an early model tank destroyer.

---

[98] Little, *Selective Service and American Society*, 40.

During the training period, Stubinger became one of the mechanics for the tank destroyers. His capabilities, and that of his fellow mechanics, was demonstrated in unit records denoting the battalion's maintenance section was "considered the best of any battalion in the TD BUTC (Tank Destroyer Basic Unit Training Center)," scoring an impressive 490 out of 500 points on the rating scale used in the assessment. Later in their training, the battalion received the newer M18 Hellcats—a minimally armored tank with top speeds of more than fifty-five miles per hour and armed with a 76mm cannon.

For the next several months, the battalion conducted field exercises and maneuvers at Camp Swift, Texas, in addition to field training at Fort Knox, Kentucky. Despite the war in Europe having ended during their training, the battalion anticipated serving in the Pacific. They left Kentucky by rail and arrived in Seattle, Washington, in late December 1944 to prepare for overseas deployment.

Lt. Col. Allerton Cushman, who served as the battalion's commander, wrote in the February 1946 edition of *The Field Artillery Journal* that the 671st "arrived in Leyte (Philippines) in the summer of 1945 and immediately began intensive training ..." In his article, Cushman goes on to explain that the battalion received the newer M-36 Tank Destroyers while in the Philippines and began training as "corps artillery, infantry assault guns," learning the "technique of adjusting fire ... exactly the same as conventional field artillery ..." [99]

While still training, the atomic bombs were dropped on Japan, thus heralding the end of the war and rendering unnecessary the need for the continued service of the battalion. Stubinger boarded a troopship in early January 1946, returning to the United States and receiving his discharge at Ft. Leavenworth the following month.

After the war, Stubinger came back to Russellville and reunited with his wife. The veteran was later employed as the shop foreman for

---

[99] Cushman, *The Field Artillery Journal*, 70.

Vanosdoll Motors and American Motors in Jefferson City. In 1991, his wife passed away, and he later remarried; however, Stubinger passed away on January 28, 1994, and was laid to rest in the cemetery of St. Paul's Lutheran Church in Lohman. With no children to carry forth his story of service to the country in World War II, Stubinger's extended family hopes that they can take up the mantle of preserving and sharing his proud legacy of service to the nation he loved.

"I didn't get to know Ted until later in life," said Beth Rockelman, the veteran's great-niece. "I wish I could have known him much sooner and have had the opportunity to learn more about what he did when he was younger, especially during the war." She added, "He was such a wonderful man, and I believe that he and many others deserved a lot more recognition than what they got when he came home from the war." *(Photograph courtesy of Dorothy Rockelman)*

Lawrence "Larry" Diggs – *Columbia*

World War II became a major turning point in the desegregation of the United States military when African American service members continued an honored legacy of military service in newly established organizations such as the Tuskegee Airmen. It was also during this period that the United States Marine Corps first began inducting African American recruits into an elite group that became known as the Montford Point Marines. Lawrence "Larry" Diggs of Columbia explained that he was raised on Mississippi Delta farmland but was living in Chicago when he received his draft notice and was inducted into the Marine Corps on October 14, 1943.

"Before World War II, blacks had not been allowed to serve in the Marines," said Diggs. "During the induction process, there was no rhyme or reason to how they selected us for a specific branch of service; they just pointed out a few of us and said, 'You're going to be Marines'—I didn't have any choice in the matter."

From Chicago, Diggs and his group of fellow inductees traveled by bus to Jacksonville, North Carolina, and from there were taken to nearby Camp Lejeune. Upon their arrival at the camp, they were transferred to a segregated training area known as Camp Montford Point.

"We didn't have barracks or anything like what the white Marines had," recalled Diggs. "During our training, we lived in tents, and all of our instructors were white."

For several weeks, they underwent basic training, which Diggs described as being "brutal" at times. During this timeframe, in addition to learning drill and ceremony and conducting maneuvers, they trained with weapons such as the M-1 rifle, mortars, grenades, all of which was supplemented by instruction on the effective use of bayonets in combat.

"Most of our instructors didn't want black Marines and didn't support the idea of integration in the military, so they tried to drill us hard enough to break us down and make us give up, but that only made us more determined to succeed," he affirmed.

When his initial training was finished in the early weeks of 1944, Diggs was assigned to the 7th Ammunition Company. He was soon transferred to the island of Guadalcanal in the southwest Pacific to complete jungle warfare training and additional instruction on the operations of several types of machine guns. In early September 1944, he boarded an ammunition ship in preparation for the Battle of Peleliu. Peleliu, in the Palau Islands, became part of the island-hopping campaign in the Western Pacific, implemented to capture areas of strategic importance held by the Japanese forces. The Battle of Peleliu began in mid-September 1944, with Marine forces conducting an amphibious assault against Japanese troops who were concealed across the island through a network of underground caverns.

As Diggs explained, "We were attached to the 1st Marine Division and sent as replacements for Marines that had been lost in the fighting. When we got to Peleliu, we watched from the ship as the Navy bombarded the island; there was smoke everywhere, and they had knocked down most of the trees."

Serving as a rifleman, Diggs became part of a group of Marines ordered to go ashore for the assault. Departing the ship aboard amphibious duck boats, as soon as the Marines hit the beach, they quickly dug foxholes while mortars fell around them like hail in a thunderstorm. The battle for the island continued for several weeks, with Diggs and his fellow Marines experiencing hand-to-hand combat and using devices such as flamethrowers to drive the entrenched Japanese soldiers from their network of caverns. Other times, they had the unenviable responsibility of burying the dead and decaying Japanese corpses. In spite of all the hardships, Diggs possesses some humorous reflections from his time in a combat environment.

"We all wore green colored undershirts, but we had this one guy named Douglas, who was a scout and who liked to wear white undershirts that weren't Marine Corps issue. He was a great scout, and one time, while surveying enemy positions, he stole a Japanese bike and rode it back into camp."

Diggs went on to explain that when the scout returned to camp at dusk, he jumped into his foxhole and removed his outer shirt, but when a crab crawled across his body in the dark, he let out a holler in surprise.

"The Japanese shot up a flare and saw him in his white undershirt," Diggs said. "They started shooting at us, and he's lucky that one of our own guys didn't kill him for giving away our position." Grinning, he added, "He survived, and it was all funny enough after it was over."

The battle for the island came to an end in late November 1944, and Diggs remained on the island for several months, serving as a truck driver delivering supplies and training other soldiers to serve as drivers. He returned to Montford Point in the spring of 1945, where he remained until receiving his discharge on May 11, 1946. Returning to Chicago, he was eventually hired by the United States Postal Service and went on to retire with thirty years of service. The married father of five children moved to Columbia in 1980, where he and his wife continue to enjoy their retirement years.

Recognition for the achievements of the Montford Point Marines came in 2012, when Diggs joined nearly four hundred of his fellow Marines at a ceremony in Washington, D.C., to collectively receive bronze replicas of a Congressional Gold Medal.

The period of World War II was a "different time," the veteran admits, but he remains contented in knowing that the efforts of he and his fellow black Marines during the war helped inspire desegregation of the military and moved the country forward in the spirit of civil rights.

"Once I became of age to enter the service, I had no choice—they got me right after I turned eighteen," he chuckled. "But once I was there, I made the best of it." He concluded, "They didn't want us in the Marine Corps; they weren't ready for us, and they did their best to make sure that we didn't succeed. We just performed the best that we could and were determined to prove them wrong." *(Photograph courtesy of Larry Diggs.)*

Leonard O. Taggart – *Windsor*

When making annual preparations for the approaching Memorial Day, Tim Theroff, general manager of Riverview Cemetery in Jefferson City, was strolling through the cemetery grounds when he observed a grave with military markings that had not been decorated with a small U.S. Flag.

"The headstone showed that the veteran had been killed in action, but since he did not have a traditional VA marker, it had been inadvertently overlooked by the volunteers who place flags on the graves," said Theroff.

Contacting the Silver Star Families of America for additional information on the veteran buried there, Theroff discovered it was a soldier who possessed a fascinating story of military service spanning the National Guard and U.S. Army in addition to connecting the Missouri communities of Jefferson City, Windsor, and Clinton. Born on March 23, 1918, in Jefferson City, Leonard O. Taggart was raised in a family of six siblings. Sadly, a two-year-old brother died in 1927, followed by his mother, Dena, who passed in 1936; both were buried in Riverview Cemetery. The young Taggart went on to attend local schools before moving with his family to the small city of Windsor, where he was employed by the International Shoe Company.

The June 9, 1959, edition of the *Clinton Eye* reported that Taggart became a member of "Battery E, 128th Field Artillery Regiment and (was) with the Clinton National Guard unit when it was inducted into federal service on November 25, 1940." The unit was later redesignated Battery B, 231st Armored Field Artillery (AFA) Battalion and "trained at Ft. Jackson (South Carolina), Camp Blanding (Florida), Camp Chaffee (Arkansas), the Mojave Desert, California and at Camp Cook (California)," the newspaper further noted. Operating as an organic unit under the 6th Armored Division, the 231st AFA participated in several major campaigns of the war in Europe following their arrival overseas in 1943, which included locations in England, France, Luxembourg, Belgium, and Germany.

The *Windsor Review* reported on March 30, 1944, that Taggart and his brother were both serving overseas. They wrote, "Cpl. Kenneth Taggart and Cpl. Leonard Taggart are now in England, not together but where they will be able to see each other occasionally…"

Taggart was with the 231st AFA when the 6th Armored Division entered France through Utah Beach in July 1944, the month following the initial D-Day landings. Their impressive legacy of combat included the Battle for Brest in addition to the Battle of the Bulge, the latter of which Taggart would not experience. On August 3, 1944, the *Windsor Review* wrote, "Tuesday's Kansas City Times gave a long list of Missourians that were recently in action against the Germans in France, most of them were from old National Guard units. Listed from Windsor were Sgt. Bates Griffith and Pvt. Leonard Taggart."

However, it was the battery's efforts to help establish a bridgehead that would lead to the memorialization of Taggart's name. During operations at Han-sur-Nied, France, on November 11, 1944, the half-track Taggart was operating was hit with an enemy round, severely wounding the twenty-six-year-old soldier from Missouri.

"George Taggart received a message Sunday from the War Department saying his son, Cpl. Leonard Taggart, had been seriously wounded in action on November 11 in France," reported the December 7, 1944 edition of the *Henry County Democrat*. The newspaper added, "Wednesday morning Mr. Taggart ... received a second message from the Adjutant General's office stating his son ... died November 12 in France as a result of wounds received in action on November 11." The paper also reported that the death of Taggart represented the ninth Gold Star (military death) of the war for Windsor, which, according to the 1940 census, was a community of only 2,373 residents.

The remains of the veteran were initially laid to rest in a military cemetery in Lorraine, France.

"George L. Taggart has been notified that the body of his son ... arrived in New York from Europe aboard the United States Army Transport Oglethorpe Victory," reported the *Windsor Review* on July 22, 1948. "The final destination requested by his father is Jefferson City, Missouri, the former home of the Taggart family."

Taggart's return was part of a program in operation from 1947 until the 1960s, which afforded certain next of kin of those killed in WWII to have the remains of their loved ones repatriated to the United States at the expense of the government for burial in a local cemetery or national cemetery. Funeral services for Taggart were held in Jefferson City on August 22, 1948, with members of the Windsor American Legion post participating. The veteran was then laid to rest in a grave alongside his mother in Riverview Cemetery.

A second memorialization for the fallen WWII soldier came on June 7, 1959, with the naming of a new National Guard armory. It was on this date the French-Taggart Memorial Armory was co-named in honor of both Taggart and the late Alva A. French, also a member of the former Battery E, 128th Field Artillery, who was killed in action.

Tim Theroff of Riverview Cemetery is hopeful a traditional-style military marker can someday be obtained for Taggart's grave to make it more discernible as a veteran's gravesite. Although his headstone is eligible for a small veteran's medallion, the Department of Veterans Affairs does not provide markers for graves of this era in cemeteries where the veteran already has a private headstone.

"He is truly a hero and deserves to be recognized for his service with a flag on Memorial Day," said Theroff. "His headstone is easily overlooked, and someday I won't be here to ensure this is done. I want to make sure that those who come after me can continue to honor his memory, just as he deserves," he added. *(Photograph courtesy of JC Vandergiff)*

Doris Van Wickel – *WAC to CIA*

Bruce Berger of Jefferson City, Missouri, has a number of reasons to take pride in the memory of his mother. Not only did she demonstrate her patriotism while supporting her country in the Women's Army Corps in World War II, years later, after her husband passed away, she was also able to raise three sons while at the same time completing a career in an American intelligence agency. Born November 19, 1915, in Brooklyn, New York, Doris Van Wickel was the daughter of Jesse Van Wickel, who was at the time serving as a Foreign Service Officer for the United States. Due to his chosen career field, his daughter was exposed to many cultures while growing up in several different countries.

"My mother lived in several places in her youth to include Shanghai, China; Jakarta, Indonesia; The Hague; Netherlands East Indies; and England," said Berger. "Until 1939, most of her time was spent outside of the United States," he added.

Records maintained by Van Wickel indicate that in the early 1930s, she attended the Malvern Girls' College in Great Malvern England and later completed coursework at George Washington University in Washington, D.C., and Columbia University in New York. During her early years abroad, she acquired proficiency in seven languages to include German, French, Dutch, and Chinese. She also worked for companies in Holland before returning to the United States, where she was hired in 1941 by the Military Intelligence Division of the War Department in New York.

"The work she did with the War Department was confidential," said Berger. "In 1942, she became an assistant economic analyst with the Board of Economic Warfare in Washington, D.C. There she acted as an assistant chief for the Southwest Pacific Unit and researched conditions of the occupied Netherlands, East Indies, and Malaya."

In October 1943, she made the decision to enlist in the Women's Army Corps (WAC)—an organization created during World War II to allow women to support the war effort by serving in non-combat positions. As Berger explained, his mother completed her WAC boot camp at Fort Des Moines, Iowa. Military records indicate Van Wickel was discharged at the rank of technical sergeant on February 16, 1945, and the following day was appointed a second lieutenant. She remained on active duty as an intelligence research analyst until February 18, 1946, spending her entire period of military service at the Pentagon and achieving the rank of first lieutenant.

"While my mother was with the WACs, she met my father in Washington, D.C. after he whistled at her as she walked into a hotel," said Berger. "Apparently, they dated for awhile and then married." He added, "My father had served in the Army and after the war worked for the Census Bureau. My mother was eventually discharged from the WACs after she became pregnant with my oldest brother."

The family remained living in the Washington, D.C. area where Van Wickel Berger's first son, Ken, was born in 1946; a second son,

Darrell, born in 1948; and Bruce, the youngest, was born in 1949. Sadly, Berger explained, his father passed away from Hodgkin's disease in January 1953, leaving behind their mother to raise three young boys.

"After my dad passed, my mother worked a couple of months for the Census Bureau and was then hired by the Central Intelligence Agency (CIA) in the spring of 1953," Berger said. "She went on temporary duty assignments to places like Iran, Hong Kong, and Thailand while us boys went to boarding school at Girard College in Philadelphia."

The intrigue of their mother's new chosen career field soon drew the boys into an exciting adventure when she brought them to live in Saigon in early 1962. While her sons were attending school during the day, Van Wickel Berger was involved in operations that remain shrouded in relative secrecy.

"She never talked too much about what she did and always joked that if she told us, she would have to kill us," Berger chuckled.

Berger and his brothers have pieced together many facets of her service in Vietnam, which included her involvement in coordinating flights for "Air America"—a covert passenger and cargo operation operated by the CIA during the Vietnam War. The pilots, Berger noted, would deliver goods needed by various hamlets and bring their products back into towns, collecting military intelligence during the process. When the situation in Saigon grew more dangerous in early 1965 following bombings of locations such as a movie theater, Van Wickel Berger sent her children back to California to live with her brother. In 1967, she was sent to Udorn, Thailand, where she worked closely with the 7th Radio Research Field Station and was involved with radio intercepts.

"My mother returned to the United States in 1970 and worked at the CIA headquarters in Langley, Virginia, retiring later the same year," said Berger. "She then went on to work for them as a contractor for a couple of years before retiring to Florida."

The former member of the WACs and CIA agent passed away in 1989 from emphysema and was laid to rest alongside her husband in Arlington National Cemetery. As Berger went on to explain, although his mother may have at one time embraced the possibility of a "traditional" lifestyle of raising a family, the adventure that became her life demonstrates she was a woman before her time.

"When my father died, I think that my mother felt the American dream wasn't really holding true for her—being married, having a nice house, and raising children. But," he paused, "I'm not really sure that ideal would have lasted for her." He continued, "My mother would joke during the 1960s and 1970s, at the time when women were burning their bras for equality as part of the women's liberation movement, that she was working as a field operative for the CIA in several war zones. She was a trailblazer as a woman, not only because she served her country in uniform in the WACs, but she went on to demonstrate the value women could offer by working for the CIA at a time when women really had to fight to get a job that wasn't just clerical in nature." *(Photograph courtesy of Bruce Berger)*

James T. Blair Jr – *Jefferson City*

Military service has often been embraced as a platform for launching many a successful political career. However, the late James T. Blair Jr. was already making his ascension up the political ladder when World War II erupted, since he had already served as the city attorney for Jefferson City and completed two terms in the Missouri House of Representatives. Heeding the nation's call to arms, he suspended his political aspirations and left his private law practice to join the U.S. Army Air Forces in the spring of 1942, initially becoming a captain assigned to their intelligence division. After saying his goodbyes to his wife and two children, he departed for training at Miami, Florida, in mid-May 1942. The direction of his military journey would soon shift and align with an interest developed years previous while attending college.

"When a student at Cumberland University, Tenn., he took flying lessons and later received a pilot's license," reported the *St. Louis Globe-Democrat* on March 19, 1943. "He enlisted ... and was commissioned last May..."

On November 7 and 8, 1942, less than six months after entering active military duty, Capt. Blair demonstrated he was not only capable of distinguishing himself in political circles but as a military officer as well. It was during this time that he "operated planes carrying army troops from England to North Africa," noted the March 19, 1943 edition of the *Daily Capital News*.

The newspaper added that Blair was awarded an Air Medal for these missions because they were "(c)arried out despite bad weather and communication conditions and enemy fighter activity…" The article also reveals that this was the "longest massed, unescorted non-stop troop carrier mission successfully performed by the Army Air Forces."

According to the website of the Army Air Corps Library and Museum, as a member of the 9th Troop Carrier Command, these flights served as a precursor to the Allied drive across Egypt and Libya, followed by the campaign in Tunisia and the invasions of Sicily and Italy.[100] Maj. Blair then accompanied the 9th Air Force on their move to England in October 1943. The following April, his father, James T. Blair Sr., a renowned attorney and former member of the Missouri Supreme Court passed away. At the time of his father's death, Blair's two brothers were also serving in the military.

The 9th Air Force would fulfill a crucial role in planning and executing the air assault up to and including D-Day. The *Moberly Monitor-Index* reported on September 22, 1944, that Lt. Colonel Blair was awarded a Legion of Merit by Dwight D. Eisenhower for "organizing the pathfinder group of airborne troops which participated in the invasion of France."

As executive officer for the Pathfinders unit, and one of the first behind enemy lines in the hours prior to the main invasion, Blair explained in an article appearing in the August 1944 edition of *Air*

---

[100] Army Air Corps Library and Museum, *9th Air Force*, https://armyaircorpsmuseum.org.

Force: The Official Journal of the U.S. Army Air Forces, a few details regarding their unenviable mission.

"Our job, briefly, is to do for troop carrier planes taking troops into enemy territory what (Royal Air Force) pathfinders do for their night bombers—mark the target so the main forces can find it without delay and without error." He added, "In other words we go first—and we've got to be right."[101]

Surviving the harrowing missions of the Pathfinders, who went on to prepare the way for the seaborne troops in the invasion, Blair later encountered an old friend who was on assignment in France in the weeks following D-Day.

Duke Shoop was at the time serving overseas as a war correspondent for the Kansas City Star. He had recently been part of a group of Navy Seabees and war correspondents who made a narrow escape after they came under attack by German forces while traveling in France.

In October 1945, shortly before receiving his discharge, Lt. Col. Blair attended the wedding of his close friend, Senator Bennett Champ Clark, to British actress Violet Heming. Clark, himself a veteran of World War I, had the distinction of being a founding member of the American Legion and served as the organization's first national commander when it was formed in 1919.

Following Blair's return to Missouri, he briefly served as mayor of Jefferson City before resigning the position after being elected to the office of lieutenant governor. He became governor in 1956, serving one term. The *Moberly Monitor-Index* reported July 12, 1962, that he maintained his interest in aviation and, while governor, often took control of the Highway Patrol's plane when flying around the state.

---

[101] Air Force: The Official Journal of the U.S. Army Air Forces, *Blazing the Trail on D-Day*, 21.

After the war, Blair also received a commission as a colonel with the Missouri National Guard and served as their senior legal officer. In a depressing twist of fate, the veteran and his wife died unexpectedly in 1962 from carbon monoxide poisoning in their home. Senator Edward Long made a speech on the floor of the Missouri Senate on July 12, 1962, honoring the legacy of his fellow public servant and friend.

"Jim Blair won the respect and affection of his fellow Missourians through a lifetime of devoted public service," Long said. "It will serve as a memorial to a great Missourian—one for all of us to emulate."

Many years earlier, during a time when Blair was making headlines for his accomplishments while serving in World War II, the *Daily Capital News* in their September 28, 1944 edition praised the abilities and acknowledged the potential of the future governor.

"When Lt. Col. Blair is given a job to do, it is so well performed that he wins signal distinction because of the way he does it." *(Photograph courtesy of Myrna Blair)*

Peyton Russell – *Mexico*

For many years, David Russell of Lohman, Missouri, has stored a worn military trunk once belonging to his late father, Peyton Russell. Recently, he and some friends were able to pick the lock on the trunk that contained items accrued during his father's lengthy military career, including diaries that chronicled his service during World War II. When growing up, Russell recalls his father sharing little information about his time in the Army during the war even though he would later go on to serve more than thirty years as a battalion commander in the Missouri National Guard.

"I spent a lot of time with my father at the armory in Mexico when he was in the (National Guard)," said Russell's son, David. "But he really kept quiet about his service in World War II, so I really didn't know many details of his war experiences."

Born in 1918 and raised in Kentucky, Peyton Russell graduated with a bachelor's degree in mathematics from Murray State University in 1940, registered for the draft, and began teaching for a local school. His career in education was interrupted when, according to records accessed through the U.S. National Archives and Records Administration, Russell was ordered to report for a physical and was subsequently inducted into the U.S. Army on October 9, 1941, nearly two months prior to the Japanese attack on Pearl Harbor.

The twenty-three-year-old recruit was sent to Fort Benjamin Harrison, Indiana, where, he explained in his diary, he was given "a mental test, oath, classification, got uniforms issued... (and received) two shots after eating." Several days later, Russell and several recruits boarded a train, arriving at Fort Sill, Oklahoma, on the afternoon of October 15, 1941. That evening, he wrote, "(I) bunked with five others in a tent (and) nearly froze sleeping under two blankets."

He was assigned to the 32nd Field Artillery Battalion and settled into the routines of Army life for the next three months. This cycle of instruction included equestrian training since mounted soldiers could serve as observers for the field artillery and haul light artillery pieces. In early January 1942, nearly a month after the United States entered World War II, Russell trained for several weeks at Camp Papago Park in Phoenix, Arizona. From there, he continued his training at Camp Hydle at Point Reyes, California, until receiving orders for Alaska in August 1942, boarding a troopship in Oakland, California.

Days later, the battalion disembarked the ship at Adak Island, Alaska. In their camp, the whir of air raid sirens became a regular part of their duty day because of the threat of attack from Japanese planes. In early October 1942, Russell wrote, "Three bombs dropped within 500 yards and machine gun bullets within 25 feet of my tent." The following day he scribbled in his diary, "Bombs at 4 a.m., didn't get up, southwest of camp."

For several months, Russell remained at his Alaskan duty station performing what he described as "routine Army duties," much of which seemed to consist of digging drainage ditches. However, on March 31, 1943, he again boarded the USAT St. Mihiel bound for Ft. Lewis, Washington, and then traveled to Ft. Sill, Oklahoma, for officer's candidate school.

In early 1944, the young second lieutenant was sent to California to complete desert maneuvers with the 491st Armored Field Artillery Battalion and received a promotion to first lieutenant on June 20, 1944. Following a brief period of leave, Lt. Russell and the battalion boarded a troop ship in New York and sailed for England. The battalion arrived in France in December 1944 and began providing artillery support as the Allied front pushed west into Germany, assisting such entities as the 4th Infantry Division in the recapturing of several cities that had been previously held by German forces.

Russell's diary in the spring of 1945 chronicles the passage of the battalion through various German communities and, on May 6, 1945, he wrote of their arrival at a "gasthaus" (German-style inn) near the small Austrian city of Gallneukirchen. It was here, he stated, "We enjoyed the end of the war... picking up saddle horses to ride shows" in addition to "souvenir pistols."

In the months that followed, Russell was transferred to the 144th Field Artillery Group and served with the occupying forces until returning to the United States in December 1945. He was discharged from the Army in early 1946 and, in June the same year, moved to Mexico, Missouri, to take a job with A.P. Green Firebrick Company until retiring in 1983. The veteran married in 1949 and later enlisted in the Missouri National Guard. He retired from the National Guard at the rank of lieutenant colonel with more than thirty years of service to his credit. Sadly, the veteran passed away on December 11, 2003, and was laid to rest in Elmwood Cemetery in Mexico.

While growing up, David Russell recalls spending time with his father as he performed his duties at the Missouri National Guard armory in Mexico. Despite the time they were together, David explained, his father rarely discussed his WWII service but offered a glance into his early military service through his diaries.

"I don't think he talked about it much because he likely didn't think his service was all that interesting or as important as the soldiers who participated in D-Day, the Battle of the Bulge or other major battles," said David Russell. "It was certainly not that he was ashamed of his service in any way, it was that he was a very humble man. Because of this," he added, "I really didn't know much about that period of his military career and this is why it is important for veterans to share their stories before they are lost." He concluded, "I am glad he kept a diary because it helped me to understand what he did during the war and ensures his story is in some way preserved." *(Photograph courtesy of David Russell)*

Dr. Cortez Enloe Jr. – *Jefferson City*

In decades past, the Enloe family of Mid-Missouri produced a respected line of physicians and dentists. Additionally, many members of the family established a legacy while serving in the military, including Captain James Enloe, who commanded a company of troops from the Russellville area during the Civil War, and his nephew, Roscoe Enloe, a Jefferson City soldier killed in WWI and for whom a local American Legion post is named. One such individual whose name has essentially faded from the collective memory of the community is that of Dr. Cortez Enloe Jr., a man whose education and experience carried him across the globe and helped inspire a character named "Doc" in a once-popular comic strip.

Born in Jefferson City in 1910, Cortez Ferdinand Enloe Jr. was the grandson of the aforementioned Captain James Enloe and a 1928 graduate of Jefferson City Senior High School. He soon made the decision to follow the example set by his father, a respected physician, by enrolling at the University of Missouri in Columbia.

"I went to Culver Military Academy (Indiana) and the University of Missouri, but my father's savings were wiped out in (the Stock Market Crash of) 1929," said Enloe Jr. in an interview appearing in the April 15, 1987 edition of the *St. Louis Post-Dispatch*. Graduating with his bachelor's degree in chemistry in 1932, he soon chose to continue his medical education overseas. "Medical school was $450 a year then at Washington (University in St. Louis), but at Heidelberg (Germany) it was $100," he further explained in the previously mentioned article.

Departing Missouri in the fall of 1932 to begin his studies at the University of Heidelberg, Enloe Jr. continued to follow his father's lead, who had "returned from doing research work there and in Austria several years ago," reported the *Jefferson City Post-Tribune* on September 26, 1932. While studying in Germany, he met his wife and traveled to Jefferson City in 1933 for their wedding. The couple then returned to Heidelberg so that Enloe could resume his studies. The following year, the joy of his recent marriage was tempered by the death of his mother, whom the August 16, 1934 edition of the *Jefferson City Post-Tribune* described as "one of the most gracious women of the capital city."

He graduated cum laude with his medical degree from the University of Berlin in 1937 and, two years later, joined the medical staff at St. Anthony's in St. Louis. From there, he went to New York to work on a penicillin research project and, after the U.S entered WWII, enlisted in the Army Air Corps to train in aviation medicine. An article appearing in *Nutrition Today*—a health magazine founded and edited by Dr. Enloe after the war, noted in Volume 21, Issue 1: "His service included administrative positions of high responsibility such as those of Assistant Surgeon of First Fighter Command (and) Medical Inspector of the First Air Force (Continental USA) ...." The doctor was later involved in combat operations, the magazine further explained, as a combat flight surgeon of the First Air Commando Force during the airborne invasion of Burma, participating in thirty-nine combat missions and "in combat operations behind enemy lines in Central Burma."

While serving in the Southeast Asian nation, he spent two months behind Japanese lines and suffered from a severe bout of dysentery. Enloe also became the medical advisor to Admiral Louis Mountbatten—a famed British naval officer admired by Winston Churchill, who led a successful military campaign against the Japanese, resulting in the recapture of Burma during WWII. Enloe's military service, noted the previously cited article in *Nutrition Today* magazine, resulted in what the Mid-Missouri medical professional claimed his "greatest distinction" when he became the "prototype for the character 'Doc' in Milton Caniff's comic strip 'Terry and the Pirates,' based upon his commando exploits in Burma."

As the years passed, his meteoric career included not only founding an internationally renowned nutrition magazine but, according to a biography from the Air Force Academy, he "went to Europe with the U.S. Strategic Bombing Survey Group (after WWII) and interrogated nearly all the doctors from Hitler's higher headquarters inquiring about the health of the German nation during the war…" He witnessed atomic testing in the 1950s while president of a medical advertising agency and went on to earn recognition in boating as well. The WWII veteran was awarded the 1967 New York Yacht Club Medal "for his work in establishing and promoting power yacht racing activities…" reported the January 11, 1968 edition of *The Capital* (Annapolis, Maryland) newspaper.

A broad collection of achievements and interests certainly could bestow upon Dr. Enloe the title of Renaissance man, never resting on his laurels nor shying away from a new challenge. One final endeavor, however, never came to fruition since it was cut short by his passing—a book about his military experiences. Dr. Enloe was the recipient of thirteen military decorations from the Army, Air

Force, and Navy, becoming "one of the most decorated medical officers in the American Armed Forces" in WW II. Sadly, he "died suddenly of a heart attack in 1995 before completing his book about the First Air Commando's," explained the Air Force Academy Library in biographical notes about the late veteran.

A longtime resident of Annapolis, Maryland, Dr. Enloe said for years that he wished to be buried in Arlington National Cemetery—an honor he had earned through his World War II service. However, hours before his passing, he informed his daughter, Margaret Enloe, that he wished to have his body returned to his native Missouri and interred in Enloe Cemetery near Russellville.

His life, as demonstrated by his achievements, served as an example to many aspiring physicians and military medical professionals; however, as he noted many years ago, success came from adherence to the advice of his father—simple words with enduring applicability. In an article appearing in the November 29, 1972 edition of the *Evening Sun* (Baltimore, Maryland), Enloe sagely affirmed, "I remembered that my father had once told me, 'If you want to be a success, erase the distinctions between yourself and people of great achievement.'" *(Photograph courtesy of Jeremy P. Amick)*

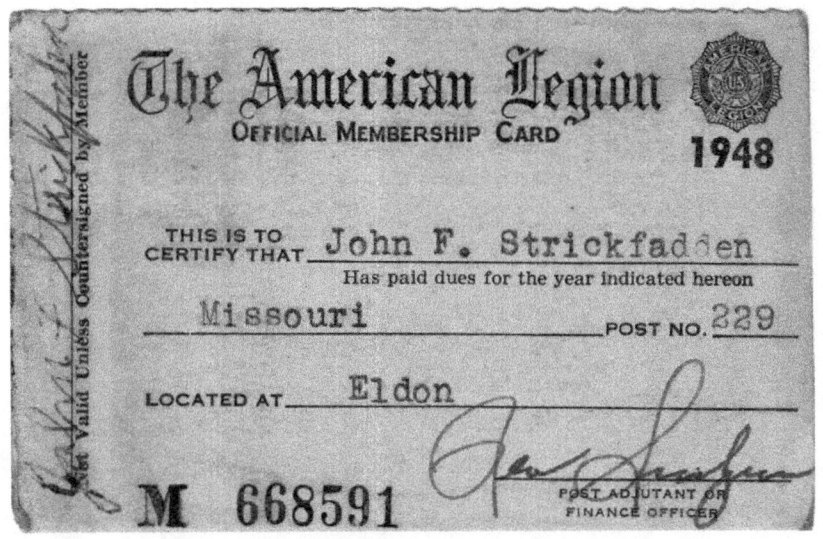

John Strickfaden - *Eldon*

John Frank Strickfaden was a U.S. Navy veteran of World War II and, following his military service, became very active in the American Legion. He was a member of the American Legion Post in California, Missouri, but in the late 1940s transferred to Post 229 in Eldon, Missouri. Strickfaden held several offices within the American Legion throughout the years and, in 1948, represented Post 229 as a delegate at the thirtieth annual convention of the Department of Missouri in Kansas City, Missouri. According to the September 7, 1948 edition of the *Moberly Monitor-Index*, it was during this convention that a resolution was passed to petition Congress to make the home of the late General John J. Pershing, who passed away a few months earlier, a national shrine.

In his civilian endeavors, Strickfaden was employed as an automobile mechanic and passed away on September 5, 1965, at the age of fifty-six. The veteran was laid to rest in the California City Cemetery in California, Missouri. Pictured his membership card for the American Legion Post 229 in Eldon for the year of 1948. *(Photograph courtesy of American Legion Post 5)*

Velma Strickfaden - *Eldon*

Mrs. Velma Strickfaden was a member of the American Legion Auxiliary and active with the unit at Eldon Post 229 for many years. In 1948, she was a delegate representing the auxiliary for her post at the Department of Missouri's thirtieth annual convention of the American Legion held in Kansas City, Missouri, in early September 1948. Mrs. Strickfaden married her husband, John, in 1940, prior to his induction into the U.S. Navy, followed by his subsequent service in World War II. She passed away in 1990 and is interred in California City Cemetery in California, Missouri.

Pictured above is Mrs. Strickfaden's membership card for the American Legion Post 229 in Eldon for the year of 1948, the same year as the department convention in Kansas City. The auxiliary was founded in 1919 and, according to the website of the American Legion, has become the "world's largest women's patriotic service organization" and honors "the sacrifice of those who serve by enhancing the lives of our veterans, military, and their families, both at home and abroad."[102] *(Photograph courtesy of American Legion Post 5)*

---

[102] The American Legion, *My Auxiliary Member Portal*, https://auth-member.legion-aux.org.

Leonard Jaegers – *Meta (Part 1)*

The mission of the Silver Star Families of America—a Missouri-based non-profit—has always been to remember, honor, and assist the wounded, ill, or dying of our Armed Forces from all wars. In this spirit, the story of one local veteran truly personifies this endeavor and features a young man suffering a grievous wound in combat during World War II, who was able to overcome adversity and live a long, productive life through the assistance of medical professionals. His story of love and determination begins in the rural Osage County community of Meta, where a young Leonard P. Jaegers, the oldest of seven children, grew up on his family's farm.

"When my father received his draft notice and had to report to Jefferson Barracks (St. Louis), he was engaged to my mother, Helen Wankum, who grew up near him on a neighboring farm," said Jaegers' son, Robert.

Military records indicate the twenty-one-year-old Jaegers was inducted into the U.S. Army on August 17. 1942, and, after being given a few days to travel home to help his father put up hay on the farm, returned to Jefferson Barracks to complete his basic training. In a summary of Jaegers' service written by his late wife, it was noted that the young soldier "boarded a train and headed west for Denver." His wife went on to note that he was assigned to the military police department; however, after volunteering to serve in the kitchen and impressing the mess sergeant with his culinary abilities, Jaegers was sent to cooking school at Ft. Riley, Kansas.

"Dad said that he thought that he had it kind of easy being a cook and decided that he wanted to get into some of the 'rough' stuff," said James, another of Jaegers' sons. "That's when he volunteered to be a combat engineer, and the Army sent him to Ft. Leonard Wood for more training," he added.

The new duty assignment provided the soldier with a slate of new skills soon identified as those needed to replace the combat losses from fighting during the Battle of the Bulge. He departed Ft. Leonard Wood on Christmas Eve of 1944, bound for Paris, Texas, for six weeks of infantry training. In early February 1945, Jaegers received a brief delay en route to his next duty assignment, affording him a few days back home to visit with his family and fiancée.

His wife wrote, "On the last night of his leave, we went to a dance, and Leonard asked the band to play 'Over the Way Waltz,' and we danced and danced. Little did we realize that this would be the last time that we would ever dance together again," she solemnly explained.

Boarding a train in Jefferson City, Jaegers said his goodbyes to his fiancée and family and made the trip to Camp George E. Meade, Maryland. Two weeks later, he was transferred to Camp Shanks, New York, and boarded a transport ship bound for France. Shortly after his arrival in LeHavre, France, he was processed as a replacement soldier with Company F. 310th Infantry Regiment of the 78th Division.

"Mom's records state that our father and several of his fellow soldiers boarded boxcars and rode the train for several days to the front lines," said his son, Robert. "He wasn't there for very long when he became part of a mission that affected him for the rest of his life."

On April 6, 1945, after the regiment was recovering from an exhausting battle against unwavering German forces, Jaegers was in a foxhole with two of his friends when bullets began whizzing by them. His fellow soldiers were killed while one bullet penetrated Jaegers' helmet, striking him in his skull. Since Jaegers lay unresponsive and had brain matter dripping from the severe wound to his scalp, he was presumed dead, and his body removed from the foxhole and placed next to a group of soldiers who had been killed in battle.

In a fortuitous moment, a chaplain who was blessing the bodies of the deceased observed that Jaegers was still alive, calling for a medic to come and provide immediate assistance. The medic placed the brain matter back into Jaegers' skull and then wrapped the wound.

"Our father lost his memory when he was wounded and did not recall much of the fighting years later," said James Jaegers. "Dad's military records show that he was first evacuated to a field hospital in Germany and was later sent to France and then England for treatment. The chaplain sent the family a letter saying our father was alive but was in serious condition."

Jaegers was eventually transferred back to the states, arriving in New York and taking a train to Brigham City, Utah, for care at Bushnell General Hospital. The veteran's wife wrote years later, "The Red Cross nurse wrote to us about his condition."

She further detailed the seriousness of her fiancée's wound, writing, "He had more surgery on his head. ... His right side was paralyzed. He couldn't talk, walk, read or write. The nurse advised us not to come for a visit until he was a little better."

The days ahead were difficult and filled with both burdens and victories for the wounded soldier as he struggled to regain the abilities that had been torn from him. It was also a stressful period for his fiancée and his family, as they tried to determine the role they would play in ensuring his recovery.

"It was a difficult time for my father and also for our mother," said Robert Jaegers. "But in the coming years, their perseverance and love were promising in our father's recovery and greatly improved his quality of life." *(Courtesy of the Jaegers family)*

Leonard Jaegers – *Meta (Part 2)*

Sergeant Leonard P. Jaegers, after being shot in the skull on April 6, 1945, during combat in World War II, was presumed dead, followed by his body being moved to an area and laid among several other soldiers killed in action. Fortunately, a chaplain discovered the wounded Jaegers was still alive, and the immediate medical attention he received is credited with having saved his life.

"Years later, he told a family friend that while he was on the battlefield in Germany, he made the promise to God that if He let him live, he would work for Him until he died—and he kept that promise," said Jaegers' daughter-in-law, Helen.

This period was also very tumultuous for another Helen in Jaegers' life, Helen Wankum, to whom he was engaged prior to the war. When word was received that the family could come to visit the injured Jaegers at Bushnell General Hospital in Brigham, Utah, his mother, fiancée, and family friend, Bud Loethen, left their homes in

Meta and took a train headed west. The injury left Jaegers with severe memory loss, paralysis on his right side, and significant speech limitations. Upon their arrival at the hospital, the recovering soldier did not recognize his visitors, but after a couple more visits, he recalled who they were and was pleased to see them.

Years later, his former fiancée wrote of her time at the hospital, "During one of (our) visits, I told him that we were engaged, and his injury didn't make any difference to me and that one day we would be married. This information improved his attitude."

Undergoing several surgeries on his skull and brain, the next several months continued an intense regimen of physical and speech therapy followed by his transfer to a hospital in Framingham, Massachusetts. As Helen, his fiancée at the time explained in some of her later writings and recollections, he would first walk by pushing a wheelchair since he was unable to grip a cane. Eventually, Jaegers' abilities improved to the extent he was allowed to return home to Meta, where his fiancée remained true to her commitment. On December 27, 1945, Leonard Jaegers and the former Helen Wankum were united in marriage and, as the years passed, became the parents of seven children.

"One thing that impresses me about our father," said his son, James, "is that although he received a military pension and didn't have to work, he wanted to get up in the morning, shave, and get dressed to show his kids that fathers were supposed to have something to do."

In addition to traveling to locations such as St. Louis to undergo physical, speech, and occupational therapy, Jaegers was described as a man that was always on the move and eventually found employment at a drug store in Meta. This job afforded him opportunities to rebuild his confidence while recovering from his injuries. With improvements in his motor skills and speech also came the return of many of his past memories; however, Jaegers would always suffer from headaches and never regained the use of his right arm. As his children explained, although he enjoyed his work at the drug store, he aspired for something more, which was achieved through the help of the love of his life, Helen.

"Our father always wanted to open a store of his own, so he and mom opened Jaegers Shoes and Apparel in August of 1959," said Robert Jaegers. "They frequently traveled to Springfield (Missouri) and loaded their station wagon with wholesale merchandise that they brought back to the store in Meta to sell." Pausing, he said, "They operated that store for twenty-six years."

Reflecting on the promise the young soldier had made on the World War II battlefields of Europe, the Jaegers' family explained that he strived to fulfill the promise of service that he had made to God.

"He and mother were always volunteering in some capacity," said his son, James. "They volunteered at least one day a week at the VA hospital in Columbia and were very involved in the church and community organizations." He added, "Years later when he and mother traveled to Texas for the winter months, they volunteered three days a week at the VA hospital in San Antonio."

In later years, Jaegers enjoyed attending military reunions and, during one such event held in Pennsylvania, met the individual responsible for having saved his life.

"(We) were surprised to meet the Army Medic who helped treat Leonard as he lay wounded on the German battlefield so many years ago," wrote Jaegers' wife in a document maintained by the family. "Not only was he surprised Dad had made it, but the fact that he could walk and talk. He stated that it was a miracle."

The eighty-nine-year-old Jaegers lived a rich life, passing away November 2, 2010. His beloved wife, Helen, passed away less than two years later, on July 25, 2012. The couple lies at rest in Hawthorn Memorial Gardens in Jefferson City, Missouri.

The courage and determination of their father has left an indelible impression on his children, but they also realize his success in overcoming great physical challenges was a team effort not achievable without the assistance of their mother.

"Our father always felt blessed with the life that he had been given," said Robert Jaegers. "He seemed to be on the move all the time and never sat still for very long. "Through great will and determination, he was able to improve." He concluded, "But it was our mother who was always there for him—it was her devotion and support that truly helped him recover from his war injuries." *(Courtesy of the Jaegers family)*

Elbert Payne - *Lohman*

On October 16, 1940, while living in Lohman, a thirty-year-old Elbert Roy Payne abided by the mandate of the Selective Training and Service Act and registered for the military draft. Less than four months later, he reported to nearby Jefferson City "for physical examination by an examining board of the armed forces for final determination of your military fitness."

The second oldest of the veteran's four children, Gary Payne, explained, "We know very little about his military service. We knew he served in several major campaigns in the Pacific, and he occasionally talked about it but never provided any great detail about where he was or what he did," he added.

Inducted into the U.S. Army at Jefferson Barracks in St. Louis on March 2, 1942, Payne remained at the post for the next several weeks to complete his basic training. On May 22, 1942, he boarded a troop ship to begin a journey that would span nearly three years of overseas service and introduce him to the woman that would become his wife. Upon his arrival on the island of Oahu, the thirty-one-year-old soldier was assigned to the Medical Detachment of the 35th Infantry Regiment under the 25th Infantry Division. While in Hawaii, he received several weeks of instruction in a specialty for which he previously had no experience. As his Army Separation Qualification Record indicates, Payne was trained as a "medical aidman" and learned to serve in an aid station, dressing wounds, administering plasma, and providing first aid in combat.

Shortly after completing jungle warfare and amphibious training at nearby Schofield Barracks, "the 25th Infantry departed Oahu on 25 November (1942), arriving at Guadalcanal on 17 December 1942," reported a history compiled by the 25th Infantry Division Association.[103] The division spent the next several months assaulting and securing areas of the island once held by Japanese forces, earning a Presidential Unit Citation for their valorous actions. During the campaign, Payne provided first aid for wounded soldiers while attached to a rifle company within the division.

"The one thing I remember him saying about his time on Guadalcanal was they were always soaking wet—it was hot, humid, and there were huge mosquitoes and jungle rot to contend with," said Gary Payne.

During the summer, the division became part of the drive to remove Japanese forces from the Northern Solomons, with the 25th Infantry participated in seizing the island of Vella Lavella in a campaign beginning August 15, 1943. Once successfully completed, the island was turned over to New Zealand forces on September 18, 1943, while Payne and his fellow soldiers were sent back to Guadalcanal a few weeks later.

"While my father was overseas, he was given leave in New Zealand and attended a local dance that was put on for the soldiers there,"

---

[103] The 25th Infantry Division Association, *A Brief History of the 25th Infantry Division*, https://25thida.org.

explained Gary Payne. "It was at this dance that he met Bette, a local woman who would later become my mother," he smiled. "They traded letters back and forth until he got back home."

The 25th Infantry Division Association notes the move was made to New Caledonia in February 1944 to conduct additional training exercises. "The training lasted throughout the summer and into late fall," the association explained. "Maneuvers and landings were conducted ... in preparation for the anticipated invasion of the island of Luzon in the Philippines."

Arriving in Lingayen Gulf on January 11, 1945, the division became part of the amphibious assault landing on Luzon. The next few weeks were spent clearing the central plains region of enemy resistance while Payne assisted the wounded in a battalion aid station.

"There was a time that dad and I were watching a war movie, and I asked him if he wore the Red Cross armband on his uniform since he was a medic," Gary Payne said. "He stated that they didn't wear one because that made them a target for Japanese riflemen." His son added, "My father also mentioned that there was a time he and his fellow soldiers noticed their rations were disappearing. It wasn't long after that they caught some Japanese soldiers who had built tunnels under palm trees and were sneaking into their camp at night and stealing the food."

On April 20, 1945, after having spent two years and ten months overseas, Payne was sent back to the United States. He received his discharge at Jefferson Barracks on June 9, 1945, after achieving the rank of Tech 3 and having earned four Bronze Service Stars for his participation in several major campaigns of the war. Shortly after the war ended, the veteran brought his fiancée from New Zealand to the United States, where the couple were soon married and went on to raise four children. Payne finished a career as a postal clerk in Jefferson City while also operating a farm near Russellville.

The veteran passed away in 1990, and his wife died fourteen years later; both were laid to rest in the cemetery of St. John's Lutheran Church in Stringtown, Missouri. His son recognizes that buried with his father were scores of military stories that can now only be pieced together through blurred recollection and military records.

"He would have nightmares about his service right up until he passed away," said Gary Payne. "I can remember the times working on the farm years ago when we'd be shoveling wheat into the bin, and I'd ask him about his service. He might share a little bit about what happened but never in great detail." He added, "At the time, I didn't think much about it, but as you get a little older, you want to know more about what your parents went through." Pausing, he concluded, "I know it's too late to be asking the question now, but it's nice to know that there are records that can help show what he did back in the war." *(Photograph courtesy of Gary Payne)*

William Kromer – *Jefferson City*

William Kromer mirthfully recalls that when graduating from high school in Lacrosse, Wisconsin, in the spring of 1944, he had entered the waiting game and fully realized the likelihood of being drafted into the military for WWII service. In preparation for this imminent circumstance, he made the decision to try to enlist in the U.S. Navy.

"When I went through all of the tests for the Navy, they found out I was color blind, and I couldn't enlist," said Kromer. "After that, I just waited until I was drafted, which wasn't too much longer," he chuckled.

The draftee became a member of the U.S. Army on September 27, 1944, and, following a brief period of induction at Fort Sheridan, Illinois, was sent to Camp Fannin, Texas, for basic infantry training. It was there, the veteran explained that he and scores of other young recruits had their training shortened because of events unfolding in Europe.

"When the Battle of the Bulge took place (beginning in mid-December 1944), they folded up our operation because they needed us overseas as replacements," Kromer recalled. "They shipped us out of New York on the *Queen Elizabeth*—nothing but first class all the way!" the veteran jokingly remarked of their spartan accommodations aboard the ship. He added, "There were so many people on the ship, they were only able to feed us twice a day, and it seemed like there was a continuous line of soldiers going through the chowline. The mess hall was actually set up in the area of the ship that had once been the swimming pool."

Arriving in Europe in mid-February 1945, the Battle of the Bulge had ended, but he and his fellow soldiers were soon traveling across France to meet up with various units in dire need of replacement soldiers. Kromer noted that he was quickly placed with Company G, 354th Infantry Regiment of the 89th Division, shortly after they had crossed the Mosselle River and were fighting their way toward the Rhine River.

"The night before I got to my new company, they had a couple of guys that had been killed in their foxholes by a (German) sniper," Kromer said. "After the captain told me that, I made sure that I was digging my foxhole as deep as I could go!" he affirmed.

As the 354th prepared to cross the Rhine during the latter part of March 1945, often under the camouflage of an acrid smokescreen or the cover of the evening's darkness, it was not enough to fully mitigate the persistent threat from German troops on the other side.

"We went across near St. Goarhausen on assault boats that were basically made out of plywood," Kromer explained. "There were about twelve men going across on each boat with two or three guys that took it back and forth." With perceptible heaviness, he added, "When I went across, one guy got shot in the ear, and another took a bullet in his shoulder."

When the Rhine crossing was finally accomplished—despite the occasional pockets of lingering resistance they continued to encounter—Kromer and his fellow soldiers sensed that the war was drawing near an end as the "opposition was kind of thinning out." The regiment soon made their movement into central Germany "through Wiesbaden and then east toward Frankfurt and onto the Frankfurt-Berlin autobahn," wrote an unidentified author in a regimental history distributed to the soldiers of the regiment after the war.

"We were in Zwickau, Germany, when the war ended," said Kromer. "Prior to this, we had been guarding a bridge into the town ... and the town was full of German soldiers." He noted, "As soon as the Germans got word that the war was over, they came to us to surrender, and there were so many turning themselves in that we couldn't handle it at first."

Throughout the weeks that followed, the veteran remained in Germany as part of the occupational forces and was scheduled to transfer to the South Pacific to help with the war against Japan; but when the atomic bombs were dropped in August 1945, and Japan surrendered, Kromer was sent to Styer, Austria to help guard prisoners of war.

"While I was over there, I tried to visit my grandparents who were living in Germany (Kromer's father was first-generation American)," he said. I got as close as seventy-five miles from them but they were living in a sector controlled by the Russians, so I never did get to see them."

In the summer of 1946, the veteran had earned enough points to return to the United States, and he received his discharge from the Army on July 26, 1946. In the years after the war, the veteran moved to Jefferson City, Missouri, married, helped raise three children, and worked more than forty years at the former Hotel Governor.

The Second World War was certainly one of the most exciting periods in Kromer's years of experiences, but rather than dwell on the fleeting moments of the time he spent in uniform many decades past, he chooses to view his service to the nation in a most humble, casual manner.

"I just figured that I had to fight for the country and try to survive to raise a family someday," he calmly admitted. "I was just one of many basic infantry guys over there taking orders and doing whatever they said to do." With a wry grin, he concluded, "I was lucky because there are several times that I could have been killed, I guess … if whoever we were fighting against knew how to shoot a little straighter."

The ninety-two-year-old veteran passed away on July 1, 2019, and is interred in Riverview Cemetery in Jefferson City. *(Photograph courtesy of William Kromer)*

James Rackers - *Taos*

Missouri veteran James Rackers may have received his draft notice after World War II officially concluded; however, his subsequent military experiences would carry him to both a historic Missouri military training site and to an overseas city that was decimated less than two years earlier by an atomic bomb that brought an end to the war in the Pacific. Raised near the community of Taos, Missouri, Rackers finished an eighth-grade education at nearby St. Francis Xavier School and spent the next few years helping his parents work their farm. The war came and went during this period, but the draft finally caught the young man and pulled him from his country surroundings.

"I had gotten a six-month deferment because of the farm work, but they finally got me," he recalled. "I was inducted into the U.S. Army in December 1945 at Ft. Leavenworth (Kansas), and then they sent me to Camp Crowder for training," he added.

Located near Neosho, Missouri, Camp Crowder is now a Missouri National Guard training site comprising more than 4,300 acres.

During WWII, it became a major Signal Corps training site that grew to encompass nearly 43,000 acres and, by some estimates, was home to more than 40,000 troops during the height of the war.

After completing his basic training at the southwest Missouri post, Rackers began a regimen of Signal Corps training as a lineman, learning to scale the poles to hang communications wires. But as his training progressed, he was assigned as a truck driver within the 3247th Signal Base Maintenance Company.

"We were only at (Camp) Crowder for a few months before they said they were going to shut down the camp since the war was over," said Rackers. "A lot of the barracks there were already sitting empty."

His company soon loaded trucks and convoyed to Camp Polk, Louisiana, where, Rackers explained, they were told they would be watching prisoners of war. Instead, they received orders a couple of weeks later, sending them to Ft. Dix, New Jersey.

"We weren't there very long ... just long enough to do some machine-gun training, if I remember correctly," Rackers said. "Then we got orders for Japan, and they sent us by bus to Grand Central Station in New York. From there," he continued, "we took a troop train all the way to Camp Stoneman in California."

A week following their arrival on the West Coast, Rackers and his fellow soldiers boarded troop ships, spending the next two weeks sailing for their destination of Yokohama, Japan. While aboard the ship, the young soldier recalls becoming "so seasick I thought I was going to die." Following their arrival in Japan in November 1946, where they were to serve as part of the occupational forces, Rackers was assigned to a U.S. Army camp situated near the base of Camp Fuji. As it became his duty during his stay at Camp Crowder, he served as a truck driver and began hauling many items to include fifty-gallon barrels of heating oil and lumber used for a specific purpose.

"There was a Japanese man living there who had actually been raised in the United States," said Rackers. "He owned a sawmill, and I would take a team of Japanese workers—many of them former Japanese soldiers—to pick up lumber at the sawmill and to bring it back to the camp."

The lumber, he went on to explain, was used to crate and package military equipment to be shipped back to the United States. Once completed, Rackers and his crew would then haul the crates to locations where they would be unloaded from his truck and loaded on waiting ships for final shipment overseas.

"Our camp was about twenty miles or so from Hiroshima, and we were able to visit the area and take photographs," he said. Little did he realize in the moment, his exposure would have lasting effects on his health and that of many of the soldiers with whom he served.

During the summer of 1947, the U.S. Army continued to trim down its force structure since the world was no longer at war. Rackers soon received notice that he would be returning home. In June 1947, he boarded a troop ship bound for Ft. Lawton, Washington, receiving his discharge from the military on August 6, 1947. He returned to the farm to help his father and was able to "save enough money to buy a tractor." In 1951, he married his fiancée, Mardell, and the couple went on to raise four children. Through hard work and perseverance, he and his wife have "made a decent living" by running their own farming operations.

Years have passed since his service in the U.S. Army ended, but the consequences of his overseas service emerged through respiratory problems he has developed, which are attributed to his exposure to ionizing radiation. Many of his fellow veterans have, sadly, passed from cancers and other related ailments from their own service near areas such as Hiroshima. The veteran has continued his service as a life member of the VFW, serving two terms as commander of his local post. When reflecting on his extensive past, Rackers affirms that moments from his brief time in the U.S. Army have never faded and are sculpted into his permanent memories.

"For a farm kid, I got to see a lot of the world and learned a lot of things that I didn't know when I left home for the Army," Rackers said. "Pausing, he added with a grin, "The one thing I sure do remember quite clearly is they didn't pay us a whole heck of a lot back then. I made a dollar a day. That's all I got. But it was all a valuable experience." *(Photograph courtesy of James Rackers)*

James D. Ellis – *Kansas City*

The period of World War II has left us with many stories of heroism, often that are associated with individuals so filled with patriotism and a voluntary spirit that they chose to serve their nation despite any obvious threats to their safety. Sadly, many of these bold personal narratives come with the death of the servicemember and loved ones left behind to mourn an unexpected loss. One such tale originates from Kansas City, Missouri, and describes James D. Ellis—the only member of the Missouri Highway Patrol to have lost his life while serving in the military. Though his passing is now decades in hindsight, it has inspired one organization to share his story and seek ways to honor his memory by beautifying his final resting site.

"Before entering the army … Captain (James) Ellis was in charge of the fingerprint department at the Lee's Summit highway patrol office and before that was stationed at the patrol's headquarters at Jefferson City," reported the *Maryville Daily Forum* on March 19, 1943.

Prior to his decision to enlist in the U.S. Army during World War II, Ellis served as a lieutenant with the Missouri National Guard's Battery D, 129th Field Artillery Regiment, which became known as "Truman's Own" since it was the regiment with whom President Harry S. Truman served during the First World War. Records obtained from the Missouri State Highway Patrol confirm that Ellis attended the patrol academy in 1935, followed by his assignment to General Headquarters in Jefferson City, where he was serving when he married the former Kathleen Hufflines in 1936.

The twenty-nine-year-old trooper was transferred to Lee's Summit in August 1937 and, less than three years later, made the decision to leave his position as a citizen/soldier with the Missouri National Guard to serve his country as an officer in the U.S. Army. Granted a leave of absence from his patrol duties on June 30, 1941, Ellis "was assigned to the Philippines and served in the field artillery," wrote retired Col. Fred M. Mills, former superintendent of the Missouri Highway Patrol.

Records accessed through the U.S. National Archives and Records Administration establish that Ellis was promoted to captain and assigned to the 88th Field Artillery Regiment. The regiment, as noted in the book *World War II Order of Battle* by Shelby L. Stanton, was "partially activated at Ft. Stotsenberg, Philippines," on April 19, 1941.[104]

Trevor Nevitt Dupuy's book *Asiatic Land Battles: Japanese Ambitions in the Pacific* summarizes the horrid struggle that soon ensued in the Philippines. As Dupuy explained, by December 1941, "[General] MacArthur's force consisted of 13,000 American troops, plus 12,000 excellent Filipino soldiers ... (and a) Philippine Commonwealth Army [that] consisted of about 100,000 (poorly trained) men." The Japanese were focused on capturing Luzon, the principal island of the Philippines, and as Dupy further explained, they had "nearly 60,000

---

[104] Stanton, *World War II Order of Battle*, 376.

combat troops (and were) supported by the powerful Japanese Third Fleet." [105]

Former Trooper Ellis, now an artillery officer in the U.S. Army, would experience the nightmare that quickly followed. On December 8, 1941—the day after much of the U.S. fleet was crippled at Pearl Harbor—Japanese planes destroyed many American aircraft during an attack of Clark Field, Luzon. A couple of days later, Japanese landings began on the northern coast of Luzon.

Overwhelmed by the violent Japanese assaults and lacking adequate reinforcements, U.S. troops soon had to withdraw south toward Bataan. In the coming weeks, supplies began to diminish, and the lack of food weakened those who struggled to keep up the fight. On April 3, 1942, the Japanese launched their final attack and, on April 9, 1942, the 88th Field Artillery Regiment along with the other American forces surrendered.

Much has been written about the "Bataan Death March" that followed, during which hundreds of Allied survivors were forced to march in sweltering heat to prisons in Manila. Though much suffering occurred during this timeframe, Ellis, who was wounded in combat prior to the surrender, "remained behind on Bataan in a Japanese prisoner of war camp at Cabcaben, which also served as a field hospital," explained James Erickson.

"A file from the National Archives and Records Administration indicates Ellis later died from malaria on October 16, 1942, in Ward 12—the officer's ward—of the Cabanatuan #1 POW camp hospital," explained Erickson, whose own father, Capt. Albert Erickson was held in the same ward during a portion of his three and a half years of imprisonment by the Japanese. He added, "I do not know that my father and Capt. Ellis knew one another, but it seems probable."

---

[105] Dupuy, *Asiatic Land Battles: Japanese Ambitions in the Pacific*, 13.

The Sunday News and Tribune reported on July 11, 1943, "Capt. J.D. Ellis, formerly fingerprint expert of the Highway Patrol in Jefferson City, died in a Japanese prison camp according to word received here yesterday by friends,"

The artillery officer's body was eventually returned to the United States and interred in Floral Hills Cemetery in Raytown, Missouri. His wife, with whom he never had any children and who never remarried, passed away in 1986 and is buried in the Lee's Summit Historical Cemetery.

Fred Mills is a past president of the Missouri Association of State Troopers Emergency Relief Society (MASTERS)—a benevolent fund that provides aid to a trooper's immediate surviving family member (wife or husband) and children if he or she is killed in the line of duty. As he explained, MASTERS wishes to honor Ellis's memory by connecting with any relatives to work together to improve and maintain the trooper's gravesite.

"We feel that it is important that Trooper Ellis' story becomes a permanent part of the Patrol's history," Mills said. "It is our wish to honor his unselfish service for not just maintaining, but living the Patrol's motto of 'Service and Protection.' MASTERS was formed in 1979 with the commitment to support the families of troopers who died in the line of duty, and while Ellis's death was not a Patrol line-of-duty death, he is the only trooper to have died while on military leave." Mills added, "As such, we feel that we have a moral responsibility to honor his sacrifice and work toward providing a grave marker that recognizes both his Patrol and military service." *(Photograph courtesy of the Missouri State Highway Patrol)*

Richard Carroll – *Jefferson City*

Within the small community of Chariton, Iowa, in the spring of 1942, a seventeen-year-old Richard Carroll approached his parents in the weeks after graduating high school with a patriotic appeal—for them to grant him the permission to enlist in the United States Marine Corps and serve his nation in World War II.

"I had an older brother in the Navy, one in the Army, and the other was on the draft list getting ready to be called up," Carroll recalled. Grinning, he added, "I guess I decided to go into the Marines because I wanted to do something different than my brothers."

Achieving the blessing of his parents, the young Iowa man traveled to Des Moines and became a Marine recruit on July 27, 1942. A few days later, he reported to San Diego to begin several weeks of basic training.

"We spent about a week on the rifle ranges at a place called Camp Elliott," said the veteran. "I didn't do so well on the range because all we had in our family was a .22 rifle, but we could never afford to buy the shells for it. In fact, there, at Camp Elliott, was the first time I ever fired a weapon."

Early in his enlistment, Carroll indicated he had wanted to serve in the tank corps; however, in late September 1942, he was sent to a mustering station at North Island (San Diego Bay), where he was informed that he would receive training as an aviation machinist mate. The young Marine arrived at the former Naval Air Technical Training Center in Norman, Oklahoma. It was here that he was first exposed to the world of aviation, spending the next three months learning to repair and maintain the aircraft being used by the Marine Corps in the Pacific.

"I discovered that there are a lot of parts on an airplane," Carroll laughed. "That's where I first learned about the nine-cylinder Wright (Whirlwind) engines—I didn't know an engine could have an odd number of cylinders before I got to that school," he added.

In early January 1943, he briefly returned to North Island before boarding a troop ship destined for New Caledonia—an island grouping in the South Pacific. He remained there for the next three weeks where, instead of performing aviation work, he helped spray-paint buildings on the base.

"They finally sent me to the New Hebrides and assigned me to the headquarters squadron for the 1st Marine Aircraft Wing," he recalled. "One of the most profound things I remember is about a month after I arrived, a plane came in and landed that looked like a seagull; it was the first F4U (Corsair) assigned to the squadron."

Since he was new to the squadron, Carroll was not given the authority to work on any aircraft and instead spent the first several weeks of his assignment supporting the aircrews by delivering supplies and maintenance equipment to wherever it was needed.

"One day, the line chief came up to me and asked if I had ever worked on a dual-engine aircraft," he explained. "I said 'no,' because I've never even been close to one before."

Despite his lack of experience, Carroll was assigned crew chief for the Douglas DC-3 (dual-propeller airplane) used by General John T. Moore, who at the time was serving simultaneously as chief of staff of the 1st Marine Aircraft Wing and Marine Air South Pacific.

"I did the job as crew chief for more than a year and had full responsibility for the plane to make sure it was ready to go whenever the general needed to fly somewhere, which included places like Australia and Guadalcanal," Carroll said. "When we returned from a flight, I would ensure the plane was fueled and checked that all necessary repairs were performed."

Following a one-month furlough back in the states in August 1944, the young Marine returned to San Diego and was then sent to Memphis, Tennessee, for several weeks of training to learn to work on dive-bombers. From there, he was sent back to San Diego and boarded a troop ship bound for a second overseas assignment.

"This time I was sent to Mindanao in the Philippines and placed in a dive-bomber squadron," he said. "While I was there, they told us to get our things packed and loaded us on an LST (landing ship tank) that was going to take us to China."

Surviving a typhoon during which their LST sustained damage, Carroll arrived in Sing Tao, China, only days before the war with Japan ended. It was here, he recalled, that he saw his first and only Japanese soldier, who had been captured and imprisoned by locals. The military soon began the process of discharging personnel since there was no longer a war to fight, and Carroll was sent home in

December 1945, receiving his discharge in San Diego several weeks later.

Returning to Iowa, he soon married the former Cumalene Wood, whom he had met prior to the war. The veteran earned his law degree from Drake University by utilizing his veteran's benefits and later moved to Jefferson City, where he was employed as legal counsel in the insurance industry. The father to a son and daughter, Carroll has enjoyed retirement since 1994. The years have revealed to Carroll many benefits yielded from his time in military service during World War II—one of the most important, he affirms, being the determination to see things through to the end.

"I was shocked when they told me I was going to school for aviation maintenance and not the tank corps, but it all worked out," he said. "It was a great experience for me, and it taught me that whatever needed to be done, to go ahead and get it done." He added, "That' the reason I ended up in law school and despite the difficulties I may have experienced there, the military had instilled in me that I was going to do it right and finish what I started." *(Photograph courtesy of Richard Carroll)*

James Thompson – *Marshall*

Growing up diagnosed with dyslexia, James Thompson faced many challenges in his early learning experiences, which tempered his ambitions toward pursuing an education in future years. Additionally, while in the eleventh grade in the fall of 1944, he received his draft notice and believed it to be the end of any formal education; instead, the military later provided the spirit and resources to earn a master's degree.

"I was eighteen years old when I received my draft notice for the U.S. Army and left Columbia by bus on October 20 (1944)," said the veteran. "When we arrived at Jefferson Barracks (St. Louis), we were given another physical, issued our uniforms, and the next morning put on a train to Camp Crowder."

For the next few weeks, he underwent his basic training followed by lineman training, instruction as a radio operator, and cryptographic training.

"The first sergeant came and got me and said there's a guy (in civilian clothes) who wants to interview you," Thompson said. "After that, I was in the Office of Strategic Services (OSS)—the forerunner to the Central Intelligence Agency (CIA)," he added.

Serving as "the first organized effort by the United States to implement a centralized system of strategic intelligence and the predecessor (to the CIA)," the OSS was established on June 13, 1942, and conducted many covert functions such as receiving and decoding enemy communications, noted the website of the OSS Society.

In the summer of 1945, Thompson received orders for overseas service but was first given several days leave back home. He then took a train to California and, from there, sailed aboard a troop ship to the island of Eniwetok. His journey ended with his arrival at Clark Air Base in the Philippines, where he spent the next several months as a cryptographer.

"The OSS was disbanded because the war was over," said Thompson. "I can remember that in late November 1945, there were about six of us transferred from the Philippines to Tokyo, Japan, at the headquarters of General Douglas MacArthur who was there as oversight for the occupational forces."

The veteran explained that he was part of a group that processed messages sent to and from Sixth Army and MacArthur's headquarters. While there, he was later promoted to sergeant and placed in charge of the code room, which had the responsibility of decoding message traffic. While in Japan, his enlistment expired but he chose to remain there as a civilian to continue the work he enjoyed at McArthur's headquarters. However, in June 1947, he returned to the United States and was able to enroll in college at the University of Missouri despite having not completed his high school education a few years earlier.

"In 1951, I earned my bachelor's degree in psychology," recalled Thompson. "While I was at MU, I was informed that since I had held the rank of sergeant in the Army, I could complete one semester of ROTC and qualify for commission as a second lieutenant in the Air Force upon graduation."

The former soldier began his Air Force career as an officer when assigned to Bangor, Maine, administering entrance exams for new recruits and draftees. It was here that he met the former Barbara Longfellow while taking courses at the University of Maine and the two soon married. The couple went on to raise three sons. From there, he was briefly transferred to Tinker Air Force Base in Oklahoma before receiving assignment to Wheelus Air Base in Tripoli, Libya, spending time as an administrative officer for the 580th Air Materiel Assembly Squadron.

"I became the adjutant for the base administrative officer at Selfridge Field (Michigan) in 1959," he explained. "I made captain while I was there and became the administrative officer and later the commander for the 753rd Radar Station at Sault St. Maria, Michigan."

He would later attend the first class of the Defense Intelligence Agency in Washington D.C., as the various military service branches learned to combine their intelligence gathering capabilities. From 1962 to 1966, he was stationed in Ramstein, Germany, gathering intelligence on the Soviet air capabilities. In Germany, he took courses through the University of Southern California, earning his master's degree in systems management. He was then transferred to Little Rock, Arkansas, for a year, followed by his assignment to Vietnam. During the war, he was stationed in Nha Trang and briefed pilots prior to their aerial missions.

"I was given my base of choice when returning to the states in 1969, so I chose Whiteman Air Force Base," said Thompson. "I spent the last few months of my career there and retired as a major with twenty years, one month, and one day of service," he grinned.

His military career, he explained, was a collection of unique experiences that did not follow a linear path. As a child, he further noted, he would never have imagined the opportunity for advanced education or the option of pursuing his interest of becoming a member of the military.

"When I was younger, the military was something I always wanted to do, and I never believed I could join the Army or Air Force because of my dyslexia," he said. "My ambitions weren't all that high as a child, but then I was drafted. I encountered people who I admired and inspired me to achieve." He concluded, "When it was all said and done, I not only got to serve both in the Army and Air Force but this young man," he said, pointing to himself, "who didn't finish high school, was able to earn a master's degree ... all because of the military." *(Photograph courtesy of James Thompson)*

Central Missouri Women's Post 496 – *Jefferson City*

When the American Legion was established in 1919, it offered membership to women who served in various military support roles during World War I, such as those who toiled in Europe as Army nurses. Additionally, wives and daughters of veterans were extended membership in the organization's auxiliary. In the years that followed, however, groups of women veterans in communities throughout the United States began banding together to form their own American Legion posts.

"The Central Missouri Women's Post No. 496, The American Legion, held a banquet on Thursday evening at the Governor Hotel commemorating its first anniversary," reported the August 24, 1947 edition of the *Sunday News and Tribune*. "This Post, which is composed entirely of ex-service women, was presented its temporary charter in September 1946 …"

Records maintained by the American Legions Post 5 in Jefferson City indicate the women's post held their first meeting on August 21,

1946, and, during a ceremony on December 11, 1946, installed their first group of post officers. Beulah (Marche) Means, who served as a corporal with the Marine Corps in World War II, became the post's first commander. Months later, on April 14, 1947, the post received its permanent charter and began holding its monthly meetings at the home of the Roscoe Enloe American Legion Post 5 at 111 Madison Street, which is now the site of the Cole County Historical Society Museum. The Central Missouri Women's Post 496 was preceded in birth by the St. Louis Women's Post 404 in St. Louis, which was established in the early months of 1946. Post 404 remains an active organization in the St. Louis community and surrounding areas.

"Miss Louise Davidson, 38 years old, 1109 West Miller Avenue, Jefferson City, was killed Friday when the automobile she was driving struck a machine driven by Harry Leedman ... Webster Groves," noted the *St. Louis Post-Dispatch* on March 7, 1954.

Davidson, one of the founders and charter members of Post 496 in Jefferson City, was a native of Hartsburg, a veteran of the Women's Army Corps in World War II, and employed as a clerk with the Missouri Department of Health at the time of her death. In recognition of Davidson's contributions to the post, state, and nation, her fellow veterans submitted a request to the American Legion Department of Missouri to have the post renamed in honor of their departed friend. On August 6, 1954, approximately five months after her passing, the Central Missouri Women's Post 496 was officially re-designated the Louise E.M. Davidson Post 496.

Throughout the next several years, the post remained actively involved in the community, hosting concerts at the former Simonsen Auditorium with famous recording artists of the period to include Hank Snow and Ernest Tubbs. The women of the post also participated in Memorial Day ceremonies and raised money for such causes as the purchase of crutches for individuals afflicted with polio. Declining participation and membership, the death knell of many an organization, brought the demise of Post 496 a little more than two decades after its post-World War II origins.

"The Louise E. M. Davidson Post No. 496 ... voluntarily returned their Charter to Department Headquarters and requested that it be canceled, so that their members would be free to transfer their membership to Roscoe Enloe Post No. 5 in Jefferson City," noted a letter dated November 7, 1967, from Aubrey W. Sullivan, adjutant for The American Legion Department of Missouri. In the letter, Sullivan further explained to the members of the disbanded post, "The Charter was submitted to and canceled by the National Executive Committee, in session, on October 19, 1967."

Many women who were members of the erstwhile post became actively involved in other American Legion posts throughout the Central Missouri area, contributing their talents and efforts to continue to help with initiatives in their communities.

A number of years would pass, however, before a woman veteran would lead the organization on the national level. On August 24, 2017, during the 99th national convention of the American Legion held in Reno, Nevada, Denise Rohan, a U.S. Army veteran from Wisconsin, was elected national commander for the organization's two million members. Although Central Missouri no longer boasts a women's American Legion post, others have sprung up throughout Missouri in recent years to include Heartland Women Veterans Post 1107 in Independence and Women Veterans of Southwest Missouri Post 1214 in Springfield. Despite the loss of their post due to waning membership, many members of the former Louise E. M. Davidson Post No. 496 in Jefferson City transferred to the local Roscoe Enloe Post 5, bringing with them a dedication to serve and support their fellow veterans, regardless of gender.

In the January 1921 edition of the *California Legion Monthly*, Minnie Allen penned an article titled "The Women's Work in the Legion." In her writing, she stressed that ex-servicewomen (of World War I) should "make it known to the public that they served and made sacrifices" while also working with their male counterparts to progress the Legion mission of assisting all veterans in need. The time is past when women are to have honorary offices only. They must be efficient, active members—alive to their responsibility. It truly behooves every one of us to inform ourselves on the work of the Legion." Allen added, "Look around in your own post and watch for your opportunity to help." [106] *(Photograph courtesy of American Legion Post 5)*

---

[106] Allen, *California Legion Monthly*, 16.

Jack Sandwith – *Slater*

There are a number of reasons an individual might choose to enlist in the military—a sense of duty, money for college, or the pursuit of a career. Regardless, Jack Sandwith explained that his own decision to enter the military in the heat of World War II was at the behest of his two older brothers, both of whom were drafted.

"My two older brothers were preparing to leave for the service and told me to come with them on a little vacation," Sandwith grinned. "They then instructed me to say that I wanted to be in the infantry so that we could all serve together."

Making the decision to leave during his junior year of high school in Baxter Springs, Kansas, the aspiring soldier enlisted in the U.S. Army but soon discovered that even the best of plans may undergo unexpected changes.

"Somebody decided that all of us brothers probably shouldn't all be serving together," he said. "They placed one of my brothers in the Marines, one in the Air Force, and they kept me in the Army," he chuckled.

The seventeen-year-old arrived at Camp McCain in Grenada, Mississippi, in December 1942, where he underwent several weeks of basic training. While there, he was assigned to the 149th Combat Engineer Battalion and soon traveled to Ft. Pierce, Florida, for amphibious maneuvers.

"While we were training in Florida, they would take us out three miles or so and put us in rubber boats," said Sandwith. "We would then try to make an assault on Ft. Pierce as part of our exercises," he added.

The young men of the battalion then traveled to Camp Pickett, Virginia, receiving an introduction to the type of assaults they were to perform on the beaches of Normandy the following year. It was here the soldiers participated in two mock amphibious invasions aboard landing craft in the Chesapeake Bay. Days after Christmas 1943, the battalion boarded troop ships at Camp Kilmer, New Jersey, and became part of a large convoy that zigzagged across the Atlantic Ocean for several days. Destined to join the battle raging in Europe, they arrived in Liverpool, England, and continued their training by performing maneuvers along the English coast.

"We then ended up moving up to Peyton, England—south of London—where groups of us lived in homes with local residents," said Sandwith. "That's basically where we stayed until the invasion," he sagely recalled.

Scores of accounts exist that chronicle the horrors of D-Day, much of which was experienced by Sandwith on that fateful morning of June 6, 1944. Arriving at Omaha Beach by landing craft with the first wave of troops, the veteran noted that the opening stages of the planned assault were less than glorious.

"It was low tide when we came in, and our landing craft ran aground," said Sandwith. "We had a company of men on board, and the back gate would not come down to let us off." Solemnly, he added, "When we jumped off the craft, we dropped into twelve feet of water, and I had to cut off the stuff I was carrying to keep from drowning."

The bodies of dead American soldiers were strewn throughout the water and along the beach, but Sandwith made it to shore through the crossfire of German machine guns. He navigated through a minefield by using a path worn in the sand and followed a trail up the cliffs of Normandy, where he and other troops began clearing out German machine gun emplacements. When he paused from the action, he noticed his boot was full of blood and later discovered he was shot through the ankle. A medic wrapped the wound, and Sandwith continued in his battlefield service, later receiving his first Purple Heart for the injury.

"When we began pushing toward Germany, I would help clear minefields," said Sandwith. "I used a flamethrower to burn the grass off the minefields, and then you could see the patterns of the mines the Germans had laid out." He added, "Once we knew where they were, we could neutralize them."

In April 1945, following his company's crossing of the Rhine River, Sandwith and two of his fellow soldiers sought shelter in an old building after they came under attack by German mortars. When mortars struck the building, his fellow soldiers were killed while Sandwith was blown through a window.

"I spent seven-and-a-half months in the hospital and lost my left eye because of that incident," he said. "That became my second and final Purple Heart."

Receiving his discharge from the Army at Camp Chaffee, Arkansas, in 1946, the former soldier completed a fascinating career building levees in Holland that had been damaged from the war, constructing dams throughout the United States and later assisting in the construction of a water reservoir in Colorado.

The widowed father of five children notes that even if "mayhem" seems most aptly to characterize his time in World War II, he realizes it was a collection of frenetic events never again to be experienced.

"I had never been in a situation like that in my life, and we sure encountered some tough fighting," he affirmed. "I was just a young kid who had a machine gun in his hands." With a grin, he concluded, "I was only 5' 5" when I went in and weighed about 105 pounds. Honestly, I didn't think I could do much more than shoot a gun. I just wanted to help—that's all." *(Photograph courtesy of Jack Sandwith)*

Hubert Rothove – *Folk*

A twenty-year-old Hubert Rothove left his father's farm near the Osage County community of Folk to travel to the county seat of Westphalia on June 30, 1942, registering with his local draft board. After doing so, he returned to his work on the family farm and continued dating the former Regina Brendel, a friend of his sister that he had met when attending a picnic in nearby Rich Fountain. Like many a young man, he carried in his mind plans for the future; but as the months passed and he busied himself tending livestock and assisting in the cultivation of crops, any ideas he possessed were placed on hold when he received his notice to report to Jefferson Barracks for his pre-induction physical.

"When World War II erupted, his life changed forever when he was inducted into active service with the U.S. Army on January 4, 1943," stated his daughter, Marla Markway.

Although much of the veteran's experiences remain something of a mystery since he is now deceased, Rothove's family has pieced together sections of his military experience using notes from soldiers who served in the same battalion as their father in addition to brief conversations he shared with his children decades ago. Following his induction, the first several weeks of Rothove's military service were spent at Ft. Eustis, Virginia, for basic training with an anti-aircraft battalion. From there, he went on to complete several weeks of instruction as a cannoneer at Camp Stewart, Georgia, learning to operate a halftrack and other military vehicles under combat conditions.

"When he finished his training and just before he deployed overseas, they gave him a little bit of leave, and he returned home and married our mother on July 27, 1943, at Holy Family Church in Freeburg," explained Marla Markway.

Assigned to Battery B, 467th Anti-Aircraft Artillery (AAA) Automatic Weapons Battalion, Rothove returned to Camp Stewart following his wedding, where his battalion loaded their halftracks on railcars. Traveling to the Desert Training Center in California, it was here they underwent several months of training with the Ninth Armored Division.

"Records we've found show they were sent to Camp Pickett, Virginia, for amphibious training, said Paul Rothove, one of the veteran's sons. "Then they were sent to Ft. Dix, New Jersey, to prepare for their shipment overseas aboard the *Esperance Bay* (an English freighter built in Scotland in 1922)," he added.

Discharge papers reveal Rothove arrived in England on January 31, 1944 and, for the next few months, conducted amphibious training and target practice in locations throughout the English countryside. On June 1, 1944, they left their marshalling area and boarded landing craft in preparation to cross the English Channel for the most famed beach landing of the war.

"We couldn't estimate how far from shore we were, but at 07:00 a.m. (on June 6, 1944, D-Day), a boat pulled near and again a man with a megaphone yelled at us: Go on in, good luck," wrote Hyman Haas, a sergeant with Battery A, 467th AAA. "Well, that started us off," he added. "We began our run onto Omaha Beach."

Paul Rothove recalled, "Many years ago, when I was around ten or twelve years old, it was the anniversary of D-Day, and my father came home early from work and mentioned that back during the war, his halftrack took a shell during the landing, and because of the damage, he received a new halftrack the next day. That was about the only time I recall him speaking to us about his service."

With the chaos and the carnage of the D-Day landings soon behind them, the battalion began a determined advance toward Germany, functioning primarily as mechanized infantry. They eventually broke out of Normandy but continued to encounter fierce resistance. When the Battle of the Bulge unfolded a few months later, they helped in defense of the city of Luxembourg and later Bastogne.

"His unit was essentially converted to infantry during the Bulge, and after it was over, they returned to an anti-aircraft capacity," said Paul Rothove.

The battalion's half-tracks provided anti-aircraft defenses for several river crossings, including the capture of a critical bridge at Remagen, Germany, in mid-March 1945. Later the same month, the battalion helped liberate U.S. prisoners held at an airport in Frankfurt, Germany, and shortly thereafter witnessed more devastation when U.S. forces liberated Dachau concentration camp. When the war ended in May 1945, Rothove's battalion remained in Europe for several months, performing occupational duties such as border patrols. On December 23, 1945, the twenty-three-year-old veteran received his discharge and reunited with his wife in Osage County. He and his wife moved to St. Louis where he graduated from Ranken Institute of Technology before moving to Jefferson City.

"My father was the sole owner of Rothove Construction Company and built houses for about ten years," said his daughter, Marla Markway. "He later became a journeyman electrician and worked for Capital City Electric Company," she added.

The father of four sons and two daughters, Rothove passed away from a massive heart attack in 1983 when only sixty years old and was laid to rest in Resurrection Cemetery in Jefferson City. When asked of the significance of her father's World War II service to their family, Marla Markway explained, "He rarely mentioned his experiences in the Army, but he experienced a deep camaraderie with his fellow soldiers—it was a bond that was meaningful, and they continued to support one another in the decades after the war."

Rothove's son, Paul, added, "If you don't write things down, such as our father's military experiences, the living memory disappears with the person. That's why it is important to keep records because it is the only way we can understand their sacrifices and learn from history." *(Photograph courtesy of Marla Markway)*

Paul Hofius – *Jefferson City*

Paul Hofius possesses an impressive family legacy of military service dating back to the Revolutionary War and including later conflicts such as the War of 1812, the Civil War, and World War I. Many of his relatives were compelled into military service because of their country's call to arms—an obligation that led to Hofius' own service in the U.S. Navy during the waning days of World War II.

"I received my draft notice (in 1945) after beginning my senior year at Sharpsville High School in Pennsylvania," said the veteran. "I decided to go ahead and enlist in the Navy since my family used to visit Lake Eerie, and I liked being around the water," he added.

After graduating in late spring 1946, Hofius was sent to boot camp at Bainbridge, Maryland, and from there received assignment to the USS *John W. Weeks*—an Allen M. Sumner-class destroyer named for a former Secretary of War. When arriving at his new duty station, Hofius was among a group of newly trained sailors questioned by a chief boatswain's mate whether any of them knew how to type.

Although none immediately admitted they possessed such ability, a fellow sailor professed that Hofius had such skills.

"I guess it all worked out because they assigned me to administrative tasks in the ship's office for my duty," he grinned.

The USS *John W. Weeks* remained in port at Charleston, South Carolina, and on January 1, 1947, was assigned to a new destroyer squadron. Five weeks later, the ship sailed to the Naval Ammunition Depot in North Charleston to take on ammunitions for use in various maneuvers and tactical exercises in the Atlantic during the weeks that followed.

"It was after World War II had ended, and many of the experienced sailors were already discharged," he said. "There were a lot of new sailors with no experience, and these exercises were used to teach them their duties."

As Hofius recalled, their homeport was changed from the Naval Minecraft Base in Charleston to the Naval Repair Base in New Orleans in March 1947. Since their new base was located 321 miles up the river, it was a leisurely journey to the Gulf of Mexico and back since they had to travel slowly as not to create large wakes on the shoreline.

"The skipper of our ship was a very interesting officer," explained the former sailor. "During one inspection of the ship's firemen, he walked by the sailors who were standing in a line along the deck, stopped in front of each sailor, and then threw their sailor's hat overboard." Shaking his head, Hofius concluded, "He never explained why he did it, but they all seemed to think their hats were either too small or in bad condition."

During the summer months, the USS *John W. Weeks* participated in a number of two-week training cruises to locations such as Jamaica and Cuba to help train Naval Reservists. In late 1947, Hofius was detailed to work for the commander of the Destroyer Division 162 and was transferred to the destroyer USS *Wallace L. Lind*.

"While working for the commander on the Lind, I did a lot of clerical duties such as recordkeeping," he said.

His two-year commitment ended when he was sent to U.S. Naval Air Station at Pensacola, Florida, receiving his discharge in June 1948. While there, he was encouraged to join the Inactive Naval Reserve for four years after being advised that if another war broke out, he would maintain his rate (career field) and be the last recalled to service.

"I had returned to Pennsylvania and was working at a local Westinghouse plant when the Korean War broke out," Hofius explained. "I was recalled into the Navy, and I did maintain my rate, but I was not one of the last called back to active duty."

Returning to active duty on April 20, 1951, he reported to the Naval Air Station in Norfolk, Virginia, where he spent the next seventeen months processing discharges, enlistment extensions, and reenlistments for enlisted personnel. Following his discharge on September 16, 1952, he returned to Pennsylvania and enrolled in college.

"I married my fiancée, Noreen, in 1953, and I went on to earn my degree in industrial management through Ohio State University," he said. "I have to say, I was glad to have been in the service because it made it much easier to get an education, and it paid for virtually my entire degree."

As the years passed, Hofius and his wife raised five children while he went on to complete a lengthy career with the Westinghouse Corporation. His employment eventually resulted in his transfer to Jefferson City, where he retired in 1988. The years have been filled with many wonderful experiences for the veteran, but more recently, in 2017, he encountered a resurgence of memories related to his military service during a Central Missouri Honor Flight trip.

"Initially, I was hesitant to go on the Honor Flight but was encouraged to do so by friends and family—and I am glad that I went!" he exclaimed. "It was really worthwhile to travel to Washington, D.C., and see all the war memorials, and it brought back a lot of memories for me." With a broad grin, he added, "One of the best parts of the Honor Flight was being there … seeing all the sites with those who had also served. Being in their company during those moments we visited the memorials was truly something special." *(Photograph courtesy of Paul Hofius)*

Vernon Sommerer – *St. Louis*

As the sixth of twelve children growing up on a farm in rural Cole County, the world once appeared mighty small to Vernon Sommerer during the harsh and unforgiving days of the Great Depression. But in 1946, his view of global affairs changed with the intense lessons that came while serving as a guard for the war crimes trials in Japan after World War II. The nineteen-year-old Sommerer was inducted into the U.S. Army at Jefferson Barracks on April 29, 1946, but was soon transferred to another military post because of an unanticipated supply shortage.

"They didn't have any uniforms for us at Jefferson Barracks, so they shipped us over to Ft. Leavenworth, Kansas, to get uniforms," the veteran recalled. "Since I had been assigned to armor [tanks], they sent me to Ft. Knox (Kentucky) for six weeks of armored basic training."

When his initial training was completed in early summer, he returned home for a brief period of leave, assisting with the threshing on the family farm. He then reported to Ft. Lawton, a former U.S. Army post located in Seattle, where he remained for several weeks awaiting his next duty assignment.

"I finally got orders for overseas service and took a troop ship to Yokohama, Japan," Sommerer said. "Just like the Army, even though I had trained in the armor, they assigned me to the 720th Military Police Battalion in Tokyo, and then I was detached to the War Ministry Building, where they were holding the International Military Tribunal for the Far East (IMTFE)."

Sommerer went on to explain that the "Far East" designation was for the trials convened in Japan following the conclusion of the proceedings held in Nuremburg, Germany. For the next several months, he would live and work in the War Ministry Building while former Japanese military and political leaders were prosecuted for crimes committed during WWII.

"We were placed on four shifts at the War Ministry Building," recalled Sommerer. "There were two-day shifts and two-night shifts, each one of which was six hours." He added, "There was another group of military police who would transfer those being prosecuted from the courts at the War Ministry Building to nearby Sugamo Prison, where they were held when not on trial."

As the veteran went on to explain, Sugamo Prison was where Hideki Tojo—who served as Prime Minister of Japan during World War II—was hanged on December 23, 1948, after being condemned and sentenced to death by the IMTFE. Sommerer further noted that although his military service unfolded after the end of the war, he and many of his fellow soldiers were exposed to depressing and unexpected circumstances caused by a disease that has since been eradicated in the United States.

"One of our company commanders, a fine young man who was probably in his thirties, had been assigned to our outfit for several months when his wife and his several children made it over to Japan." With a sad pause, he added, "He then came down with polio and lived about a week. It is a reminder that we as a country have much to be thankful for, and polio is not one of our worries."

When there was a break in court proceedings, the accused, such as Shigenori Tōgō, the former Minister of Foreign Affairs for Japan during WWII, were escorted by military policemen to a prisoner holding room where they received their noon meal and visited with their family. Tōgō was later convicted of war crimes and died in Sugamo Prison in 1950 while serving a twenty-year sentence.

During his overseas service, Sommerer met Dr. Kobashi, a Japanese man who had earned his medical degree while living in the United States prior to the war. Since the Japanese medical community did not recognize his medical credentials from the states, he was employed as a translator after the war.

"Dr. Kobashi and I became close friends, and we bummed around together during our free time," said Sommerer. "I recall one time when he brought his daughter to meet me, who was a school teacher, and then asked me right in front of her if I'd marry her." He added, "I wasn't able to think of anything to say ... I was too shocked."

Silence may have been the saving grace for the young soldier since they never married.

In late September 1947, he departed Japan aboard a troop ship, returning to the U.S. after having completed his military commitment. When the ship arrived in San Francisco Harbor in the late afternoon, the personnel onshore responsible for processing returning troops stated it was too close to their quitting time.

"We had to spend another night aboard the ship and wait until the next morning to process out of the military," said Sommerer. "They pulled the ship far enough away from shore so that no one would be tempted to jump ship and swim to shore," he chuckled.

Receiving his discharge on October 4, 1947, the veteran returned briefly to Mid-Missouri before moving to St. Louis, where he went on to marry, raise one daughter and complete a thirty-nine-year career with General Motors. When discussing his service in a country which, only months prior to his arrival, had been an avowed enemy of the United States, Sommerer acknowledges the intensity of the experiences were quite memorable for a young man coming from an insulated farm community in rural Missouri.

"The situation during the war crimes trials in Japan was much different than it had been during the war—the political climate was completely different," he said. "You would have expected the Japanese people to have hated us, but they were very kind, cordial, and welcoming to us soldiers." He added, "I had a lot of fun and interesting times while I was there and enjoyed the entire experience." *(Photograph courtesy of Vernon Sommerer.)*

CHAPTER 4
KOREA & VIETNAM

Gerald Westfall - *Jacksonville*

Gerald Westfall proudly points to a row of framed photographs hanging on a wall behind him—an impressive demonstration of his family's legacy of military service. It is a story that includes a great-grandfather who died from Civil War injuries, his father who served with the U.S. Army in WWI, a brother killed while serving with the U.S. Air Force in 1967, and, more recently, the service of his sons, both of whom are Air Force veterans. This heritage, he explained, includes his own enlistment with the Air Force during the period of the Korean War. Raised on a farm near the community of Lone Tree, Iowa, Westfall graduated from high school in 1947 and began working on his father's farm. Three years later, in December 1950, he recognized the likelihood of being drafted into the military.

"With the Korean War going on, I realized I didn't want to be drafted into the Marines or Army and have to sleep on the ground," he grinned. "Instead, I decided to enlist in the Air Force."

Inducted at Cedar Rapids, Iowa, on December 27, 1950, the twenty-one-year-old farmhand boarded a train and traveled to Lackland Air Force Base in Texas to complete his basic training.

"Our boot camp was supposed to have been two months long, but with the thousands of troops coming through there for training, it was cut down to only four weeks so they could get us all through," he recalled. "Close order drill is really about all I learned while I was there."

He was then sent to nearby Ft. Sam Houston in San Antonio for a U.S. Army-hosted medical training program. During the two months of training that followed, Westfall qualified as a surgical technician, learning various emergency procedures, the operating room, and sterilization techniques.

"They must have just pulled my name out of a hat because I don't know how I was selected for (medical training)," Westfall mused. "I guess that's just where they thought I belonged because I sure didn't have that kind of background."

In early April 1951, he received orders for overseas service, but not for Korea, where the war was in full swing. Instead, he boarded a troop ship and crossed the North Atlantic to Bremerhaven, Germany. From there, he processed through a Replacement Depot and was sent to Royal Air Force (RAF) Burtonwood. Located north of Warrington, England, the former RAF Burtonwood was once the largest military airfield in Europe and was transferred to the U.S. Army Air Forces in 1942. When the Air Force was founded in 1947, they assumed control of the base for nearly two decades.

"I went to work in the hospital, and it was really a great assignment," Westfall affirmed. "There were only three nurses for the surgical department, so those of us who were surgical technicians had to assume a lot of their responsibilities such as suturing minor wounds."

With the Cold War between the U.S. and Soviet Union continuing to boil, anti-aircraft battalions designated to protect the base in case of an aerial attack traveled to the northern coast of England during the summer months for training exercises.

"During their exercises, I would go along with them and run the dispensary," he noted. "It was interesting to witness because they would tow targets behind aircraft and then use a radar-guided firing system to shoot at them."

His assignment in England also included a brief deployment to Greece to assist those injured during a major earthquake that struck the region in the summer of 1953.

"They sent a group of medical personnel to southern Greece, and we took trucks to the town of Petros," said Westfall. "We were there for about a week when they decided they didn't need us anymore." With a grin, he added, "They sent us back to Athens to meet a plane, but the doctor in charge of our group arranged so we could stay there for a week on R&R (rest and relaxation)."

Returning to RAF Burtonwood, Westfall finished his two and a half years overseas duty in November 1953, receiving an early discharge because of the massive reduction in U.S. forces in the months following the Korean Armistice Agreement. Following his arrival stateside, he returned to farming and in September 1957, married his fiancée, Shirley Simpson. The couple moved to Jacksonville, Missouri, in 1964, where they raised four children. As the years passed, Westfall completed a lengthy career as a rural mail carrier.

He and his wife have since relocated to Jefferson City, which has allowed them to enjoy their golden years while being closer to family. In recent years, Westfall explained, he has enjoyed not only reflecting on his own experiences in the United States Air Force but also watching his children follow the example he set decades earlier.

"I have always been proud of my country, and I think that I am like a lot of veterans in that I would go back and do it all over again if I were physically able to do so and I was needed," he boldly noted. "It has also been rewarding to watch my children grow up and serve their country in uniform as well," he added. "My oldest son served as a pilot in the Air Force and now flies for the airlines, and my youngest son served with a hospital unit in the Air Force." Pausing, he concluded, "I also have a great-grandson who is a Marine, which truly makes this veteran proud that his own family has made the decision to continue to serve." *(Photograph courtesy of Gerald Westfall)*

Alonzo "Mack" Gross – *Tipton*

Alonzo "Mack" Gross was raised on a farm near Tipton, never making it far from home until he was hired by the Missouri Highway Department and began traveling throughout the state painting bridges. Although this employment introduced him to a life away from familiar surroundings, it was not until receiving a certain letter in the mail that his outlook on the world became unexpectedly broadened.

"I got my draft notice in July 1952 and reported to Kansas City for my pre-induction physical," explained the veteran. "I passed everything just fine, and that's where I was inducted into the U.S. Army," he added.

Gross went on to complete nearly eight weeks of basic training at Fort Riley, Kansas and was then selected to attend two weeks of leadership training, receiving an introduction to leading soldiers in addition to training on a number of foreign weapons.

"At that time, we all pretty well knew we were going to Korea," he said.

In September 1952, he departed Fort Riley and traveled by train to Camp Stoneman, California, where he spent only a couple of days. He then boarded a troop ship in San Francisco bound for Japan. Following his arrival overseas, he was sent to the once-embattled island of Iwo Jima for chemical, biological and radiological (CBR) warfare training, acquiring an introduction to decontamination procedures in the event that CBR-type weapons were employed by enemy forces.

"After about two or three weeks at Iwo Jima, I was sent to Korea and assigned to the front lines with the 9th Infantry (Regiment) of the 2nd Infantry Division," recalled Gross. "Since I was a little stockier back then, they assigned me to carry the BAR (Browning Automatic Rifle—a .30-caliber machine gun fired from a bipod)."

As Gross went on to explain, his unit spent approximately three months on the front lines, repelling enemy advances from the protection of foxholes and bunkers. A harsh recollection, he explained, was when enemy soldiers were killed after becoming entangled in the protective wires that had been strung to protect the U.S. troops.

"The Chinese troops would often get drunk on a bunch of Saki (alcohol) and then try to rush our lines," he said. "We only got one hot meal a day when we were on the front lines, and they often liked to plan their attacks during those times we were eating."

The American soldiers were later pulled back and placed in reserves, receiving a temporary break from combat while training new soldiers who were sent to replace the combat casualties. Additionally, this time was used to send soldiers such as Gross to various leadership courses. After a few weeks, they were again sent to the front lines for another cycle of harsh combat duty. The soldiers of the regiment took turns manning listening posts a short distance forward of their lines, observing troop activity and watching for any attempted attacks. If an enemy advance was spotted, Gross said, the observers were essentially "sitting ducks" since they might not be able to make it back to the safety of the American lines.

"I was getting tired of toting that heavy BAR all over the place, and I guess the company commander somehow caught wind of that," Gross explained. "I was summoned to company headquarters and informed that I was being transferred to the military police."

By this point in his military experience, the Korean Armistice Agreement had been achieved, and Gross received assignment to the 558th Military Police Company at Yong Dong Po to provide security for the headquarters of the 8th Army Division.

"This assignment was much more relaxed," he chuckled, "and I spent a large part of my time performing traffic control and guarding military conferences." He continued, "On the front lines, the only showers you got was bathing with water from your helmet, but in Yong Dong Po, we had the privilege of showers with hot water—which was great!"

Located in a former Japanese military academy used in the Second World War, Gross explained that his new duties brought him in close proximity to such renowned military leaders as Generals Douglas MacArthur and Matthew Ridgeway. The ferocity of war had not dissipated in his new assignment since Turkish troops serving in the vicinity shot Koreans caught stealing discarded U.S. rations. Their bodies were then strung up along a fence and left to decay as a warning to others; however, the U.S. troops were under strict orders forbidding removal of the corpses.

When approaching the end of his two-year period of service in late May 1954, the corporal was sent to Fort Carson, Colorado, and received his discharge from the U.S. Army on June 10, 1954.

"I had the opportunity to reenlist and make sergeant, but I was ready to get home and make some money," he said.

As the years passed, he married, raised children, and eventually went to work for the Missouri Department of Corrections, retiring in 1987 after nearly thirty years of employment. The time he spent overseas during the war, he affirmed, was an eye-opening experience for a young man who once lived a life relatively sheltered within the confines of his state.

"I was raised on a farm, and other than working for the highway department in a few places around the state, I hadn't seen much of the world," he said. "My time in Korea gave me an outlook on how fortunate I was to have been raised in a free country." He added, "And I remember seeing those Korean women go out there after battles to pick up the brass left from shells just to make things like chairs and benches—and many of them got killed! It showed me that so little could mean so much to some people." *(Photograph courtesy of Mack Gross)*

Lloyd Parr – *Jefferson City*

A nineteen-year-old Lloyd Parr traveled to Memphis, Tennessee, in June 1951 to begin his training as an aircraft machinist mate for the U.S. Navy. The Denver area native had been in the service for less than a year but was unknowingly preparing to embark upon a journey that would introduce to him his lifelong partner and set the stage for a worldwide adventure.

"After I joined the Navy in (October) 1950, I did my boot camp at San Diego and was then stationed at Moffett Field near San Francisco," said Parr. "I was then sent to Jacksonville, Florida, to take some tests to determine my aptitudes, and the Navy decided I should be an aircraft mechanic," he grinned.

While in training at Memphis, the young sailor learned to work on the reciprocating engines used in most of the Navy's aircraft of the period. During a weekend break, Parr took a trip to Texas with two of the sailors that were in training with him.

"One of the guys I was in training with was from Texas and convinced us to go down there with him," Parr said. "After we got there, he said that he had a cousin that lived down the road, and he introduced us." He added, "That's the first time I met Fran, and we began dating."

Completing his aircraft maintenance school in August 1951, the sailor was transferred to Naval Air Station North Island in San Diego. For the next eighteen months, he managed a hobby shop on the base. In December 1951, he took leave and traveled to Woodville, Texas, where he and Fran were married. While on the West Coast, he and his wife lived together off base. However, in June 1953, Parr received orders for a new duty assignment and boarded a troop ship destined for Iwakuni, Japan. Upon arrival, he was transferred to the USS *Kenneth Whiting*—a seaplane tender.

"The ship was moored in the harbor and served as a maintenance and fuel facility in addition to a control tower for military seaplanes," he said. "I was assigned to the engine maintenance division while I was there."

As Parr explained, the pilot of one of the aircraft they had repaired offered to let some of the sailors fly with him on a brief trip to Hong Kong. Although Parr wished to go along, he had cut his finger while working on an engine and was suffering from lead poisoning after washing his hands in aviation fuel.

"Several of my friends took that trip," he said. Pausing, he solemnly added, "The plane flew into the side of a mountain and killed everyone on board. Our ship then sailed for the Ryukyu Islands carrying corpsmen and other sailors to recover the bodies of the seventeen who lost their lives in the crash."

While assigned to the Whiting, Parr participated in a cruise to the South Pacific. The crew later sailed to Pearl Harbor, during which the ship was damaged in a typhoon. Following repairs to make the vessel once again seaworthy, they returned to the West Coast to go into dry-dock for more extensive repairs. In September 1954, Parr was discharged from the Navy after four years of service, and he, Fran, and their young daughter moved to Denver. For a short time, the former sailor went to work doing survey work with the Denver Water Board, but in 1957, after the board closed their engineering department, Parr sought a different employment option.

"I enlisted in the Air Force in 1957 and was sent to Okinawa early in my enlistment to calibrate radar facilities," he said. "After that, I was stationed in Glasgow, Montana, as the NCOIC (Non-Commissioned Officer in Charge) of an engineering department."

Later in his tenure with the Air Force, Parr and his family lived in Turkey, where he worked in NATO Headquarters to assist with the monitoring of the construction of Turkish and Greek airfields. This was followed by his transfer to Little Rock, Arkansas, in addition to temporary duty in locations such as Korea.

"I got orders for Vietnam and was stationed there for about eleven months between 1970 and 1971," Parr explained. "We were located at a small base airbase just off the coast in Tuy Hoa." He added, "One of the jobs we had was to maintain and calibrate electronic navigational aids used by aircraft during landings."

The veteran finished out his sixteen-year Air Force career with the Civil Engineering Center at Wright-Patterson Air Force Base in Ohio, retiring in 1973. During his career, he and his wife became parents to four children and, following his retirement, moved to Mid-Missouri. With twenty total years of military service under his belt, Parr went to work for the Missouri Department of Transportation, spending twenty-six years with the agency and retiring as the director of their aviation program. Possessing an extraordinary collection of experiences to reflect upon during their golden years, Parr and his wife are grateful for the opportunities they were provided through the military.

"We saw many things that made lifelong impressions on both of us," said Fran. The history of Turkey was amazing for me because we had the opportunity to stand on the ruins of places that we had read about in the Bible. "That," she excitedly affirmed, "was truly an incredible experience." With a pause, Parr added to his wife's comments, "Yes, it was quite interesting to live and work within cultures that were vastly different than ours, but returning to the United States was something we always enjoyed. They were experiences that provided us with a greater appreciation for this country." *(Photograph courtesy of Lloyd Parr)*

Jeremy P. Amick

Gene Steenbergen - *Russellville*

Raised on a farm south of Russellville, Missouri, Gene Steenbergen recalls the many years he studied at Valley Home School—a one-room schoolhouse that no longer exists. After completing the eighth grade, he transferred to Russellville High School in the fall of 1945, around the time that the Japanese surrendered aboard the USS *Missouri* in Tokyo Bay, heralding the end of World War II. With the worldwide conflict now in hindsight, life in his rural community began to return to a level of normalcy as Steenbergen went on to graduate in 1949. However, the Korean War exploded the following year, placing many recent high school graduates in a position to make a critical decision.

"I did some work locally until they began drafting everybody in Cole County in 1951—that's when the war was really getting pretty bad," Steenbergen said. "I heard that every fourth person they were drafting was being put in the Marines, and I didn't like those odds."

Certain it was only a matter of time before he was drafted into military service; he chose to exercise a little choice in his destiny and enlisted in the U.S. Navy on September 1, 1951. Days later, he was at Great Lakes, Illinois, to undergo several weeks of basic training.

"They gave us a bunch of tests whenever we enlisted, and I guess they decided from the results that I would make a good machinist mate," he explained. "I stayed at Great Lakes for sixteen weeks of additional training and learned a little bit of everything, such as how to use lathes and other tools for machine shop type of work," he added.

In early April 1952, the newly trained sailor was assigned to the USS *Sperry*—a submarine tender that had been commissioned during World War II. At the time, it was anchored in San Diego to provide refit and repairs for submarines.

"There were several hundred sailors assigned to the ship, and we all lived on board," said Steenbergen. "It had a huge machine shop and foundry; basically, we could reproduce any mechanical part that might be needed to repair a submarine."

The former sailor went on to explain that the USS *Sperry* was essentially a floating repair platform that could support ten types of U.S. Navy submarines, and they maintained detailed blueprints and schematics for all of them.

"My job was that of a mechanic—if a certain part needed to be repaired or replaced, we'd go and remove it; when it was repaired, we'd go and put it back on," he said.

Steenbergen further noted that unlike the more recent submarines, which are powered by a nuclear reactor, the vessels they worked on utilized diesel engines for propulsion, which required that overhauls of the engines be conducted on a routine basis.

"In 1953, we sailed to Pearl Harbor and put the USS *Sperry* in drydock for several weeks," recalled the veteran. "While the ship was being blasted and repainted, we really didn't have anything to do but pull guard duty." Grinning, he added, "That was kind of like a big vacation for us."

With their repairs completed in late September 1953, the crew sailed for the island of Chi Chi Jima, located approximately one hundred and fifty miles north of Iwo Jima. It was here, Steenbergen noted, the U.S. Navy planned to establish a submarine base, but the actual implementation never occurred.

"We spent about two weeks on the island and had the opportunity to do some exploring," he said. "The Japanese had worked for years preparing the island for World War II battles, and there were tunnels from one end of the island to the other. There were still boats sunk just off the shore and torpedoes laying on the beach ... all left over from World War II."

Several days later, the USS *Sperry* departed the island and returned to San Diego, arriving in harbor in late October 1953. After having spent nearly three and a half years assigned to the ship, he received his discharge from active-duty service with the U.S. Navy in August 1955.

"I had a reserve obligation for another four years, but since the Korean War had ended by that time, I was never called back up," Steenbergen said.

Returning to Mid-Missouri, he married Lina Scrivner in 1956 and went on to attend Jefferson City Junior College for two years, becoming a member of the school's final graduating class prior to its closure in 1958. He then used his GI Bill benefits at Lincoln University before transferring to the University of Missouri-Columbia, graduating with a degree in civil engineering in 1962.

"I went to work for the Missouri Highway Department and retired in 1989 after twenty-seven years with them." With a chuckle, he added, "Now, I have been retired from the state longer than I worked there."

A member of the American Legion, VFW and Disabled American Veterans, Steenbergen enjoys playing music with several groups and provides entertainment at local senior living facilities. Though now far removed from circumstances that first inspired his entry into the military, he insists his service on a submarine tender provided him with benefits of decades-long impact.

"I grew up on a farm, so that's about all that I knew as a young man," he said. "It was quite an experience for me to see a lot of the country and places overseas and to even cross the International Date Line." In conclusion, he added, "The experience was also beneficial considering the educational benefits it provided because without them, I would have never been able to afford college, which then helped me with the career I pursued. But most importantly, it was really an enjoyable experience." *(Photograph courtesy of Gene Steenbergen)*

Harold Westhues - *Glasgow*

Harold Westhues does not hesitate in acknowledging the early lessons in hard work he accrued while growing up on a farm near the small town of Glasgow, Missouri. These experiences, he asserts, were a driving force behind his resolve to work his way through college and were later supplemented by the invaluable training and education he received while serving with the U.S. Army during the Korean War.

"While I was attending the University of Missouri (in the early 1950s), the Korean War was going on, and I realized that I might be drafted—some of my friends had already been drafted," said Westhues. "Because of this, I decided to complete the ROTC (Reserve Officer Training Corps) program and get my commission as an officer."

Graduating with his bachelor's degree in finance and marketing in 1953, he was commissioned as a second lieutenant in the U.S. Army and, in August the same year, was sent to Fort Sill, Oklahoma, for artillery school. He remained there for nearly sixteen weeks receiving instruction in battle planning and the operation of the 105mm howitzers.

"They taught us all aspects of the howitzers, including how to serve as a forward observer and calling in artillery on defined targets," Westhues said. "When we graduated training, they lined us up and told us where our duty assignment would be; half were going to Europe and the rest to Korea." Pausing, he added, "When they announced my name, it was for Korea."

Following a few days of leave back home in Glasgow, Westhues traveled to California and boarded a plane to travel to his overseas assignment. They made brief stops in Honolulu and Wake Island before finally arriving in Yokohama, Japan. From there, the group rode a bus to a military base in Tokyo, where they received a week of indoctrination training to prepare them for their approaching duties. Japanese trains then transported Westhues and a group of his fellow soldiers to the port in Sasabo, Japan, stopping briefly in Hiroshima so they could witness the devastation from the atomic bombings a few years earlier. They then boarded a transport and sailed to Pusan, Korea.

It would take another locomotive ride followed by a trip in the back of a military truck before Lt. Westhues finally arrived for duty with his new unit—C Battery of the 555th Field Artillery Battalion—in late December 1953. The armistice resulting in the cessation of hostilities in the Korean War had been signed a few months earlier. At the time of his arrival, Westhues' battery was in reserve but continued to undergo a comprehensive regimen of training to ensure they were "prepared to fight in case combat broke out once again," Westhues said.

Shortly before the armistice in July 1953, an estimated 70,000 Chinese soldiers attacked the sector the 555th Field Artillery helped to defend, and the artillerymen were simply overwhelmed by sheer numbers. When the battle came to a close days later, the battery had incurred fifty-eight casualties, either killed or captured.

"One of my earliest duties was to teach classes to these soldiers—these heroes—who had been completely overrun during some of the most intense fighting of the war," he said. "I learned by working with these men ... listening when they wanted to talk, and I grew as an officer rather quickly because of it."

The "Triple Nickel," which the 555th was nicknamed, later moved under the centralized command structure of the 3rd Infantry Division. Under this new configuration, they provided light artillery support alongside the Greek Expeditionary Forces, the latter of whom fulfilled the role of infantry.

"We were moved to a location in the Ch'orwon Valley and setup in old artillery positions there," Westhues said. "I was a forward observer with a team of three other soldiers—a Jeep driver, a sergeant, and a corporal." He added, "My job was to coordinate with the Greek infantry and identify reference points in the valley in case we had to call in artillery strikes on enemy targets." Westhues continued, "The Chinese forces were out in front of our positions and had us outnumbered five to one. Part of our responsibilities were to detect and monitor any enemy troop movements and also to continue our training to maintain our skills."

In December 1954, Westhues' overseas assignment ended, and he was sent to Fort Lewis, Washington, where he remained for the next several months to help stand up a new division for service in Alaska. The young officer received his discharge as a first lieutenant in May 1955. After returning home, the veteran was employed by Glasgow Savings Bank for eight years before moving to Jefferson City in 1967, spending the next forty-one years in service as president of Jefferson

Bank of Missouri. He married Donna in 1970, and the couple raised two sons, Rick and Dan.

When speaking of his military experience from decades past, Westhues sagely explained that it was a period of valuable lessons with enduring relevance during his career in the banking industry.

"In my situation, I knew that failure was not an option. I took my commission (as an officer) seriously, and I learned a lot about how to administer and run an operation ... and how to make sound decisions using good judgment." Reflecting on the soldiers with whom he served, he added, "I was proud of them—they were all great men. They made me a better person, and even under the harshest of conditions, they found a little humor in their circumstances and managed to make the situation better." *(Photograph courtesy of Harold Westhues)*

Henry Dahl – *Jefferson City*

The service of all veterans is deserving of remembrance and recognition but the contributions of Cold War veterans, who served as a deterrent to Soviet threats in decades past, often goes unrecognized. One local veteran wants to ensure that not only are those with whom he served remembered for their service in times of relative peace but that the role played by an iconic Cold War bomber is never forgotten. Raised in a small town in Iowa, Henry Dahl and a friend learned that the G.I. Bill of Rights was set to expire on January 31, 1955, and decided they should hurry and enlist in the Air Force so they could qualify for some educational benefits.

"I settled on the Air Force because I was interested in mechanics and wanted to learn about aircraft," Dahl recalled. "But when we got to Omaha to swear in, there were so many people there with the same idea, they delayed our induction until February 3, which meant we wouldn't qualify for the GI Bill."

The Air Force explained they could back out of their enlistment because of the delay, but Dahl chose to pursue the military career path and was soon on his way to Lackland Air Force Base in Texas for his basic training. From there, he traveled to Chanute Air Force Base in Illinois in early April 1955 to begin several weeks of training on reciprocating engines.

The veteran explained, "I was there for about six months, and we learned the theory of engine operation and how to tear down, rebuild, install and operate B-29 (Superfortress) engines."

The airman was then transferred to his first duty assignment at the newly established Little Rock Air Force Base in Arkansas, where he remained for the next several months maintaining the engines on the Boeing KC-97 Stratofreighter, a refueling aircraft. In the early weeks of 1956, he returned to Iowa for a short period of leave before reporting to his next and final duty assignment at Ramey Air Force Base in Puerto Rico. Upon arrival, Dahl noted, he was assigned to the maintenance crew of the Convair B-36 Peacemaker—a strategic bomber with six reciprocating engines and four jet engines.

"The plane was the predecessor to the B-52, which became widely known because it is still used by the Air Force," said Dahl. "The B-36 had a wingspan of 230 feet, was 162 feet long, and held 32,000 gallons of fuel … just to give you an idea of how massive it was."

An article by Daniel Ford appearing in the April 1996 edition of *Air & Space Museum* magazine noted, "Each airplane had 336 spark plugs, and after a flight lasting a day and a half, a mechanic would have to haul a bucket of replacement plugs to the airplane to service all six engines." [107]

The serial number for Dahl's aircraft was "711," and he remained with the same plane for the duration of his time in Puerto Rico. The

---

[107] Ford, *Air & Space Museum*, https://airspacemag.com.

veteran mirthfully recalled that the aircraft shook so intensely when idling on the ground that it was nicknamed it "Ol' Shaky," and Dahl was granted permission to paint its new nickname on its nose. He added, "Our job, as part of the maintenance crew, was to keep the aircraft on flying status, ready to go. We were part of the Strategic Air Command (SAC), and there was a B-36 in the air at all times in the region of Puerto Rico as part of SACs strategic bombing mission."

Early in his assignment, Dahl added, the B-36s were equipped with conventional bombs; however, the aircraft was later updated to carry and deploy the significantly more destructive hydrogen bombs, the latter of which weighed 43,000 pounds each. The former airman went on to explain that one of the most intense experiences of his Air Force career came with the looming threat of destruction from Hurricane Betsy, which approached Puerto Rico in August 1956.

"We knew it was coming, but like most hurricanes, it came early, and we had just enough time to get to the plane off the ground during the calm of the eye of the storm," he said. "I had only the clothes on my back and a couple of bucks in my wallet, and we stayed the next week at Biggs Air Force Base (Texas) before returning to Ramey."

Dahl recalled that although there was much destruction across areas of the island, Ramey Air Force Base fared comparatively well since many of the structures on base were built out of concrete. He remained in Puerto Rico until late August 1958, departing the base during the time the B-36s were being phased out and replaced with the newer B-52s. Following his discharge, Dahl traveled to St. Louis to attend Bailey Technical School, earning several certifications.

As the years passed, Dahl married his fiancée, Dona, and they have since raised two sons. His military experiences and subsequent education later led to his being hired by Central Electric Power Cooperative in Jefferson City, with whom he went on to retire as their telecommunications director after forty-two years of employment. The veteran's personal Cold War experiences, though bursting with interesting circumstances and stories, are not the focus of his recollections; instead, Dahl affirms, he is dedicated to ensuring the role fulfilled by the aircraft he supported years ago is never forgotten.

"That's my main objective and interest—preserving the legacy of the B-36," he stated. "It has become a relatively unknown aircraft because of the B-52, but I want the public to understand the critical role it served as a deterrent to Soviet aggression during the height of the Cold War." He added, "The B-36 was labeled the 'Peacemaker' because it never had to fire a weapon or drop a bomb in a time of war. It was my pleasure to have had the opportunity to work on and around the aircraft, and I want to share its story while I'm still around to furnish the information." *(Photograph courtesy of Henry Dahl)*

Bill Buehrle – *Jefferson City*

"My Sailors are students, and I am their teacher. I guide and influence the lives of these young men and women. In the final analysis, I will determine the quality of these sailors"—poignant affirmations of "The Chief Petty Officer's Pledge" that have for decades defined the life and work of local U.S. Navy retiree Bill Buehrle. A 1955 graduate of Jefferson City Senior High, Buehrle was fully prepared to marry his fiancée after high school, but being unable to locate suitable employment to support a family, he looked to the military for the means to achieve financial stability.

"I enlisted in July 1956, and they sent me to basic training at Great Lakes (Naval Training Station) in Illinois," he explained. "Then," he added, "It was on to several months at basic sonar school in Key West Florida, learning basic electronics and using sonar equipment to locate submarines."

Upon completion of his initial training in May 1957, the following month Buehrle married his fiancée, but the couple soon said their temporary goodbyes when Buehrle received assignment to the USS *Bearss* (DD-654)—a Fletcher-class destroyer built during World War II moored in Portsmouth, Virginia, for an overhaul.

"The guy I relieved wasn't assigned to the ship once I got there and before he had left, had basically torn apart the weapons systems and sonar," said Buehrle. I had to put them back together, and that was a great education because I had to learn everything quickly."

While assigned to the ship, the sailor went on to participate in several cruises in locations including the Mediterranean and the North and South Atlantic. However, he affirmed, the most interesting was the crew's participation in "Operation Argus" in 1958.

"They sent us with a group of ships somewhere off the coast of South Africa," recalled the veteran. "They detonated nuclear missiles high in the atmosphere; it was the brainchild of some scientist that believed that the detonations would form a shield that would interfere with the electronics of Russian weapons," he added.

Following the series of atmospheric nuclear tests, Buehrle explained, the USS *Bearss* navigated to a location under the detonation area where scientific personnel used equipment to measure radiation levels. This, Buehrle maintained, likely caused some of the cancers he and his fellow sailors experienced in later years.

"The long and short of it is I'm still here, and that's all that counts," he grinned.

In 1960, the sailor and his wife welcomed their first and only child, a daughter they named Karen. The same year, Buehrle reenlisted and received orders to serve as an instructor for anti-submarine warfare at the Fleet Training School in Norfolk, Virginia. His next assignment came in March 1965, when he was sent to the Fleet Training Group at Guantanamo Bay, Cuba, spending the next year assessing the combat capabilities of the crews of various naval vessels and achieving the rank of chief petty officer.

"My commander thought I needed more education, and I was sent to a twenty-six-week advanced electronics course in Key West in the summer of 1966," said the former sailor. "Halfway through, they pulled me out of the course and reassigned to the Bureau of Naval Personnel in Washington D.C." He continued, "That was probably the most important and rewarding assignment of my career. I was the guy that assigned enlisted personnel to their duty stations, whether it was a duty on ship, shore, in recruiting, or to a school," he said. "What I did in that position impacted a lot of careers."

Sadly, in 1971, an unexpected personal tragedy struck when the Buehrle's lost their ten-year-old daughter to Ryes Syndrome at the Bethesda Naval Hospital. The following year, the grieving father was transferred to the Naval Material Atlantic Command in Norfolk.

"My job was to train both civilian and naval personnel on the planned maintenance for equipment used in the Trident sub program, which was a new type of missile being developed," he said. "That's what I did until retiring with my twenty years of service," he added.

Throughout the next several years, the veteran lived in Virginia and was employed by defense contractors until forming his own consulting company in 1981. In 1983, he went to work as a program and department manager for Computer Sciences Corporation, remaining there until 1996.

"My wife's health was really beginning to decline at that time, so we sold our home and moved back to Missouri," he said. Sorrowfully, he added, "I became her caregiver for the next few years, and she passed away in 2003, on the same day our daughter died, thirty-two years earlier."

The veteran has since met and married Rosalie, and the couple continues to reside in Jefferson City. His decades of service to the nation, Buehrle sagely explained, were defined by his responsibility as a chief petty officer to provide the greatest guidance possible to up and coming sailors based upon his own treasure of experiences.

"The military gave me purpose in life," he proudly affirmed, "and a satisfaction that I could use my God-given skills to help others better themselves. And," he continued, "I learned how to manage projects, and it seems like I'm still managing several aspects of my life to this day by using the lessons provided by the Navy." He added, "As our pledge states, 'I am a Chief Petty Officer in the United States Navy … I serve my country and her people with pride and honor.' And I am certainly proud that I had the opportunities that I did in the service." *(Photograph courtesy of Bill Buehrle)*

Dennis Oppenheim – *Jefferson City*

As a first-generation citizen of the United States, Dennis Oppenheim learned at an early age that opportunities might present themselves in the most unexpected fashion. Raised by Danish immigrants in the bustling city of Chicago, he soon discovered the valuable lessons provided to him through service in the Cold War-era armed forces.

"I started high school in Chicago in 1953 but decided to quit school in 1955 and went to work for a year," Oppenheim recalled. "On my eighteenth birthday (March 1956), I was required to sign up for the draft but decided to enlist in the U.S. Army the following month," he added.

As the veteran explained, the Army offered a three-year enlistment period, whereas the Navy and Air Force required a new recruit to commit to a term of four years. Shortly after signing his enlistment papers in April 1956, he boarded a bus for Fort Leonard Wood to complete eight weeks of basic training. Upon graduation, he was granted twelve days of leave to return home before reporting to his next duty assignment at Fort Bliss, Texas.

"They placed me in the 550th Field Artillery (Battalion), and I started out training as a launcher crewman with the 'Honest John' rocket," Oppenheim said. The MGR-1 Honest John was a nuclear-armed surface-to-surface rocket developed in the early 1950s and later adapted to use conventional and chemical warheads. It is considered the first tactical nuclear weapon of the U.S.

Following his arrival at the Texas base, the decision was made to convert his military occupational specialty to that of atomic warhead specialist, and he was sent to Fort Sill, Oklahoma, to learn the skills associated with his newly appointed duty assignment.

"It was supposed to be a four-week course that they crammed into two weeks," he said. "In order to launch the rocket, you have to complete a sequence of steps using boxes with switches and lights. During the training, we had to demonstrate that we were able to complete the entire launch sequence in five minutes."

The young soldier returned to Ft. Bliss for a number of months to continue refining his skills as part of a rocket crew; however, his battalion was sent to White Sands Proving Grounds in New Mexico, where they spent approximately nine months performing launch exercises. While in New Mexico, he was able to finish the high school studies he had deserted a few years earlier by earning his GED. Once the battalion returned to Ft. Bliss from their training at White Sands, there was little downtime to be enjoyed since Oppenheim, and a small group of soldiers was sent to Fort Bragg, North Carolina, for a unique training assignment.

"They sent us to Fort Bragg to make a training film for the airborne troops to demonstrate the use of the 'Little John,'" Oppenheim said. The MGR-3 Little John, he explained, was a smaller artillery rocket system designed for deployment in airborne assault operations.

Weeks later, he returned to Ft. Bliss, but the battalion was soon on their way to the country of Panama for another unexpected opportunity—the testing of a new warhead design for the Honest John.

"We spent a couple weeks in the middle of the jungle," he recalled. "The warhead we tested would come apart near the target and shoot out a bunch of smaller balls that flew in different directions and then exploded." He added, "We had targets set up and fired two separate test rockets while we were there to measure the amount of damage they could inflict on enemy forces."

The exercise in Panama would become his final temporary duty assignment since he returned to Ft. Bliss and finished out the remainder of his enlistment in April 1959. Despite the offer of reenlistment and travel to Turkey to teach the rocket system to Turkish soldiers, he admitted he was homesick and ready to return to Chicago. For more than eighteen years, Oppenheim was employed by the Chicago Transit Authority and, in 1976, married his fiancée, Jan. Wishing to leave the "rate race" of Chicago life and to raise their children in a quieter environment, the couple moved to Jefferson City in the summer of 1977.

"I worked for the Department of Corrections for about eighteen months and then went to work for the old Capital City Water Company, spending twenty-two years with them," he said. "In 1981, I enlisted in the Missouri National Guard and became a cook until retiring from there in 1998."

In addition to having worked part-time as a cook at St. Peter Interparish School and with Jefferson City Public Schools, Oppenheim and his wife have volunteered with Operation Bugle Boy—a nonprofit organization that honors veterans, military members, and first responders. When asked about the impact of his service with the U.S. Army during a Cold War period that was sandwiched between the Korean and Vietnam Wars, the first-generation American asserts that it was for him an honor to have had the opportunity to serve the nation that was first home to his parents.

"I just love this country and everything it represents," Oppenheim said. "I loved being in the Army and all of the wonderful people that I came into contact with because of it." In mirthful reflection, he concluded, "We all came from different backgrounds and communities but learned how to work together to get the job done. To this day, I can still remember all the names of most of the people that I served with." *(Photograph courtesy of Dennis Oppenheim)*

Ray Mabury - *Piedmont*

After graduating from high school in the southeast Missouri community of Piedmont in 1957, Ray Mabury began working for a local shoe manufacturing company. When considering the possibilities for the future and recognizing the reality of a flat job market in the region, he made the decision to pursue a different employment opportunity by joining the United States Air Force.

"I enlisted in 1958 and ended up buying four years of service instead of two," the veteran chuckled. "Had I waited to be drafted, it would have been two years, but since I chose to volunteer, it was a four-year enlistment," he paused to explain.

The first stop in his journey was Lackland Air Force Base in San Antonio for several weeks of basic training followed by his transfer to Sheppard Air Force Base in Wichita Falls, Texas. It was at the latter base he received training as an aircraft maintenance technician, learning to work on the B-52 Stratofortress, KC-135 Stratotanker, and the C-130 Hercules.

"It really wasn't any type of specialized training but rather general maintenance of the aircraft," said Mabury. "When I finished that in early 1959, they sent me to my first and only duty assignment at Seymour Johnson Air Force Base in Goldsboro, North Carolina."

Seymour Johnson Air Force Base was part of an organization known as the Strategic Air Command (SAC), which, through their long-range bombing capabilities, served as a deterrent to the nuclear threats posed by the Soviet Union. Each SAC base, Mabury explained, had two bombers in the air at all times, carrying nuclear bombs in case they were called for a long-range offensive operation.

"There were regular alerts conducted, and I was part of the ground crew that would run out and pull the chocks from under the wheels of the B-52s so they could taxi down the runway for their mission," Mabury explained.

The former airman went on to note that he had to keep uniforms and spare clothes packed in a bag, along with a toolbox, ready to go in case they were deployed to a "safe area" during an emergency. In such a situation, he explained, he would be flown from the stateside base to a location in the Pacific, where, as part of a mobility team, he could be sent to repair bombers. During the early months of his assignment at the North Carolina base, Mabury worked on the flight line in support of one of the B-52s. However, in later months, he was moved to a hangar to perform periodic inspections on the aircraft's eight massive engines.

"Since the planes were each loaded with two nuclear bombs, I had to wear a dosimeter all the time to measure for any potential exposure to radiation," Mabury said.

Even if his daily maintenance duties, accompanied by the occasional alert, appeared to be in any way a routine, an event unfolding in January 1961 demonstrated the ever-present dangers that faced the airmen even during training exercises.

"At the time, I was recovering from a car crash that happened four months earlier and had been on some light duty since I had gone through plastic surgery to rebuild damage to my jaw," he said. "On January 24, 1961, during my recovery, one of our B-52s broke apart in midair near the base with two nuclear bombs on board."

Mabury went on to explain that the bombardier was able to eject one of the bombs, which descended to the ground using a parachute, while the other plummeted into a muddy field, many of its components disintegrating while remaining pieces became buried many feet below the surface.

"Three airmen were killed in the crash, and I was sent out to the area as part of the recovery team," the veteran recalled. "Many years later, I learned that a single switch prevented the detonation of the second nuclear bomb. That was disturbing to learn how close we came to such a devastating explosion," he remarked.

Upon returning to his regular duties, Mabury received his discharge from the Air Force in August 1962. In the years following his service, he married, raised four children, and eventually settled in Jefferson City, where he retired in 2013 as Manager of Sales for Farm Bureau Insurance Company. While living in Jefferson City, he and his wife began attending First Baptist Church. As part of a Sunday school class, they made a trip to an area restaurant with fellow church members, one of whom, Mabury discovered, shared a unique historical connection.

"[I went] with Jerry Kemple to a restaurant for dinner and made conversation along the way," said Mabury. "The subject of military service came up, and I learned that he had been in the Air Force and stationed at Seymour Johnson Air Force Base during the same time I was there." The veteran continued, "Then, I found out that he worked in armament and loaded the bombs on the B-52s. He was part of the very crew that was sent out to retrieve the bombs from the B-52 that had crashed in a field."

Pondering the unexpected encounter, Mabury concluded, "I really think that it's interesting that all those years ago, I worked on the same flight line in the vicinity of Jerry while stationed in North Carolina and also scoured the same fields after the B-52 broke apart, yet we never met each other. And somehow, through sheer chance, we came to know each other all these decades later." *(Photograph courtesy of Ray Mabury)*

Jerry Kemple – *Jefferson City*

Heeding the experienced advice coming from an older brother serving in the U.S. Air Force, Jerry Kemple made the decision to enlist after graduating from Smithfield High School in Ohio in 1958, clinging to hopes that he could acquire technical training that might benefit him in the coming years. Traveling to Lackland Air Force Base in San Antonio, Texas, in July 1958, to complete his basic training, Kemple was at Lowry Air Force Base in Denver, Colorado, a few weeks later for instruction on becoming a special weapons mechanic.

"The training really appealed to me because I thought it would be a good career field to get into," said the veteran. "I spent six months there and learned how to work on various types of armament like the .50 caliber machine guns and 20mm cannons," he added.

Finishing the training in late January 1959, he was sent to his first duty assignment at Seymour Johnson Air Force Base near Goldsboro, North Carolina, and attached to the 4241st Armament and Electronics Maintenance Squadron.

"The first six months there," he said, "we were busy with preparations to receive the new B-52Gs ("Stratofortess"—a long-range strategic bomber) from the factory," said Kemple. "Most of what we did during that time was updating and converting the temporary hangars and facilities that had been built back in World War II."

Several months later, after the B-52s were received, Kemple was transferred to the 53rd Munitions Maintenance Squadron and began working on the four .50 caliber machine guns used on the bombers in addition to performing maintenance on the release systems used for the nuclear armaments on the aircraft.

"They conducted an exercise with the B-52s that they called 'Cocked Pistol,'" recalled Kemple. "The B-52s took off from Seymour Johnson and flew at a very low altitude to a designated spot somewhere off the coast to see if they could penetrate the air defense radar."

As the former airman recalled, one of the B-52s made its rendezvous point over the ocean but then disappeared. To Kemple's knowledge, the wreckage of the aircraft and the remains of the crew have never been located. In addition to his maintenance duties, Kemple served as a member of crews loading bombs on the planes prior to their missions and later removing the bombs upon their return. He noted that as part of the Strategic Air Command (SAC), the base had a mission to keep nuclear-armed aircraft in the skies twenty-four hours a day in case they were called to strike a Cold War target.

"A component of this SAC mission included our plane making a flight circle from Seymour Johnson to Thule, Greenland, and then back to the base," explained Kemple. One of these missions, he explained, resulted in deadly consequences for the crew involved.

"On January 21, 1961, one of our B-52s was on their mission to Thule and attempted an aerial refueling," said Kemple. "There was a fuel leak observed during the refueling process, and the aircraft was ordered to return to Seymour Johnson," he added.

Approximately twelve miles from base, the plane exploded. Five members of the crew successfully evacuated the aircraft prior to the explosion, while three died because of the incident.

"There were two nuclear bombs aboard that aircraft, and one of the bombs parachuted to the ground and was recovered," he said. "The other nuclear bomb plummeted to the earth and some of its primary components became buried in the swampy ground below."

Attempts were made to excavate the bomb but were later abandoned due to groundwater flooding. The University of North Carolina at Chapel Hill has estimated the primary section of the bomb to be entombed at a depth of 180 feet, where it remains to this day. Estimates indicate each of the nuclear bombs from the incident possessed 250 times the destructive power of the atomic bombs dropped on Hiroshima in WWII.

"All the pieces of the B-52G were collected, and I helped reconstruct the plane on base so that the investigators could determine the cause of the crash," said Kemple. "I believe the crash was attributed to defective wing spars that cracked during the flight."

Receiving his discharge from the Air Force in March 1962, Kemple went on to utilize his GI Bill benefits to earn a bachelor's degree in electrical engineering from the University of Tennessee in 1967. The same year as his graduation, he married his fiancée, Joyce, and the couple has since raised two daughters. As the years passed, the veteran was employed by the Westinghouse Electric Corporation and later returned to college, earning his master's degree in business administration from the University of Georgia in 1975. He eventually transferred to Jefferson City with his job, retiring as a manufacturing engineer from ABB in 2002.

It may not have been abundantly clear when he was attempting to map out the direction of his life after high school, but Kemple has since realized that his service with the Air Force bestowed upon him opportunities that later morphed into his chosen career field.

"The service gave me the opportunity to think about going to college and provided me the financial resources to do so," he said. "When I graduated from high school, three students out of my class of 56 students went to college. Most of my classmates went to work in the steel mills in Ohio; the problem with that choice was the steel mills closed several years later." He concluded, "I am fortunate to have made the decision that I did and appreciate what resources the Air Force provided to help me become successful in my own career pursuits." *(Photograph courtesy of Jerry Kemple)*

William Miller – *Crawford County*

Many factors went into William Miller's decision to enlist in the U.S. Air Force following his graduation from Steelville High School in 1948; considerations including a lagging economy, a father who served in WWI, and an older brother wounded in WWII. It became a choice that led to a twenty-six-year career, and none of which would have been possible, he affirmed, without the support of his wife.

"I studied what the Air Force did and how they did it before I went to enlist," said Miller. "It seemed like the right place for me, and it turns out it *was* the right place for me," he grinned.

Completing his basic training at Lackland Air Force Base in Texas, the Crawford County native went on to finish aircraft maintenance school at an airbase in Mississippi. He was then sent to Germany, where he assisted in the overhaul of engines on transport planes used during an iconic moment early in the Cold War.

"During the Berlin Airlift, the Soviets blockaded sections of Berlin, and I was sent to a station in Hahn, Germany, to work on the planes that were used to fly relief missions," he said. "We were located near the area of the city that the Russians had taken, and that was certainly an eerie feeling."

When his assignment in Germany ended, he returned to the U.S. and became a maintenance instructor and supervisor with the Air Force Maintenance School, a position that included temporary assignments at Scott Air Force Base, Illinois, and in France, Germany, and England. In 1955, Miller married his fiancee, Gerry, and the couple would go on to raise a son and a daughter during his Air Force career. The year following his marriage, he decided to leave the enlisted ranks and applied for Officer Candidate School (OCS).

"I was accepted and graduated from OCS, receiving my commission as a second lieutenant," he recalled. "That's when I was sent to Navigator Training School at Harlingen Air Force Base (Texas) and graduated first in my class."

Miller remained at the school as an instructor and later moved to the section that developed the curriculum for the navigator training. From there, he received a transfer to Anchorage, Alaska, where his duties included participation in patrols along the coast to watch for Soviet activity in the region. The next several years of the airman's career are too numerous to detail, but he climbed through the officer ranks, serving as a training officer and later working in operations and planning. One of the greatest achievements of his career came in the late 1960s when he was one of sixty Air Force officers selected for Armed Forces Staff College.

"The college was at Barksdale Air Force Base, Louisiana, and tailored for top-level management in the military," he explained. "The curriculum covered a range of fascinating topics such as conference techniques, law, and conduct of international relations, public affairs, and systems analysis ... to name but a few."

Upon graduation in 1969, Miller was issued a set of orders for overseas service in support of the Vietnam War. Traveling to the Philippines, he received several days of jungle training to prepare him for his wartime service.

"On one evening of the training, they sent us out to the jungle, and we had to stay the night there without being caught, which was to help train us to evade the enemy and not become a prisoner of war," he said. "I found a spot and was sleeping when I was awakened by a tap on the shoulder."

As Miller went on to explain, the officers running the school paid local Filipino scouts a small sum of cash for each one of the concealed trainees they were able to discover. After a couple weeks in the Philippines, Miller arrived at his new assignment in NaKhon Phanom, Thailand. His duties became those of a wing plans officer, working in the office during the day and flying missions at night.

"We had some special forces teams on our base, and part of our duties were flights using primarily C-123s, patrolling along the Ho Chi Minh Trail, and searching for enemy convoys smuggling in weapons and other items used in the war effort," he said. "Once a target was located, we would call in strikes and direct aircraft to destroy it." Miller added, "If we needed a war plan for a particular area where we were operating, I would also write those plans as part of my job."

When his one-year tour of duty ended in 1970, he returned to the U.S. and was assigned to the Headquarters for Air Training Command in San Antonio, working in the office of the Inspector General. He finished out the remainder of his career in a weapons acquisitions program before retiring in 1974 at the rank of lieutenant colonel. In the years that followed, the veteran worked for a number of engineering and construction companies. When reflecting upon his time in the Air Force, the veteran affirms it would not have been such a fruitful and productive career without the support of a very special woman in his life.

"We have great children, and my wife deserves much of the credit for that because while I was in the military, I had to be away from home much of the time," he maintained. "It's unbelievable what she accomplished." He added, "It's not easy to have a good family life while serving in the military, but we did just that, and it is because of the dedication and patience of my wife, Gerry." *(Photograph courtesy of Jeremy P. Amick)*

Arnold Sandbothe – *Lake Ozark*

Born in 1940 on a farm in Maries County, Arnold Sandbothe came of age in a family of seven brothers and three sisters, watching as two of his older brothers left for service in World War II while another was wounded during the Korean War. As the years passed and he went on to graduate from Vienna High School in 1958, it seemed like only a matter of time before he and his other brothers would fulfill the family legacy of serving in the military.

"After high school, I spent some time working construction jobs in St. Louis," said Sandbothe. "While I was up there, I decided that I would also serve and joined a local engineering unit of the Army Reserve," he added.

Completing his boot camp at Ft. Leonard Wood, the young soldier anticipated receiving orders to remain at the fort to complete advanced training in a military engineering specialty; instead, he was handed orders for finance school at Ft. Benjamin Harrison, Indiana.

"I was shocked that I wasn't staying for engineering school, but when one of the officers asked me who I knew to get in that school, I realized it would be alright," he grinned.

He returned to St. Louis for a few months after completing his finance training but soon decided to return closer to home, moving to Jefferson City when he was hired full-time at the former McGraw-Edison Company. In April 1960, he transferred to the Missouri National Guard and was assigned to Company B, 735th Ordnance Battalion, which in late 1962 transitioned to the 1035th Ordnance Company.

"My older brother Ray, who had been wounded in Korea, was working full-time in the state headquarters for the Missouri Guard and told me about a full-time job as a federal technician in the warehouse. I applied and was hired, and worked there for about a year when I was offered a promotion to work in the stock control section for the United States Property and Fiscal Office for the Guard."

Continuing his full-time work for the National Guard while taking college accounting courses in the evenings and drilling with the 1035th on weekends, he was encouraged to consider Officer Candidate School (OCS). He was accepted for OCS and completed his training in June of 1966. Receiving his commission as a second lieutenant, he had to make a critical career decision.

"There was not a compatible officer slot for my full-time federal technician job at that time … and if I waited for one to come available, I might be passed over for appointment," he said. "So, I became a second lieutenant with the 1035th as my drilling unit and was eventually hired full-time with the Missouri Credit Union League."

His full-time employment with the credit union required him to relocate to Kansas City, and, for a number of years, he commuted to Jefferson City to drill with his unit on the weekends. When a command and control headquarters element was organized in Kansas

City, he received a transfer to a slot as a captain in the early 1970s. While living in Kansas City, he met and married Linda Nolker Huyett in 1977. Throughout the next few years, his military career continued to progress while he fulfilled several leadership roles until receiving appointment as commander of the 205th Military Police Battalion in the summer of 1986.

"I had completed my branch training as an ordnance officer, but the new position required that I take my basic and advanced course as a military policeman," said Sandbothe. "I became a major and eventually a lieutenant colonel before leaving the MP Corps of the Missouri National Guard in 1989."

Working full-time with the credit union and performing his part-time military duties as a commander with the military police, Sandbothe realized he would have to be at least halfway finished with Command and General Staff College (CGSC) if he wished to qualify for promotion to colonel.

"During my battalion command time with the MP Corps, I spent many of the few free weekends I had taking CGSC courses and, by the time I left my command there, I had finished a college degree in addition to CGSC."

Although qualified and selected for promotion to colonel, the state did not have any available officer slots at that grade. Sandbothe then made a decision that led him back to where his military career began—the Army Reserve.

"I transferred to the Army Reserve and was able to receive promotion to colonel," he said. "I stayed with them until retiring from the military in 1994 with credit for thirty years of service. Also," he added, "I worked for the Missouri Credit Union Association for thirty-two years before retiring as senior vice-president in 1998."

The veteran has come to recognize the distinct moments that appear to define the differences between the years he spent as an enlisted soldier and those as a commissioned officer, each of which seems to provide him with specific types of memories.

"As an enlisted soldier in my early-to-mid-20s, I was a typical enlisted soldier who had quite a bit of fun but did what I had to do," he said. "But I really didn't grow up until I went to OCS, and they made a gentleman out of me—if that was possible!" he laughed. "I am proud of my fellow Guard members who I met and served with over the years. Working together made each of us better citizens.

However, the most important aspect of his military career has not been the climb through the various ranks but fulfilling a legacy that began with his father and has been carried forth by him and his brothers.

"My father was in WWI, and each of my six brothers served in the military in some capacity," he said. With a chuckle, he added, "When you think about that, I had no choice because what an embarrassment it would be if I hadn't served as well." *(Photograph courtesy of Arnold Sandbothe)*

Tom LeComte - *Taos*

Tom LeComte's decades-long military career spanned the U.S. Navy, U.S. Army, the National Guard of two states, and the Army Reserve, and included service as an enlisted man, a warrant officer, and, finally, a commissioned officer. When describing the breadth of his impressive experiences, LeComte asserts that this entire period was punctuated by the year he spent in combat as a helicopter pilot during the Vietnam War. Born and raised in a small community in Wisconsin, LeComte graduated from high school in 1960 and made the decision to enlist in the U.S. Navy. Completing his basic training in San Diego, the eighteen-year-old enlistee traveled to Memphis, Tennessee, to attend nine months of advanced training as an aviation electronics technician.

"There was a lot of math in the course," said the veteran, "and we covered everything from basic electronics to operating and repairing advanced radar equipment used on various types of aircraft."

He returned to San Diego in late spring of 1961 to complete a three-month course in advanced electronics and was then transferred to the former Naval Air Station at Barber's Point, Hawaii, where he was assigned as a crewmember with a naval patrol squadron.

"We operated throughout the Pacific and even flew the Sea of Japan aboard the P-2V Neptune—a patrol plane used primarily to search for Soviet submarines and to track ships that we suspected to be Russian," said LeComte. "I started out as an electronic countermeasures operator and then worked up to a radio operator."

As the former sailor explained, their Cold War service often placed them in situations where Soviet fighter jets would intercept their aircraft.

"They would fly up next to us, and we would just wave at them," he mirthfully recalled. "They wanted to let us know that they were watching us."

Finishing his enlistment in June 1964, LeComte returned to Wisconsin and began working for a local company. He started taking flight lessons at a nearby airport in his spare time; however, when a friend told him that he had joined the Army and was going to receive training to become a helicopter pilot, the former sailor found a new career direction.

"I enlisted in the Army in the fall of 1967 to attend helicopter flight school," said LeComte. "I figured there was no need to pay for flight training when the Army would provide it to me for free. He added, "The worst part was that I had to go through Army basic training at Ft. Polk, Louisiana."

After his basic training, he attended his primary flight training at Ft. Wolters, Texas, in early 1968. He then transferred to Ft. Rucker, Alabama, where he was trained to pilot a historic aircraft that would help define the Vietnam War—the UH-1 Iroquois helicopter, referred to as the "Huey."

"I graduated my flight training in April 1968, became a warrant officer, and spent several weeks at Ft. Eustis, Virginia," he said. "But that September, I got orders for Vietnam and was assigned to the 189th Assault Helicopter Company at Camp Holloway (near Pleiku in Central Vietnam)."

Initially, he explained, his duties were that of a co-pilot flying a range of missions from troop insertions, resupply and delivery, and medical evacuations when needed. However, after only two months in the country, he progressed to being a pilot in command of his own helicopter.

"There were times we would go out with gunships and drop CS gas [tear gas] canisters that would pop and dispense, forcing enemy troops to flee from inside their cave networks," he said. "Once the enemy bolted from the caves, the gunships took care of the rest."

During the balance of his tour, LeComte spent a portion of his time piloting a gunship and, in September 1969, returned to the United States for reassignment to Ft. Carson, Colorado. It was here that he left the ranks of warrant officer and received a direct commission as an officer.

"I ended up leaving the Army in 1971 and two years later became a full-time maintenance officer with the Colorado National Guard," said LeComte.

Several years later, in 1981, he met and married Patty Henke, and the couple soon moved to Iowa when he was hired as a facility commander with the Iowa Army National Guard. Leaving the National Guard in 1990, Tom, his wife, and their two children moved to Taos to be closer to his wife's family. Throughout the ensuing years, he finished his military career in the mid-1990s, retiring as a lieutenant colonel with the Army Reserve and later working five years with the State Emergency Management Agency in Jefferson City.

When looking back on a military career that included time with several components of the military, LeComte explains that much of the success he experienced in the latter years of his service was a direct result of his early aviation encounters during the Vietnam War.

"Several years ago, when I was with the Iowa National Guard, we flew missions in Alaska alongside a unit from another state that was made up of younger pilots who, unfortunately, were not performing very well," said LeComte. "A general came to me and said, 'The reason you Iowa [National Guard] pilots do as well as you do is that you are all Vietnam vets and know how to handle tough situations.' The general also said that the new pilots coming out of flight school didn't have the experience that we did."

Pausing, LeComte added, "The time I spent in Vietnam was filled with some interesting situations and certainly put my head on straighter. When you see people die, lose friends in combat while working seven days a week, fifty-two weeks out of the year, it tends to have quite an impact." *(Photograph courtesy of Tom LeComte)*

John Clark - *Columbia*

With a beaming grin that shrouds the hardships he has endured, local veteran John Clark recounts his experience as a prisoner of war in Vietnam and how it has fortified his faith in family, God, and nation. Born on January 1, 1940, as the first baby of the decade in Boone County, Clark began attending the University of Missouri-Columbia (MU) in 1957 following his graduation from Hickman High School.

"I thought that when you went to high school in Columbia, it was just natural you then went to MU," Clark joked.

While attending the university, Clark participated in the Air Force Reserve Officer Training Program program, rising to the rank of cadet commander among 2,200 cadet corps members. The aspiring airman graduated as the "distinguished military graduate" in 1962 with a degree in mechanical engineering, at the same time receiving an appointment as a second lieutenant in the Air Force. He immediately began his initial flight training at Reese Air Force Base in Lubbock, Texas, a thirteen-month intensive program where students were introduced to flight in a small jet trainer and progressed to the T-33 (T-Bird)—a Korean War-era fighter. Finishing the program as a distinguished flight graduate, Clark went on to complete survival training. He was then assigned as a pilot with a medical transport unit. However, he soon had a realization that led to a change in the direction of his career.

"I learned that in the Air Force, there is a division between flying propeller- driven aircraft and jets," he said. "It was kind of a jet arrogance."

Clark was accepted into the RF4C program at Shaw Air Force Base in South Carolina in 1965 and soon became qualified on the jet.

"It was a monstrous plane with unbelievable performance," he stated.

He was then assigned to Royal Air Force Alconbury in Huntingdon, England, where he spent two years flying in support of NATO operations. But in late 1966, he received an assignment to Vietnam that would forever change his outlook. Assigned to fly reconnaissance missions over North and South Vietnam, Clark flew more than eighty missions before a fateful event on March 12, 1967.

"It was a routine day as far as the war went," he explained. "We were out performing a weather recon and flew right into a flak trap."

Clark's plane was struck in the belly, and he was forced to eject. Though his parachute opened, the plane's close proximity to the ground led to moderate injuries to his neck and shoulders, including spinal compression. Attempting to evade capture as he had been trained, Clark was quickly apprehended by locals who turned him into North Vietnamese Army (NVA) authorities. Throughout the next six years, the captured Airman was detained in prison camps such as the "Hanoi Hilton" and confirms many of the widely held suspicions regarding the treatment of American prisoners of war (POWs).

"They (the North Vietnamese Army, also referred to as the "NVA") were bagging several guys a day," Clark explained. "They looked for opportunities to torture prisoners and make them confess to (alleged) crimes they had committed. It's really hard to project the actual deprivation, fear, and pain a person endures under such horrible circumstances," he added.

Toward the end of the war, Clark notes that public sentiment toward the treatment of POWs lead to somewhat better conditions, such as placement in "propaganda camps" where they were allowed care packages every month. On February 28, 1973, Clark's six-year internment came to a close when he was among a group of twenty prisoners released "as a gift of the NVA to Henry Kissinger."

Returning to the Mid-Missouri area, Clark remained on active duty until 1978, then joining the Air National Guard and retiring as a colonel in 1992. He went on to earn an MBA from the University of Missouri. In 1987, he became a water engineer for Columbia, from which he retired in 2000.

"I retired (from Columbia) six years early because I wanted to get back the six years I had spent in prison camps," Clark said.

With his characteristic convivial demeanor, those unfamiliar with Clark's history would never suspect the weight of hardship he has overcome, but he does not hesitate in sharing the lessons born of his experiences.

"When you're in such a situation, you realize how fortunate you are to be an American," he said. "It also helps shed light on the intolerance and selfish, simplistic thoughts of greed that come from those who have never had to suffer for something they truly care about." *(Photograph courtesy of John Clark)*

David Hunter – *Jefferson City*

Many might consider three Purple Heart medals and a Bronze Star for valor from service in the Vietnam War to be quite an impressive distinction. However, for Marine Corps veteran David Hunter, these recognitions are simply a byproduct of an intense set of experiences that were the beginning of a maturing period for a young man seeking some direction in his life. Growing up in the community of Harriman, New York, Hunter left high school before he could graduate in pursuit of "something a little different." He then stopped by his local recruiting office to take the first step in embarking upon a life of adventure.

"I wanted to go somewhere, and I wanted to get there quickly," said Hunter. "I actually thought I would join the Navy, but their recruiter was out of the office when I stopped by, but a Marine Corps gunny [gunnery sergeant] came over to me and said, 'Come on—I'll buy you a beer.'"

Enlisting in the Marine Corps in April 1965, the eighteen-year-old recruit completed boot camp at Parris Island, South Carolina, followed by several weeks of advanced infantry training at Camp Lejeune, North Carolina. Receiving assignment to the 5th Marine Regiment of the 1st Marine Division at Camp Pendleton, California, he was soon engaged in training to prepare for deployment to Vietnam. In late April of 1966, the freshly trained Marine arrived in the Gulf of Tonkin aboard the USS *Princeton* and was soon engaged in "Operation Hastings"—a major military operation that pushed the North Vietnamese Army back past the demilitarized zone (DMZ).

"We lost Marines in Hastings, but we killed a lot of North Vietnamese regulars," he said. "The North Vietnamese were professionals who knew how to fight and stood nose-to-nose with us in combat," he added.

Serving in several locations throughout Vietnam as a member of battalion-sized sweeps, search and destroy missions and combat along the DMZ, Hunter noted he was first wounded during a mission on July 23, 1966, when a rocket-propelled grenade struck the ground less than ten feet away.

"The detonation wounded one of the guys on my team, and when the battle was all over, I was bleeding from several places," he recalled. "They considered me walking wounded, and I was treated by a corpsman for several shrapnel wounds. Several days later, I was evacuated and treated in the infirmary aboard the Princeton for infection of those wounds."

Quickly returning to duty with his battalion, in the late summer of 1966, they began moving north toward Da Nang while conducting minor sweeps, company-sized drills, and ambushes. Weeks later, he was transferred from 3rd Battalion to 2nd Battalion of the 5th Marines.

"We locked fists with the 22nd North Vietnamese Regiment in an area called Phu Loc 6 prior to Christmas (of 1966)," said Hunter. "We fought them all the way through Christmas, and I survived by the grace of God," he added.

On December 16, 1966, he braved enemy fire to retrieve much-needed ammunition and medical supplies from a helicopter that crashed in a rice paddy. For this, he earned a Bronze Star medal for valor. On the same day, while on a patrol, he saw a North Vietnamese soldier stand up and the flash of the muzzle blast from his rifle.

"I remember lying on the ground and had a bullet in my chest stuck between my ribs," he explained. "Fortunately, I was wearing a flak jacket, and the bullet hit magazines I was carrying, then nicked the corner of a grenade hanging from my suspenders, and tore up the button of my jacket."

A corpsman was able to remove the bullet on the spot, and Hunter was later evacuated to An Hoa, where he received five stitches from the bullet wound. The incident earned him his second Purple Heart. He would go on to earn a third Purple Heart on April 10, 1967, during a search and destroy mission known as Operation Union II, when he received shrapnel wounds to his back from a 120mm rocket. He left Vietnam in late 1967 and, after a brief time back in the states with the 2nd Marine Division, he returned to Vietnam in April 1969 and completed a tour as the platoon sergeant for Company A, 11th Engineers, 3rd Marine Division.

"The most intense thing that happened to me on my second tour was when I was operating a bulldozer at Vandergrift Combat base, and a rocket struck next to the dozer," he said. "It blew me off the dozer, and I ended up with a ruptured left eardrum, permanent hearing loss, and it dislocated my right shoulder."

After Vietnam, he finished his high school education through night classes. Hunter remained in the Marine Corps, transitioning from the enlisted ranks to warrant officer and eventually becoming a commissioned officer, retiring in 1989 as the captain in command of the Marine Corps Detachment at Ft. Leonard Wood. For fifteen years following his military career, he was a field supervisor for two telephone contractors.

The married father of four humbly explained that when looking back on his experiences in Vietnam, he often focuses on moments touched with humor rather than the loss and injury so often associated with service in a combat environment.

"Even when I was a kid, I was a clean freak, but you didn't get much time to wash or shave when you were on the move in Vietnam—and that really bugged me," he asserted. "And those canned rations they fed us ... they were nasty; there is no other word to describe them." With a grin, he added, "And in every circumstance when I was wounded, it was because there was nowhere to go to avoid the situation, and the first question that came to mind was whether or not my fellow Marines got the guy that did that to me." *(Photograph courtesy of David Hunter.)*

John Bailie – *Jefferson City*

In the years following his Vietnam War service, John Bailie developed something of a "flag fetish," resulting in the decoration of a room in his basement with various forms of *Old Glory*. The veteran went on to explain that this love for the U.S. flag came with the realization of the true nature of sacrifice made by his fellow soldiers, many of whom did not return from the war. A 1962 graduate of Port Hueneme High School in California, Bailie jovially noted that he "bummed around a little" after high school until eventually finding employment as a machinist with Allis Chalmers near the community of Oxnard.

"I met Barbara while I was out there, and we married on June 1, 1966," said Bailie. "Two months later, I received my draft notice, and a month after that, I was inducted into the U.S. Army at Los Angeles."

The newly married draftee was sent to the former Fort Ord, California, to complete several weeks of basic training. He remained at the post for advanced training as a field lineman, learning to install communication systems. Upon graduation from his initial training in January 1967, he received orders for his first duty assignment—overseas service in Vietnam.

"They sent me over on a commercial aircraft out of Travis Air Force Base and flew me into Bien Hoa Air Base," he recalled. "While there, I was briefly assigned to a holding company before being sent to my new unit, which was B Company, 1st Battalion of the 44th Artillery located seven and a half miles from the DMZ (demilitarized zone) in *Đông Hà*."

Because there was little need for field linemen in his new assignment, Bailie was designated a radio operator—a position for which he received on-the-job training. In the early days of his new position, he discovered that radio operators did not stay in the hooch receiving and forwarding radio communications; instead, they served with a platoon that went out on patrols.

"Our unit was supporting the Air Force base," said the veteran. "We were like perimeter guards, and we had an M42 Duster (self-propelled anti-aircraft gun similar to a tank) with twin forties (40mm guns) that we used to patrol and secure the perimeter and prevent the enemy from setting up attacks."

The base became ground zero for nightly mortar attacks from an enemy gun that was installed on a rail car on a nearby mountain. Once the gun was fired, the rail car was pulled back into a cave in the side of the mountain face, essentially concealing the immense weapon.

"It was a hot area," said Bailie, "and we got into a lot of firefights. One thing that I discovered quickly is that I didn't want to be a radioman because they are usually the second man the enemy tries to kill during an attack; the first is the officer or person in charge of the group," he added.

A little more than halfway through his overseas tour of duty, Bailie was granted two weeks of leave and was able to travel to Hawaii to spend time with his wife. When returning to Vietnam, he approached his sergeant about reclassifying in a military job that might afford him a promotion and the opportunity to earn more money.

"The only thing they had available was motor pool clerk, so I got a promotion to E-4 and began maintaining the records on all of the equipment in our company," he said. "Then, in early January 1968, just before the Tet (Offensive), my time in Vietnam was up, and they transferred me to Ft. Hood, Texas.

For the next several months, he and his wife lived in an apartment near the Army post while Bailie continued his work as a motor pool clerk. In his new duty assignment with 1st Battalion, 66th Armor Regiment, the soldier helped track the maintenance and readiness status of the battalion's armored personnel carriers until receiving his discharge on September 13, 1968. Returning to Oxnard, he was reemployed with Allis Chalmers until a steel strike and economic downturn inspired his move to a nearby Oldsmobile dealership, where he was employed as a parts manager. In 1974, he and his wife moved to Jefferson City to be nearer to his wife's sister and her husband.

He was briefly employed as a parts manager at a local Cadillac dealership before being hired at the former Westinghouse Electric, which later became ABB. In 2006, he retired from ABB with approximately 30 years of service. In the years prior to his retirement, he and his wife raised a son and daughter.

Bailie has only recently begun speaking about his service in Vietnam, a hesitance that stems from the disparaging treatment he and his fellow veterans received when coming home from the war. The veteran also noted that although he was not what one would call a "flag waver" prior to his service, an experience on his return from Vietnam secured his passion for the nation's flag.

"There is a room in my basement that I have chosen to decorate with different U.S. flag memorabilia because it is something I respect and enjoy," said Bailie. "It stems from when I was at Da Nang [Vietnam], waiting to come home from the war." He continued, "There were a hundred or so coffins of my fellow servicemen draped with the U.S. flag, all who were also waiting to come home for the last time. That memory," he paused, "… that memory sticks in my mind, and I think it was that moment that secured my respect for the flag and all who served under her." *(Photograph courtesy of John Bailie)*

William Lipskoch – *Taos*

During his one-year combat tour in South Vietnam in the late 1960s, William Lipskoch witnessed the loss of friends and fellow soldiers, leaving him with memories he chose to suppress for a number of decades. However, he joyfully maintains that one unforgettable moment from the war never to be forgotten is the young Vietnamese woman he met and married during his overseas deployment. Born and raised on a farm near the small Osage County community of Hope, Lipskoch graduated from high school in nearby Linn in 1961. For the next couple of years, he worked at a couple of automotive garages in the area before enrolling at Linn Technical Junior College (now State Technical College of Missouri).

"I actually received my draft notice in January 1965, but I was granted a deferment until May so that I could graduate from Linn Tech," Lipskoch said. "Right after graduating, I was inducted into the U.S. Army and sent to Ft. Leonard Wood for my basic training," he added.

While in basic, he received orders to attend aviation electronics school and, in late July 1965, began nineteen weeks of advanced training at Ft. Gordon, Georgia. While there, he learned the fundamentals of radios and electronics and later underwent technical simulations to ensure he and his classmates could diagnose and repair radios and associated equipment. Graduating in late December, he received orders for deployment to Vietnam but was able to enjoy a few days home during the Christmas holiday. He then flew to Oakland, California, spending a couple of days in orientation prior to boarding a flight bound for Vietnam.

"We flew into Saigon, and I eventually got orders for the Mekong Delta," recalled Lipskoch. "They sent me to the military base at Soc Trang in South Vietnam sometime around the second week of January 1966, and I was assigned to the 336th Assault Helicopter Company."

As part of his duties, the young soldier often accompanied the helicopter gunships during their flights to various landing zones in the region. During these missions, they dropped off ARVN (Army of the Republic of Vietnam) troops for combat operations. While the gunships were awaiting the return of the ARVN troops, Lipskoch worked to ensure the radios on the aircraft remained operational.

"Other times, when I wasn't repairing any issues that the crew chiefs identified with the radios, I was helping to work on the helicopters," he explained. "While I was there," he solemnly added, "we lost some good soldiers on helicopters that were shot down."

One moment that has remained forever emblazoned in his Vietnam reflections happened a few weeks after his arrival at Soc Trang when an aircraft returned from an intense and deadly mission.

"A helicopter was bringing some ARVN troops that had been on a mission back to the base," he explained. "Several had been killed, and some were missing legs, and others were missing arms ... and they threw all the bodies in a big pile." Following a brief pause, he added, "It was something I had never seen before and an image I have never forgotten."

During his off-duty hours, he occasionally visited the enlisted club, where he met a young Vietnamese woman named Rita Bui. She sold tickets that the soldiers used to purchase drinks and other items at the club. In the evenings, she and the other Vietnamese locals working on the base were driven back to their nearby village in a military truck guarded by military police.

"I went to see her at the club whenever I could and then began walking her to meet the truck that carried her back to their village in the evenings," he said. "We began dating, and about eight months later, I asked her to marry me. At first, her mother didn't want her to leave Vietnam, but she eventually gave her permission."

His initial overseas deployment was scheduled to end in January 1967, but he volunteered to extend for several months to remain in Vietnam so that he could complete the paperwork necessary to marry Rita and bring her back to the states. In a private ceremony at the base on April 1, 1967, they were married by a military chaplain. When his extended tour came to an end in mid-May 1967, he and his new wife returned to the United States and initially settled on his parent's farm in Hope. As the years passed, they raised three daughters and a son. Lipskoch worked several years at a Ford dealership after the war but eventually went on to retire from CenturyLink after thirty-five years of employment.

The couple now resides in the community of Taos, and both have actively supported the Central Missouri Honor Flight and Operation Bugle Boy. As Lipskoch explained, the camaraderie he experienced when going on an honor flight several years ago, coupled with seeing for the first time the Vietnam Veterans Memorial in Washington, D.C., inspired him to open up about his own military service.

"Meeting Rita was a blessing from the war, but after witnessing the helicopter crashes in Vietnam and losing friends over there—and then coming home only to be spit upon and called names at the airport in California—I really didn't want to talk about the experience for the longest time," he said. He continued, "But I can't say enough good things about going on the Honor Flight and the service they provide for veterans. It is an inspirational group of volunteers that has encouraged me to speak and share more about my own service in Vietnam." *(Photograph courtesy of William Lipskoch)*

Rita (Bui) Lipskoch – *South Vietnam to Taos*

For the last several decades, Rita Lipskoch has never wavered in counting the blessings she has been bestowed. Coming of age in a small village in South Vietnam during the embattled period of the Vietnam War, she left her meager surroundings and moved to the United States after marrying a soldier who served with the U.S. Army. Born in the Catholic village of Xuan Hoa, located near the larger city of Soc Trang, South Vietnam, the former Rita Bui grew up in a family of 16 children. She would often spend her days helping her parents in their farming endeavors of growing such staples as rice, fruits, bananas, coconuts, mangoes, vegetables, in addition to raising ducks, chickens, and pigs.

"We went to a local Catholic school as kids," recalled Rita. "I wanted to become a doctor, but my parents could not afford to send me to school in the city for that specialty; so, basically, I was stuck in Xuan Hoa," she added.

Communist infiltration increased in the area surrounding her village as the Vietnam War progressed, and, on one occasion, Viet Cong soldiers abducted the priest from their church, murdering the clergyman. Emboldened by their numbers, the communist soldiers began entering the village at night to capture young men to serve with their forces while also kidnapping girls to sell into prostitution.

"Several of us became members of the South Vietnamese Army and were trained on shooting rifles and being soldiers," she explained. "But after the Communists came and killed several of the people from our village and put their bodies in the school for everyone to see, my mother decided to send me away for my safety."

Living with family in the nearby city of Soc Trang, a relative informed her that jobs were available at the local military base. She was soon hired to work in the building that housed the enlisted club, selling tickets that soldiers used to purchase drinks and other items. In the mornings, a military truck would pick up several Vietnamese workers in town, including Rita, and drive them to the military base at Soc Trang. Guarded by armed military policemen, the truck would likewise transport the workers back to their village in the evenings.

"There was a young soldier who would come in the club during his breaks, sit on a stool and visit with me while I was working," said Rita. "At first, I didn't realize he was interested in me until he started walking me to the truck that would take me back home in the evenings," she added.

William Lipskoch, a U.S. Army draftee from Osage County, Missouri, was serving at the U.S. Army base in Soc Trang when he met Rita in 1966. After dating for eight months, he asked for the young Vietnamese woman's hand in marriage.

Rita recalled, "When he first asked me to marry him, I told my mother, and she didn't want me to go because then she wouldn't have anyone around. But, after I told her that I would be able to live and work in the U.S. and send her and my father money to help support them, she finally agreed."

The couple married on April 1, 1967, during a small ceremony on the base performed by a U.S. Army chaplain. Several weeks later, Lipskoch received his discharge from the military and returned to the United States to settle in Osage County, beginning the next chapter of his life with his new wife. As the years passed, Lipskoch was employed by a local communications company, while Rita focused on the commitment made to her parents. She worked several jobs throughout the years but was hired by the Missouri Department of Revenue in December 1974, from which she retired in May 2005.

In addition to her full-time employment in state government, she worked many hours a week at the Gerbes Super Market in Jefferson City from 1992 until 2015, sending money home to her parents and helping to ensure her own children received a college education.

"In 1991, I finally returned to Vietnam and visited my parents," Rita said. "They were basically living in a chicken house, and I helped them purchase a new home." She continued, "There had also been a tornado that knocked the old church off its foundation, and I made quilts that were raffled off so that I could send money to Vietnam to help rebuild the church."

In 1998, Rita's mother passed away at eighty-nine years of age and was laid to rest in the cemetery of the church she had attended as a child and youth. Although she was unable to return to Vietnam for the funeral, in 2014, she felt as though God was encouraging her to return home one last time.

"I watched the fluctuations in airfare and finally got a good rate in May 2014," she explained. "While in Vietnam, I had the opportunity to visit with my father." Pausing, she added, "I am glad that I went when I did because he died the following year when he was 107-and-half years old."

She and her husband have, in recent years, been active participants in organizations supporting veterans such as Operation Bugle Boy and Central Missouri Honor Flight. The Vietnamese native has used her culinary skills to provide treats for many of these events as a demonstration of her appreciation for the sacrifice veterans made in her native land.

"I love the United States and am forever thankful for everything that veterans have done for me and my people," she affirmed. She elatedly added, "And I truly believe that God sent Bill to Vietnam because I had prayed many times that I would someday meet a good man and have a better life. Well … God answered my call." *(Photograph courtesy of Rita Lipskoch)*

Denny Banister – *St. Louis*

When Denny Banister graduated from college in Warrensburg in 1966, the young man's life could have taken many interesting directions. Only recently married to his fiancée, Madelyn, with whom he had grown up in St. Louis, the young man chose to pursue a long-held interest in the military by enlisting in the U.S. Navy.

"They sent me to San Diego in May 1967, for boot camp," recalled Banister. "While I was there, I was selected to serve as a journalist because of the broadcasting and radio experience I had acquired during and after college," he added.

After completing his basic training, he received orders to report for Rota, Spain, arriving in the country in late summer 1967. Several months later, his wife joined him at their new overseas home.

"They assigned me as the station manager for the radio station on the base," he explained. "The naval base was very interesting, and the radio station was located down by the pier." He further noted,

"We were part of the Armed Force Radio and Television Service and carried their transcribed programming."

Additionally, Banister went on to explain, he spent much of his time as a disc jockey and developing local programming.

"One memorable moment was when I interviewed an admiral with the Spanish navy and the interview was conducted through an interpreter. On another occasion, I interviewed for the base newspaper a prince in the line of Spanish royalty."

On other occasions, the sailor was called upon to host and introduce various entertainment acts who were visiting the military base during USO shows. During what became a three-year assignment in Spain, Banister's wife gave birth to their son on Christmas Day of 1968.

"My family and I were able to get some time off and travel to Austria, Switzerland, and Germany—we really got to see a nice chunk of Europe," he said. "But then I received orders for Guantanamo Bay, Cuba, in the summer of 1970, so my wife and son went back to St. Louis while I finished the next two years of my assignment."

While in Cuba, he was once again assigned to the Armed Forces Radio and Television Service, working as the radio station manager and as a member of the television evening news team.

"I remember when I arrived at Cuba, and they were ferrying me to the station, I thought to myself, 'Here I am, serving during the Vietnam War and spending my time as a journalist, while many of my friends are in the Vietnam War.' It was a surreal moment," he added.

The United States soon began to draw down forces as the end of the Vietnam War approached, and, in September 1972, Banister received his discharge from the Navy. When returning to St. Louis to reunite with his family, his parents were in the process of retiring to the Lake of the Ozarks. During a trip to visit them, a voice he heard over his car radio soon shifted the direction of his post-military career.

"We were going to see my parents when a guy I used to broadcast with during college came on the radio station in Fulton," he said. "So, I stopped by the station to see him and the general manager there was another guy I had worked with in commercial radio."

Banister would spend the next six months working at the station in Fulton, followed by five years with KLIK in Jefferson City. Missouri Farm Bureau then hired him in 1976, where he would go on to retire as assistant director of public affairs after thirty-five years of employment.

"I had been out of the Navy for eleven years and working for Farm Bureau when I realized that I really missed the service," explained Banister. "Initially, my decision to leave the Navy was because I was tired of being away from my family, but when I was working in radio, there were no holidays, and you were always moving to other stations if you wanted opportunities for advancement."

Enlisting in the Navy Reserve in St. Louis in 1983, Banister remained in the service until retiring on this sixtieth birthday in August 2004, having completed a combined twenty-eight years of military service.

"The Navy Reserve offered me several fascinating opportunities like working temporary orders at different naval broadcasting facilities and covering events like Fleet Week and air shows with the Blue Angels—the Navy's flight demonstration team." He added, "I also got to go on sea duty frequently."

As the veteran sagely explained, his experiences have made it difficult for him to share with others his own story of military service.

"As a journalist, it was part of my job to tell the stories of others," he said. "If you focus on yourself, then you're missing the story." He added, "But while I was in the Navy, I never stopped learning. I had the privilege of working with individuals from many professional backgrounds, and I learned from them, taking those new skills back to my full-time employer. It all tied together quite well." *(Photograph courtesy of Denny Banister)*

Libby Shull – *Tebbetts*

As a young lady coming of age in the small community of Angelus, South Carolina, Libby Shull settled on the intent of someday becoming a nurse. Upon graduation from high school in 1963, she chose to pursue this professional goal by enrolling in a nurse training program at Presbyterian Hospital in Charlotte, North Carolina.

"It was a residency program at the hospital, and they had a dorm on the campus where we stayed," said Shull. "It was great hands-on training that gave us the experience we needed and resulted in a three-year diploma," she added.

Following completion of the program in 1966, she continued to work at the hospital for the next three years. However, when another nurse with whom she occasionally chatted made the suggestion they should consider joining the military, Shull agreed it might be a good opportunity.

"I wanted to serve my country during the Vietnam War and we spoke to several recruiters but decided on the Air Force," she recalled. "After joining, I was sent to Sheppard Air Force Base in Texas in January of 1969 for three weeks of indoctrination training to learn how to wear a uniform, salute and all the basics of serving as an officer."

One aspect of the training that shines brightly in her reflections was being taken to the field with several of her fellow medical trainees and performing triage on the casualties of a simulated aircraft crash. Appointed as a second lieutenant, her first duty assignment was at the former England Air Force Base in Louisiana, where she worked in a small hospital with "maybe two-dozen beds." Three months after her arrival, the chief nurse approached her and asked if she had signed up for "worldwide duty."

She explained, "I had been issued orders for Clark Air Base in the Philippines," she chuckled. "I was assigned to the Med Surg (medical-surgical) and the Neurointensive Care Unit while I was there."

Although the hospital provided various types of medical care to personnel from all military branches, Shull recalled that the most difficult aspect of the hospital's mission included receiving, treating, and stabilizing seriously wounded troops coming out of the combat zones of Vietnam. On some occasions, there were patients who had succumbed to their wounds and injuries while being transported from Vietnam; their remains had to be processed upon their arrival at Clark Air Base prior to being sent back to the United States.

During her fifteen-month tour of duty in the Philippines, she lived in a barracks building with many Air Force officers assigned to the base and became acquainted with a pilot named Walter Shull. The two became friends and remained in contact after she was reassigned to the base hospital at Blytheville Air Force Base in Arkansas in late 1970.

"Walt had been assigned to an Air Force base in California, but he and I were able to visit one another on occasion while I was stationed in Blytheville," Shull said. "In 1971, we were engaged and planned to be married in December of that year, but Walt got orders for Vietnam, and we had to delay our marriage." She added, "I received my discharge from the Air Force in the fall of 1971 and spent the next year working at a hospital in South Carolina."

In December 1972, after Walt returned from his service flying rescue missions in Vietnam, the couple married. As Shull explained, prior to their marriage, they had agreed that she would leave the Air Force since it was unlikely that they would be stationed together while both were on active duty.

She explained, "Once we were married, I accompanied him on his duty assignments in places like Florida, Alaska, Utah, Scott Air Force Base, and at Shaw Air Force Base in South Carolina. I did some part-time nursing work at hospitals near the bases and later stayed home to raise our two sons during their early years."

Her husband received a transfer to Shaw Air Force Base, South Carolina, in the late 1980s since her parents, who lived nearby, were in declining health and passed shortly thereafter. Following Walt's retirement in 1991, the couple moved to Mid-Missouri, settling near the community of Tebbetts. The former Air Force nurse worked a number of years for a home healthcare company and later retired from the Cole County Health Department in 2011. She continues to volunteer at Capital Region Medical Center and proudly explained that one of her sons retired from the Air Force while the other remains on active duty.

When discussing her rather spontaneous decision to join the military during the Vietnam War decades ago, Shull maintains that it set the stage for an unexpected adventure that provided her with the means to support those who fought in combat.

"At that young age, I thought of it as an adventure and also realized that it would give me the chance to do my part during the war," she affirmed. "The time in the Philippines really was an eye-opener because there were some heavy casualties coming through the hospital and many who never survived the war." Meekly, she added, "But you always felt needed and realized you were participating in a calling. It was so very gratifying to be able to help the ones that you could, but at the same time heartbreaking because of those you could not help." *(Photograph courtesy of Libby Shull)*

Walter Shull – *Tebbetts*

Walter Shull became interested in aviation after his parents purchased for him and his twin brother flight training hours at the airport in Jefferson City while they were still in high school. A few years later, when attending college at Central Methodist University in Fayette, he went on to finish the requirements to earn his civilian pilot's license, which was a decision that soon influenced the direction of his military career. Graduating from college in January 1967, Shull soon received notice to report for the military draft. In an effort to have some choice in his service branch, he tested for the Air Force and was soon accepted into their pilot training program.

"My initial officer's training was at Medina Air Force Base in San Antonio, followed by pilot's training at Williams Air Force Base south of Phoenix," he said. "While in Arizona, they brought in all different types of aircraft, and that's when I became interested in the HC-130 because of the various types of missions it could perform."

The HC-130 is an airframe based upon the Lockheed C-130 and was designed to refuel helicopters, conduct search and rescue operations, and was even employed to assist in the retrieval of the Apollo astronauts once they returned from space.

"Since I finished second in my class, I had the choice of the type of aircraft I wanted to fly, so I chose the HC-130 ... and I am sure glad that I did," he affirmed.

Following several months of training on the C-130 at Seward Air Force Base near Nashville, he completed rescue school at Eglin Air Force Base in Florida. The young pilot then volunteered for service at Clark Air Base in the Philippines. While there, he flew missions to rescue downed pilots off the coast of South Vietnam.

"My first eighteen months of flying was primarily over water instead of the land," he said.

During these rescue missions, the HC-130 would serve as the airborne mission commander while jets flew in formation, offering protection. A helicopter accompanied the group, which could be refueled by the HC-130 and could enter the area where the downed pilot was located. While in the Philippines, Shull met an Air Force nurse named Libby. After he was transferred to Hamilton Air Force Base in California in November 1970, he continued to maintain contact with Libby, who had been transferred to an Air Force base in Arkansas.

"We were engaged to be married but had to delay the marriage because I got orders for Vietnam in December 1971," he explained. "I spent about a year in Vietnam doing rescue missions over the land. When I came back, Libby and I were married in December of 1972 and decided it would be best if she left the Air Force since we would probably not be stationed together while we were both on active duty," he added.

Shull went on to complete a number of Air Force assignments throughout the U.S. during the next few years that included the rescue of fishermen stranded at sea, searching for lost hikers, and retrieving weather balloons in descent so the information collected could be analyzed before being contaminated by certain elements present at lower altitudes.

"After we were married, I was transferred to Eglin Air Force Base in Florida and flew rescue aircraft while also serving as an instructor pilot," he said. "In 1977, I was transferred to Elmendorf Air Force Base, Alaska, where I worked in the rescue coordination center."

In Alaska, the center coordinated more than four hundred missions a year, including the rescue of the passengers and crew of the MS Prinsendam—a Dutch cruise ship that suffered an out-of-control engine fire in October 1980 off the coast of Alaska. Although the Coast Guard took the lead in the rescue of the more than five hundred people aboard, the Air Force helped coordinate and provide resources for the effort.

During their moves, Libby often worked part-time at local hospitals while raising their two sons. The family moved to Scott Air Force Base in 1981, remaining there for the next six years, where Shull worked as director of operations command and control for Headquarters Air Rescue and Recovery Service and later the 23rd Air Force.

"From 1987 to 1988, we were at Hill Air Force Base, but I requested a humanitarian transfer to Shaw Air Force Base in South Carolina since Libby's parents were in declining health," he said. "Unfortunately, both of her parents soon passed."

He remained at the base to run the command post for the 363rd Tactical Fighter Wing until retiring at the rank of lieutenant colonel in 1991. Since his parents were still living, the family chose to move to Mid-Missouri and settled in the Tebbetts area. Shull went on to work nineteen years for the Missouri Department of Natural

Resources before "retiring for good in 2011." Since that time, he has been actively involved in the Optimist Club and continues to support such organizations as Operation Bugle Boy and Central Missouri Honor Flight.

Proudly sharing details of the service of his two sons, both of whom are Air Force veterans, Shull maintains that his own time in uniform was full of many unique experiences that have left him with unforgettable lessons and memories.

"It was probably the best job in the world—I got to fly airplanes and help save lives," he excitedly remarked. "Very few rescues we conducted were ever identical and plans frequently changed, so every day was interesting since we had to learn to improvise ... especially during the combat missions." *(Photograph courtesy of Walter Shull)*

Everett Markay Jr. – *Jefferson City*

When attending Helias Catholic High School during the early 1960s, Everett Markway Jr. recalls a dynamic teacher who inspired a lasting passion for the sciences. It seemed a natural conclusion that following his graduation from high school in 1963, he should pursue a degree in chemistry at Lincoln University.

"Our family didn't have a lot of extra money for me to go to school so enrolling at a local college, where I could live at home while attending classes, seemed the best choice for me," said Markway.

Graduating with his bachelor's in chemistry in May 1967, he married the former Marla Rothove, his high school sweetheart, the following September. Although he was now eligible for the military draft, he began taking graduate chemistry courses at the University of Missouri-Columbia.

"I made it through one year of graduate school while also working a short time as a feed chemist at the Missouri Department of

Agriculture laboratory before my draft notice finally arrived," said Markway. "I completed my induction at Jefferson Barracks and began my basic training at Ft. Leonard Wood in January 1969," he added.

The weeks he spent at Ft. Leonard Wood provided a number of interesting experiences for the young soldier, such as performing suicide watch of a trainee in a restroom before the troubled soldier was transferred from the post, in addition to guard duty outside a post exchange on a rainy evening armed with a rifle and no ammunition. Finishing his basic training in late March 1969, he received orders for his next duty assignment and, after a brief furlough to visit his wife and family in Jefferson City, reported to Ft. Detrick, Maryland, to work in the U.S. Army Biological Defense Research Center.

"I did not attend advanced individual training like most soldiers but entered a special science and engineering classification system," said Markway. "I had already met the requirements to attend Officer Candidate School (OCS), but since I would be working in the lab for the remaining two years of my duty, I declined OCS since I would likely have been slotted as an infantry officer instead of the Chemical Corps."

Ft. Detrick, he described, was not "the usual Army fort"—it consisted of civilian scientists, military scientists, and medical personnel working in tandem to develop defensive biological warfare research. The primary focus of their scientific endeavors was to develop measures to prevent the adversaries of the U.S. from utilizing biological agents as a means to overwhelm military and civilian populations. Working in the Physical Sciences Lab in an internal fenced complex maintained by security police, while also protected by an outer fenced perimeter with military policemen staffing the gates, Markway performed fundamental research primarily with cell membranes of non-lethal bacteria under the guidance of a senior research scientist.

Initially residing in the enlisted barracks for single soldiers, Markway's wife moved to the area in May 1969, and the couple soon found off-base housing in the nearby community of Frederick. While stationed in Maryland, the couple's first child, Laura, was born. In addition to his daily scientific duties while stationed at the post, Specialist Markway volunteered to serve as a member of the fort's honor guard, participating in military funerals in rural western Maryland.

"It was a particularly somber and humbling experience to provide honorary funeral details for grieving families of soldiers who had been killed in Vietnam," said the veteran.

Memorial Day weekend of 1970, three weeks after the Kent State shootings, provided an enduring memory since Markway was called out in full riot gear to help respond to anti-war demonstrators protesting outside the post's main gate. The military police, he noted, were able to maintain the fort's perimeter security without incident. Completing his two-year active-duty commitment on January 13, 1971, Markway and his family returned to Jefferson City. Shortly before his discharge, a friend informed him of a chemist position open at the Missouri Highway Patrol Crime Laboratory. Applying for the vacancy, he was soon hired and went on to complete a thirty-one-year career with the agency.

"It was a rewarding career, and I analyzed physical evidence in more than 10,000 cases, which were primarily drug cases," he said. "During my career, I also testified more than four hundred times in seventy-seven counties in the state and am proud of doing my part to fight the scourge of drug abuse."

Markway and his wife welcomed their second and final child, Greg, in 1974. During the early-to-mid-1970s, the veteran returned to school and, in 1976, earned his master's degree in criminal justice administration from Central Missouri State University. The son of a Marine Corps veteran who served in the Pacific during WWII, Markway asserted he was "gratified and honored" to have made the Central Missouri Honor Flight in 2016, seeing the nation's war memorials in Washington, D.C. While there, he had his photograph taken in front of the WWII memorial while holding pictures of his late father and father-in-law, both WWII veterans.

Service to the public, Markway said, was a natural progression of experiences beginning in college and carrying through his post-military career with the Missouri State Highway Patrol.

"At Ft. Detrick, our efforts were dedicated to keeping up with the Russians and others who were developing biological weapons, testing for vaccines and antidotes for our military and civilian populations in case we were attacked," he said. "And looking back on my career that preceded and followed, it was a collection of public service experiences—working in the lab while in college, my biological work in the military, and then with the crime lab." He added, "That seemed to be my mission and my background and was the appropriate path for me." *(Photograph courtesy to Everett Markway Jr.)*

Gerald Hoechst – *St. Louis*

A 1962 graduate of Mehlville High School in St. Louis, Gerald Arthur Hoechst went on to attend Central Methodist University and graduated with his bachelor's degree in education in 1968. He was drafted into the U.S. Army on August 2, 1968, and is pictured while serving as an equipment maintenance specialist with HHD, 720th Military Police Battalion in Long Binh, Vietnam. Several months prior to his arrival in Vietnam, the base at Long Binh had been infiltrated by Vietcong during the Tet Offensive. Following his discharge on April 1, 1970, Hoechst returned to St. Louis and was for many years employed with United Van Lines in Fenton, Missouri. The former U.S. Army sergeant passed away on March 22, 2001, when only fifty-six years old, and is buried in Jefferson Barracks National Cemetery. *(Photograph courtesy of Judy Thompson)*

Stanley J. Adams – *Millersburg*

In May of 1968, when Stanley Adams received his military draft notice, he was not taken by surprise since many of his friends had already been called into service for the Vietnam War. Little did he realize that within a few months, the boy from Mokane would become a man when embroiled in combat thousands of miles from home, experiencing deprivations and a loss of friends that he would struggle to forget in later years. Through the encouragement of family, he has since rekindled many of his military friendships and penned a book in hopes of preserving the history of the unique group of soldiers with whom he served.

"I was inducted into the Army in June of 1968, and went to Fort Leonard Wood for my basic training and then on to Fort Ord in

California for my AIT (Advanced Individual Training) as an infantryman," Adams recalled. "By late November, I was on an airplane heading to Vietnam," he added.

Assigned to Company B, 4th Battalion, 9th Infantry Regiment of the 25th Infantry Division located near Tay Ninh, Vietnam, Adams explained that the regiment was called "Manchu," which stood for "Dragon Men," in the lexicon of Vietnamese locals. The dragon, explained, was a component of the 9th Infantry Regiment crest. Upon his arrival in Vietnam, the barely twenty-year-old "replacement" soldier was advised that the Manchus were always in the thick of the fight, and his chances of making it home were slim. These admonishments would nearly become a reality three weeks later when he was caught in a major battle that has never disappeared from his reflections.

"Word came around that we were to build a patrol base camp 9.5 miles south of Tay Ninh City, west of the South Vam Co Don River about half a klick away from the Cambodian border," wrote Adams in his book *Mokane to Mole City*. He added, "The site was a flat, wide-open area in the rice fields that became hard and dusty during the dry season."[108]

The camp, which was designated "Mole City" by the soldiers stationed there, became ground zero for a bloody battle unfolding on December 22, 1968. While on a listening post near the camp, Adams and three of his fellow soldiers observed enemy movement and were nearly discovered. They quickly gathered their equipment and returned to Mole City to report their observations.

"Shortly after we returned to camp that night ... the radar squad on the tower sent word down the bunker line that they could see a tremendous amount of enemy movement down the wood line and ditches with the starlight scope," Adams wrote. "Three of our boo-

---

[108] Adams, *Mokane to Mole City*, 26.

by-trap grenades went off at the entrance to the ditch, in the vicinity of our earlier (listening post)."

The details of the nightmarish episode that developed are enough to fill a book and have become a large part of Adams' aforementioned book. Portions of the camp were overrun by the North Vietnamese Army (NVA), and many U.S. soldiers whom Adams had only begun to know were killed in action.

Adams wrote, "We had to fight to the finish, no matter the outcome. If it came down to it, I guess we would've fought to the last man standing, like the Alamo. None of us knew how this was going to end, and we were all very scared."

Their savior came at daybreak, with gunships and helicopters continuing to drive the enemy forces back into nearby Cambodia. This was the first and most intense combat experience of Adams' year served in Vietnam, although the coming months were accentuated with death and despair from combat patrols in addition to assorted battles and skirmishes.

"You became callous to it all and tried not to get close to anyone because you just never knew if and when they might be killed," Adams said. "I will never forget my sergeant telling me, 'You won't hear the round that gets you, so why worry about it?'"

Returning to the states in late 1969, Adams finished out the remaining six months of his two-year draft period with a unit at Fort Carson, Colorado. When back in Missouri, he met Rita through mutual friends, and they married in November 1974. As the years passed, the couple raised two daughters, and he went on to retire from Ameren UE.

"I was looking through some of his pictures from Vietnam and believed the worst tragedy would be for him not to see his buddies ever again," said Rita. "I did some research on the internet and found that the Manchus were having reunions, so we began attending several years ago."

During the reunions, Adams was encouraged to see a counselor at the VA, who advised him to make notes of his dreams of Vietnam as a means of coping with the disturbing memories. While doing this, he also noticed while attending reunions, many of his friends were passing away. From the encouragement of his wife and daughters, he resolved to write a book of his experiences.

"It was a very stressful experience, and it was like I was reliving these battles every day when writing the book," he said. "When it was finished, many of those dreams dwindled away, but some of the memories I can never be rid of." Pausing, he added, "I remember when I got ready to leave Vietnam back in 1969, my captain encouraged me to reenlist. I decided to leave the Army because I knew I would be sent back to Vietnam. I'm a believer that you only get so many chances in life."

Autographed copies of Adams' book are available through www.luckysnipe.com. *(Photograph courtesy of Stanley and Rita Adams)*

Leonard Rutledge – *Jefferson City*

While a student at Lincoln University, where he was a member of the school's Reserve Officer Training Corps (ROTC) program in the late 1960s, Leonard Rutledge was accepted into an ROTC flight program. This introductory aviation training later helped inspire and shape the direction of his twenty-nine-year military career, which was punctuated by service in both Vietnam and the Gulf War.

"The ROTC flight program began at Lincoln in 1966 and was considered a six-credit-hour course," said Rutledge. "The school contracted with Jefferson City Flying Service, and it provided fifty hours of flight time in a Cessna 150," he added.

Upon graduation in 1968, he earned his Bachelor of Science degree and was commissioned a second lieutenant in the U.S. Army. He then traveled to Fort Sill, Oklahoma, for several weeks training at the Field Artillery Officers Basic Course.

"Aviation wasn't considered a branch at that time, so I selected the field artillery as my branch," said Rutledge. "Once my branch training was completed, they sent me to Rotary Wing Flight School at Ft. Wolters, Texas, for six months of training to learn to fly the TH-55—a training helicopter."

Realizing he was destined for service in Vietnam since aviators were in high demand, he was sent to Hunter Army Airfield near Savannah, Georgia, spending the next several months in training learning to pilot the UH-1 Iroquois (Huey), the helicopter that was considered the workhorse of the Vietnam War. When his initial aviation training was completed in July 1969, he returned home for thirty days of leave. It was during this brief respite that he was introduced to Quinetta, who would later become his wife.

"They flew me out of San Francisco on a commercial aircraft bound for Vietnam in August of 1969," said the veteran. "After spending a couple of days in a reception area at Long Binh, they assigned me to the 116th Helicopter Assault Company stationed in Cu Chi."

The previous year, while Rutledge was training at Ft. Sill, he was introduced to a new maintenance record-keeping system used by the U.S. Army—an experience that influenced his early service in Vietnam.

"I was initially given the assignment as officer of the motor pool and told by the commander that as soon as I squared away the motor pool, I could fly missions," he said. "They had failed several inspections prior to this because they weren't familiar with the new inspection system, but after I passed my first inspection, I began flying," he added.

Assigned platoon leader for his company, Rutledge began flying missions to fire support bases. He transported troops engaged in combat assaults with the 25th Infantry Division, many of which occurred along the Cambodian border. Additionally, Rutledge explained, he frequently flew "ash and trash" missions, transporting beer, hot meals, chaplains, and other individuals and equipment to firebases.

"As a platoon leader for the 'Yellow Jackets' (the name assigned to his platoon), I was responsible for six aircraft and their crews and flew about seven hundred combat hours during my tour. Later in my tour, our company moved to Chu Lai, where they were located when I left."

Returning stateside in the summer of 1970, Rutledge married Quinetta and was transferred to Ft. Wolters, Texas, receiving appointment as an instructor pilot to train aspiring aviators on the TH-55. He finished out his active-duty commitment in 1972 with the Second Armored Division at Ft. Hood, Texas. Returning to civilian life, he went to work for the Missouri Department of Corrections. Within months following his discharge from active duty, a friend serving as a helicopter pilot with the Missouri National Guard convinced Rutledge to join since they were in need of aviators.

"One of the selling points for me to enlist in the Army National Guard was the extra money and the additional retirement," he grinned.

For the next several years, he worked full-time for the state while also serving in the National Guard. In 1990, he participated in the second deployment of his military career when he was sent to Saudi Arabia with the 1267th Air Ambulance Company during the Gulf War.

"We had missions to fly to field hospitals to either drop off patients or pick them up to transport to other hospitals," Rutledge recalled. "There were other missions we performed, such as flying an officer from Third Armor Division around to locate places where they could move hospitals."

During his National Guard experience, he achieved the rank of captain but, in 1981, converted to a warrant officer slot because of a lack of available commissioned aviation officer slots. In 1998, he retired from the National Guard as a Chief Warrant Officer Four with more than 4,000 flight hours and twenty-nine years of service. The father of one daughter, Rutledge retired in 2006 from his full-time position with the Missouri Department of Corrections. The veteran explained that in 2016, he not only had the privilege of induction into the Army ROTC Hall of Fame at Lincoln University but also made a special trip that reconnected him with his early years in the Army.

"The College of the Ozarks extended an invitation for me to join their Patriotic Education Program in 2016," he said. "As part of the program, twelve Vietnam veterans—including myself—and twelve students made the trip." "While in Vietnam, we were able to visit many of the sites where several of us had served decades earlier, and it was a dynamic experience to be able to share stories, tears, and memories not only with the veterans in our group but also with the students." He added, "The trip reminded me of one of my life's lessons—to always enjoy life and make the best of it. Also, remember the good days and learn from the bad days … and then forget the bad days." *(Photograph courtesy of Leonard Rutledge.)*

Noland Farmer – *Henley*

Beginning on a small dairy farm in Henley, moving forward with service with the U.S. Army in Vietnam, and ending with a lengthy career in the Missouri National Guard, the life and experiences of Noland Farmer are like many whose stories of military service followed a twisted and unpredictable route. Born just days following the end of World War II, Farmer went on to graduate from Eugene High School in 1963 and embarked upon his employment endeavors when hired by the state.

"I did that for about a year and found out I wasn't going to get rich," he chuckled. "One of the guys I worked with said that he could get me a scholarship at Lincoln University if I wanted to pursue my education."

Enrolling at the university in 1964, Farmer not only attended classes but participated in the Reserve Officer Training Corps (ROTC) program while working part-time for the state at the Division of Welfare.

"With the Vietnam War going on, I figured it would be a matter of time before I was drafted and thought that if I was going to be sent, I might as well go as an officer," he explained.

In the spring of 1968, he graduated with his bachelor's degree in agriculture with a minor in biology and was commissioned a second lieutenant in the U.S. Army. He began his active duty commitment several months later when he was sent to Ft. Knox, Kentucky, for armored officer basic course. He spent the next four months learning all aspects of the operation and maintenance of tanks. When his training was finished in 1969, he received his first duty assignment with an armored cavalry squadron at Ft. Carson, Colorado. He was appointed the supply officer with overall responsibility for managing the fuel, ammunition, rations, and clothing for the squadron.

"In November (1969), my orders came down for Vietnam," he said. "I was flown to the base a Phu Bai, and, after in-processing, I was sent to the base at Hué." He added, "They found out that I had an education and background in agriculture and assigned me to a civil affairs unit."

Lt. Farmer helped lead a team of soldiers responsible for teaching South Vietnamese civilians various aspects of farming, including methods used to grow corn, raise chickens, and gardening. Additionally, he mirthfully recalled, an unofficial element of his duties was taking care of the commanding general's banana tree. A few months into his overseas duty, he was granted a compassionate reassignment to return home for a family emergency. For the remainder of his enlistment, he served at Ft. Leonard Wood in a section that processed soldiers apprehended for AWOLs (Absent Without Leave).

"My two-year commitment ended in November 1970, and I received my discharge from the Army," he said. "I came back home and was working as a microbiologist for the Division of Health when I received a letter from the United States Army Reserve, stating I had four years left on my reserve obligation."

When Farmer explained the letter to his brother-in-law, which also noted he would be assigned to a reserve unit for training, it was suggested he enlist in the Missouri National Guard as an officer with the 1035th Heavy Equipment Maintenance Company since they were short a platoon officer. In April 1971, he joined the Guard and became the platoon leader for the company's Service, Evacuation and Supply Section, which recovered ground equipment in need of repairs in addition to providing repair parts for the company during training missions.

"I was promoted to captain and became the commander for the 1035th from 1974 to 1977," said Farmer. "I worked full-time with the state until April 1979, when I went to work full-time for the Missouri National Guard," he added.

In addition to serving in a part-time military capacity with the Command and Control Headquarters in Kanas City for three years, the soldier's assignments included service as the executive officer for the 735th Maintenance Battalion in Jefferson City. His full-time military duties with the National Guard included working at the Combined Support Maintenance Shop from 1979 to 1993 when it was located on Industrial Drive prior to the Missouri National Guard headquarters move to the east end of Jefferson City near Algoa.

"Following the move, I was promoted to colonel and became the Surface Maintenance Manager responsible for the ground equipment for the Missouri National Guard with the exception of aviation assets," he explained.

Retiring in 1996, Farmer worked ten years for the Missouri Department of Natural Resources before his final retirement in 2008. The married father of two children jokingly explained, "These days, I spend time with my wife, Mary, do a little hunting and a little fishing—but as little as possible because I'm retired!"

There are many aspects of his military career that possess enduring qualities, the most important of which have been the friendships he fostered during those years.

"I met a lot of great people in the military, especially in the 1035th!" he exclaimed. "Many of these people have remained my friends throughout the years, and, in fact, one guy I've know for 50 years is still my insurance agent." He added, "The 1035th was a collection of professional talents. Anything you needed to seek advice on was available in that unit—bankers, plumbers, electricians, welders, carpet salesmen ... basically all trades and careers fields. That's why I loved the guard; it was full of professionals." *(Photograph courtesy of Noland Farmer)*

Sharon Grant – *Jefferson City*

There were many states that Sharon Grant called home while growing up since she had to move when her father, who served in the U.S. Navy, changed duty assignments. As she approached adulthood, her father retired from service and settled his family in Iowa, where his daughter went on to graduate from high school and later chose to pursue her own interest in serving her country.

"After I graduated in 1966, I attended community college in Marshalltown, Iowa, and then transferred to University of Northern Iowa," Grant explained. "This was during the Vietnam War, and I soon decided I wanted to do something to support all the young men being sent overseas."

Having worked in a dental office during her senior year of high school, the U.S. Army promised her training as a dental hygienist. In January 1969, she enlisted in the Women's Army Corps (WACs), which had been established as an auxiliary unit of the U.S. Army during World War II to afford women opportunities to serve in non-combat roles. Almost immediately, she was sent to Ft. McClellan, Alabama, the first permanent home for the U.S. Women's Army Corps Center. She remained on the military base for several weeks to complete her basic training and was then transferred to San Antonio, Texas, for the basic dental course.

"During that particular course, we were taught basic dental procedures and learned to assist the dentists in their responsibilities," she explained.

The young soldier was then transferred to Fort Rucker, Alabama, where she worked in a dental clinic for several weeks until her next dental training course came available. In December 1969, she returned to San Antonio to complete the U.S. Army school in dental hygiene. When she arrived at the school, it was days before the two-week break for the Christmas holiday. Rather than stay in the barracks and strip floors, she volunteered to work in the dental clinic—a decision that introduced her to a renowned politician of the era.

"President (Lyndon) Johnson, who was no longer president at that time, came to the clinic for some dental work," she said. "That was an exciting opportunity because I got to assist with the procedure," she excitedly added.

She remained in training in San Antonio through the early spring of 1970, receiving detailed dental instruction in cleaning teeth and fluoride application. From there, she was transferred to her first permanent duty assignment at Fort Rucker, Alabama.

"That's where the Army was doing advanced flight training for Huey pilots," said Grant. "I was assigned as a dental hygienist at the dependent clinic, where we treated the spouses and children of the service members."

While there, she met Thomas Barnett, a native of Indiana who was in flight training. The couple soon began dating, and when the aviator received orders for deployment to Vietnam, they both agreed to get married after he returned from his overseas service.

"Tom was sent to Vietnam in the summer of 1971," she recalled. "His helicopter was shot down during a rescue mission that he volunteered for in September; he was the only one of the crew to survive the crash." Tearfully, she added, "He was paralyzed and died a month later from pneumonia in a hospital in Vietnam."

The loss of her boyfriend became a wound that never fully healed, but Grant continued to immerse herself in her duties at the dental clinic at Ft. Rucker. Months laterhowever, she followed in the footsteps of her beloved Barnett when deploying to Vietnam in March 1972. Arriving in Long Binh, she spent several months working at a clinic as part of the WAC detachment at the base. Then, after the detachment returned to the United States, Grant transferred to a regular Army unit in Saigon that was in the process of turning their equipment over to the South Vietnamese.

"I lived in a hotel at Saigon, and a couple of times a week, I flew to several jungle provinces with an advisory team that was training the South Vietnamese Army," she related. "I supported a dental surgeon that was part of the team, and we provided dental care during these missions for both Americans and occasionally the South Vietnamese."

For her "untiring efforts" and willingness to volunteer for the advisory teams as part of the 38th United States Medical Group Staff, Staff Sergeant Grant was awarded a Civil Actions Medal.

Leaving the country in December 1972, she returned to the United States and remained in the Army until 1975, completing additional service at the Presidio of Monterey and in Okinawa. In the years following her discharge, she has encountered difficulties related to her service in Vietnam, which has left her with emotional trauma that she has addressed through counseling. She went on to pursue an education, using her GI Bill to earn a master's degree in social work. Her master's thesis was published and widely embraced since it was the first large-scale study to review health outcomes for women who served in the Vietnam War. She was later employed by the California Youth Authority in Sacramento and taught in the local schools there for five years.

In 2002, after experiencing some health issues, she moved to Jefferson City to be closer to her sister. The mother of one daughter, Grant explained that although she has encountered her own challenges related to post-traumatic stress, she remains proud of her service and the support she and other women provided during the war.

"I was really in a unique position in Vietnam because there were so few women who served there," said Grant. "We fulfilled important roles in the war, and I think we became a valued part of history." She concluded, "The nation was divided back home during the war, and there was a lot of eighteen- and nineteen-year-olds being sent overseas to fight, but I felt patriotic and just wanted to do my part." *(Photograph courtesy of Sharon Grant).*

Greg McManus (left) – *Springfield*

As a young boy of five or six years of age, Greg McManus recalls attending an aviation event in the Kansas City area and growing infatuated by the aircraft and the pilots who flew them. It was at this event, he noted, that a pilot picked him up, placed him in the cockpit of his plane, and explained to him the controls of the aircraft, which became the initial inspiration that would lead to his lengthy career in aviation.

"I can still remember vividly the details of that experience and how it provided me the interest to someday pursue becoming a pilot," McManus said.

Graduating from high school in Wheaton, Illinois, in 1967, McManus already possessed his commercial pilot's license, having spent hours working at nearby Mitchell Field trading out labor for flight time. The following December, he enlisted in the U.S. Army after he was advised he could fly under a three-year enlistment, whereas the Air Force and Navy required four years of college prior to flight school.

"They sent me to basic training at Ft. Polk, Louisiana, in March of 1968," he said, "and then on to Ft. Wolters, Texas, for primary flight training." He added, "When I arrived at Texas, I was thinking the entire time I would be flying airplanes, but when they placed me in the rotary wing (helicopters), I said 'something's wrong because I signed up to fly airplanes.'"

As McManus discovered, the needs of the Army generally prevail, and he remained in rotary-wing training for the next several weeks. After learning to pilot helicopters such as the OH-23 Hiller and TH-55, he transferred to Hunter-Stewart, Georgia, where he was introduced to the aircraft that would see wide use in the Vietnam War—the UH-1 Iroquois "Huey" helicopter.

"It certainly had a lot more power than the other helicopters we flew in training," said McManus of his early experience aboard the Huey.

With his training complete in the early weeks of 1969, the young pilot was pinned a warrant officer and returned home to visit his family on two weeks of leave before making the trip to California for deployment to Vietnam. Shortly after his arrival overseas, he was assigned to 162nd Assault Helicopter Company stationed in Dong Tam, Vietnam. As the veteran recalled, his introduction to overseas service was rather brusque.

"My second week there, I was co-pilot aboard a Huey, and we got shot down," McManus recalled. "The caution lights came on, and we were able to land in an open area." He added, "We yanked the radios and weapons from our helicopter, and a helicopter in our formation followed us down and picked us up."

In the weeks after his arrival, the young pilot began flying missions as the primary pilot on a UH-1C—a variant of the helicopter designed for the gunship role and equipped with two 7.62mm mini-guns, 2.75-inch rocket launchers, 40mm cannon, and two door gunners firing M-60 machine guns.

"We were kind of on-call and would support a number of missions that included troop insertions, troop extractions, and providing cover for medevacs," he said. "Our gunship was also equipped to lay down smoke screens prior to the troop ships landing to insert troops."

On March 5, 1970, the young warrant officer participated in a flight that later earned him the award of the Distinguished Flying Cross. On this date, he was flying a single gunship at night on a mission north of Chau Duc when he discovered an enemy convoy infiltrating South Vietnam along a trail from the Cambodian border.

"Without hesitation, (McManus) attacked the enemy, completely disregarding the hail of tracers which rose to meet him," noted the orders dated June 25, 1970, which announced the presentation of the award to McManus. "He fired his rockets the entire length of the convoy, confusing the enemy and scattering the troop column."

The aviator would go on to attack and destroy an armored vehicle towing a large artillery piece, all while negotiating the helicopter through continued machine gunfire. He eventually expended all his ordnance and sustained significant damage to the aircraft, necessitating it be flown to a remote Special Forces site where it was later recovered.

His tour in Vietnam ended early April 1970, the closing moments of an experience that resulted in the award of thirty-seven Air Medals, two Distinguished Flying Crosses, and nearly 1,000 combat flight hours. Returning to the United States, McManus later enlisted in the Missouri National Guard and went on to complete the second combat tour of his career while in Iraq from 2006 to 2007. He finished his career in 2009 as a chief warrant officer five with forty-one years of service and 16,200 flight hours, possessing a legacy that includes several fascinating experiences on which he can now reflect in his retirement. He asserts, however, that some of the most enjoyable moments have been when he was able to inspire a new generation of aviators ... just as he was inspired as a child.

"I was very lucky to have been part of the military and to have worked with such a great group of people who were always there for you when you needed them," he explained.

He added, "Many times in the past, the National Guard participated in public events where we would demonstrate our aircraft to the public. These events," he continued, "were very important to me because it gave me the opportunity to teach children and our youth a little about aviation and hopefully inspire some of them to consider pursuing it as a career someday.

"For me, carrying forth that inspiration I received as a child was both rewarding and memorable." (*Photograph courtesy of Greg McManus*)

James "Ed" Smith – *Springfield*

While growing up in the Springfield, Missouri area, James "Ed" Smith notes that a friendly rivalry existed between him and a cousin. When he learned that his relative made the decision to sign up to fly helicopters in the U.S. Army, Smith convinced himself that he was not going to be bested.

"I had already completed my solo flight in a fixed-wing aircraft, and when I heard of my cousin's enlistment, I told myself, 'If he can do it, so can I,'" Smith mirthfully recalled.

At the time, Smith was two years into a four-year apprenticeship with a local company but left his vocational training and enlisted in the U.S. Army in February 1967, two years following his graduation from high school. Days later, he arrived at Ft. Polk, Louisiana to complete several weeks of basic training. He was then transferred to Ft. Wolters, Texas, where he spent the next six months in initial flight training. It was here they learned "avionics, aerodynamics, pre-flight procedures, take-off, landing, and navigation," said the veteran. While at Ft. Wolters, Smith learned to fly the Hiller OH-23 Raven—a primary helicopter trainer.

"I was then given two weeks of leave before reporting to Ft. Rucker, Alabama, in November 1967," said Smith. "That's where I spent the next several months learning to fly the UH-1." (The Bell UH-1 series Iroquois helicopter has a single engine and became known as the "Huey.")

Although he experienced many memorable moments during his training with the Huey, Smith noted that an incident occurring only days prior to his graduation at Ft. Rucker nearly ended his aviation career—if not his life.

"We had just departed an LZ (landing zone) and were about three hundred feet in the air as part of a 6-aircraft formation," he said. "I was number two in the formation and had an engine failure while I was on the controls—it was just me and another student, no instructor, in the helicopter." He continued, "We finally spotted an open field on a thirty-degree slope, and I was able to maneuver the Huey to the ground. It was a hard landing, and the right skid was downhill parallel to a terrace, and another skid above the terrace and the Huey was level when the landing was finished. God provided a good landing spot," he affirmed. "Any further downhill, there would have been nothing to keep us from rolling over."

Smith and his co-pilot walked away from the landing unscathed and went on to graduate several days later. A week after graduation, the young warrant officer was on his way overseas, arriving at Camp Evans in central Vietnam in June 1968—a site that had months earlier been taken over by the 1st Cavalry Division.

"I was assigned to Bravo Company, 227th Aviation Battalion, and we flew the grunts (infantry soldiers) to wherever they needed to go in Vietnam to fight the North Vietnamese," said Smith. "We also transported the beans and bullets to wherever they were fighting," he added.

The threats of battle were not limited to below the jungle's canopy, the pilot soon discovered, and many missions resulted in damage to the Hueys from enemy fire. On one occasion, he explained, his helicopter was struck by eight .50 caliber rounds, one of which nearly severed their tail rotor drive shaft. It was on February 27, 1969, however, that Smith became involved in a situation that not only highlighted the threats to aircraft in the Vietnam War but demonstrated the mettle and dedication of the American aviators.

"After lifting off from a mission where we had delivered ammo, we heard a call that a Loach (Hughes OH-6 "Cayuse"—a light, single engine helicopter) had just departed an LZ (landing zone) and was shot down," recalled Smith. "Evening was approaching, and I looked around the area and saw them going down, so I set the Huey down near them and picked up the pilot and co-pilot of the downed helicopter." He added, "They would have been on the ground overnight, which really put them in a dangerous situation," Smith said. "For that, I was awarded a Distinguished Flying Cross."

Returning from Vietnam in the summer of 1969, Smith became a helicopter instructor pilot at Ft. Wolters, Texas for the remainder of his enlistment. In 1970, he married Linda, whom he met while serving in Texas and months later received his discharge from the Army. The Vietnam veteran was later hired full-time by the Missouri National Guard, serving more than thirty years until retiring as a Chief Warrant Officer Five in early 2007. While with the National Guard, he qualified on a number of aircraft to include the UH-60A Black Hawk and C-12F Huron, in addition to accruing 10,648.9 flight hours.

The recipient of forty-three air medals from his Vietnam service, Smith also deployed to Iraq for a year prior to his retirement, where he served as a liaison between his aviation unit in Kuwait and the brigade in Balad, Iraq, for whom they provided maintenance and aviation support. Now several years into retirement and with an extensive military career to his credit, the veteran maintains that his service as a warrant officer has provided many opportunities throughout the years.

"I enjoyed being a warrant officer because, although I didn't want to go to school to be a captain or major, it gave me the chance to maintain my association with aviation and to fly many different types of aircraft."

Shifting his thoughts back to his intense flight experience in Vietnam, Smith concluded, "If you flew helicopters in the Army during that timeframe (the late 1960s), you were going to Vietnam." He added, "And you didn't go out on a mission and say, 'Today I'm going to rescue somebody'—that's not the way it happened because you never knew what each day would bring." *(Photograph courtesy of Ed Smith)*

Laughton Smith – *Jefferson City*

The 1960s were a tumultuous period for U.S. naval forces embroiled in intelligence-gathering operations during the Cold War. Dangers abounded for Navy personnel that included tragedies such as the USS *Thresher*—a nuclear-powered attack submarine lost on a sea trial because of an electrical system malfunction, claiming the lives of one hundred twenty-nine sailors and civilians. Such catastrophes did not appear to influence the decision of one aspiring Missouri sailor, who, despite any perceived hazards in pursuing such a calling, forged ahead to become an officer and entered the submarine forces.

Growing up in Jefferson City in the 1950s, Laughton Smith assumed the reflection of many young children of the era. He attended a local Presbyterian church and actively participated in the Boy Scouts, helping conduct classes in boating during summer camps.

"'Laughton,'" being a rather high-sounding name for such a natural guy, gave way to 'Smeed' early in Smeed's grade school years," noted a brief bio for Smith in the 1965 edition of *The Lucky Bag*—the yearbook for the United States Naval Academy. The yearbook went on to explain, "Laughton has always had a winning personality, with a bright smile and heartwarming enthusiasm."

Graduating Jefferson City High School in 1960, Smith hoped to attend the U.S. Naval Academy; however, fellow classmate Jim Ayers—the principal nominee—was selected. In the interim, Smith attended classes at the University of Missouri-Columbia until the early summer of 1961, when he received his own appointment to the academy.

"There were several of us from Jefferson City who graduated around 1960 and ended up going to a military academy," said Ayers, a childhood friend of Smith. "Laughton and I went to the Naval Academy while a classmate of ours, Robert Davenport, went to the Air Force Academy and was lost in Vietnam." He added, "Joe Hemmel from Helias also went to the Air Force Academy a year ahead of us and was lost in 1967."

Additionally, William Hentges, a 1959 graduate of Helias High School, went on to receive his commission and graduate from the U.S. Air Force Academy in 1963.

In 1965, Smith graduated from the Naval Academy and went on to serve as a lieutenant junior grade at Groton, Connecticut. On April 8, 1967, the young sailor embarked upon yet another great adventure of his life when marrying the former Jane Victoria Graham at the Immanuel Episcopal Church in Wilmington, Delaware, the bride's hometown.

"We were only a grade apart at the academy, so I saw him often," said Ayers. "We both ended up assigned to nuclear submarines during our naval careers."

The April 9, 1967, edition of the *Sunday News and Tribune* reported that Smith "will report in late April to the nuclear submarine 'Scorpion' which is homeported in Norfolk, Va." The article also explained that following their honeymoon in Vermont, the couple would reside in Norfolk.

The USS *Scorpion* was a 3,500-ton nuclear attack submarine, and although "the Navy had always portrayed the 252-foot-long sub as a gleaming showpiece," it was long overdue for an overhaul, as noted in the book *Blind Man's Bluff: The Untold Story of American Submarine Espionage*. The authors added, "(T)he crew had taken to calling her the 'USS Scrap Iron'" because of mechanical issues such as "oil leaks in the hydraulic systems and seawater seeping in through the propeller shaft seals."[109]

During the early months of 1968, the "Scorpion was one of only four of the Atlantic Fleet's submarines that were still waiting to be refitted with ... safety features" that were identified following the loss of another nuclear submarine, the USS *Thresher*, nearly five years earlier. Despite not having these safety upgrades completed, the U.S. Navy continued to have the submarine perform Cold War missions.

On May 27, 1968, the U.S. Navy conveyed that the USS *Scorpion* was missing and that they had last radioed their position six days earlier. The June 6, 1968, edition of the *Charlotte News* (Charlotte, North Carolina) reported, "At that time ... the sub was 365 miles south-southwest of the Azores, approaching the pinnacles and gulfs of an underwater mountain range."

The May 29, 1968 edition of the *Jefferson City Post-Tribune* reported that Laughton Smith, who was serving as the submarine's communications officer, had written his sister weeks earlier that their "craft was having trouble with its communications equipment" and that he had been busy "getting the equipment back in shape."

---

[109] Sonntag, *Drew & Drew, Blind Man's Bluff*, 98.

Speculation abounded as to the cause of the mysterious disappearance of the submarine with a complement of ninety-nine crewmembers. It was the height of the Cold War, and an initial suspicion was that it had been torpedoed by a Soviet submarine or surface vessel, while others believed it might have struck an underwater mountain or ridge.

Following a five-month search, the wreckage of the vessel was eventually located in more than ten thousand feet of water four hundred miles southwest of the Azores (in the mid-Atlantic), where more than eight dozen sailors remain in their watery grave. Although the Navy prepared a report in 1968 detailing its findings regarding the submarine's loss, it was withheld from the public for a quarter-century.

"This week, the Navy released a report saying the Scorpion may have been destroyed by its own torpedo," reported the *Springfield News-Leader* on October 29, 1993. "The report concluded of the accident, 'The torpedo was released from the tube, became fully armed and sought its nearest target, Scorpion.'"

James Ayers sorrowfully explained, "Of the four of us from the Class of 1960 in Jefferson City who went on to our respective military academies, I was the only one who survived my period of service." He added, "Laughton's loss truly struck a chord within me because he was my best friend in high school, and our families had been so close. He was only twenty-six when he disappeared, and it is easy for the community to forget that. I want to make sure that the community is aware of his service to the nation and remembers his sacrifice in addition to all others who died during their service as well."

Joe Dresselhaus – *Kansas City*

Following his graduation from a Kansas City, Missouri, area high school in 1967, Joe Dresselhaus was frequently turned down for jobs by employers concerned they would lose him to the draft. This reality, he explained, motivated his decision to complete a stint in the military so that he could approach an employer and say, "Now that I've been to Vietnam, will you give me a job?"

Enlisting in the U.S. Army in April 1969, Dresselhaus was soon on his way to Ft. Leonard Wood, Missouri, for his basic training. From there, he traveled to Ft. Sill, Oklahoma, where he received several weeks of training in artillery.

"At (Fort) Sill, we learned to fire everything from the 105s up to the 175s (105mm and 175mm howitzers)," he explained. "It wasn't any type of training that I selected. The Army chose it for me because I guess they figured that's where they needed me."

During his training at Ft. Sill, the young soldier accepted an offer to become a "Shake 'n Bake sergeant"—an intensive course of training in a combat specialty that allowed inexperienced soldiers to receive a rapid promotion to replace non-commissioned officers retiring from the Army or those who became casualties in Vietnam.

"I remained at Ft. Sill for several more weeks and trained as a 17E40 [the Military Occupational Code for a Field Illumination Crewman]," he said. "They taught us how to operate an infrared searchlight that illuminated an area so that you could see in the dark through special scopes," he added.

Graduating from training in March 1970, Dresselhaus was on his way to Vietnam less than a month later. Although a soldier in the U.S. Army, he was attached to an element of the 1st Marine Division stationed in a camp on Hill 270 southwest of Da Nang.

He explained, "The hill was on a saddle, and if you followed the saddle out, you'd hit the Cambodian and Laos border," he said. "We were like a plug in the middle of the road to stop the movement of enemy troops. The only way off the hill was to repel or by helicopter."

During his time in the camp, one of Dresselhaus's primary duties was to light up the perimeter at night with his infrared searchlight, at which point the Marine Corps snipers and riflemen could spot enemy troops through their Starlight scopes. He and his fellow Marines were later transferred to a site known as Namo Bridge, which spanned the Song Ca De River, to protect the bridge from destruction by enemy forces since it was along a major route used by American troops. It was here that the soldier received the first of two overseas injuries.

"To keep the enemy from sneaking up and setting satchel charges to destroy the bridge, we'd drop concussion grenades into the water in the course of the evening," he said. "One evening, I pulled the pin and threw a grenade, and it went off almost immediately because it didn't have a fuse in it." He continued, "I woke up in the battalion aid station with ruptured eardrums. Had I held on to the grenade for another second or so, I would have been killed." Pausing, he added, "I was back at work the next day."

The final stage of his assignment in Vietnam was on Hill 65, which was again located southwest of Da Nang with the 1st Marine Division. It was during this timeframe, he noted, the Marines were beginning to rotate back to the United States as the U.S. Army arrived to take their place.

"I was coming back to Hill 65 from a trip to Da Nang while driving a Jeep with another soldier riding in the passenger seat," Dresselhaus said. "I'm not sure what happened—whether we hit a mine or what—but the Jeep rolled several times, and the passenger and I were pinned underneath."

It was approaching dark, he went on to explain, and their M-16 rifles were thrown clear of Jeep so they couldn't defend themselves if attacked. Additionally, they were unable to reach the radio to call for help.

"Fortunately, some of our Marine friends showed up and were able to get us out from under the Jeep before it turned dark," he said. "I was evacuated to the USS *Sanctuary* (hospital ship) in Da Nang Harbor and, thanks to the strength of my leg and Army combat boots, no bones were broken, but it stretched and tore every tendon in my left foot."

The soldier was sent back to the United States and finished out his enlistment at Ft. Leavenworth, Kansas, receiving his discharge in April 1971. After returning to Kansas City, a friend encouraged him to apply for a position with the Kansas City Police Department (KCPD), from where he retired in 1996 as a homicide detective after twenty-five years of service. Shortly after his retirement from the KCPD, he and his family moved to Jefferson City, where he was employed for fourteen years investigating murders for the Missouri

Attorney General. The married father of four children has since permanently retired.

In reflecting on his time spent in the Army while assigned with the Marines in the Vietnam War, Dresselhaus noted there were incidents that provided him with an enduring level of appreciation for the country that is his home.

"When I was with the Marines at Namo Bridge, there was an elderly Vietnamese man who brought his granddaughter—a young girl who was probably 12 or 13 years old and needed medical attention. She had been shot through the hand and what was most unforgettable was that she wasn't in shock … she was calm through it all. We realized that at her age and at that point in the Vietnam War, she had never seen a day of peace in her country, and they were accustomed to such situations." He added, "That experience is one that has stuck with me over the years and made me appreciate just how well we have it in this country." *(Photograph courtesy of Joe Dresselhaus)*

Don Cryderman – *Springfield*

Possessing an impressive military career spanning nearly forty years and including service on the home front as a single father, Don Cryderman has experienced multiple duty assignments in both the Army Reserve and National Guard. When reflecting on the details of these frenetic years, he admitted, "It's hard to keep track of it all—all the dates and places can be confusing."

Raised near Sacramento, California, Cryderman moved to Springfield, Missouri, with his family following his graduation from high school in 1969. The seventeen-year-old soon went to work at a local grocery store but quickly realized his chances of being drafted.

"I had a low draft number, so I tried to join a local reserve unit in the fall of 1970, but they had a six-month waiting list to get in," he recalled. "Finally, I got a call from them on January 28, 1971, and became an artilleryman with Battery A, 3rd Battalion of the 75th Field Artillery."

Like all new recruits, he was soon on his way to boot camp, learning the basics of performing as a soldier while stationed at Ft. Campbell, Kentucky. From there, he traveled to Fort Sill, Oklahoma, in May 1971 for several weeks of artillery school, learning how to operate the 105mm howitzers. When he returned home in early summer, he continued working for Consumer Markets in a full-time capacity and spent the next three years as a reserve artilleryman, working with his battery's self-propelled 155mm howitzers during drill weekends and summer training periods. In the three years following his initial enlistment, he primarily served as a forward observer, calling in targets to his fellow artillerymen operating the howitzers.

In 1972, he married and discovered how to balance home life and his job with the grocery chain along with his part-time military obligations. He served in several capacities with his artillery battalion in Springfield for the next several years, with the exception of a fifteen-month break in service in the mid-1970s. Ascending through the enlisted ranks, he eventually achieved the rank of master sergeant and served two years as an operations sergeant for the battalion. However, any plans for the future were soon deflated when personal tragedy struck his family, and he needed to demonstrate his resiliency as a father.

"My wife passed away unexpectedly in 1987, and I was left to raise our two sons and daughter on my own," he sorrowfully recalled. "The kids were three, four, and eleven at the time, and I quickly had to become 'Mr. Mom.' It was a very difficult and trying period for us."

Through the support of his church and gracious members of his community, he learned to tend to his family while continuing his full-time employment with the grocery chain and his part-time military obligations.

"I was promoted to first sergeant and did that for three years until the battalion was deactivated," Cryderman said. "Following a major reorganization, we became a transportation unit."

The next few years brought many significant changes in his military career as he trained to become an instructor and taught transportation courses at Fort Riley, Kansas. The reserve soldier later spent two years helping to train ROTC cadets in the state of Washington.

"I was sent to the Regional Training Institute (RTI) at Ft. Leonard Wood in 1998 to jointly train soldiers alongside National Guard instructors," said the veteran. "Later that same year, I transferred to the National Guard because I could only do twenty-six years with my rank in the Reserves while the Guard did not have such a limitation."

The following year, his full-time career of nearly thirty years ended when Consumer Markets closed its doors. Despite this setback, opportunity came knocking weeks later when the National Guard offered him a full-time job with their facilities section of the training site at Ft. Leonard Wood. In November 2006, the fifty-five-year-old soldier received notice he would deploy to Afghanistan early the next year. Completing three months of preparation training at Ft. Riley, Kansas, he arrived in the country in April 2007 as part of a team of embedded trainers.

"We were there for a year," said Cryderman. "I spent about three months as a transportation advisor for the Afghan army. The final nine months," he added, "I served as the advisor for the sergeant major for an Afghan battalion."

Returning to Missouri in the spring of 2008, he remained with the Missouri National Guard at Ft. Leonard Wood until retiring in 2011. The following year, he met the former Dee Dee Mehmert, whom he married in 2013, and moved from his home in Waynesville to live with his new wife in Jefferson City. Since then, he has become involved with the American Legion Post 5, serving three years as post adjutant. Years earlier, he learned to balance a full-time job in the grocery industry and a part-time job in the military while also raising his children. During this chaotic period, Cryderman explained, he evolved as both a parent and a soldier and now, in his retirement, seeks to honor his fellow veterans in recognition of those who have assisted him.

"There were so many people that did so many things to help me when my wife passed away, and I haven't forgotten that," said Cryderman. "Now, Dee Dee and I participate in the Legion Riders and like to help with the motorcycle escorts for the Central Missouri Honor Flight and also ride in the funeral processions for veterans. These are just little ways," he added, "that I am able to give back to the community in acknowledgment of those individuals who have been such a great support to me." *(Photograph courtesy of Don Cryderman)*

Leon DeLong – *Jefferson City*

Leon DeLong has made many lasting memories during his thirty-four years of service in the Missouri National Guard, retiring at the rank of Chief Warrant Officer Four in 2008. What many people do not realize, however, is that his military experience began with his enlistment in the Navy during the heart of the Vietnam War. A 1966 graduate of Jefferson City High School, DeLong stated, "Like everybody else in '66 and '67, you either went to college or you were drafted." He added, "I didn't want to be drafted, so I decided to enlist in the Navy."

His Uncle "Stubby" had served in the Navy and advised the young high school graduate that if he wanted to see the world and not "sleep in a ditch," then he should join the Navy. DeLong mirthfully added, "It made perfect sense to me!"

Traveling to Great Lakes Naval Training Center in Illinois in early summer 1967, DeLong completed his basic training. He then came home for a short period of leave before returning to Great Lakes to begin several weeks of training to become a machinist mate.

"When I took all of the testing during the enlistment process, I guess it showed that I had the aptitude to serve as a machinist mate," said DeLong. "In that position, you were responsible for the lifeblood of the ships—making the electricity, running the engines ... those kinds of responsibilities."

Finishing his initial training in early 1968, the sailor received his first official duty appointment when assigned to the USS *Norton Sound* (AVM-1)—a World War II-era seaplane tender that was later converted to serve as a missile-launching platform. Boarding the ship at Port Hueneme, California, DeLong noted the ship was used to launch and track missiles in the research and development phase; however, it was an intriguing process that he was not able to witness since he was "down in the hole (engine room)" performing his duties as a machinist mate.

Six months later, he received orders for his next duty assignment aboard the destroyer USS *Hull* (DD-945), which he boarded in San Diego. During the Vietnam War, the USS *Hull* would go on to complete six deployments.

"I reported to the ship in mid-1968, and it wasn't long before we were leaving the West Coast for Vietnam," said the veteran. "We operated out of Yankee Station (a site used to launch strikes) in the Gulf of Tonkin," he continued, "and we fired thousands of five-inch shells in support of our ground forces."

As DeLong went on to explain, his service in Vietnam was often a trying experience during which he learned to "sleep while standing up," since they would fire the guns of the ship all day long and spend most of the night taking on ammunition and other supplies they had expended. Briefly returning from their Western Pacific service in the summer of 1969 to undergo boiler repairs and other minor maintenance procedures, DeLong said they soon returned to sea and were on their way to what became his second and final cruise in support of the Vietnam War.

According to a website dedicated to the history of the USS *Hull* (DD-945), the ship remained in Vietnam from July 1969 through February 1970, again supporting the war effort with its five-inch guns and complement of more than two hundred sailors. In 1970, while in San Diego after returning from Vietnam, DeLong married Beki, whom he met in 1968. Additionally, when approaching the end of his enlistment, the Navy sent him to an air-conditioning and refrigeration (AC&R) school to help prepare him for his return to civilian employment.

"While I was in the AC&R, my son was born," DeLong said. "When I finished school in 1971, that's when I returned to Missouri with my family."

Despite his AC&R training, the young veteran could not find employment in that industry and soon went to work for DeLong's, Inc., making culvert pipes with his father, who was at the time the plant foreman. However, in 1973, friends who previously worked at DeLong's informed him of full-time employment opportunities available with the National Guard.

"I enlisted in the National Guard as a specialist (E-4) in 1973 because some of the guys I used to work with had enlisted and ended up getting full-time jobs as technicians," said DeLong. "I was hired as a technician in 1974 and retired more than three decades later as a chief warrant officer 4," he added.

The married father of two children explained that although his military career is often associated with his Missouri National Guard experiences, it was his naval service during the Vietnam War that introduced him to the contrasts of a combat zone while also bestowing the most enduring of his military memories.

"Other than working your tail off 24/7, there were certainly some enjoyable aspects to serving in Vietnam, such as the liberty ports we got to visit and some of the interesting sites that we got to see." "However," he added, "one thing I found odd was our surroundings at one point while we were anchored in DaNang Harbor. All hell broke loose whenever we fired the ship's big guns, and over on a hillside in the distance, you could see tracer rounds going off." Pausing, he added, "Yet in the middle of all of this, you could hear music coming from the nearby Enlisted Club, and the Vietnamese people were in small boats fishing around our ship as if that was just the norm for them. That," he concluded, "was confusing to me and made me realize how messed up war can be." *(Photograph courtesy of Leon Delong)*

Bill Farr – *Springfield*

I have enjoyed As a young man, Bill Farr pursued an interest in public service by volunteering as a firefighter in a rural district and later became a reserve police officer in a small community. This was followed by appointment as state fire marshal for Missouri and, more recently, as director of Cole County Emergency Management. These were opportunities, he explained, that progressed from the initial inspiration he received when just a young soldier in the U.S. Army. When graduating from high school in Springfield, Missouri, in 1968, Farr began working for a local automotive parts supply company, gaining practical work experience that would unexpectedly shape the direction of his approaching military service.

"It was pretty evident with the Vietnam War going on that I was going to be drafted at some point," said Farr. "So, in the end, I made the decision to go ahead and volunteer for the draft," he added.

Inducted in Kansas City in October 1969, he was sent to Fort Jackson, South Carolina, to undergo his basic training to become a soldier in the U.S. Army. For the next several weeks, he endured the regimen of many a fellow soldier by participating in "forced marches" and field exercises that introduced the trainees to the vexing bites of the notorious sand fleas.

"Since I had worked in a supply capacity with the automotive parts company back home, they made me a 76 'Yankee' (76Y is a former U.S. Army designation for supply specialists). It was a situation where I didn't have to complete any further training. They just assigned me that specialty."

Presuming he was destined for deployment to Vietnam, Farr was sent to Ft. Lewis, Washington, in late January 1970, to await his next set of orders. A week following his arrival, a sergeant came into the barracks where he was staying and read a list of names, which happened to include Farr's.

"The sergeant told us to go down to supply and draw some Arctic gear because we were being sent to Fairbanks, Alaska," he recalled. "It was decent weather when we left Seattle, but when we arrived in Fairbanks two or three days later, it was pitch black, minus forty degrees and waist-deep snow."

Upon his arrival in Fairbanks, he was detailed to the supply section of Company A, 171st Infantry Brigade stationed at Fort Wainwright. Initially established as an airfield by the U.S. Army Air Corps in 1939, the fort has since become a testing site in the development of cold-weather gear and equipment and is also home to the Northern Warfare Training Center. An important role of the brigade, Farr noted, was the maintenance, security, and operation of Nike Hercules missile sites situated along the Alaskan mountain ranges, providing a network of Cold War air defenses against the potential threat of attack by Soviet aircraft.

Farr explained, "It was just the supply sergeant and myself in my section and, looking back, it was pretty good duty. We had medics, office support staff, vehicle maintenance personnel, and infantry in the company, and we operated the supply room that supported all of them."

In addition to his regular duties supporting the logistical needs of the company, the brigade conducted frequent war games with their counterparts in the Canadian military. The soldiers also participated in such exercises as snowshoe training, learning to perform their duties in an operational cold-weather environment.

"Summers were beautiful, but the winters were tragic," he chuckled when reflecting on his military experiences. "One time, we had a blizzard, and there were some soldiers that had gone to town but couldn't get back to post for three or four days. The snow was piled higher than the street signs."

While stationed in Alaska, Farr transitioned from the company level to supply positions in both the battalion and brigade, eventually becoming an acting sergeant. In July 1971, he was provided an early discharge to returned home to begin vocational training. In the years following his return to Springfield, the veteran married, became father to two children, and embarked upon a continued career in public service by becoming a volunteer firefighter. Elected fire chief of his rural department in 1976, he later acquired law enforcement certification and became a reserve officer for the community of Republic, Missouri.

"I was hired as the first full-time fire chief of Republic in 1983," Farr said. Three years later, I was hired by the state fire marshal to oversee the investigation of fires in twenty-six counties in southwest Missouri."

In 1994, Farr moved to Jefferson City to accept a deputy chief position with the state fire marshal. The next year, after the unexpected death of the state fire marshal, he was appointed to the position by then-Gov. Mel Carnahan. Retiring in 2005, he was hired as director of Cole County Emergency Management in 2008, remaining in the position until retiring earlier this year.

When contemplating his many years invested in public service, Farr remarked of his U.S. Army experience, "It was a scary time in a young person's life, especially with everything going on with the Vietnam War. But, I felt that I had a responsibility, and the good Lord decided to send me to Alaska. The Army gave me experiences I will never give up and important lessons I have always cherished ... like helping others, which is something doing my entire life." *(Photograph courtesy of Bill Farr)*

Larry Alderson – *Grant City*

When Larry Alderson finished his high school education at Worth County R-1 near Grant City, Missouri, in the spring of 1966, he felt that his greatest competency was in drafting. He went on to spend a year in drafting courses at a local business college before applying his skills while employed in the office of a farm implement company in Independence.

"I was there for about eight months or so when I got my draft notice," said Alderson. "That's when I went and talked to an Air Force recruiter, and he advised me to take my induction physical and then come see him." He added, "The recruiter said he'd take care of everything else from there."

The recruiter was true to his word, and Alderson was inducted into the U.S. Air Force in Kansas City on July 25, 1968. He was then sent to Amarillo Air Base, Texas, to complete several weeks of basic training. As Alderson explained, he was one of the last classes to finish their training at the base before it was deactivated later that year.

"After basic, they sent me to Lowry Air Force Base in Denver, Colorado, for the weapons mechanic course," he explained. "That lasted several months, and we mostly learned to maintain, load, and unload the guns, missiles, and rockets used on different types of aircraft."

His first permanent duty assignment came in January 1969 when he received orders for England Air Force Base near Alexandria, Louisiana. For the next eighteen months, he helped load and unload the munitions from fighter aircraft used to train members of the South Vietnamese air force.

"It seemed like everyone I had gone to basic with was getting orders for Vietnam to load bombs on F-4s (Phantoms)—and that, I was told, amounted to fourteen-hour days spent in the hot sun," he said. "But I had a friend that came back from Vietnam, who had been on gunships. and said if I volunteered for that duty, you get air-conditioning and chow hall privileges."

Volunteering for the gunship mission, Alderson spent several weeks in the Airborne Weapons Technician Course at Lockbourne Air Force Base (now Rickenbacker Air National Guard Base) in Ohio. He learned to load and maintain the weapons on the AC-119K Stinger—a side-firing gunship fulfilling several roles such as defense of ground positions, armed reconnaissance, and interdiction. His next stop was Spokane, Washington, for a couple of weeks of survival training before traveling to Clark Air Base in the Philippines for additional survival training focused on jungle-like conditions. From there, he flew into Cam Ranh Bay, Vietnam, in October 1970 and hitched a ride on a small plane to his duty assignment at Phan Rang Air Base, South Vietnam.

"I spent my first month there in training and then flew an actual mission as a gunner," he said. "During that first mission, there was a sergeant that reviewed my performance to make sure I was prepared to do my job on the AC-119K," he added.

The veteran noted he was responsible for loading and maintaining the weapons on the AC-119K. It had both a Starlight and infrared scope used by the pilot to maneuver the aircraft to line up the four mini-guns or the two 20mm guns to fire on a target. Additionally, the gunship had a rudimentary onboard computer that calculated wind speeds to ensure better accuracy in firing.

"They sent me to the airbase in Nakhon Phanom in Thailand, and we began flying mostly night missions from there," he said. "We were doing about five missions a week and attacking enemy trucks that were running from North Vietnam and Laos along the Ho Chi Minh Trail carrying weapons and supplies." Alderson added, "On one mission, after we had transferred to Da Nang, we had a journalist flying with us," Alderson said. "On that night, artillery was fired at us and came up behind the cockpit and in front of the wing, exploding above us. That," he continued, "would have been deadly had it hit our wing or the fuselage."

In other situations, the former airman recalls, artillery exploded in close proximity, creating the sound of "pinging" from shrapnel striking against the aircraft's metal exterior.

Completing more than one hundred missions, he returned to the states in October 1971 and was assigned to McConnell Air Force Base in Kansas, where he maintained mini-guns on the F-105 Thunderchief. During a special function at the base, he was presented a Distinguished Flying Cross for demonstrating "professional competence" and "aerial skill" in a dangerous mission in Vietnam on April 22, 1971.

"I was able to get an early discharge in May 1972—about a month early—to return to Missouri and enroll in college," he said. "I was accepted at Missouri Southern State College (now University) in Joplin and used my GI Bill to graduate in 1976 with my bachelor's degree in Environmental Health Technology."

The veteran moved to Jefferson City in 1979 and went on to retire from the Missouri Department of Natural Resources in 2004. He and his wife, Deborah, have remained active with Roscoe Enloe American Legion Post 5, which, he recognizes affords him opportunities to continue his service.

"Like most, I am proud of my military service and would do it again if I wasn't an old man," he laughed. "It's nice that I can still serve with organizations like the American Legion Riders to support events such as welcoming back veterans who have gone to Washington, D.C., with the (Central Missouri) Honor Flight."

He concluded, "When I signed up for gunships in Vietnam, I thought it sounded exciting, but I quickly realized how dangerous it really was when we started encountering anti-aircraft fire. I was one of the lucky ones that made it safely through; unfortunately, there were too many air crews who weren't so lucky." *(Photograph courtesy of Larry Alderson)*

CHAPTER 5
COLD WAR & BEYOND

Charles Guthrie – *Lexington*

For decades, Charles Guthrie has striven to serve others; whether it be through holding an elected office in Saline County or planning events to honor veterans, he is always "on-the-go." He explains that his passion comes from a decision stemming back to 1973, when, as a young man, he chose to serve his country by enlisting in the U.S. Navy.

"My father had served with a Navy construction battalion and helped build an airstrip on Iwo Jima during World War II," Guthrie said. "He was part of my inspiration to join the Navy myself," he added.

Following his enlistment in February 1973, he traveled to Great Lakes, Illinois, for his basic training. Located near Chicago, the training site had a reputation of being ground zero for brutally cold winters; however, the former sailor noted they were blessed with "mild" weather. At the end of his initial training, the newly trained sailor received orders for Little Creek, Virginia, for assignment aboard a landing ship tank (LST). While at home for two weeks of leave prior to reporting to his new duty station, Guthrie received notice of a "modification" to his orders.

"My new orders indicated I was to report to Newport, Rhode Island, for service aboard the light cruiser USS *Little Rock* (CLG-4)," he recalled. "After I reported to the ship in the summer of 1973, we sailed to Gaeta, Italy, to relieve the USS *Springfield* as the new flagship for the Sixth Fleet."

At the time, the sailor was unassigned to a naval rate (duty position), but there was a call for volunteers to work in the laundry aboard the USS *Little Rock*, which seemed more appealing to many young sailors who otherwise might have been placed to work with the cooks on the mess deck.

"I initially worked in the laundry and later became a ship store operator," Guthrie recalled. "The store was similar to a mini-Walmart—we sold items like cameras and stereo equipment. Sometime during my initial enlistment, I also spent time as a clerk in the sales office doing bookwork and tracking inventory of items we sold in stores on the ship."

During the remainder of his two-year enlistment, the sailor remained aboard the ship as it sailed throughout the Mediterranean. As Guthrie explained, they had an admiral aboard who served as a "goodwill ambassador" to foreign nations, "wining and dining" dignitaries when they visited foreign ports.

"I had a two-by-six contract, meaning that I enlisted to serve two years on active duty and six years in the reserves," he said. "So, when I received my discharge from the Navy in the early summer of 1975, I joined the Navy Reserve unit in Kansas City."

For the next several years, Guthrie worked a number of jobs around Saline County while continuing to train with his Naval Reserve unit on the weekends and in the summer months. In 1979, he married Brenda, and the two have since raised a son and a daughter. In addition to owning and operating a jewelry store for several years, Guthrie was elected a commissioner for Saline County, serving three terms totaling twelve years. He finished out his career as the produce manager at a local grocery store, retiring in 2009.

"While I was working full-time, I remained in the Navy Reserve and made a career of that," said the veteran. "It gave me a lot of opportunities to serve on several different ships including light cruisers, destroyers, destroyer tenders, fast frigates, LSTs, and an aircraft carrier."

Guthrie maintains that although serving aboard the aircraft carrier USS Enterprise was a unique experience since the ship was so large that he felt lost the entire time he was aboard; it was another ship—one named for his home state—that has become the source of his most profound military memories.

"While in the reserves, I had the privilege of serving aboard the battleship USS *Missouri*, which is now in Pearl Harbor," he said. "That experience I view as one of my greatest accomplishments ... not only because of its name but the role it played in hosting the surrender of the Japanese in World War II." He added, "Also, it was very inspiring to be able to walk on the same deck that General Douglas MacArthur and President Harry S. Truman walked on so many years earlier."

On another occasion, the sailor served aboard the George Phillip, a guided-missile frigate that operated off the coast of Columbia to interdict ships suspected of transporting drugs. On May 1, 1996, Guthrie retired from the U.S. Navy Reserve with more than two decades of service to his credit and has an impressive list of awards to include a Navy and Marine Corps Achievement Medal.

The former sailor has remained active in his retirement, having served on the board of directors for the former Show Me Honor Flight program in Sedalia. Several years ago, Guthrie was appointed by Governor Jay Nixon to serve on the commissioning committee for the new USS *Missouri* (SSN780) submarine. In modest contemplation, Guthrie maintains that the initial inspiration of his father's naval service has been supplemented by a number of his own unique naval experiences, both of which continue to motivate his desire to honor his fellow veterans.

"I'm not bragging, but serving in the Navy was a labor of love ... and there have been more good times than bad," he said. "There's always going to be bumps in the road when you serve in the military, but you learn to adapt to the bumps." He concluded, "I have always believed in what the late JFK said: 'Ask not what your country can do for you — ask what you can do for your country.' *(Photograph courtesy of Charles Guthrie.)*

Jeremy P. Amick

American Legion Department of Missouri Convention - 1977

The Fifty-Ninth Annual Convention of the American Legion Department of Missouri was held in Jefferson City from July 15-17, 1977. During the event, the Distinguished Service Award was presented to Senator Stuart Symington. The award was created in 1966 with the first "living" presentation made in 1967 to former President Harry S. Truman and the post-humous award going to General of the Armies John J. Pershing.

A veteran of World War I, Symington was a member of the American Legion Post 158 in Jackson, Missouri. During WWII, he entered public service with the Surplus Property Board and later became the nation's first Secretary of the Air Force. In both 1948 and 1956, he was presented the General H.H. Arnold Award as Aviation's Man of the Year and, in 1957, received the Wright Brothers Memorial Trophy. From 1953 to 1976, he was elected to serve as a Democratic United States Senator from Missouri. *(Photograph courtesy of American Legion Post 5)*

Steve Diemler – *Jefferson City*

Inspired by his father and two uncles who served in the Marine Corps, Steve Diemler enlisted in the delayed entry program during his senior year at Helias Catholic High School. The week following his graduation in May 1973, the recruit headed to basic training to begin an adventure that years later culminated in a daring escape from Kuwait during the opening stages of the Persian Gulf War.

"Once I finished my basic training at MCRD [Marine Corps Recruit Depot] in San Diego in August (1973), they sent me to the Marine Communications and Electronics School at Twentynine Palms, California," he said.

For the next few weeks, he was introduced to basic electronics, followed by the fundamentals of digital logic. The class was then divided into separate training groups—several Marines were sent to radio training while Diemler and others were sent to radar school.

"It was during the radar fundamentals course that we learned to work on the ANTPS-32," he explained. "It was a long-range, air search, three-dimensional radar system. It had the capabilities of identifying the range, direction, and height of aircraft," he added.

When the training was completed, he transferred to the Marine Corps Air Station at Tustin, California, which was a sub-unit of the Marine Corps Tactical Systems Support Activity (MCTSSA) at Camp Pendleton, California. While there, his 20-man unit tested new defensive radar equipment being introduced into the Marine Corps. Additionally, the crews used the radar to track aircraft on training missions originating from the former Naval Air Station Point Mugu, while Diemler helped troubleshoot any problems that arose, performing the necessary repairs. While assigned to the station, the young Marine met Rita, whom he married in January 1975. The following May, the couple welcomed their first son, Sean.

In April 1976, Diemler left Tustin when his sub-unit was sent to Camp Pendleton to rejoin the Tactical Systems Support Activity. It was from here that he finished out his enlistment and received his discharge from the Marine Corps on May 30, 1977.

"My wife, son, and I returned to Jefferson City, and I began attending Lincoln University full-time while also working full-time as a repair technician for a local office supply company," Diemler said. "After finishing my junior year in the summer of 1980, we went on a trip to California to visit my wife's family, and I stopped by Camp Pendleton to visit some of the guys I had worked with in the Marines."

During his visit to the base, Diemler was advised of a contract position with ITT Corporation—the company that built the radars he had worked with in the past. They were in need of instructors to teach the systems to foreign nations who purchased such equipment through foreign military sales contracts. He was soon hired by the company and sent to Kuwait in the fall of 1980. The day after his arrival, Iran began bombing oil tankers in the Persian Gulf in what became known as the Iran-Iraq War. From that point forward, Diemler explained, the Kuwait Air Defense, which would normally shut down around 2:00 p.m., began operating on a twenty-four-hour cycle.

Briefly returning to the ITT plant in California in the fall of 1981, he traveled back to Kuwait in 1982. His second son, Joshua, was born in Lancaster, California, in September 1982, shortly before his family joined him in Kuwait City.

"Although I first helped teach the radar system to Kuwaiti nationals, I later became one of the tech reps that helped maintain the two radar sites," he said. "Our third son, A.J., was born while we were living in Kuwait in 1985," he added.

During the summer months, his family returned to the United States while Diemler remained in Kuwait. Fortunately, his family was back in the states in August 1990 when Iraq invaded Kuwait and Diemler and other westerners became trapped; they were ordered to remain in Kuwait City and denied permission to leave the country by the Iraqi military.

"I didn't want to go to the America Embassy because the Iraqi military was watching it, and if they wanted to capture you, then you're already caught if you were there," he said. "I ended up connecting with other contractors, and, through their connections, plans were made for us to escape into Saudi Arabia."

Diemler, American contractors, and other Arabic locals formed a convoy of thirteen military vehicles that escaped watch by the Iraqi military and began the "seventy-something-mile" trek across the desert. Eventually, Diemler observed dots on the horizon that soon formed into a fearful reality as they approached.

"I realized they were Iraqi tanks," he said. "I thought for sure the Iraqi's would open fire on us, but the guide kept going and drove us right between them. As we passed by, there were soldiers sitting around, and our guide stopped everyone after we got a mile or so past them."

The guide informed the group to wait there because he had to go back and find a vehicle that had been lost from the group.

"When the guide returned with the vehicle," Diemler explained, "he said that it had been stuck in the sand, and the Iraqi soldiers helped push it out. He also said the soldiers told him, 'That Saddam Hussein is crazy and we don't want to be here.'"

The group finally made it to the safety of the Saudi Arabian border and, with the help of a member of the Associated Press in their group, were provided airline tickets back to the United States to reunite with their families. Diemler eventually settled in his native Jefferson City and spent several years in law enforcement. In early 2019, he retired from the Missouri Department of Social Services, where he was employed as an investigator for Medicaid fraud.

The greatest danger of his past career, the veteran noted, came with his service as a contractor in the years after his discharge; however, Diemler affirms that both his own military service and that of his children help highlight what has been the greatest source of his professional pride.

"All three of my sons have gone on to become Marines just as I followed in my own father's footsteps," he said. "That certainly makes me one proud father," he grinned. "And the old saying 'Once a Marine, always a Marine' is the reason that I chose to be a member of the Marine Corps League—it doesn't matter what you did while you were in the service because it was a title that you had to earn." *(Photograph courtesy of Steve Diemler)*

Patty LeComte – *Taos*

Graduating from Blair Oaks High School in 1973, Patty Henke LeComte of Taos laid the groundwork for her career when accepting a job as a civilian personnel clerk at the Missouri National Guard headquarters in Jefferson City. It was during this timeframe that an officer with whom she worked provided the initial encouragement for her to enlist, thus becoming the first step in a three-decade military career.

"I joined on the buddy system, and me and a girl that I was friends with went to basic training at Ft. Jackson, South Carolina, in September 1975," LeComte said. "After eight weeks there, they sent us to Lowry Air Force Base in Aurora, Colorado, for photography school."

During the thirty-two weeks of advanced training she received in photography, she learned not only how to operate the "old box-style cameras," but to mix the chemicals used to develop film in the pre-digital age followed by an immersion in all aspects of working in a "dark room." At a time when the Women's Army Corps (WAC) was fading from existence and women were integrated into the regular U.S. Army, she returned to Missouri in the summer of 1976 and began drilling with a unit in Jefferson City. The following year, she decided to move to Colorado and transfer to the Colorado National Guard. Months later, she was hired full-time as a clerk at the headquarters for the Colorado National Guard.

"I did that for a couple of years and then transferred to the 147th Medical Hospital in Aurora (Colorado) to work as a full-time training NCO (non-commissioned officer)," she said. "I had to go to Ft. Sam Houston (Texas) to receive training to become a combat medic."

In the late 1970s, she met Tom LeComte—a Vietnam veteran who was then serving in the Colorado National Guard—and the two were married in 1980. The following year, Tom became a facility commander with the Iowa National Guard, and the couple soon made the move to a new state.

"I transferred to a medical unit with the Iowa National Guard and was there for almost ten years," LeComte said. "We had our son, Josh, in 1988, and two years later, we moved to Taos after Tom retired from the military," she added.

LeComte soon went to work as a secretary at Blair Oaks Elementary School before being hired on full-time as a training NCO with the Missouri National Guard's Counterdrug Task Force in 1992. The program, she explained, is designed to foster a relationship between the National Guard and local law enforcement agencies throughout the state to help reduce the presence of illicit drugs.

"In my full-time capacity, it was my job to manage all of the training for the counterdrug program and supervise several soldiers at the central office in addition to intel analysts in the field," said LeComte. "In a part-time capacity, I drilled on weekends with the 35th DISCOM (Division Support Command) at the Blue Armory in Jefferson City."

She and her husband adopted their daughter, Lena, in 1996. In 2005, she made the decision to retire from the National Guard and mirthfully noted that she "took off" for the next year "because it felt great to do so." She then worked briefly for both the State Emergency Management Agency and the Missouri State Highway Patrol.

"From 2007 to 2008, I worked as a contractor with the Missouri National Guard Family Program at the Blue Armory," said LeComte. "Then, I continued work as a civilian contractor for the National Guard backfilling a position for a soldier who deployed to Kosovo and later helped track military awards for units that had fallen behind because of their deployments," she added.

She eventually made the decision to permanently retire in 2013 but has remained actively involved in a number of voluntary endeavors. Since 2006, she has assisted her friend, Judy Minard, in operating the Mid-MO Family PX—a food pantry located at the Blue Armory for military members and veterans in need.

"It has been very fulfilling to work with the pantry and to assist those who have fallen on hard times," said LeComte. "We are fortunate to have been assisted in our mission by several wonderful organizations including the Boy Scouts, Calvary Lutheran High School, VFW and Ladies Auxiliary, Heroes Cares, Operation Bugle Boy, and several private donors."

In addition to her and her husband's careers in the armed forces, LeComte comes from a very patriotic family with a proud legacy of military service. Her father served during the Korean War; an uncle was killed in WWII; a brother served in the Army; another of her brothers served in the Navy, and her son spent many years in the National Guard and deployed to Afghanistan. Three decades of uniformed experience to her credit, LeComte notes that just as those who have served tend to relate, the relationships she has fostered while in the military are some of the most valued of her reflections.

"I spent half of my married life in uniform, and although it was difficult at times because of having to be away from my family, I still miss the people I served with, the structure, and all of the good memories that come with it." She added, "They always say the military is like one big family, and it truly is. The friendships last a long time, and I still keep in touch with many of the people I served with here and even those from the Colorado and Iowa National Guard." *(Photograph courtesy of Patty LeComte)*

Vickie Davenport – *Jefferson City*

During the Vietnam War, explained local veteran Vickie Davenport, many military members returning from the war were showered with disparaging labels such as "baby killers" and "warmongers." Serving with the U.S. Army during this period, she recalls receiving such negative treatment when in uniform, which is why only in recent years she has begun to acknowledge to others her past military service. While living with her mother in Texas in 1972, Davenport briefly attended a secretarial school while at the same time trying to find a job. Prospective employers told her that she did not possess the experience needed to be hired, and she soon chose to focus her sights on an alternative employment path.

"I enlisted in the Women's Army Corps (WAC) on October 24, 1972," said Davenport. "By doing so, I figured I would gain the experience the employers were looking for, have a roof over my head, get paid, earn some money for college, and also serve my country," she added.

The predecessor to the WAC—the Women's Army Auxiliary Corps (WAAC)—possessed no military status and made "available to the national defense the knowledge, skill, and special training of the women of the nation," read Executive Order 9163, signed by President Franklin Roosevelt in May 1942. However, on July 3, 1943, the WAC bill was signed into law, granting military status to the organization.

"Within days, I arrived at Fort McClellan (Alabama) for basic training, she said. "That's where I spent the next several weeks learning military protocols, marching, formations, trained with gas masks—basically everything except for weapons training."

According to a section of the Ft. McClellan website dedicated to the post's history during the years of 1917-1999, the Women's Army Corps Center was established at the post in 1954 and became "a receiving, processing and training center for all female inductees to the Army." [110]

"We were completely segregated—it was all women that we trained with in addition to those who trained us ... with the exception of some men who worked as maintenance for our facilities," she said.

Davenport mirthfully recalled that since she was only five feet, two inches tall when she arrived at basic training, and the Army did not tailor the clothing she was issued, she often wore uniforms that were much too large for her. In January 1973, after completing her initial training, she returned to Texas for a few days of leave and married her fiancée, who was at the time on active duty in the Air Force. Days later, she traveled to Ft. Dix, New Jersey, for advanced training as a

---

[110] United States Army Garrison, *History of Fort McClellan 1917-1999*, https://mclellan.usace.army.mil.

clerk typist. During this period, she explained, female trainees were no longer segregated from the male soldiers, although they lived in separate barracks.

For the next two months, she and her fellow WACs received detailed instruction that would allow them to perform typing and clerical duties when they received their first duty assignment. For Davenport, this came in the spring of 1973 when she was issued orders for an assignment in Germany.

"They eventually attached me as a clerk typist with the drug and alcohol rehabilitation program for the U.S. Army in Pirmasens, Germany," said Davenport. "I can remember that when I arrived there by bus, all of the male soldiers began cheering because a WAC was a rare sight to see there," she laughed.

The rehabilitation center, she noted, was housed in an old prison and the counseling rooms had once been used as the individual prison cells. For the next year, she helped maintain the confidential records with regard to the treatment provided to soldiers in the rehabilitation programs. In mid-spring 1974, Davenport requested an early discharge since her husband was on active duty with the Air Force. In April 1974, her request was approved, and she was given an honorable discharge, at which point she made her return to Ft. Worth.

"I enrolled in a local college and began using my G.I. Bill," said Davenport. "My husband and I eventually separated, and our marriage was annulled," she added.

Throughout the ensuing years, the former WAC moved to southern California, where she was employed for nearly a decade with the Trinity Broadcasting Network. She was later employed for several years in the entertainment industry, working for both Warner Brothers and Disney.

"In 2005, I moved to Jefferson City because my mother was living here," Davenport said. "I began working for the Christian Television Network in 2007 as an administrative assistant and was promoted to general manager a week later." She remained with the company until her retirement in March 2018.

When leaving the service in 1974, Davenport noted, those who served in the military—both men and women—were often subject to discouraging treatment. Because of this, she added, it was only in recent years that she began sharing her own story of service as a WAC.

"I never used to tell anybody I was a WAC because of what happened during the period of the Vietnam War ... but now it seems like everyone wants to tell you 'thank you' for your service." She concluded, "Now, after visiting on several occasions with a fellow Christian veteran about our military service, I don't mind sharing my story because there weren't a lot of people who served in the WACs." Pausing, she said, "Many things have certainly changed for the better in recent years." *(Photograph courtesy of Vickie Davenport)*

Thomas Akers – *Eminence*

The career of Eminence, Missouri, resident Thomas Akers has—in quite literal terms—risen to meteoric heights. A veteran of four Space Shuttle flights made during the 1990s, Akers recognizes that his career as an astronaut was a dream achieved through the boost provided from the training received in the United States Air Force. Born in St. Louis on May 20, 1951, Akers explained that his parents made the decision to move to the community of Eminence when he was four years old to find a quieter location to raise their family.

"I am a twin, and we have an older brother as well," said Akers during a recent interview. "My father worked in St. Louis as a carpenter and was only home on weekends while we were growing up," he added.

Graduating in 1969 as valedictorian of his high school class, he enrolled at the University of Missouri-Rolla to pursue a degree in applied mathematics, a subject he enjoyed. Additionally, he explained, the math teacher at Eminence High School planned to retire in the next few years, which was a position that interested young Akers. He went on to earn his bachelor's degree in 1973 and his Master of Science degree in 1975.

"I managed to pay for my college through scholarships and working as a park ranger at Alley Springs during the summer months," he said. "My wife and I were married while I was still in college, and shortly after I finished my education, I was talked into becoming the high school principal at Eminence and did that for the next four years."

A few months into his employment as principal, he and his wife welcomed their first child, David, into the world. Three years later, an Air Force recruiter visited the high school to recruit their math teacher to fill technical vacancies. The teacher was not interested in pursuing a military career, but Akers read the brochures left behind and decided the Air Force might offer a beneficial opportunity.

"I didn't want to be a high school principal the rest of my life and chose to enlist in May 1979," he said. "My first three months in the Air Force were spent at Officer Training School at Lackland Air Force Base (Texas) followed by my first duty assignment at Eglin Air Force Base in Florida."

Throughout the day, Akers was an air-to-air missile analyst but in the evenings taught math and physics courses at Troy State University. In 1980, while in the midst of a frenetic work schedule, his family grew with the addition of his daughter, Jessica. It was also during this period that the airman received an incentive ride in the backseat of an F-4 Phantom (supersonic jet)—a thrilling experience that not only inspired his desire to fly but would also lead to his becoming qualified to apply for the astronaut program.

"In 1982, I was selected to attend Air Force Test Pilot School at Edwards Air Force Base in California," he said. "In one of the buildings on the base, they had photographs of all of the Apollo astronauts hanging on the wall." He added, "Seeing those photos really got me interested in the potential of becoming part of the astronaut program."

Returning to Eglin in 1983, Akers worked on weapons development programs for several types of aircraft. He applied for the astronaut program through the Air Force in 1985 but was not selected. The following year, he again went through the application process; however, the program was temporarily suspended after the Challenger incident in January 1986.

"In 1987, I again applied for the program and was selected," he said. "As part of the selection process, there were approximately one hundred individuals interviewed for a final class of only fifteen astronaut candidates," he said.

As Akers explained, he remained a member of the Air Force but was assigned to NASA. Completing about a year of astronaut candidate training at Johnson Space Center in Houston, he participated in his first space flight in October 1990, assisting in the deployment of an interplanetary probe. The Space Shuttle *Endeavor* made its maiden flight in May 1992 with Akers aboard for his second mission. The astronaut would again travel to space in 1993 and 1996, finishing his NASA career after accumulating more than eight hundred hours of space flight and twenty-nine hours of spacewalking over the course of four missions.

"I left NASA in 1997, and the Air Force assigned me as commander of the ROTC program at the University of Missouri-Rolla," Akers explained. "I retired from the Air Force two years later at the rank of colonel."

The veteran remained at Rolla for a number of years, serving as an instructor in the university's math department until retiring in 2010. He and his wife now reside on a small farm near his hometown of Eminence. Reflecting on his fascinating experiences, Akers acknowledges his professional achievements were made possible through the military, a supportive family, and God's guidance and blessings.

"The greatest benefit I learned in the Air Force is the value of teamwork—each person relies on everyone else to accomplish the mission," he affirmed. "Additionally, in the scientific and engineering fields, you don't place much value on positions or titles but rather on competencies and abilities, all of which helped prepare me for NASA." He added, "And all of this would not have happened without the support of my wife, Kaye. She understood the risks during the entire time I was flying and performing space flights but never let on as to any worry. However," he concluded, "once I finally stopped flying, she told me how worried she had actually been." *(Photograph courtesy of Tom Akers)*

Alan Winemiller – *Jefferson City*

Shortly after graduating from Jefferson City Senior High School in 1973, Alan Winemiller enlisted in the U.S. Army—a decision partially inspired by the military service of an older brother. With the Vietnam War in hindsight, it may have been a relatively calm period in the military; however, the young soldier experienced a moment of intense excitement after helping thwart a possible assassination attempt against the U.S. president.

"When I enlisted, I didn't have any type of MOS (military occupational specialty) selected," he said. "I enlisted for two years and figured they would make me a cook or something like that since I wasn't going to be in for long," he added.

Traveling to Fort Leonard Wood for his basic combat training in the summer of 1973, Winemiller was advised the Army had selected him to become a nuclear weapons maintenance specialist. That fall, he left the Missouri military post and traveled to Redstone Arsenal, Alabama, to complete several weeks of specialized training. The young soldier received in-depth instruction on maintaining several types of air defense missiles in the U.S. Army's nuclear air-defense arsenal to include the Nike Hercules, Pershing, and Honest John. Many of these missiles were deployed not only stateside but throughout Europe to serve as a deterrent to Soviet aggression.

"We actually worked on the warheads, which were stored in a shop inside a magazine (fortified structure)," he recalled. "The missiles had limited life components that we had to replace on designated cycles, like the neutron generators and some of the seals." He added, "The rest of the missile, like the rocket motors, were stored at the launch sites."

When his training was finished in the early weeks of 1974, Winemiller was sent to a conventional ammunition company of the 9th Infantry Division at Fort Lewis, Washington, since he had only a little more than a year remaining in his enlistment. His company stored and maintained all of the munitions for Fort Lewis and, because their inventory did not include any missiles, Winemiller was appointed as the company armorer, storing and maintaining the M-16s used by the soldiers. Although he considered it a rather mundane duty assignment, it would unexpectedly draw him into the spotlight.

"The soldiers assigned to our company could store their personal weapons in our arms room and check them out when they wanted them," explained the veteran. "One guy in the company, whom I didn't really know all that well, came by toward the end of the workday and checked out his personal weapons."

In an interview appearing in the June 16, 1974, edition of the *Sunday News and Tribune*, Winemiller stated, "I didn't question him at first, but then he said he was going to take the weapons to Spokane, Wash., and shoot the president." The newspaper added, "Nixon was scheduled to arrive in Spokane the next day of the Expo '74 World's Fair."

Winemiller recalled, "At the end of the day, an officer would come down to account for all of the weapons, and I informed him what the soldier had said. It wasn't long after that when things really went crazy, and there were all kinds of investigators speaking with me that included Secret Service agents."

The suspect was apprehended, and Winemiller was called to testify as a witness in federal court. As he recalls, the soldier was never convicted but was discharged from the U.S. Army.

"I was congratulated for my role in preventing a potential threat on the life of a president and was told I was going to be awarded an Army Commendation Medal," he said. "I never received the medal—I guess everyone just kind of forgot about it, and I didn't ask any questions."

When the end of his enlistment approached, the soldier made the decision to reenlist when learning his military career field was eligible for a $12,000 reenlistment bonus. Signing a six-year contract, he spent the next 3-1/2 years as a missile maintenance specialist in Italy.

"Our base was near Vicenza, and we would travel on short duty assignments to missile bases throughout northern Italy to conduct maintenance of missiles on site," he said. "The Italian military was actually in charge of the security for each of the sites although we maintained the missiles."

During his overseas tour, Winemiller explained, one of the most memorable experiences was the opportunity to visit several European countries during his time off-duty. Toward the end of his enlistment contract, he was reassigned to Red Stone Arsenal, where he received his discharge from the U.S. Army in 1981.

After returning to Mid-Missouri, he worked briefly at the former Missouri State Penitentiary before being hired by a mechanical contractor that helped build several nuclear power plants. Eventually, the veteran decided to utilize his GI Bill benefits and graduated from the HVAC program at Linn State Technical College (now State Technical College of Missouri) in 1990. He was later employed as an industrial and commercial refrigeration specialist for Dillons Food Stores, installing and maintaining refrigeration equipment for several supermarkets throughout Mid-Missouri before retiring in 2016.

The father of three children, Winemiller maintains that although his military experience was "pretty normal," the U.S. Army provided him with several opportunities he otherwise would have never experienced.

"When I was stationed in Italy, there was always something to do when you were off," he said. "I got to see Austria, Germany, and Switzerland ... which is something that never would have happened had I not been in the Army. I enjoyed my military service, but I guess the time when I was recognized for helping protect the president from an assassination attempt became my fifteen minutes of fame," he chuckled. "But all in all, it was a great time, and I made a lot of wonderful memories." *(Photography courtesy of Alan Winemiller)*

Marcy Ng – *Centralia*

During her formative years in Centralia, Missouri, Marcella "Marcy" Ng humorously explained that she was raised as a "drug baby"— she was drug into church on Sunday morning or any other time the church doors were open. Raised by her grandparents, Ng affirmed that it was this early immersion in Christian faith that provided her with the foundation to help usher her through difficult times in both her military career and personal life. Graduating from Hickman High School in Columbia, Missouri, in 1974, the world began to unfold when she applied for three different universities and received acceptance letters from each one. After visiting with teachers at her former high school, she made the decision to attend the University of Wisconsin-Madison.

"There were several people in my family who had served in the medical field as nurses so I wanted to become a doctor," she said. "That all changed after I became involved in the ROTC program in college," she added.

Excelling within the military structure, Ng went on to serve as a leader in the cadet corps and was selected to attend U.S. Army Airborne School prior to her senior year at the university. It was during her ROTC training, however, that one of her instructors encouraged her to not only consider a military career but also contemplate becoming a pilot.

"When I graduated with my English degree in December 1978, I was honored with being a distinguished military graduate, commissioned a second lieutenant, and then sent to Ft. Eustis, Virginia, for the Transportation Officer Basic Course," she explained. "From there, I traveled to Ft. Rucker (Alabama) to begin flight school."

It was during her flight training that she was advised that she possessed an unexpected distinction among her training class.

"At some point, I was completing my in-processing at Ft. Rucker, and one of the clerks said to me, 'You're the first one of you all to come through here,' which was his way of saying that I was the first African American woman to go through flight school."

For the next nine months, Ng and her fellow aspiring aviators were introduced to the TH-55 training helicopters before progressing to the larger UH-1 Iroquois "Huey" helicopters that were prevalent in the skies during the Vietnam War. While in flight school, she met Dennis Ng, and shortly after her graduation in November 1979, the couple married. With little time to celebrate their recent nuptials, she was sent to Stuttgart, Germany, and received assignment to the 394th Transportation Battalion. The next three years were a medley of intriguing assignments, with Ng spending time as an executive officer in the headquarters and headquarters company in addition to fulfilling the duties of motor officer and dining facility officer. However, she recalls that not every aspect of her time in Germany is a glorious memory.

"I learned that I was the first black officer and the first woman in the unit," she said. "I served under a commanding officer who, in the nicest terms, lacked integrity, and I was eventually disqualified from flight service because of discrimination ... but I let it go because I lacked any solid proof."

Despite the stresses of this period, Ng maintains that God was always at work in her life and continued to open new doors. She returned to the United States in 1983 to complete the Transportation Officer Advanced Course and, within the next year, assumed command of her own company at Ft. Hood, Texas. Proving her competency as a leader and demonstrating her organizational abilities in her professional endeavors, her personal life grew as she and her husband became parents to three children and were blessed to remain stationed together during a large part of their individual military careers.

Her progression as an officer continued in the ensuing years while she performed duty in locations such as Korea and, in 1989, was assigned to the 7th Infantry Division (Light) at Ft. Ord, California. During this period, she was sent briefly to Panama in support of infantry brigades shortly before "Operation Just Cause"—the U.S. invasion of Panama.

"In 1991, I was promoted to major and later completed my Command and General Staff Officers Course," she explained. "I truly had an enjoyable career filled with a number of great duty assignments, but one highlight was when I was selected as executive officer and acting commander for the 24th Transportation Battalion at Ft. Eustis."

Her career eventually resulted in promotion to the rank of lieutenant colonel and included time in command of a transportation battalion at Ft. Hood. Although she continued to enjoy her career and the varied opportunities it offered, in September 2000, she made the decision to retire.

"It was time to settle down with my children," she said.

She now lives in Texas and enjoys spending time with her husband, who also retired as a lieutenant colonel. Even though she no longer maintains the frenetic schedule of an Army officer, she has gone on to serve as a director of a pregnancy center and currently manages an event venue owned by her family. Although her life, rich in treasured memories, might serve as a template of encouragement for others, Ng maintains it is her walk with God that has provided her enduring peace and established the path for her career.

"If my experiences of getting through all the hard knocks during my military career can serve as an inspiration for other black women, then that is fantastic," she said. "But there is someone else responsible for giving me the opportunities I enjoyed. There were many tough times when I wanted to give up, and so I prayed and spoke with the Lord, and he then spoke to my heart ... he encouraged me to stick it out. When I started praying and following after the Lord," she added, "that's when my career and life begin to change for the better." *(Photograph courtesy of Marcy Ng)*

Carol Jean Dameron Bailey – *California*

Growing up the daughter of a rural preacher and an electric lineman, and in a combined family of seven children, Carol Jean Dameron Bailey realized her parents would not have the financial wherewithal to send her to college. In the weeks prior to her graduation from California High School in 1976, she made the decision to enlist in the U.S. Army.

"Initially, my decision to join was motivated by my desire to earn some college money, but it later became an experience that I really enjoyed, especially the camaraderie," she affirmed.

Several weeks after graduation, in August 1976, she traveled to Ft. Jackson, South Carolina, for her basic training. At the time, she was a member of the Women's Army Corps (WAC), which had been established as an auxiliary unit of the U.S. Army during World War II to afford women opportunities to serve in non-combat roles. In the fall of 1976, Bailey was transferred to the former Fort Wadsworth, New York, where she completed several weeks of training to serve as a chaplain's assistant. As she explained, her military occupational specialty was inspired by her father's and her grandfather's careers as preachers.

"My first duty station was at Fort Leonard Wood in January (1977)," she explained. "I requested that duty location because it was closest to home."

The following month, she married a soldier who was assigned to Ft. Bragg, North Carolina. In June 1977, she was able to receive a transfer to Ft. Bragg and worked at the main post chapel and Religious Education Center, completing reports, creating church bulletins, and maintaining supplies for the chaplains. In 1978, the Army abolished the WAC, and Bailey was transferred to the Regular Army. She gave birth to her only child, a son named Robbie, in March 1980. Five months later, she was discharged from the Army after completing her enlistment and immediately joined the North Carolina National Guard.

"My husband and I began attending college and participated in the ROTC program so we could become officers," she explained. "I received my commission as a personnel officer in May 1982."

For several years, she remained in an Inactive Ready Reserve (IRR) status, completing occasional duty and correspondence courses to accrue military service credit while she accompanied her husband on his military assignments throughout the U.S. In 1985, she was promoted to first lieutenant and the following year returned to Ft. Bragg with her husband and son.

"I stayed in the IRR and worked for about thirteen years as an Army civilian," she said. "I was promoted to captain in 1989, divorced in 1991, and the following year moved to Tipton (Missouri)." She added, "I then decided to join the Missouri National Guard and performed state emergency duty during the flood of '93 and also spent time in Panama."

In 1993, she also earned her bachelor's degree in business administration from Campbell University and went on to complete additional training to improve her skills as an officer. However, in 1998, she made the decision to pursue opportunities in the Army Reserve. Soon after her transfer, she was promoted to major.

"I was assigned to the 418th Civil Affairs Battalion in Belton, Missouri, as the team chief for the telecommunications section, "she recalled. "I did a lot of summer camps at Ft. Hood, Texas, and, in early 2000, I volunteered to go with a unit deploying to Bosnia."

During deployment, she served as agriculture officer, providing farming and economic support to the local population. Her duties included coordination of seminars between non-government organizations that provided seed and farm equipment and Bosnian locals interested in pursuing agricultural opportunities. When the deployment ended in the summer of 2000, she returned to an IRR status but continued performing intermittent periods of active duty while working full-time with the Substance Abuse Program at the Tipton Correctional Facility.

"I was mobilized as part of Operation Enduring Freedom and deployed to Afghanistan in April 2003," she said. "I was there until October 2003 as the public affairs officer with the Coalition Joint Civil Military Task Force, writing press releases, coordinating dignitary visits, and writing articles and newsletters, among other tasks."

Two years later, in January 2005, she went on active-duty orders at MacDill Air Force Base in Florida. During this period, she was promoted to lieutenant colonel and performed temporary duty in Qatar as a civil affairs officer with the Civil Affairs Military Operations Center.

"I went back into the IRR in October of 2005," she paused, adding, "but then began doing short-period mobilization orders at Ft. Bragg with the Civil Affairs Command. I retired on June 1, 2010, but then did a voluntary retirement recall tour, serving until February 2011, when I retired for good," she chuckled.

Bailey now lives in her hometown of California and beams with pride when sharing that her son joined the Army Reserve in 1997 and went on to serve for nearly a decade. In recent years, she has enjoyed doing genealogy research when not assisting her mother. The years she invested in service to the nation, she remarked, were the result of not only striving to identify an avenue by which to fund her college education but have come to define her drive to succeed through her own efforts and on her terms.

"The military was something that I did on my own, and I am proud that I became the seventeenth generation of my family to serve," she said. "I completed all of the necessary schools and requirements to meet the qualifications for promotions ... and I earned it." She concluded, "When I joined the Army, I made a promise to my stepfather that I would do my best and earn my rank. I never forgot that and always gave 100 percent to completing the mission." *(Photograph courtesy of Carol Jean Dameron Bailey)*

Mark Randazzo – *Eugene*

For eighteen years, the late Mark Randazzo was associated with the 1035th Maintenance Company, accompanying them on their relocation from Jefferson City to Jefferson Barracks in 1995. He came of age with the unit, beginning his military career as a young enlisted soldier, and later attended Officer Candidate School followed by a promotion to company commander.

"The 1035th was always home for him because he was so young and impressionable when he joined the company," said Lisa Randazzo, the late veteran's wife. "He served with so many wonderful people that were good mentors for him."

Born in St. Louis and later growing up near Eugene, Randazzo attended Our Lady of the Snows Elementary School in Mary's Home and went on to graduate from Helias Catholic High School in 1981. Between his junior and senior year, he made the decision to enlist in the Missouri National Guard and began drilling as an enlisted soldier with the 1035th Maintenance Company, which was at the time headquartered at the Blue Armory on St. Mary's Boulevard and trained at the maintenance complex on Industrial Drive in Jefferson City. Through some encouragement, he enrolled at Central Missouri State University in Warrensburg (now University of Central Missouri) following his graduation from high school.

"Attendance at both Helias and Central Missouri State was not my idea, but I sure am glad my parents pushed me and made me do it," said Randazzo during a 2006 presentation to the Missouri Retired Teachers Association.

Graduating with a degree in aviation technology in 1986, the young soldier acquired full-time employment as a mechanic with the maintenance shop at the Missouri National Guard headquarters. A few years later, he was encouraged to apply for Officer Candidate School (OCS).

"We were married on September 16, 1989, a month or so after he graduated from OCS," said Lisa Randazzo. "He continued working full-time at the maintenance shop and, in March 1991, was commissioned as a second lieutenant while continuing to drill with the 1035th."

Having invested ten years as an enlisted soldier and mechanic with the 1035th, the next several years were a progression of assignments for the officer that included service as detachment commander, maintenance control officer, and, following the company's move to Jefferson Barracks, appointment as company commander on August 24, 1995. When completing his command in June 1998, he received a grand farewell at a ceremony during which he was presented a guidon (flag) from the soldiers of the 1035th in addition to a plaque that read, in part, "Your professionalism, dedication, guidance, and friendship as a soldier ... and commander have gotten us where we are. Our future successes will be based upon the foundation you've built."

His part-time military duties led to an appointment as executive officer for the 835th Corps Support Battalion, with whom he deployed to Iraq from December 2003 to January 2005. Acknowledging the sacrifices made by his wife, Randazzo stated in the aforementioned presentation to the Missouri Retired Teachers Association, "During the thirteen months I was gone (to Iraq), I missed quite a bit: my wife built a house, sold our old house and had a baby (their youngest son, Michael) the day I convoyed from Kuwait to Iraq."

In his full-time capacity, Randazzo's career advanced with assignments that included a tour with the National Guard Bureau in Arlington, Virginia, assignment as the Surface Maintenance Manager, and eventually as the Director of Logistics for the Missouri Army National Guard. In 2000, he became a major, followed by promotion to lieutenant colonel in 2006.

Sadly, the revered forty-eight-year-old officer passed away unexpectedly in 2011, leaving behind his wife and two young sons. At the time of his passing, he had compiled an impressive resume with more than thirty-one years of military service and was posthumously promoted to colonel.

"When Mark died, we were trying to decide where he should be buried," said Lisa. "I found a red deployment booklet that he had written inside that if something should happen to him, he wished to be buried in a federal cemetery."

Following discussions with the funeral home, she learned that no new burials were being made in the Jefferson City National Cemetery, but when the other federal cemeteries in Missouri were mentioned, she immediately found her answer.

"They said Jefferson Barracks National Cemetery was open to burials, and I knew that is where he would have wanted to be," she said. "He served with the 1035th at Jefferson Barracks for all those years, speaking about how he loved the area and could gaze upon the cemetery from his office there."

With a military career composed of a medley of fascinating experiences and resulting in the award of such prestigious medals as the Legion of Merit and a Bronze Star, it was his time with the 1035th Maintenance Company that remained the most influential, his wife affirmed.

"He was so young when he enlisted, and the mechanics in the 1035th were much older than him and could have been his father," she said. "You can grow up in an organization like that, and it certainly made a lasting impression on him."

Joseph, the veteran's oldest son, explained that he and his brother were quite young when their father passed away, but hearing stories about his service helps provide them with insight into the impact he made during his career.

"What's most important to us is when people speak well of our father and share with us the good memories that they have of him," said Joseph. "We appreciate hearing about the positive influence he was in the lives of others." *(Photograph courtesy of Lisa Randazzo)*

Charles Campbell – *Tipton*

Shortly after his graduation from high school in Memphis, Tennessee, in 1977, Charles Campbell chose to continue his education. He went on to earn his associate's degree in optometric technology before going to work for his father, who had become a successful optometrist in the Nashville area. For the next couple of years, Campbell listened while his father—a U.S. Army veteran of both World War II and Korea—encouraged him to consider enlisting in the military.

"My father thought that it might be a good way for me to acquire some benefits and experience," said Campbell, who now lives in Tipton. "So, I went to the recruiter and enlisted in the U.S. Army in August of 1982," he added.

As Campbell explained, when speaking with the recruiter, there was little thought given to the military specialty he wished to pursue other than avoiding an infantry assignment. When flipping through pages listing various military job fields, he pointed to the artillery and said, "That will work."

The first stop in his military journey was Ft. Sill, Oklahoma, where he spent the next few weeks undergoing his basic training. He remained at the post for several more weeks to receive instruction to qualify as a cannon crewman.

"During the training, we learned to work with the mobile 155mm howitzers," said Campbell. "Part of this included learning how to cut charges and set timers, load the howitzers, perform maintenance, and how to set up a defensive perimeter around the equipment."

When he first enlisted, Campbell specifically requested the opportunity to serve in Germany after his initial training was completed, which became a wish granted in December 1982. It was during this timeframe that he was assigned to the 6th Battalion, 9th Field Artillery Regiment at Rivers Barracks in Giessen, Germany. A few months after his arrival, they made the transition to 5th Battalion, 3rd Field Artillery Regiment. As the former soldier explained, almost immediately upon his arrival at his new duty assignment, he was placed in a section that had "nuclear capabilities."

He noted, "They wanted soldiers that had a little bit of education, and we were drug tested every week. We were working with nuclear artillery shells, and I learned to handle and assemble them by reading and studying a number of manuals," he added.

During this timeframe, Campbell acknowledged there existed the threat of a Soviet attack in the region, and their responsibility was to serve as a deterrent and to "hold the line" in case of a confrontation, providing a delay so that reinforcements could arrive. The soldiers of his battery regularly participated in the Army Training and Evaluation Program (ARTEP), during which observers from the Pentagon evaluated their abilities to load, operate and protect the nuclear-capable artillery weapons under simulated combat conditions. On other occasions, his battery participated in exercises with West German and British forces to enhance their coordination and response capabilities in case of a military emergency.

"We were in the field quite a bit, participating in different exercises and basically trained all the time," Campbell recalled. "As part of the ARTEP review, we received a U.S. Army certification but had to go through regular evaluations to maintain that certification since there were a lot of protocols associated with working around nuclear artillery."

Because of the battalion's proximity to a NATO site where nuclear artillery rounds were stored, Campbell was often part of a team of soldiers tasked to serve as part of a reactionary force to provide security for the location. In August 1984, his two-year enlistment ended, and he was sent back to Ft. Jackson, South Carolina, where he received his discharge from the U.S. Army. He then returned to Nashville and spent the next couple of years working for his father.

"One of the guys who I became friends with while in Germany and who happened to serve in one of our neighboring batteries was living in Mid-Missouri and told me that there were several employment opportunities available with the Department of Corrections," he said.

"I decided to make the move and worked a couple of years at the old Missouri State Penitentiary," said Campbell. "Then I left that and went to work for the Federal Bureau of Prisons for three years, which was interesting because I spent some time in Miami helping guard (Manuel) Noriega."

He soon returned to employment with the Missouri State Department of Corrections and, throughout the next several years, worked at several facilities to include Renz Women's Prison, Jefferson City Correctional Center, and Church Prison Farm. In 2018, Campbell retired from state employment while working at the Tipton Correctional Facility. Since retiring, the former soldier has embraced his faith and is an active member of the Seventh Day Adventist Church. When reflecting on his service in the U.S. Army, Campbell noted it was an experience that not only helped improve his temperament but provided an insight into the relationships that evolve through a close-knit working environment.

"Prior to the Army, I had a harsh personality and could be very negative at times; however, my experience in the military whittled away the rough edges and taught me how to respect others and work together to accomplish tasks in the most efficient manner. I can recall," he added, "my father saying to me before I enlisted that if I were to serve in the military, I would have something wonderful to talk about in later years, and I would become part of the special community (veterans) who would always be there for me when I needed them … and he was right." *(Photograph courtesy of Charles Campbell)*

Jeremy P. Amick

Silver Star Families of America Commendation Award

A non-profit based out of Clever, Missouri, the primary mission of the Silver Star Families of America is to support and recognize veterans who are wounded, injured, or have acquired an illness related to their service in a combat zone—regardless of service branch or military conflict. In keeping with this mission, the founders, president, and board of the SSFOA conduct an election process to select the winner for the organization's premier honor—the SSFOA Commendation Award. The annual commendation may be awarded to military or civilian personnel and departments or organizations that have positively affected the lives of wounded and ill veterans.

In 2017, the SSFOA founders selected the Kansas City Royals for this distinction because of their "unwavering support of the military community by offering discounted tickets to members of the military and their families; honoring veterans and the military in pre-game ceremonies; visiting troops at military sites such as Ft. Riley, Kansas, and Whiteman Air Force Base; hosting Memorial Day tributes; and visiting veterans at VA hospitals," the award citation read.

Steven Newton, founder and CEO of the SSFOA said, "It is pleasing to note that there are organizations in major league baseball, such as the Kansas City Royals, who appreciate the sacrifices of members of our Armed Forces and utilize their resources and notoriety to support causes benefitting these great warriors with no expectations of recognition for their efforts."

Pictured are Shawn Johnson (left) and Jeremy P. Ämick (right), volunteers with the Silver Star Families of America, discussing the commendation with Kansas City Royals icon and Major League Baseball Hall of Famer George Brett. *(Photo courtesy of Jerod Barlow)*

WORKS CITED

Newspapers

Atlanta Constitution (Atlanta, Georgia)
Austin American-Statesmen (Austin, Texas)
Bainbridge Mainstreet (Bainbridge, Maryland)
Bee (Danville, Virginia)
Belleville News-Democrat (Belleville, Illinois)
Boston Globe
Capital (Annapolis, Maryland)
Carthage Evening Press (Carthage, Missouri)
Caruthersville Journal (Caruthersville, Missouri)
Casper Star-Tribune (Casper, Wyoming)
Charlotte News (Charlotte, North Carolina)
Chattanooga Daily Times (Chattanooga, Tennessee)
Chicago Tribune (Chicago, Illinois)
Chico-Daily Evening Enterprise (Chico, California)
Chico Enterprise (Chico, California)
Climax-Madisonian (Richmond, Kentucky)
Clinton Eye (Clinton, Missouri)
Colored American (Washington, D.C.)
Columbia Evening Missourian (Columbia, Missouri)
Daily Arkansas Gazette (Little Rock, Arkansas)
Daily Capital News (Jefferson City, Missouri)
Dallas Times-Herald (Dallas, Texas)
Edina Sentinel (Edina, Missouri)
Evening Journal (Wilmington, North Carolina)
Evening Sun (Baltimore, Maryland)
Gazette (Montreal, Canada)
Henry County Democrat (Clinton, Missouri)

Honolulu Advertiser (Honolulu, Hawaii)
Honolulu Star-Bulletin (Honolulu, Hawaii)
Houston Herald (Houston, Missouri)
Jefferson City News Tribune (Jefferson City, Missouri)
Jefferson City Post-Tribune (Jefferson City, Missouri)
Kansas City Journal (Kansas City, Missouri)
Kansas City Star (Kansas City, Missouri)
Kansas City Times (Kansas City, Missouri)
King City Chronicle (King City, Missouri)
Leader-Telegram (Eau Claire, Wisconsin)
Leaf-Chronicle (Clarksville, Tennessee)
Lexington Intelligencer (Lexington, Missouri)
Macon Chronicle-Herald (Macon, Missouri)
Maryville Daily Forum (Maryville, Missouri)
Moberly Monitor-Index (Moberly, Missouri)
Morning Herald (Uniontown, Pennsylvania)
Mount Carmel Daily Republican Register (Mount Carmel, Illinois)
News-Palladium (Benton Harbor, Michigan)
Newton Daily Republican (Newton, Kansas)
Oroville Daily Register (Oroville, California)
Plattsburg Leader (Plattsburg, Missouri)
Press-Tribune (Roseville, California)
Sacramento Bee (Sacramento, California)
Salt Lake Herald (Salt Lake City, Utah)
Sante Fe New Mexican (Sante Fe, New Mexico)
Sikeston Herald (Sikeston, Missouri)
Sikeston Standard (Sikeston, Missouri)
Spokane Chronicle (Spokane, Washington)
Springfield Leader and Press (Springfield, Missouri)
St. Cloud Times (St. Cloud, Minnesota)
St. Joseph Weekly Gazette (St. Joseph, Missouri)
St. Louis Globe-Democrat (St. Louis, Missouri)
St. Louis Post-Dispatch (St. Louis, Missouri)
St. Louis Star and Times (St. Louis, Missouri)
Sunday News and Tribune (Jefferson City, Missouri)
Tampa Times (Tampa, Florida)

Tennessean (Nashville, Tennessee)
Times (Philadelphia, Pennsylvania)
Wilmington Morning Star (Wilmington, North Carolina)
Windsor Review (Windsor, Missouri)
Word and Way

Books and Articles

Adams, Stanley J. *Mokane to Mole City: A Manchu Vietnam Memoir.* (Independently published, January 2, 2019).

Allen, Minnie. *The Women's Work in the Legion.* (California Legion Monthly, January 1921).

Anderton, David A. *The History of the U.S. Air Force.* (New York, NY: Crescent Books, 1981).

Assembly. *Be Thou at Peace.* (West Point, NY: Association of Graduates, United States Military Academy, April 1989).

Bliss, Maj. Paul S. *History of the 805th Pioneer Infantry.* (St. Paul, MN: Paul S. Bliss, 1919).

Broeg, Bob. *Stan Musial.* (Garden City, NY: Doubleday & Company, Inc., 1964).

Chubb, Robert W. *Regimental History: 342 Field Artillery, 89th Division.* (Regimental Historian, 1921).

Commission on the National Guard and Reserves: Transforming the National Guard and Reserves into a 21st-Century Operational Force. *Final Report to Congress and the Secretary of Defense, January 31, 2008.* (CreateSpace Independent Publishing Platform, November 22, 2014).

Coontz, Robert E. *From the Mississippi to the Sea.* (Philadelphia, PA: Dorrance and Company, 1930).

Craighead, William M. *All Ahead Full: World War II Memoirs of an LSM 215 Veteran.* (Paducah, KY: Turner Publishing Company, 2004.)

Crowder, Enoch Herbert. *The Spirit of Selective Service.* (New York, NY: The Century Co., 1920).

Diggs Sr., Roland C. *The History & Lineage of the 203rd Engineer Battalion* (Cassville, MO: Litho Printers and Bindery, 2012).

Dupuy, Col. (Ret.) Trevor. *Asian and Axis Resistance Movements.* (New York, NY: Franklin Watts, Inc., 1963).

Dupuy, Col. (Ret.) Trevor. *Asiatic Land Battles: Japanese Ambitions in the Pacific.* (New York, NY: Franklin Watts, Inc., 1963).

Dupuy, Col. (Ret.) Trevor. *The Naval War in the Pacific: On to Tokyo.* (New York, NY: Franklin Watts, Inc., 1963).

English, Jr., George H. *History of the 89th Division, U.S.A.* (Denver, CO: Smith-Brooks Printing Co., 1920).

Fiedler, David. *The Enemy Among Us: POWs in Missouri During World War II.* St. Louis, MO: University of Missouri Press, 2003.)

Fleming, Candace. *Amelia Lost: The Life and Disappearance of Amelia Earhart.* (New York, NY: Random House, 2011).

Ford, James E. *A History of Jefferson City and of Cole County.* (Jefferson City, MO: The New Day Press, 1938).

Guttman, Jon. *Sopwith Camel* (Air Vanguard). (Oxford, UK: Osprey Publishing, 2012).

Historical Annual National Guard of the State of Missouri. *The Spanish-American War.* (Baton Rouge, LA: Army and Navy Publishing Company, 1939).

History of Kansas City, Missouri: Its History and Its People, 1800-1908 (Volume II). *Colonel George Peery Gross.* (Chicago, IL: The S.J. Clarke Publishing Co., 1908).

History of the Missouri National Guard. *Chapter III: History of the First Regiment of Infantry, 138th Infantry and Connected Organizations, 1808-1934.* (Published by the Authority of the Military Council, Missouri National Guard, November 1934).

History of the Missouri National Guard. *Chapter V: 203rd Coast Artillery (Anti-Aircraft).* (Published by the Authority of the Military Council, Missouri National Guard, November 1934).

Johnson, William F. *History of Cooper County, Missouri.* (Topeka, KS: Historical Publishing Company, 1919).

Journal of Negro History. *Robert Thomas Kerlin.* (Volume 35, Number 2, April 1950).

Little, Blanche E. *Military Methods in the Training of Boys, Wentworth Military Academy*. (Published in the School Journal, Volume 67, September 5, 1903.)

Lockmiller, David. *Enoch H. Crowder: Soldier, Lawyer and Statesman*. (Columbia, MO: The University of Missouri Studies, 1955).

Lowry, Terry. *Bastard Battalion: A History of the 83rd Chemical Mortal Battalion in World War II*. (Charleston, WV: 35th Star Publishing, 2009).

Mansfield, George C. *History of Butte County, California*. (Los Angeles, CA: Historic Record Company, 1918).

Mayo, Lida. *United States Army in World War II, The Technical Services, The Ordnance Department: On the Beachhead and the Battlefront*. (Washington, DC: Center of Military History, 2009).

McGrath, Lt. John F. *War Diary of the 354th Infantry*. (Trier, Germany: J. Lintz, 1920).

McMahon, Margaret M. *A Guide to the U.S. Army Pioneer Infantry Regiments in WWI*. (CreateSpace, November 1, 2018).

Moniteau County Historical Society. *Moniteau County Missouri History 2000*. (Marceline, MO: Walsworth Publishing Company, Inc., 2000).

National Historical Annual of Missouri. *140th Infantry*. (Baton Rouge, LA: Army and Navy Publishing Company, 1939).

Order of Battle (Volume 3, Part 3). *Regiments*. (Washington, D.C.: Center of Military History United States Army, 1988).

Philadelphia War History Committee. *Philadelphia in the World War, 1914-1919*. (Philadelphia, PA: Wynkoop Hallenbeck Crawford Co., 1922).

Rottman, Gordon. *Guam 1941 & 1944: Loss and Reconquest*. (Oxford, UK: Osprey Publishing, 2013).

Scott, Emmett J. *Scott's Official History of the American Negro in the World War*. (Independently Published, 1919).

Settle, Raymond W. *The Story of Wentworth*. (Kansas City, MO: Spencer Printing Company, 1950.)

Sonntag, Sherry, Christopher Drew and Annette Lawrence Drew. *Blind Man's Bluff.* (New York, NY: HarperCollins Publishers, 1998).

Stanton, Shelby L. *World War II Order of Battle.* (New York, NY: Galahad Books, 1984.)

Trimble, Joe. *Yogi Berra.* (New York, NY: Grosset & Dunlap, 1965).

Twenty-Second Annual Report of the National Society of the Daughters of the American Revolution, March 1, 1918 to March 1, 1919. *Special Memorials.* (Washington, D.C.: Government Printing Office, 1921).

Venzon, Anne C. (Ed.) *The United States in the First World War: An Encyclopedia.* (New York, NY: Garland Publishing Inc., 1995).

Walker, Mort. *Backstage at the Strips.* (New York, NY: Mason/Charter, 1975).

Wood, Richard E. *The South and Reunion, 1898.* (The Historian Journal, May 1969).

Online Resources

80th Infantry Division Veterans Association. *After Action Reports.* Accessed February 10, 2021. https://www.80thdivision.com/WebArchives/MiscReports.htm.

Air Force: The Official Service Journal of the U.S. Army Air Forces. *Blazing the Trail on D-Day.* (Vol. 27, No.8, August 1944). Accessed February 15, 2021. https://www.google.com/books/.

American Rhetoric. *John Jordan "Buck" O'Neil.* Accessed February 11, 2021. https://www.americanrhetoric.com/speeches/buckoneilbaseballhalloffame.htm.

Army Air Corps Library and Museum. *9th Air Force.* Accessed February 15, 2021. https://www.armyaircorpsmuseum.org/wwii_9th_Air_Force.cfm.

Army Air Forces Historical Studies No. 31. *Flexible Gunnery Training in the AAF.* Accessed February 10, 2021. https://www.afhra.af.mil/Portals/16/documents/Studies/1-50/AFD-090602-068.pdf.

Atomic Heritage Foundation. *Attack on Pearl Harbor – 1941.* Accessed January 26, 2021. https://www.atomicheritage.org/history/attack-pearl-harbor-1941.

Bryan, Jami L. *Fighting for Respect: African-American Soldiers in WWI.* (National Museum of the United States Army). Accessed January 22, 2021. https://armyhistory.org/fighting-for-respect-african-american-soldiers-in-wwi/.

American Legion. *What Legion Event Celebrates its 93rd Anniversary in May?* Accessed January 20, 2021. https://www.legion.org/moment-in-time/164267/what-legion-event-celebrates-its-93rd-anniversary-may.

Carson, Clayborne. *African Americans at War.* (Stanford University). Accessed February 11, 2021. https://web.stanford.edu/~ccarson/articles/oxford_companion.htm.

Commander, Navy Region Mid-Atlantic. *Former Naval Base Little Creek's History.* Accessed February 11, 2021. https://www.cnic.navy.mil/regions/cnrma/installations/jeb_little_creek_fort_story/about/history/naval_amphibious_base_little_creeks_history.html.

Cushman, Allerton. *The Field Artillery Journal.* Accessed February 15, 2021. https://google.books.com.

Ford, Daniel. *B-36: Bomber at the Crossroads.* (Air & Space Magazine, April 1996). Accessed February 16, 2021. https://www.airspacemag.com/history-of-flight/b-36-bomber-at-the-crossroads-134062323/.

Goldenberg, Col. Richard. *In World War I, African American 'Hellfighters from Harlem,' Fought Prejudice to Fight for Their Country.* Accessed January 21, 2021. https://www.uso.org/stories/2125-black-world-war-i-troops-fought-to-fight-for-their-country.

Great War Association. *78th Company, 6th Marines.* Accessed February 16, 2021. http://www.great-war-assoc.org/6THMarines.html.

Idaho Military Museum. *Idaho Legacy: Farragut Idaho.* Accessed February 10, 2021. https://museum.mil.idaho.gov/idaho-military-history/idaho-legacy/.

Indian Motorcycle. *History*. Accessed February 11, 2021. http://www.indian-motorcycle.lv/en/history/71-history/1940.

Jackie Robinson Foundation. *JRF Mourns the Death of Baseball Great Buck O'Neil*. Accessed February 11, 2021. https://www.jackierobinson.org/press/jrf-mourns-the-death-of-baseball-great-buck-oneil/.

Justin Museum of Military History. *Biography of Sandford Sellers Jr.* Accessed February 16, 2021. http://www.justinmuseum.com/cccpapers/sellerssbio.html.

Keene, Jennifer. *True Sons of Freedom. (American Legion Magazine)*. Accessed January 21, 2021. https://www.legion.org/magazine/240774/true-sons-freedom.

LeMoine, Bob. *Buck O'Neil*. (Society for American Baseball Research). Accessed February 11, 2021. https://sabr.org/bioproj/person/buck-oneil/.

Lone Sentry. *The Story of the 80th Infantry Division*. Accessed February 10, 2021. https://www.lonesentry.com/gi_stories_booklets/80thinfantry/index.html.

Messianic Bible. Dead Sea Scrolls. Accessed February 16, 2021. https://free.messianicbible.com/about-our-bible/dead-sea-scrolls/.

Missouri Digital Heritage. *Soldier's Records: War of 1812 – World War I*. Accessed January 8, 2021. https://s1.sos.mo.gov/records/archives/archivesdb/soldiers/#soldiersearch.

Missouri Digital Heritage, Missouri Death Certificates. Accessed January 10, 2021. https://s1.sos.mo.gov/Records/Archives/ArchivesMvc/.

National Archives and Records Administration. *The Meuse-Argonne Offensive*. Accessed January 12, 2021. https://www.archives.gov/research/military/ww1/meuse-argonne#:~:text=The%20Meuse%2DArgonne%20Offensive%20was%20the%20largest%20operations%20of%20the,and%20over%20120%2C000%20total%20casualties.

National World War II Museum. *The United States Occupies Japan*. Accessed February 12, 2021. https://www.nationalww2museum.org/war/articles/did-us-army-occupy-japan-after-world-war-ii#:~:text=The%20military%20occupation%20

of%20Japan,command%20of%20General%20Douglas%20MacArthur..
Naval History and Heritage Command. *Bayfield*. Accessed February 10, 2021. https://www.history.navy.mil/research/histories/ship-histories/danfs/b/bayfield-i.html.
Naval History and Heritage Command. *Colorado III (BB-45)*. Accessed January 21, 2021. https://www.history.navy.mil/research/histories/ship-histories/danfs/c/colorado-iii.html.
Naval History and Heritage Command. *Cruise of the Great White Fleet*. Accessed January 7, 2021. https://www.history.navy.mil/research/library/online-reading-room/title-list-alphabetically/c/cruise-great-white-fleet-mckinley.html.
Theodore Roosevelt Center at Dickson State University. *Great White Fleet*. Accessed January 10, 2021. https://www.theodorerooseveltcenter.org/Learn-About-TR/TR-Encyclopedia/War-and-Military-Affairs/Great-White-Fleet.aspx.
State Historical Society of Missouri. *Guide to American Civil War in Missouri*. Accessed June 30, 2018. https://shsmo.org/research/guides/civilwar/regiment.
The Spanish-American War Centennial Website. *2nd Missouri Volunteer Infantry*. Accessed January 8, 2021. http://www.spanamwar.com.
The 25th Infantry Division and World War II. *Japan*. Accessed February 13, 2021. https://books.google.com/.
United States Army Garrison—Fort McClellan, Alabama. *History of Fort McClellan 1917-1919*. Accessed February 16, 2021. https://mcclellan.usace.army.mil/Info.asp.
United States World War One Centennial Commission. *African-Americans – World War I Centennial*. Accessed January 22, 2021. https://www.worldwar1centennial.org/index.php/edu-home/edu-topics/588-americans-at-war/4992-african-americans.html.
University of Washington. *The Great Depression in Washington State*. Accessed January 20, 2021. http://depts.washington.edu/depress/strikes_unions.shtml#:~:text=Depressions%20often%20break%20unions.,militant%20union%20building%20to%20come.

INDEX

Abels, Herman 18
Adams, Stanley 466-469
Adkins, John (Pete) 244-247
Akers, Thomas 534-537
Alderson, Larry 510-513
American Legion Convention 520-521
American Legion Police 132-135
Amick, Elliott W. 146-149
Amick Sr., Eugene E. 123-126
Amick, Lon 215-218
Bailie, John 437-440
Bailey, Carol Jean Dameron 546-549
Banister, Denny 449-452
Batdorf, Col. Edwin 19-22
Beaman, William 232-235
Berra, Yogi 260-263
Blair Jr., James 311-314
Boehmer, Andrew 291-294
Boehmer, Louis 287-290
Boehmer, Stephen 279-282
Boehmer, Sylvester 283-286
Brett, George 558-559
Brown, Millard 127
Buehrle, Bill 402-405
Cadice, Jasper 66-69
Caffee, Lt. Arthur 38-41

Call of Missouri (painting) 62-65
Camp Weingarten 274-276
Campbell, Charles 554-557
Carroll, Richard 349-352
Central Missouri Post 496 357-360
Chalender, Walter 100-103
Citizens War Power Committee 166-169
Clark, Col. Joel Bennett 96-99
Clark, Col. John 430-432
Clay Jr., Henry Robinson 119-122
Comer, Ralph L. 182-185
Coontz, Admiral Robert E. 49
Crowder, Enoch H. 52-55
Cryderman, Don 498-501
Dahl, Henry 398-401
Davenport, Vickie 530-533
Davis, Al 219-222
DeLong, Leon 502-505
Diemler, Steve 522-525
Diggs, Lawrence 299-302
Douglas, Lon 227-230
Dresselhaus, Joe 494-497
Duss, Margaret 277-278
Duvall, Col. Andrew R. 186-189

Ellis, James 345-348
Enloe Jr., Dr. Cortez 319-322
Enloe Sr., Enoch 2-5
Enloe, Dr. Newton 104-107
Farmer, Noland 474-477
Farr, Bill 506-509
Farr, Frederick 231
Florea, George 80-83
Ford, Tirey J. 117
Foster, Charles 203-206
Garagiola, Joe 256-259
Gates, Louis A. 108-111
Grant, Sharon 478-481
Gross, Alonzo "Mack" 382-385
Gross, Col. George P. 6-9
Guthrie, Charles 516-519
Hamilton, Paul 72-73
Hearnes, Warren E. 158-161
Hoechst, Fred 136-139, 142-145
Hoechst, Gerald 465
Hofius, Paul 369-372
Hollingsworth, Jay G. 76-77
Holt, Clifford 199-202
Holt, Fay 195-198
Hunter, David 433-436
Jaegers, Leonard 325-332
Johnson, Willard Ray 194
Jungmeyer, Edwin 269-272
Karr, Coly 116
Kemple, Jerry 414-417
Kerlin, Robert T. 42-45
Kirkwood Military Academy 36-37
Krenzer, William L. 71
Langston, Robert C. 27-28

LeComte, Patty 526-529
LeComte, Tom 426-429
Lipskoch, Rita 445-448
Lipskoch, William 441-444
Lozier, Lue C. 74-75
Mabury, Ray 410-413
Malloure, Victor 78-79
Markway Jr., Everett 461-464
Markway Sr., Everett 150-153
Marmaduke Military Academy 16-17
Mathis, Clifford 154-157
McManus, Greg 482-485
Merrell, Ray 223-226
Miller, William 418-421
Missouri National Guard (Mindenmines) 128-131
Morall, Edwin S. 30-31
Mound City Jubilee 46
Muessig, Ralph 273
Musial, Stan 252-255
Ng, Marcy 542-545
O'Neil, Buck 248-251
Oppenheim, Dennis 406-409
Palmer, Charles 240-243
Payne, James E. 10-11
Parr, Lloyd 386-389
Payne, Elbert 333-336
Pitts, Elmer T. 70
Preis, Charles A. 23-24
Rackers, James 341-344
Randazzo, Mark 550-553
Reeves, Everett 56-57
Rothove, Hubert 365-368
Russell, Peyton 315-318
Rutledge, Leonard 470-473

Sansone, Charles 25-26
Salamon, Samuel J. 264
Sandbothe, Arnold 422-425
Sandwith, Jack 361-364
Schwaller, Edward 178-181
Schwaller, Joseph 170-173
Schwaller, Leo 174-177
Sellers, James 92-95
Sellers, Ovid 84-87
Sellers Jr. Sandford 88-91
Sellers Sr., Sandford 12-15
Sesenna, Enrico 190-193
Shull, Libby 453-456
Shull, Walter 457-460
Siebert, Herbert 265-268
Silver Star Families 558-559
Smith, Laughton 490-493
Smith, James "Ed" 486-489
Smith, Oscar L. 112-115
Sommerer, Vernon 373-376
Steenbergen, Gene 390-393
Strickfaden, John 323
Strickfaden, Velma 324
Stubinger, Theodore 295-298
Taggart, Leonard 303-306
Thompson, James 353-356
Tisdale, Earl 162-165
Torrey, Col. Jay 32-35
USS Missouri (BB-11) 47-50
Van Wickel, Doris 307-310
Walz Sr., Milo H. 58-61
Westfall, Gerald 378-381
Westhues, Harold 394-397
Whitehead, Don 211-214
Williams, Reuben 118
Winemiller, Alan 538-541

Young, Robert A. 207-210

CPSIA information can be obtained
at www.ICGtesting.com
Printed in the USA
FSHW010634150521
81370FS